GW00992231

MASTERING

COMPOSITION

WITH YOUR DIGITAL SLR

A RotoVision Book
Published and distributed by RotoVision SA
Route Suisse 9
CH-1295 Mies
Switzerland

RotoVision SA, Sales & Editorial Office
Sheridan House
114 Western Road
Hove BN3 1DD, UK

Tel: +44 (0)1273 72 72 68
Fax: +44 (0)1273 72 72 69
Email: sales@rotovision.com
Web: www.rotovision.com

10 9 8 7 6 5 4 3 2 1

ISBN: 978-2-940378-25-8

Designed by Fineline Studios
Art Director: Tony Seddon

Reprographics in Singapore
by ProVision Pte. Ltd
Tel: +65 6334 7720
Fax: +65 6334 7721

Printing and binding in Singapore by
Craft Print International Ltd.

MASTERING

COMPOSITION

WITH YOUR DIGITAL SLR

CHRIS RUTTER

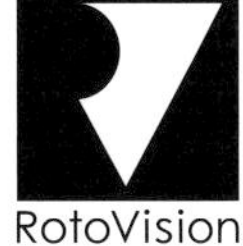

RotoVision

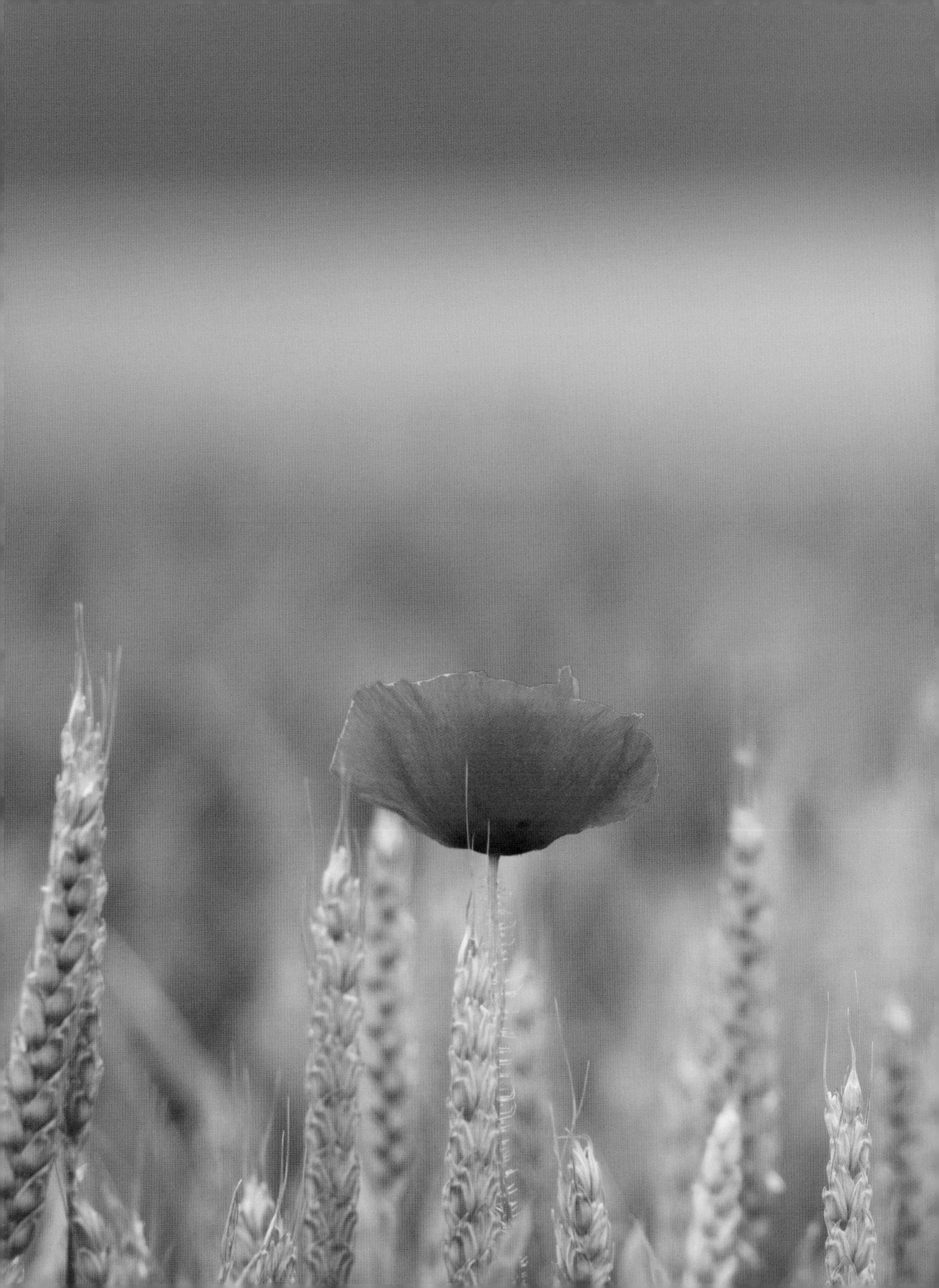

CONTENTS

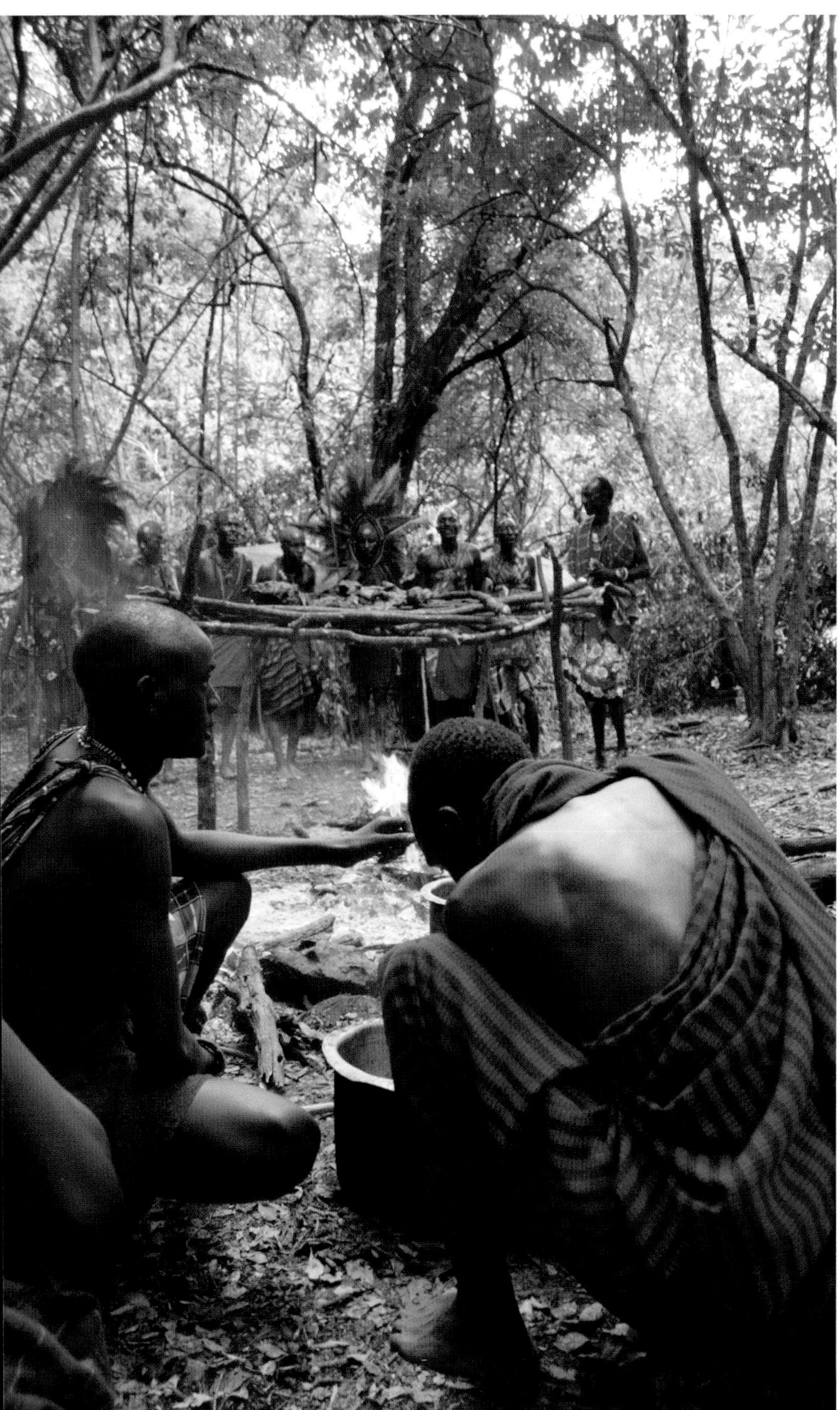

With a digital single-lens reflex camera (DSLR) you have the technology and the versatility to produce professional-looking results, with much of the convenience of a point-and-shoot camera. The rising popularity and falling cost of the DSLR has brought this ability within the reach of many, but once you've purchased your camera, how can you make the most of this technological marvel?

An understanding of shutter speeds, apertures, and exposure can help you to produce technically sound images. However, there is more to producing great images than just technical expertise; understanding how the elements of an image work together can lift your images above the crowd. The composition of the image has been at the heart of the visual arts from ancient times; indeed, many of the rules and conventions that we use today can trace their roots back to the great painters of the past. But photography, and particularly digital photography, means that anyone can produce great images quickly, simply, and relatively cheaply.

LEFT
Lens choice has a major effect on image composition. An 18mm lens on a small-sensor DSLR was used here to capture as much of the scene as possible.

OPPOSITE
Understanding how the elements of an image work together is the key to successful composition. The focal point of an image, in this case the cyclist's face, needs to have a prominent position in the frame.

The ability to "see" a great composition doesn't rely on the camera, but to translate your vision into your final image you need to know how to make the most of the many features available on DSLRs. So that's what this book is about, giving you the ability to make the most of the features of your camera, how to choose lenses, pick the right viewpoint, and arrange objects in the frame for maximum impact. We'll learn the rules and conventions that can help your composition skills, but also how to break these rules successfully.

As well as explaining how to get the most from your camera, much of this book is also about the art of seeing. Successful composition is often more about what you leave out than what you include. You can't always fit the whole scene in a single image, and even if you could, would this produce the most powerful composition? The answer is usually, no.

By concentrating on what's important to *you* about the subject, you have the power to make the viewer see the world through your eyes. This choice lies at the heart of all photography, and being able to see the picture before you even pick up the camera is one of the most important skills that any photographer can have.

RIGHT
Aperture and depth of field can be used effectively to concentrate the viewer's attention on a single, key point in an image.

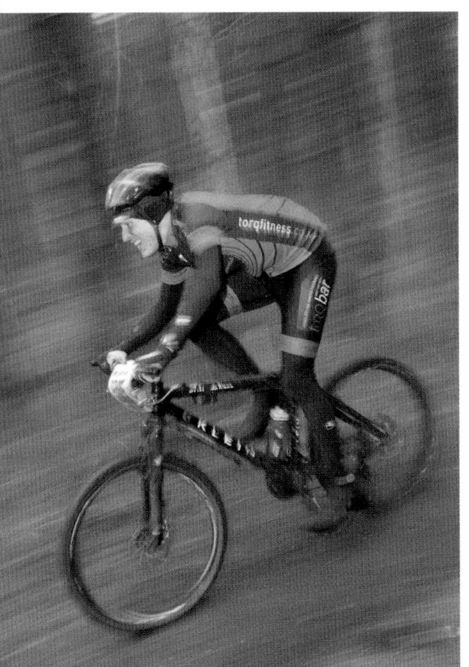

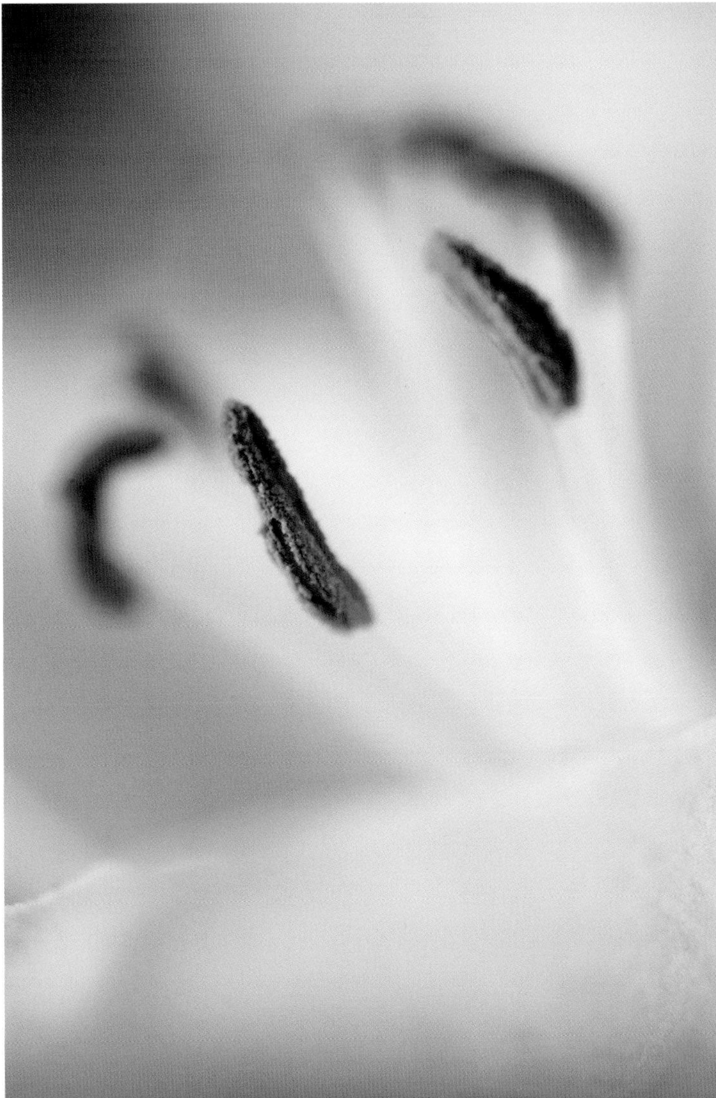

Section 1

The Digital SLR Camera

While much of the art of composition is about your vision rather than your camera, using a DSLR makes a huge difference to the way you approach a subject. So, before we look at the aesthetics of composition, let's find out about the features and technology of the DSLR.

BELOW AND RIGHT
Most DSLRs have a sensor with the same 3:2 ratio as the standard 35mm frame (A). However, as its name implies, the Four Thirds system uses a more square 4:3 ratio sensor (B).

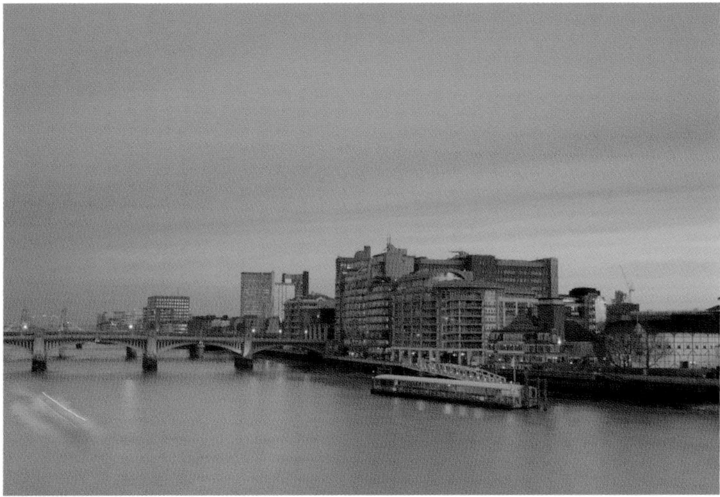

A

B

Format
Although DSLRs don't fall into the same format conventions as film cameras (35mm, medium- and large-format, etc.), the shape of the sensor influences the composition and framing of your images. Most DSLRs use the same 3:2 format as 35mm cameras, the main exception being those using the Four Thirds standard. This format was pioneered by Olympus and uses a 4:3 format sensor. The basic rules of composition and framing can be used on both formats, but the more elongated 3:2 shape gives a greater impression of width than the 4:3 format. For the majority of this book we'll be dealing with the 3:2 format, as this is generally considered the standard shape for SLRs.

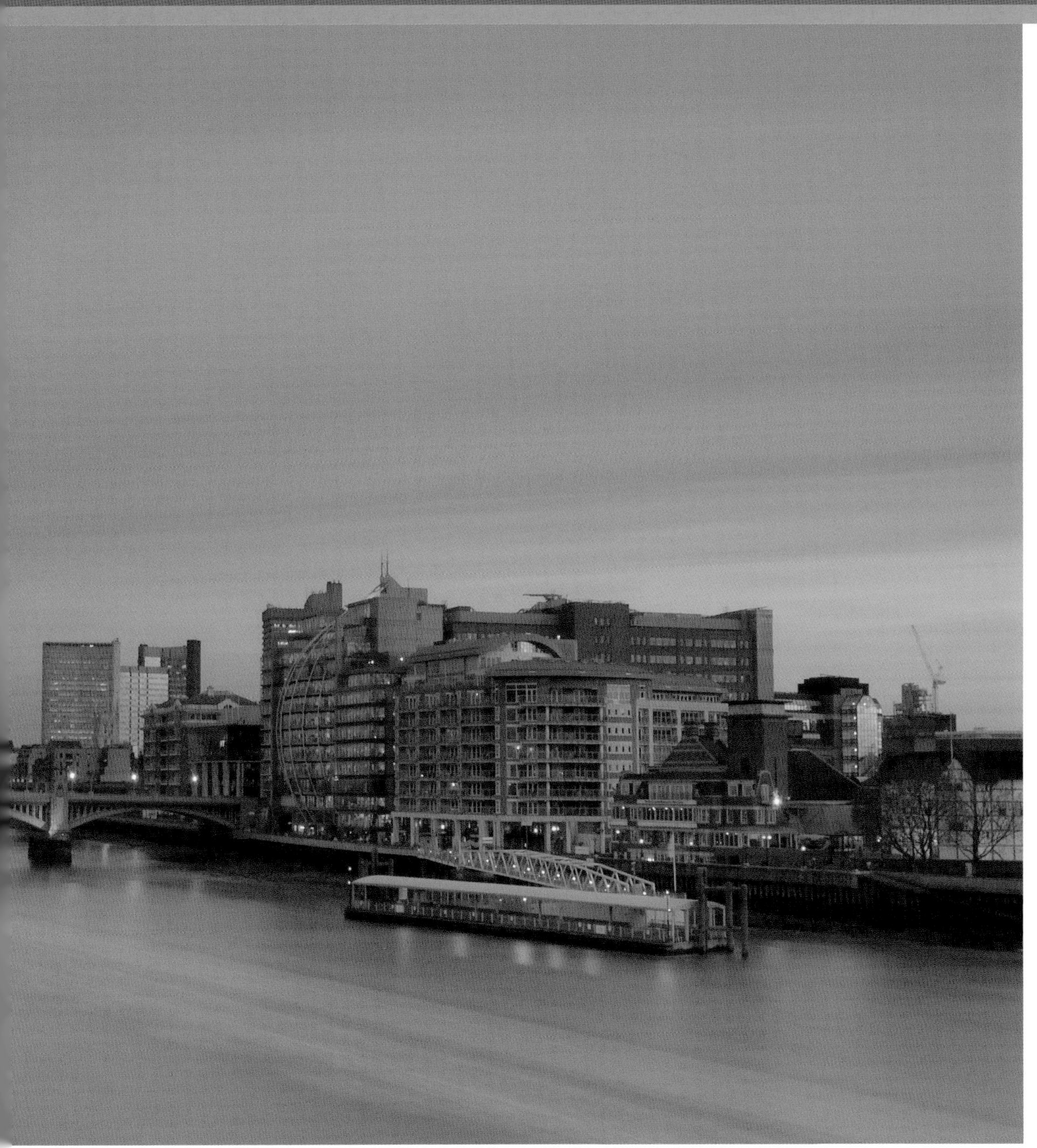

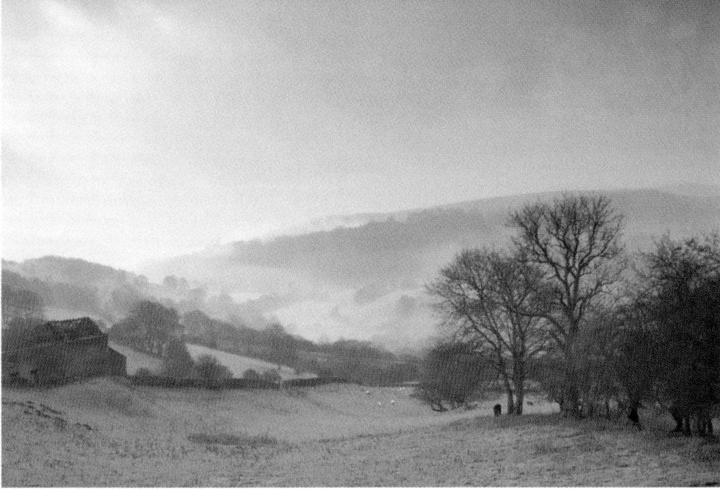

A

Viewfinder

The viewfinder is more than simply a way of approximately framing the image—it is the photographer's window on the world. Whichever camera you use, you should take the time to get to know how to visualize the final result from what you see in the viewfinder. The viewfinder lies at the heart of the design of an SLR camera, whether it's digital or film. The very name single-lens reflex refers to the optical system that enables you to frame your image through the same lens that you shoot the picture with. This is one of the greatest advantages of an SLR over almost every other type of camera around. Because you see through the taking lens, it gives the most accurate view of how the final photograph will appear.

Although the viewfinder gives a great representation of the image, it still relies on you using the view well. It's tempting to focus all your attention on the center of the image, but to make the most of your camera and improve your images, you should get into the habit of looking around the whole of the viewfinder. If you scan the area around the subject, you will notice objects or elements that could detract from the subject, and you might get ideas for new framing styles.

It is also essential to understand the limitations of the viewfinder. Few cameras show 100 percent of the area of the image. The field of view offered by the viewfinder varies between different models. Most budget DSLRs show around 95 percent of the image in the viewfinder. To find out how much of the scene is outside the viewfinder of your camera, take a shot, then compare what you can see through the viewfinder with the image shown on the rear LCD screen.

Another problem is that you see the view through the lens' maximum aperture. Consequently, you see the image with the minimum depth of field, i.e. the least amount in focus. If you take a shot at a smaller aperture, objects in front of or behind the subject you have focused on will be sharper than they were in the viewfinder.

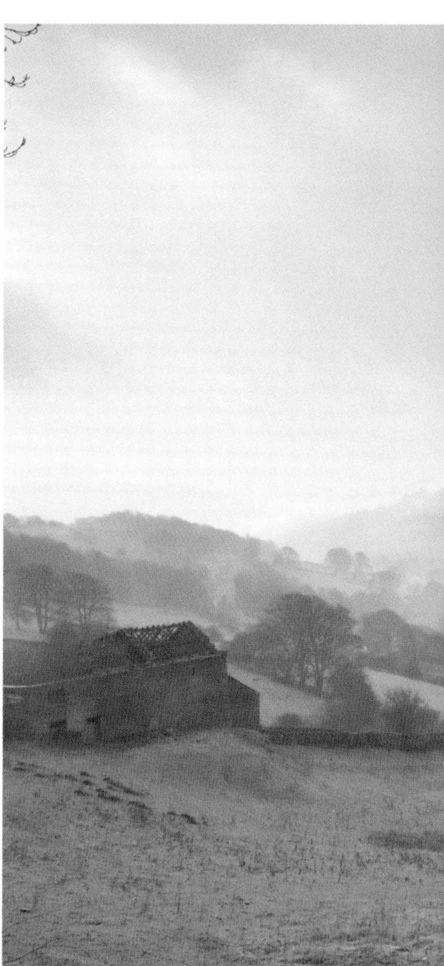

B

ABOVE
The viewfinders of most budget DSLRs show you only around 95 percent of the image (A), so you need to watch out for distracting elements, such as the branches in the top left of image B.

LCD screen

Among the most useful features of a DSLR is the ability to review your pictures immediately on the rear LCD screen. You should never rely solely on the LCD to assess your images, as it can give only an approximate preview of how the image will look. You cannot depend on it for many image-quality issues such as saturation, color, and sharpness, so do not delete images unless you're sure that they are blurred or badly exposed. The LCD is, however, an excellent aid for fine-tuning your composition and framing as it gives you the ability to judge the camera angle, lens focal length, and viewpoint. When reviewing your image on the rear LCD, take time to look around the whole frame to check the composition and framing.

Depth of field preview

As discussed opposite, one drawback of an SLR is that you view the scene through the lens at maximum aperture. Many DSLRs offer a depth of field preview facility to stop the lens down to the aperture that is set on the lens to help assess the depth of field. This feature is usually accessed by pressing a button near the lens. Using it can take some practice as, when the button is pressed, the image in the viewfinder will darken. The smaller the aperture that is set on the lens, the darker the image, making it difficult to see clearly enough to assess the depth of field. The key to using this feature is to give your eyes time to adjust to the darker image, so keep the button pressed for at least two seconds while you are looking through the viewfinder. Once you've got used to the dark image, you can start to look around the frame to check which objects will be in focus.

CHOOSING YOUR DSLR

When choosing a digital camera, don't ignore the importance of the viewfinder and other aspects of the handling. It's tempting to base your decision on resolution and the latest high-tech features, but if you can't see the subject clearly or you're not comfortable using the camera, you'll struggle to get great shots. Try to handle all the cameras in your price range before making a final decision.

The features and technology packed into DSLRs are pretty impressive. Its potential to open up new creative and picture-taking opportunities makes the DSLR one of the most powerful tools ever available to the photographer. Of course, the most creative part of a DSLR is you, the photographer, but the right camera can help you to make the most of that creativity by giving you access to all the features and functions that you need. Digital compact cameras have many of the same features, but they cannot match the combination of features and the versatility of an SLR.

All DSLRs offer a full range of exposure modes, from various automatic to fully manual options. These allow photographers of almost any level of experience to get superb results. DSLRs allow you to learn from your mistakes almost immediately by viewing the result on the LCD screen. You can also access the shooting information, such as shutter speed and aperture, by viewing the EXIF data. (To find this in Photoshop Elements, go to File Info and select EXIF or Camera Data.) These facilities make DSLRs ideal for learning about how to get the most out of the settings and features available on your camera.

Here are just a few of the options available on your DSLR and their benefits to your photography.

Aperture and shutter speed

Every DSLR gives you control over these two settings, which are at the heart of successful photography. A choice of exposure modes such as aperture priority, shutter priority, and full manual, gives you the opportunity to learn about these settings. At their basic level, aperture and shutter speed control the exposure of the image, but they also have creative applications. Shutter speed controls the appearance and recording of movement of either the camera, the subject, or both, while the aperture controls the depth of field.

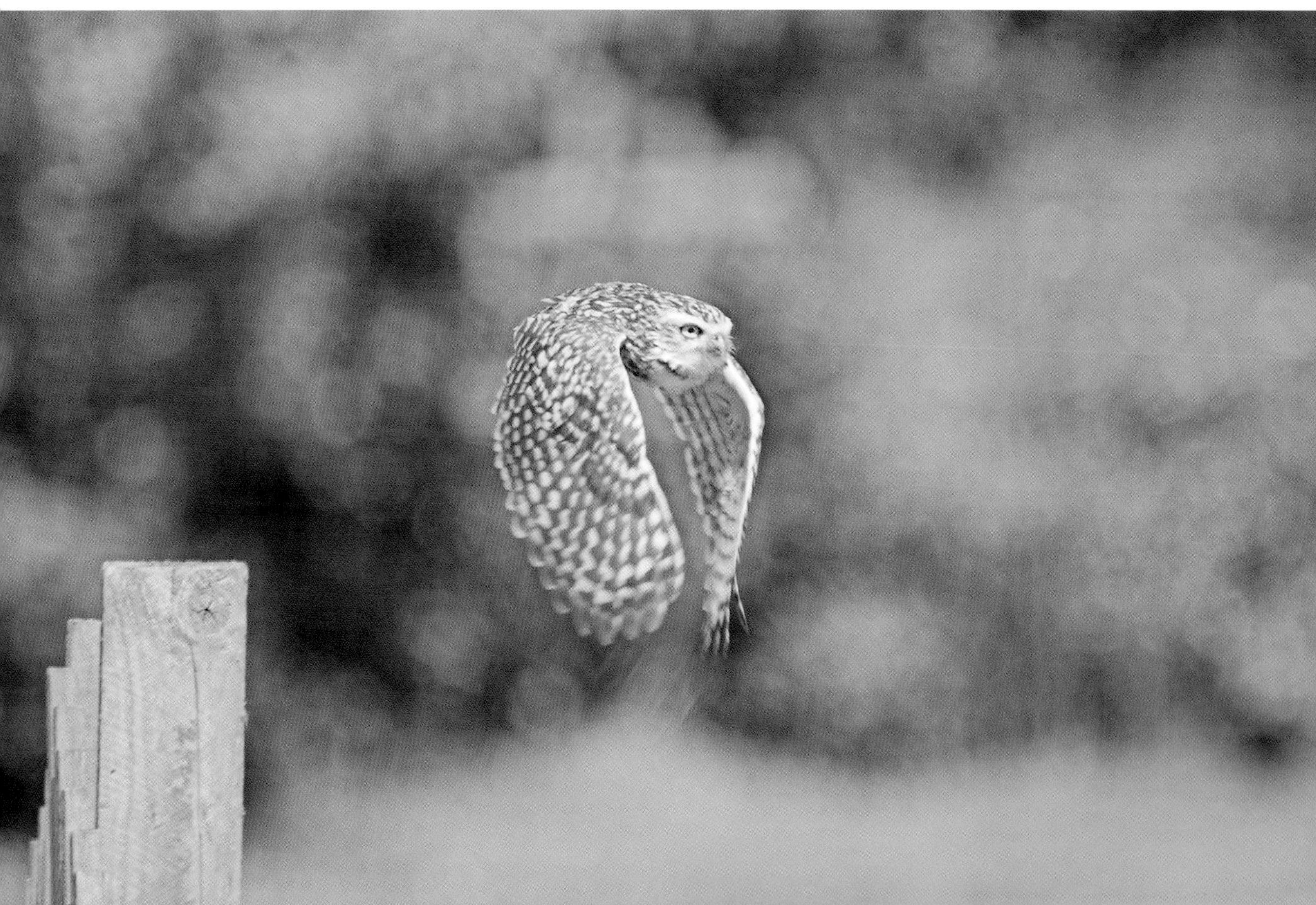

Depth of field

Once you've mastered the basics of using the aperture to control exposure, you're ready to start using it—along with the lens focal length and distance to the subject—to control the depth of field. This governs how much of the image from front to back is in focus, and can help with your composition. A DSLR is the ideal tool for utilizing this effect, because you see through the lens that takes the image, allowing you to gauge the depth of field in the viewfinder. You can also use the instant review facility on the rear LCD to help you assess the depth of field once you have taken the shot.

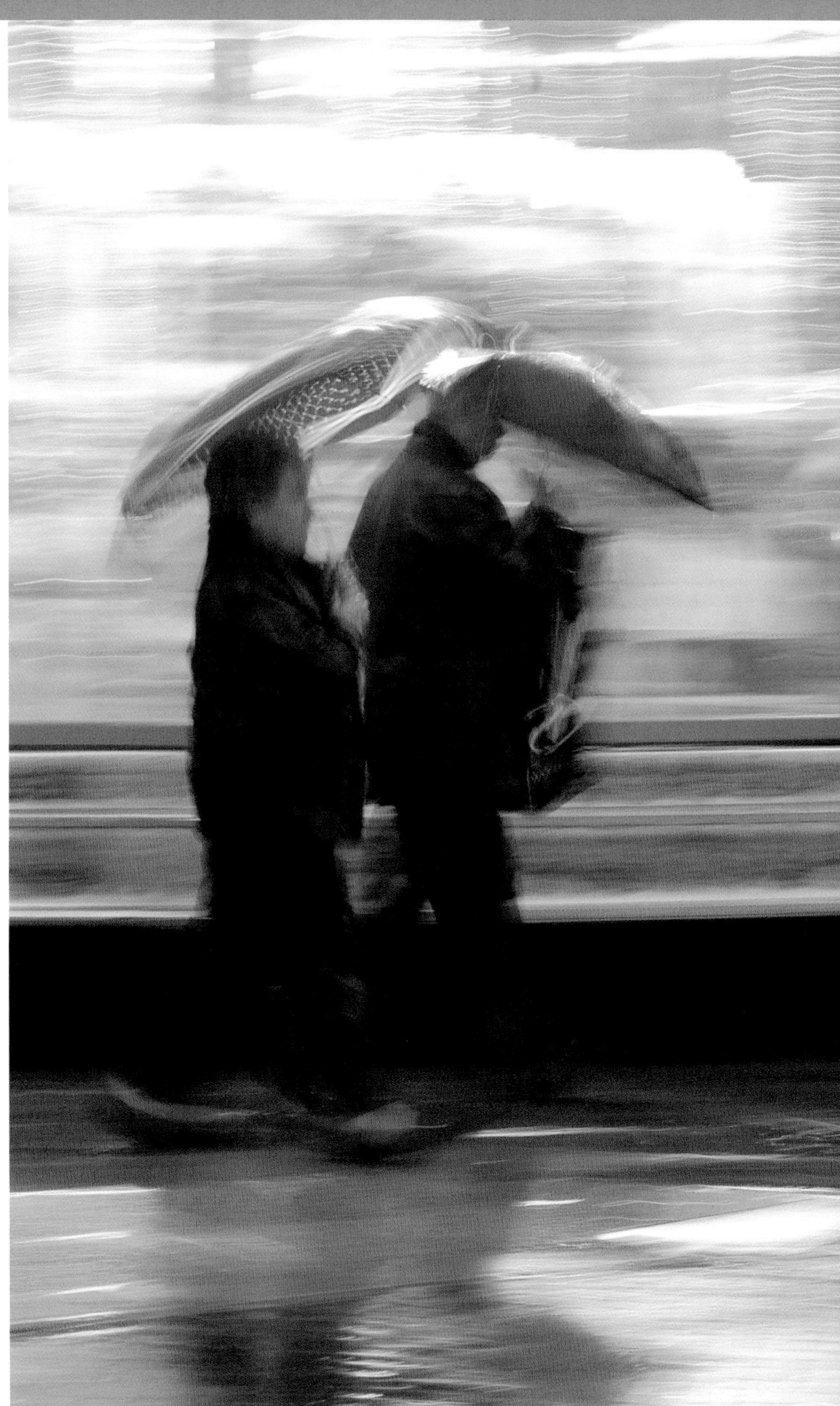

OPPOSITE AND RIGHT
With the range of shutter speeds available on your DSLR, you can choose to either blur or freeze moving subjects. A short, fast shutter speed of 1/1000 sec has frozen this owl in flight, while a long shutter speed of 1/4 sec has added a sense of movement to this street scene.

Lenses
The ability to change lenses and the massive range of lenses available, makes the DSLR one of the most versatile cameras around. Different lenses allow you to choose how much of the scene to include in your shot, and enable you to alter your viewpoint to change the perspective of your image. There are so many options, and the effects are so important to your composition, that the following section is all about choosing, using, and making the most of the lenses available for your DSLR.

Versatility
Along with lenses, there is a huge range of accessories available to help with composition and other techniques, such as flashguns, remote releases, and tripods. All of the accessories, along with the features and the quality available from DSLRs, makes these cameras suitable for shooting almost every possible subject. From sports, portraits, and low-light photography to landscapes and macro, a DSLR can produce excellent results.

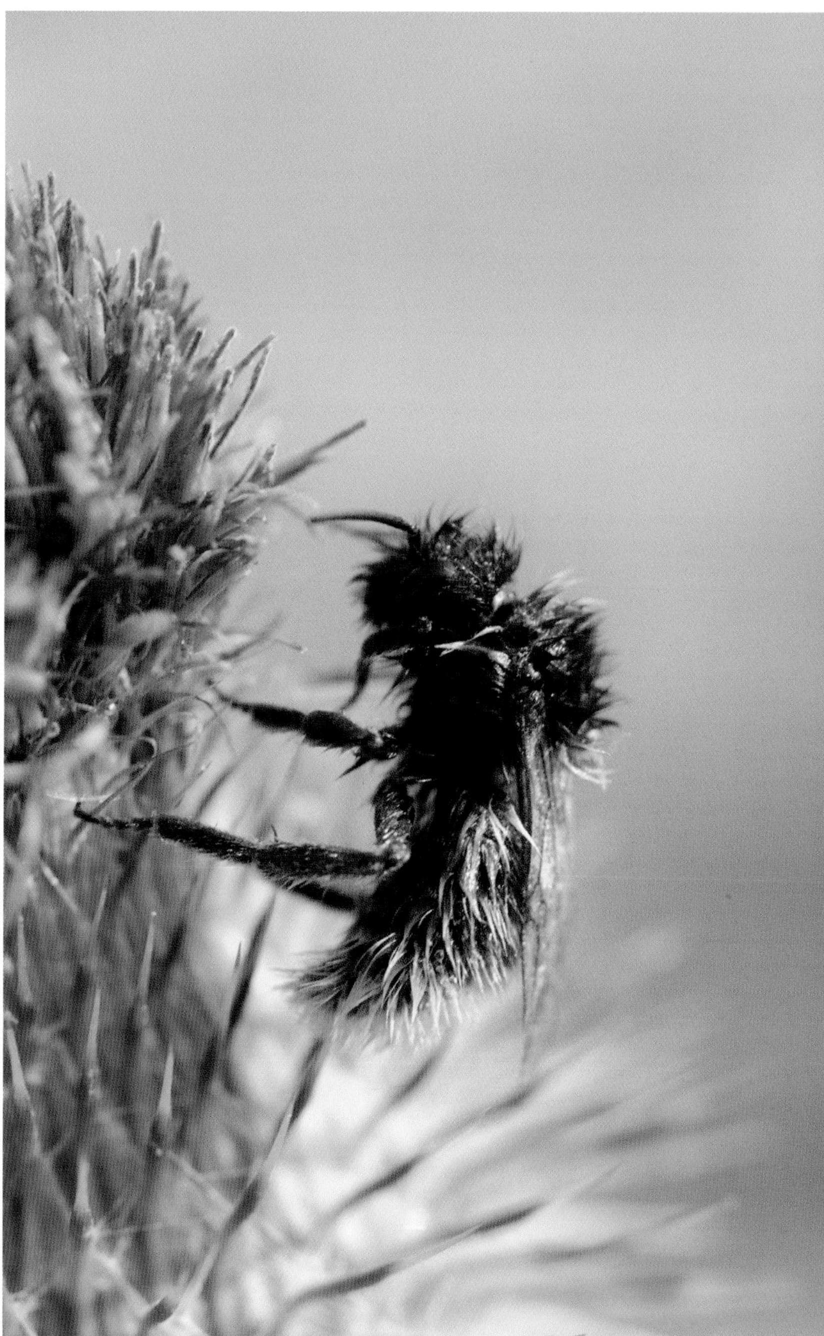

RIGHT
With a DSLR, you see through the lens that is going to take the picture, so you get a precise idea of how the image will look. This, along with the features available, makes a DSLR ideal for shooting almost any subject.

Quality
Most DSLRs are capable of producing excellent quality prints of at least 10x8in. With high-resolution models of 10 megapixels or more becoming the norm, the ability to print photo-quality 12x16in images is within the grasp of most enthusiasts. These high-resolution cameras also make it possible to crop the image to fine-tune your composition without compromising too much on image quality.

Freedom to experiment
Because you can shoot as many images as you've got the storage capacity for at little or no cost, you can experiment more than with film cameras. Once you've invested in memory cards, you are freed from having to pay for film and processing. You also save on time as, rather than waiting for images to be developed, a DSLR gives you instant feedback.

The rear LCD is the first port of call for viewing. LCD screens are really too small to accurately assess some image quality issues such as color and sharpness. To do this you really need to view your images on a high-quality computer monitor. But LCDs are useful for checking the basic composition of your images. The larger the screen the easier it is to use, and most models now offer screens of around 2½ in (6.5cm), which is enough for basic assessment.

Color or black and white
With digital images, you don't have to choose whether to shoot black-and-white or color images when you take the photograph. You can simply shoot in color, and convert them to black and white later on.

Adjust your images
Using a DSLR gives you access to all the creative options available from using the software of a digital darkroom. Once you've shot your images, there's almost no limit to the effects that you can use to adjust, enhance, and manipulate them.

BELOW
The ability to quickly and simply change your images from color to black and white gives added versatility. Even a basic composition can be made more striking by removing the color.

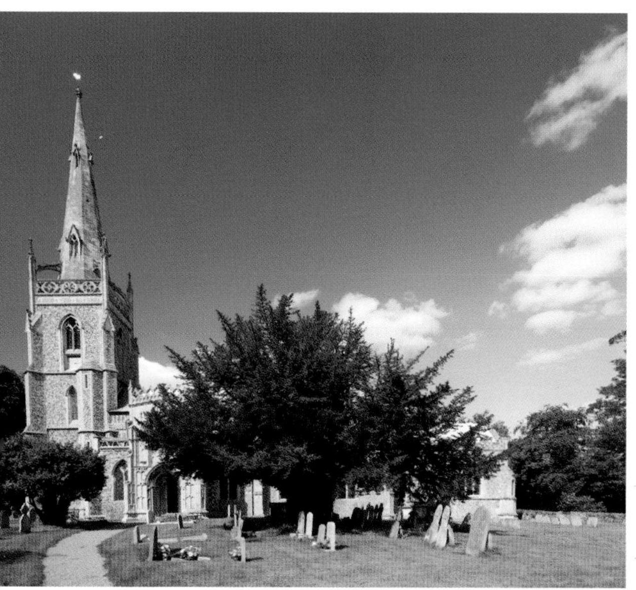

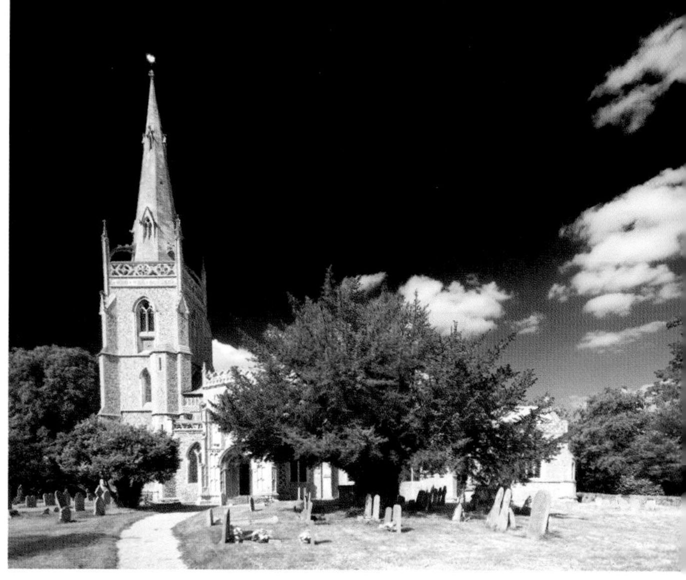

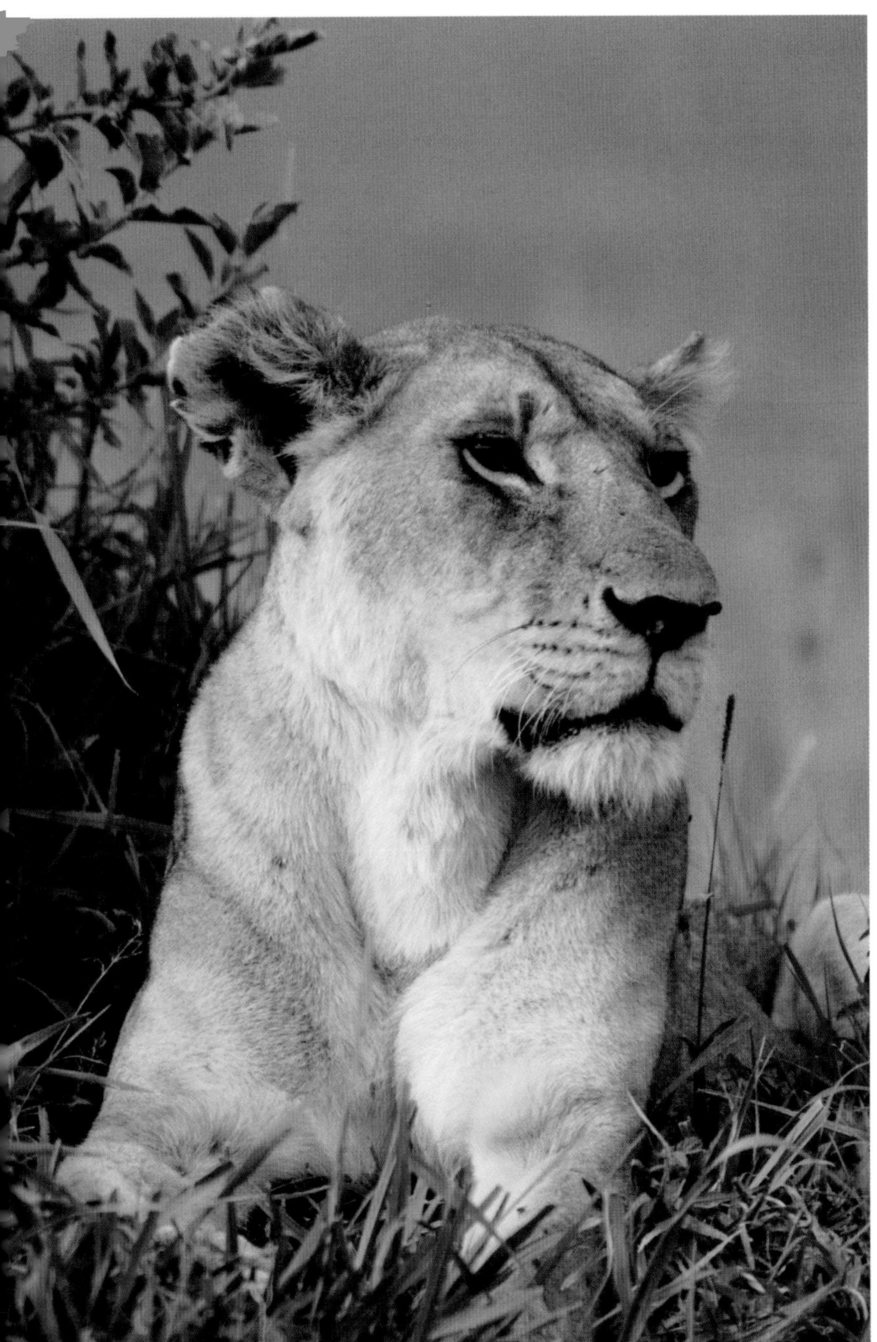

For many, the digital revolution came about because of digital compact cameras, and their popularity has brought the joys of photography to a whole new audience. While compacts are capable of good results, and some even offer many of the features previously found only on SLRs, they still lack the SLR's creative potential. DSLRs are now more affordable, and prices are falling all the time. This has led to many compact users upgrading their cameras to expand their photography.

As we saw in Key Features (see pages 10–13), the viewfinder lies at the heart of an SLR, and is the major difference between these and compact models. The optical viewfinder on those compacts that offer one (and not all do) is completely separate from the lens that takes the photograph.

All digital compacts offer a live-view feature that allows you to compose the picture using the rear LCD as a viewfinder. This shows the image from the taking lens, offering some of the advantages of an SLR viewfinder. However, it can be tricky to see in bright sunlight and lacks the sharpness and clarity of an optical viewfinder. Some manufacturers have introduced live-view on their DSLR models, giving a choice to those who are used to this feature from their compact.

LEFT
The range of features and lenses available for DSLRs makes them more suitable than compacts for tackling difficult subjects, such as wildlife.

If you are upgrading from a digital compact camera, here are some of the main differences that you'll find when using a DSLR.

Manual focus
Because you view the scene through the lens that takes the picture, it is easier to manually focus with a DSLR than with a compact camera. Even when using the live-view facility on a digital compact, it is difficult to focus accurately because of the relatively low resolution of the screen.

Depth of field
Digital compact cameras give much greater depth of field than SLRs. This is because they have much smaller focal lengths for the same angle of view. This means that more of the image from near to far will be in focus, which can be a benefit for some images, but makes it much more difficult to isolate subjects using shallow depth of field.

Interchangeable lenses
Although most compacts have built-in zoom lenses and some even offer accessories to extend their lens range, they still lack the versatility of the interchangeable lenses on SLRs. The widest options on most digital compacts are limited to a basic wide-angle, which is equivalent to around 28mm on a 35mm camera. It's a similar story when looking at the telephoto end of the zoom range.

Although many digital compacts—especially the "bridge" or crossover designs that use an electronic rather than an optical viewfinder—offer a good telephoto option, they don't have the range available to SLR users. Even those with very long zoom ranges are limited to the equivalent of around 300 to 400mm, whereas with DSLRs a host of longer lenses are available.

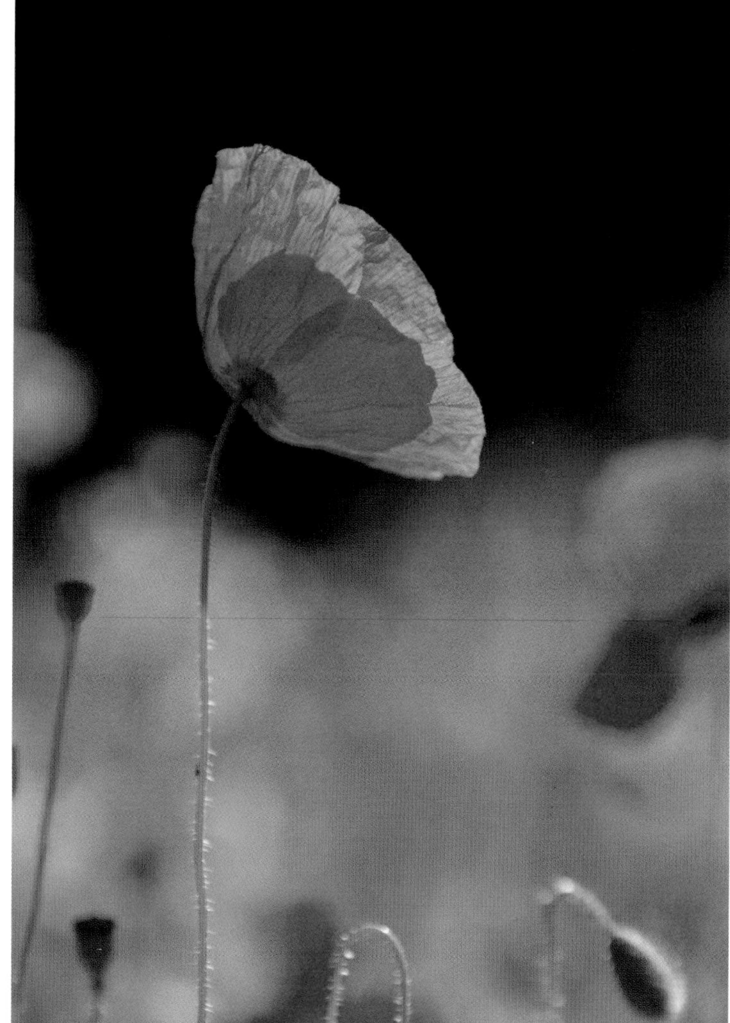

RIGHT
Using a DSLR makes achieving shallow depth of field effects much easier, allowing you to concentrate all your attention on composing the main subject.

DSLRs give you access to a vast range of accessories and gadgets to help you make the most of your photography. The accessories discussed here are the most useful for successful composition and framing.

Tripods
Primarily used to mount the camera while you're shooting with long exposures, a tripod can also help your composition. Using a tripod tends to slow you down, making you think more about the framing of your shot. This simple effect can make a huge difference to your composition, and I'd recommend that you use one whenever possible.

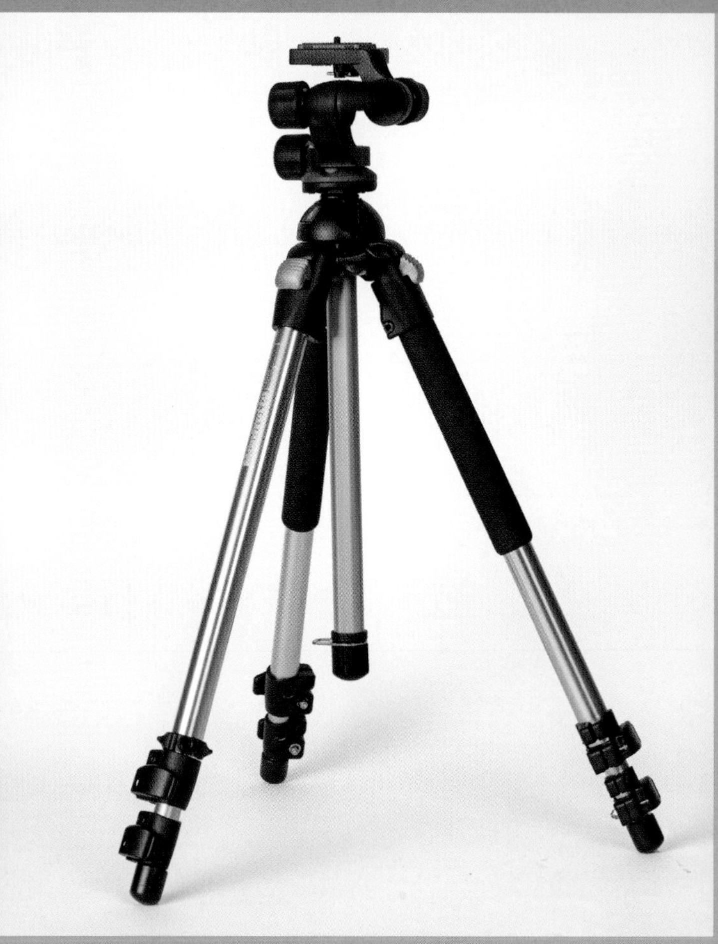

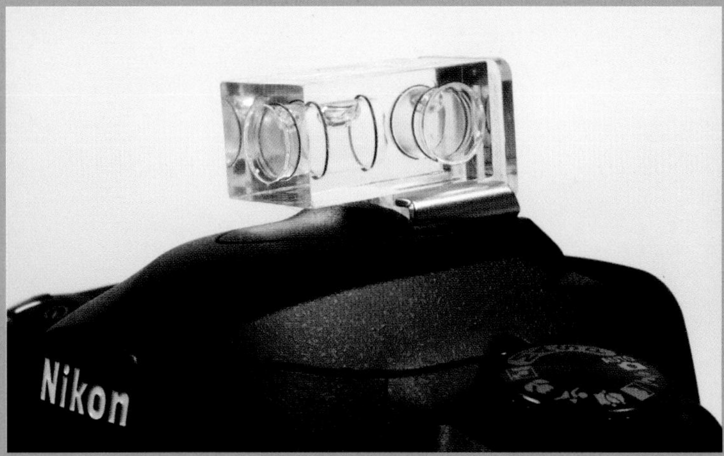

Spirit levels
No matter how careful you are, and how much time you take framing your shot, getting the camera precisely level is a challenge. The solution is to use a small spirit level to take the guess work out of the task. The most useful type fits into the standard hotshoe of the camera and gives both horizontal and vertical readings to ensure that your camera is straight and level. To use this accessory successfully, you need to mount the camera on a tripod to allow you to position it precisely. Some tripods have a spirit level built into the head, which can be used instead of the hotshoe-mounted type.

Slide mounts

It may seem strange suggesting that you use a slide mount with your DSLR, but we are not going to use it for its original application. An old slide mount makes an excellent aid to your composition, allowing you to get an idea of framing without having to raise the camera to your eye, or even get it out of your bag.

You can use a slide mount to view the scene to allow you to quickly and simply assess the best framing for your subject. To do this, close one eye, then hold the slide mount up to your open eye to visualize how the image will look. You can mimic the effect of using different lenses by the distance that the mount is from your eye. The closer it is, the wider the view (like a wide-angle lens), and the farther away, the narrower the view (like a telephoto lens).

You need to make sure that the format of the slide mount matches that of your camera, so for most DSLRs a 35mm or 2⅔x3½in(6x9cm) medium-format slide mount are ideal. If you own a Four Thirds SLR you need to use a different format to match the 4:3 aspect ratio, such as a 2⅓x1⅔in (6x4.5cm) medium-format mount.

An alternative to a slide mount is to cut out two "L" shaped pieces of card. You can use these in the same way, but with the advantage of being able to vary the format of the frame by moving the relative positions of the pieces.

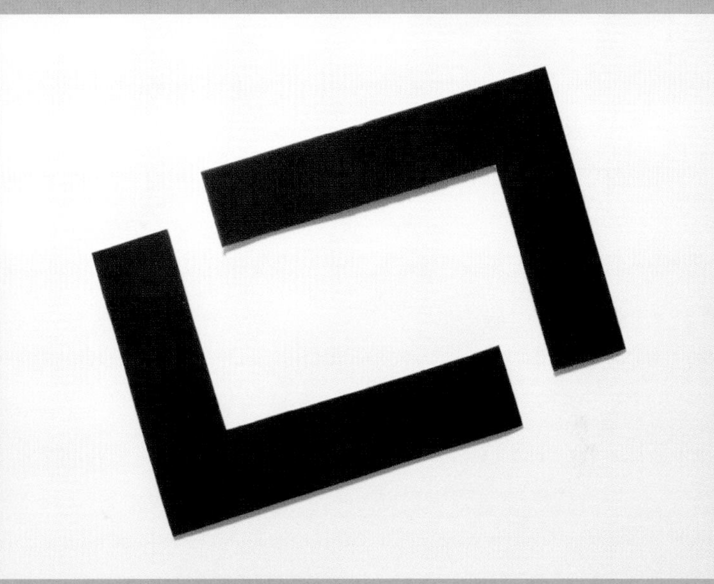

Gridded screen

Some of the more advanced DSLRs offer a facility to change the focusing screen inside the viewfinder. One of the most useful versions for composition has a grid of lines etched onto the screen giving you a handy reference for positioning objects in the frame and ensuring that horizons and buildings are straight in the frame. A few models offer an alternative method of offering a gridded screen. They overlay an electronic display onto the screen as a custom function, so negating the need to change the screen itself.

Angle finder

In normal use the viewfinder of the DSLR is perfect for composing your shots. But it can be difficult, or even impossible, to get your eye level with the viewfinder when the camera is positioned very low to the ground. The angle finder attaches to the viewfinder of your SLR, and allows you to see through the camera at a more comfortable height. It is especially useful for macrophotography. An alternative to the angle finder known as the Zigview, uses a small sensor and LCD screen that attaches to the viewfinder, giving a view similar to the live-view screen available on digital compact cameras.

Section 2

Lenses

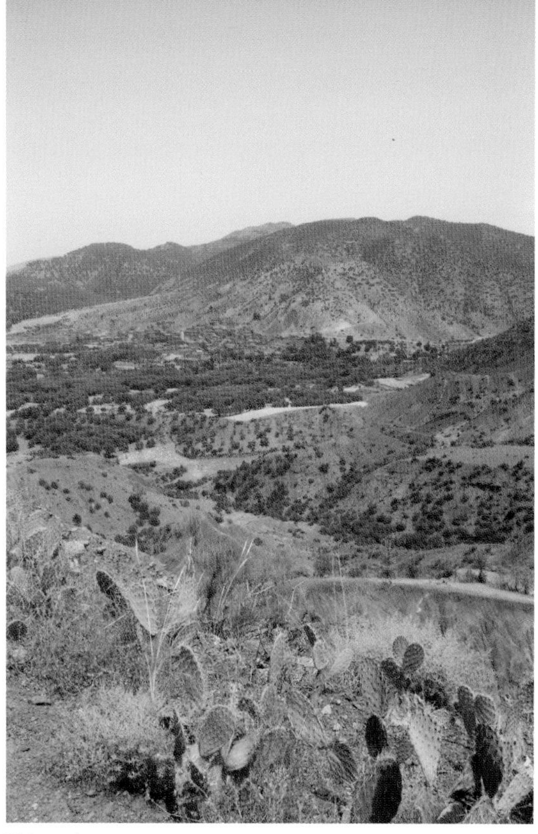

Wide-angle

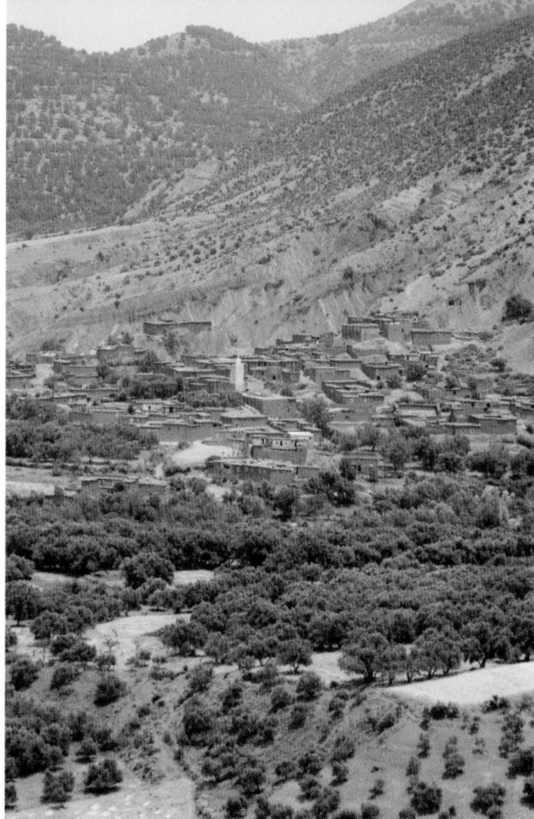

Telephoto

The ability to change the lens is one of the main benefits of a DSLR. The vast array of numbers and letters used to describe lenses can be bewildering, but there's no need to be confused; you don't need to know how all the numbers are derived, just how to translate them into the effect they will give. When it comes to composition, there's only one aspect of lenses that really matters—the focal length.

Focal length

This is usually the first set of numbers you'll come across on your lens, and is the most important aspect for composition as it tells you how much of the scene you'll be able to include in your picture. The focal length is expressed in millimeters, and technically refers to the distance between the optical center of the lens and the sensor (or the focal plane). But all you really need to know is that it tells you the magnification of the lens.

The smaller the number the more of the scene you'll be able to include, and the larger the number the narrower the view seen by the lens. Unfortunately, the optical effect of a particular focal length also depends on the size of the sensor that you are using. Because 35mm SLRs have been the most popular interchangeable-lens cameras for many years, most people use the focal lengths associated with this format to categorize the different types of lenses. Although the effect is different for many DSLRs, this has become an accepted way of expressing lens types, and you'll often see lenses quoted as "35mm equivalent." We'll learn more about how this affects DSLRs in the following pages, but for now we'll follow convention and use 35mm as the standard way of relating focal length to what you'll see through the lens.

In 35mm terms, a standard lens has a focal length of around 50mm. This is because it gives a magnification close to that of the human eye. Any lens with a shorter focal length is called a wide-angle, while those with focal lengths above 50mm are usually called telephoto.

Zoom lenses

These have two focal lengths quoted in the specification—the minimum and maximum lengths available. They allow you to choose any focal length between these two figures, making them a versatile and convenient option for most applications.

Prime lenses

These are lenses that offer only a single focal length. They have become less common with the increased popularity of zoom models. They offer wider maximum apertures and higher quality than most zoom lenses, though, and are most commonly found in specialized applications, such as macro lenses.

Other key features

Maximum aperture

The wider the maximum aperture, the more light the lens lets into the camera. A wide maximum aperture is best for composing in low-light, as you'll get a better image in the viewfinder. A wider maximum aperture will also allow you to get a narrower depth of field for creative composition effects.

Close focus

If you're interested in macro or close-up photography, look for a lens with the closest focus capability. For wide-angle lenses, it's also useful to get the closest focus possible to allow you to get very close to the subject to make the most of exaggerated perspective effects.

Perspective

You will often hear that lenses can affect perspective, but this is not true. The only thing that governs perspective is your viewpoint, i.e. how far you are from the subject. The lens determines only how much of the scene can be included in the picture. The confusion stems from the fact that to record the subject the same size in the image, you need to be closer with a short focal length lens than with a longer one. So although wide-angle lenses give the impression of exaggerating perspective and telephoto lenses of compressing it, this is governed by your position from the subject, not the lens itself.

OPPOSITE
The main effect of the focal length of the lens is the amount of the scene you can include in your shot. Switching from a wide-angle lens to a telephoto means that you can isolate individual subjects or make objects appear closer to you than they really were.

BELOW
Although the focal length of the lens doesn't directly influence perspective, it does affect the appearance of your images. To keep an object the same size in the frame, you have to change your viewpoint, so the longer the focal length the farther away you have to be. This makes objects appear closer together in the final image.

18mm

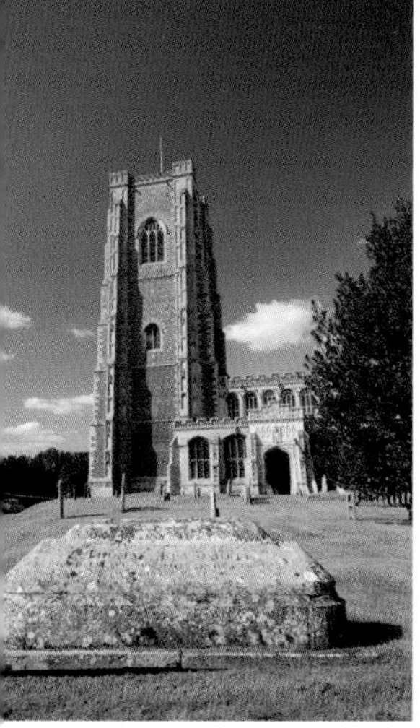

35mm

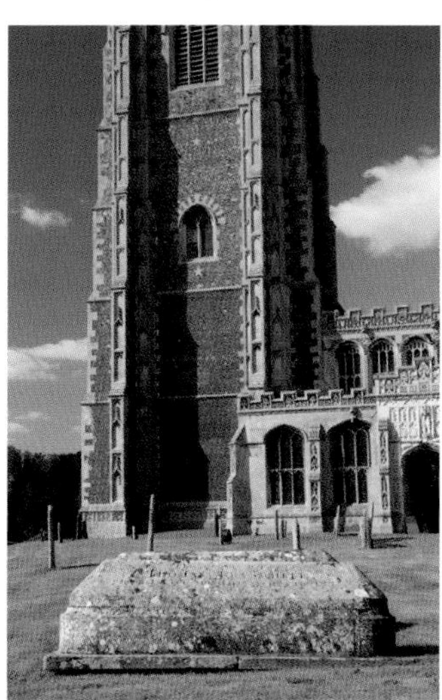

70mm

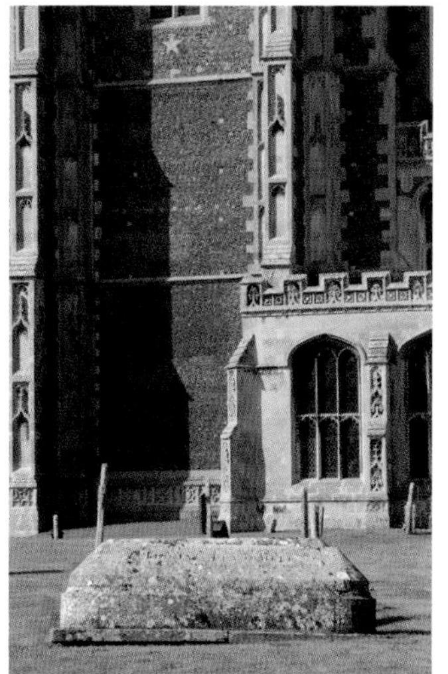

105mm

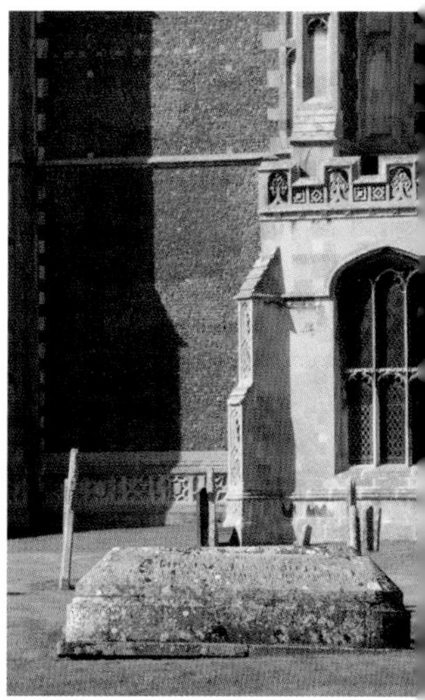

Digital cropping

Many of the most popular DSLR models use sensors that are smaller than the 35mm frame that's used as the standard for expressing the effect of different lens focal lengths. Because of the smaller sensor, the lens has a narrower field of view on these cameras than it would on a 35mm or full-frame camera. For example, if you put a standard 50mm lens on a DSLR with an APS-C sized sensor, it will give a field of view equivalent to using a 75mm telephoto lens on a 35mm camera. This effect is known as the magnification (or crop) factor (MF), which can be used to convert the field of view given by lenses on different DSLRs (see the table below). It's important not to confuse this crop factor with the actual focal length, though, as this remains the same no matter which camera you put the lens on; it's just the amount of the image that you can record that's different. When you put a lens onto a different camera the actual size of the image on the sensor or film is the same. For example, if you photograph a person using a 50mm lens on a 35mm camera so that they are 20mm high on the film, they would be exactly the same height on the sensor if you swapped the lens onto a small-frame DSLR. The only thing that changes is the amount of the scene around the person, making them appear closer in the frame.

THE EQUIVALENT FOCAL LENGTHS DUE TO THE MAGNIFICATION FACTOR (MF) ON DSLRS

Focal length on 35mm film or full-frame camera	Field of view equivalent when used on a camera with 1.5X MF	Field of view equivalent when used on a camera with 1.6X MF	Field of view equivalent when used on a camera with 2X MF
16mm	24mm	26mm	32mm
20mm	30mm	32mm	40mm
24mm	36mm	38mm	48mm
28mm	42mm	45mm	56mm
35mm	52mm	56mm	70mm
50mm	75mm	80mm	100mm
80mm	120mm	128mm	160mm
105mm	160mm	170mm	210mm
135mm	200mm	216mm	270mm
200mm	300mm	320mm	400mm
300mm	450mm	480mm	600mm
400mm	600mm	640mm	800mm
600mm	900mm	960mm	1,200mm

Some values have been rounded up or down for clarity

THE MAGNIFICATION FACTOR OF POPULAR DSLR SYSTEMS

1.5X
All current Nikon, Pentax, Sony, and Samsung DSLRs

1.6X
Canon budget and enthusiast models

2X
All Four Thirds models by Olympus and Panasonic

To get the same field of view on a small-frame DSLR as on 35mm, you need a shorter focal length, which is why you'll find that most models are supplied with a standard zoom of around 18 to 55mm. This gives a similar field of view as a 28 to 85mm on a 35mm camera.

OPPOSITE
The sensor size of DSLRs affects the amount of the scene you can include. This is known as the magnification factor.

These two shots taken with the same focal length lens show the effect of a crop factor of 1.5x.

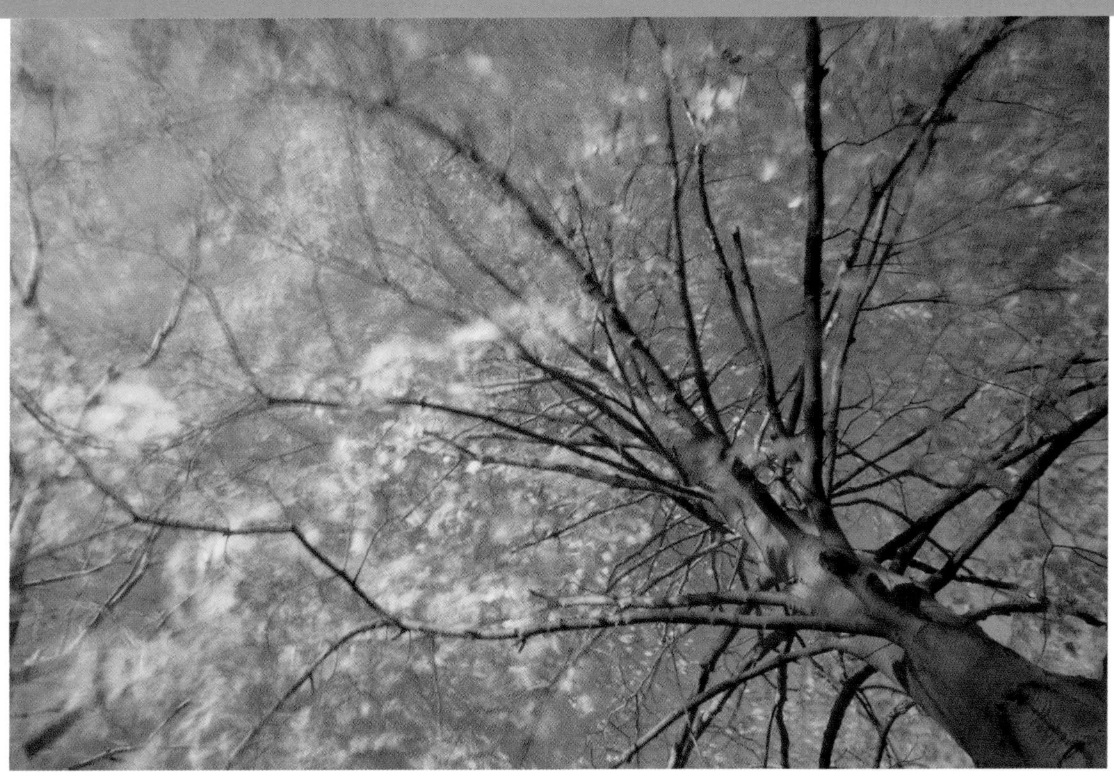

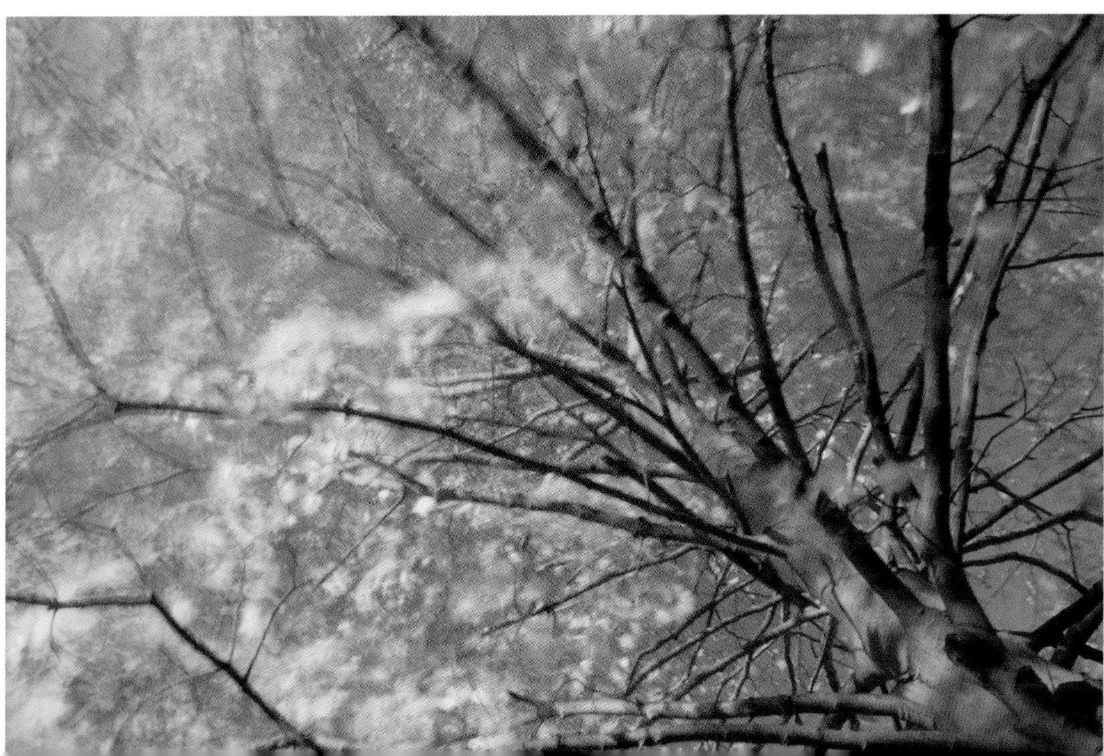

WIDE-ANGLE LENSES

The general term "wide-angle" applies to any lens with a focal length smaller than that considered as "standard" for that format. This gives a wide field of view, allowing you to include large areas of the scene in the image. Because of this wide field of view, distant objects appear smaller in the image than they were in reality. This means that you need to pay particular attention to your composition. It is easy for the subject to appear tiny in the frame, making the whole scene look empty. There are several techniques that you can use to avoid this problem in your wide-angle shots. Alternatively, you can use this sense of space to your advantage by producing minimalist shots to emphasize the sense of scale.

BELOW LEFT
Landscapes are a classic subject for wide-angle lenses. The broad field of view allows you to include many elements of the scene, including the foreground.

OPPOSITE
Wide-angle lenses are ideal for shooting in confined spaces, such as buildings.

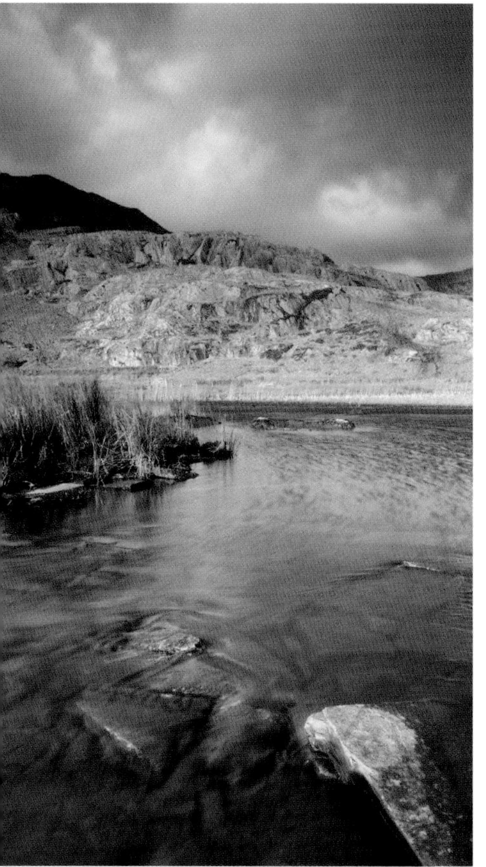

TYPICAL FOCAL LENGTHS OF WIDE-ANGLE LENSES FOR DSLRS

35mm or full-frame	1.5X MF	1.6X MF	2X MF
Wide			
28 to 35mm	18 to 23mm	17 to 22mm	14 to 18mm
Super wide			
14 to 24mm	9 to 16mm	8 to 15mm	7 to 12mm

Composition techniques to use with wide-angle lenses

Get close to your subject
When shooting with wide-angle lenses, objects tend to appear smaller in the frame compared to the normal view of the scene. If you shoot from a viewpoint that looks right to your eyes, the subject will look too small in the final image. To stop this happening, you need to get in close to your subject to make it larger in the frame.

Use lead-in lines and foreground interest
Just like the need to get close to your subject, when shooting landscapes your shots can look quite empty and lack impact. This is because even objects in the middle distance can look small and insignificant in the frame. By including an object in the foreground, you can add a sense of depth, which can be further enhanced by including lines that lead the eye into the scene.

Add a sense of scale
Because distant features can look smaller in wide-angle shots than to the naked eye, it can be difficult to show their actual scale and size. Including an easily recognizable element in the frame is an excellent way of overcoming this problem. Large, man-made structures are useful for showing the size of distant objects, such as mountains and lakes.

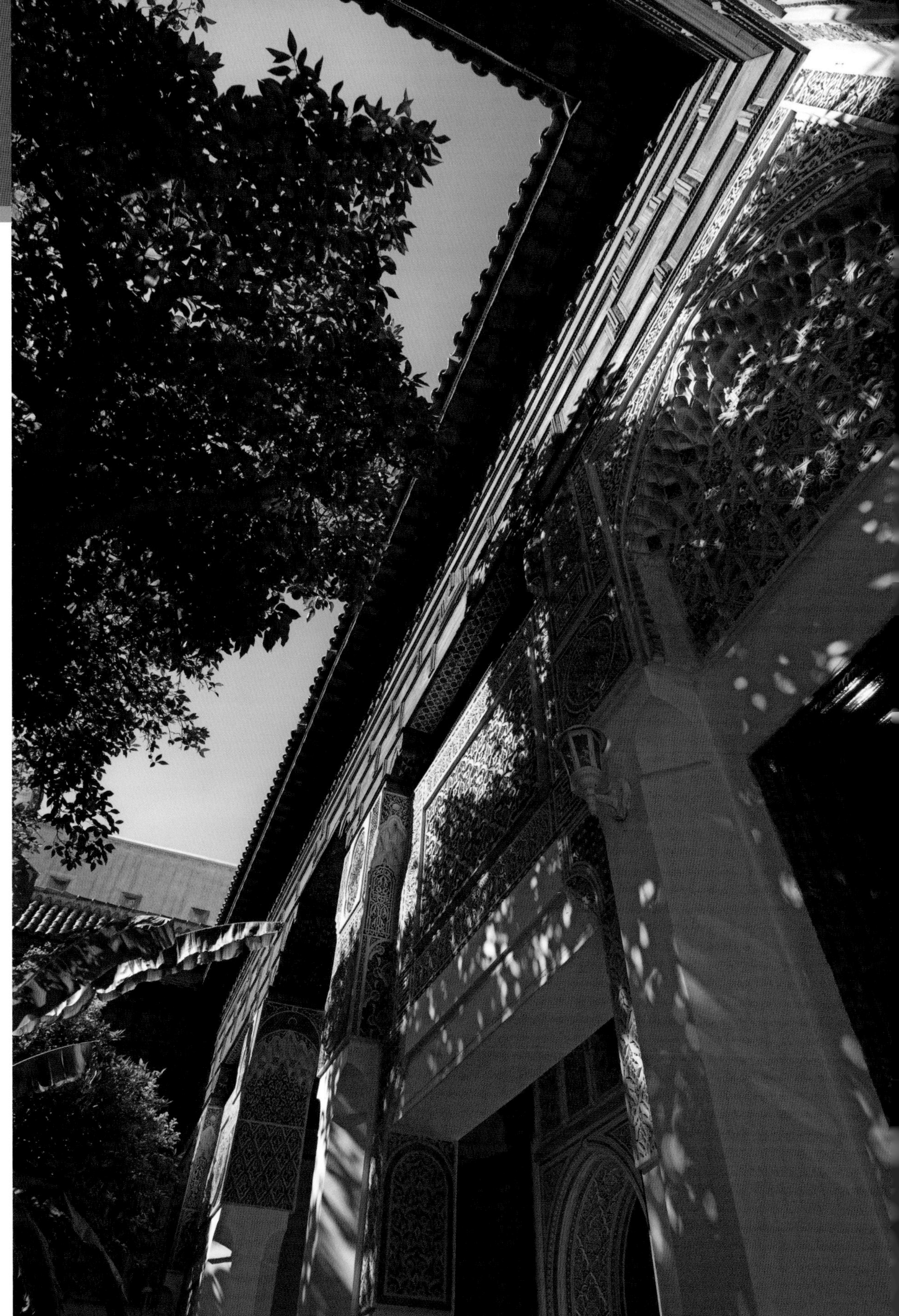

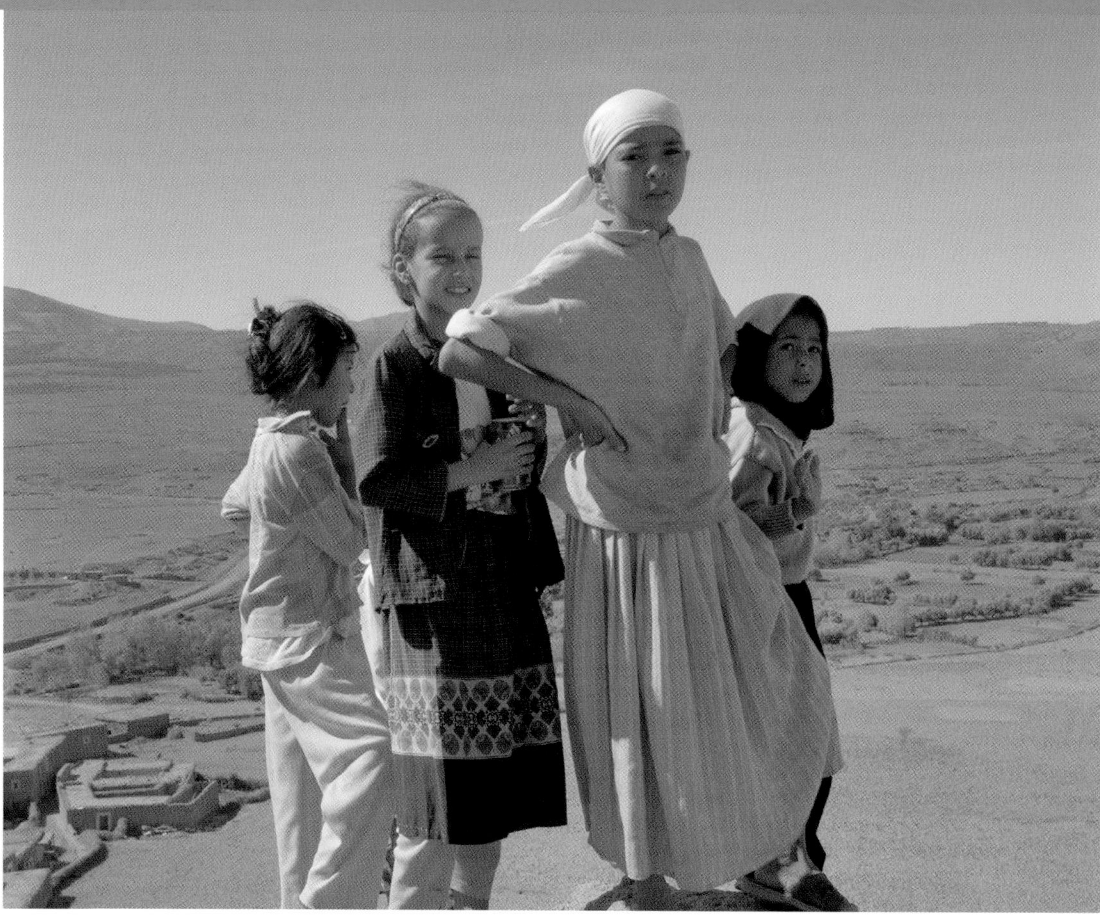

Traditionally, the standard lens for a 35mm camera has a focal length of around 50mm. This focal length is known as standard because it gives an image magnification similar to that of the human eye, so is the closest match to the world as we see it. For DSLRs with a smaller sensor than a 35mm frame, the focal length to give the same magnification is shorter. For digital cameras with a 1.5X or 1.6X cropping factor, the standard focal length is around 34mm, while for the Four Thirds system this would be a 25mm lens.

Although there are standard lenses available with these focal lengths, you will usually find them as part of the focal length range of a standard zoom. These offer the versatility of being able to change the focal length from wide-angle to telephoto in a single lens. Because of this, it's tempting to ignore this focal length as it can lack the impact of the wider or longer lengths, and use your standard zoom instead at the extreme ends of its range. However, learning how to use this familiar view can help to make your compositions much stronger, so try setting the zoom at a standard focal length and using your viewpoint to make the most of the scene, rather than relying on the zoom lens to get the framing that you want. You will find that the discipline that this technique teaches you can enhance your composition skills. Remember, your feet are the most powerful compositional tool you have.

Composition techniques to use with standard lenses

Because the standard lens gives a view similar to our own view of the world, it can produce the most natural-looking results. This doesn't mean you can ignore the composition of your standard lens shots, though.

Rule of thirds

One of the best techniques to use with images taken with a standard lens is the rule of thirds. This technique can add balance to your shots by placing subjects on imaginary lines that divide the vertical and horizontal axis into three equal parts.

Diagonal lines

Images taken with a standard lens can lack impact because the perspective of this focal length is so familiar to the human eye. To liven up your images, include elements such as diagonal lines to add energy to the composition.

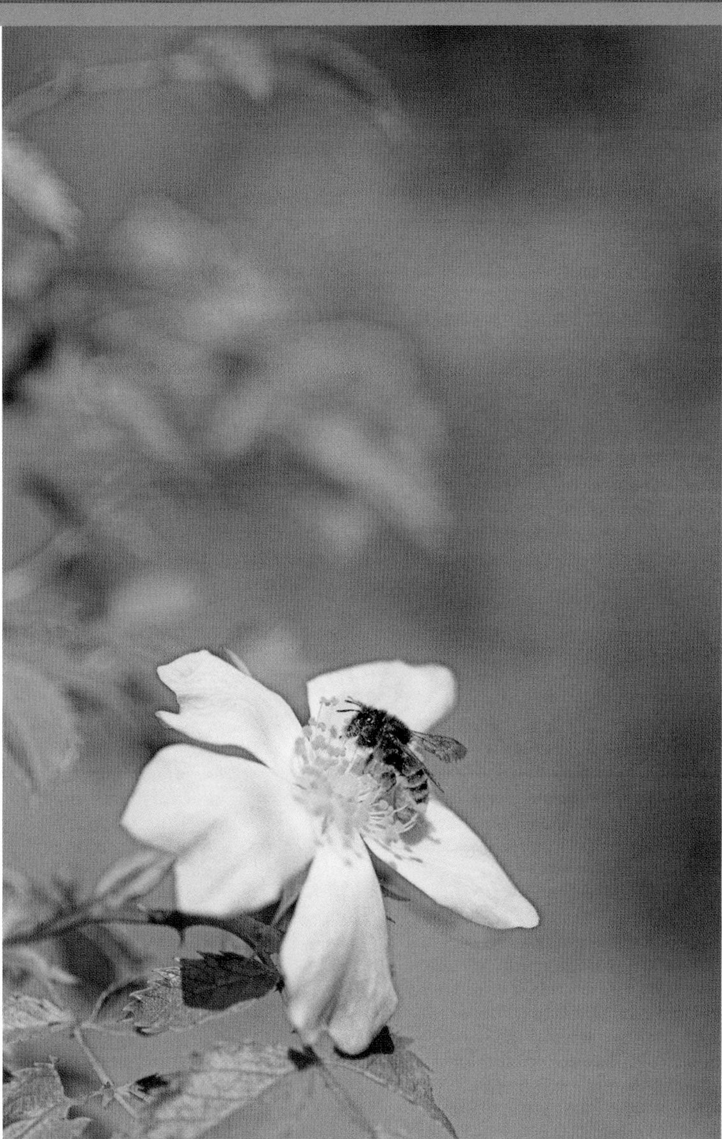

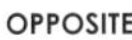

OPPOSITE
A standard zoom is ideal for shooting portraits. Using a focal length of around 35 to 50mm will allow you to shoot at the perfect distance to get the most natural-looking perspective.

RIGHT
The close-focus on most standard zooms allows you to shoot small subjects such as insects, especially when you want to include some of the subject's surroundings.

WHAT IS THE STANDARD FOCAL LENGTH?

The focal length of a standard lens for any format is approximately equal to the size of the diagonal measurement of the image. So, for a 35mm or full-frame DSLR this dimension is approximately 50mm, while the dimensions for APS-C sized and Four Thirds sensors are around 34mm and 25mm respectively.

Although the term "telephoto" actually refers to a specific design of long focal length lens, it has become a generic term for any lens longer than the standard focal length. Like a telescope, a longer focal length lens allows you to magnify small parts of the scene, so is ideal for getting close-ups of subjects that you can't normally get close to, such as sports and wildlife. Telephoto lenses can also affect the composition and framing of your images.

Because they offer high magnifications, you will often be some distance away from your subject. This viewpoint has a huge effect on the perspective of your shots, giving the impression that objects are closer together than they would normally appear. This effect can make your telephoto shots appear a little "flat," so you need to think carefully about your composition.

Many of the subjects that you'll shoot with a telephoto lens will be very distant from you so you don't have the same type of control over the positioning of objects in the scene as with shorter lenses. But you can still use many of the same composition techniques simply by moving your viewpoint or using a zoom lens to fine-tune the size and position of the subject in the frame. Because of the greater distance between you and the subject you'll often find that you have to move your own position significantly to get the right background and subject positioning. So be prepared for some exercise when shooting distant subjects, and don't just settle for the frame-filling ability of a long lens.

Composition techniques to use with telephoto lenses

"Compressed" perspective

Although not due to the lens itself, a distant viewpoint makes objects appear closer together from front to back than they do at closer distances. This effect can be exploited with telephoto lenses because they allow you to magnify these distant subjects so that they fill the frame.

Aerial perspective

Particles in the atmosphere make the color and tone of objects appear less intense the farther they are away from us. You can use this effect in your telephoto shots to enhance the sense of distance.

Subject positioning

You may not be able to change the subject's position in the scene, but you can affect how it appears by selecting where you put it in the frame. When shooting with longer lenses it's tempting to fill the frame with the main subject. But that doesn't always produce the best or most powerful composition. By using a slightly shorter lens and positioning the subject carefully in the frame, you can show more of the surroundings or environment, but still produce a strong composition.

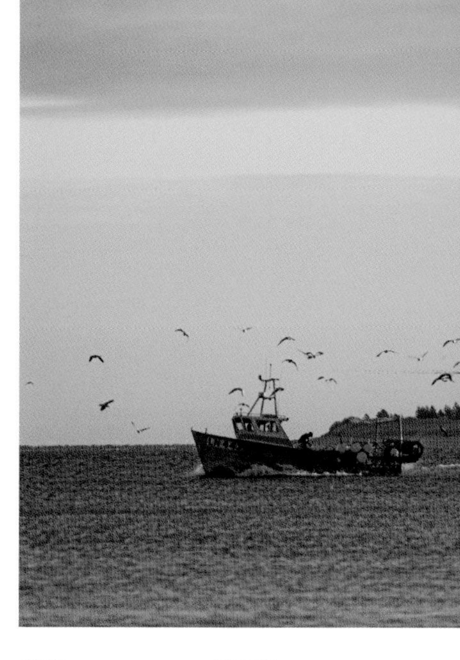

ABOVE
Using a telephoto lens allows you to pick out and isolate individual subjects in the scene, giving them much greater impact than a wider shot.

OPPOSITE
Telephoto lenses allow you to fill the frame with subjects that are difficult to get close too. Notice how the background in this shot appears to be very close to the giraffes due to the distant viewpoint.

CAMERA SHAKE

Although not a composition issue, camera shake can ruin even the most carefully composed shots. This is more of a problem with telephoto lenses because they magnify the effects of any camera movement producing blurred images. If you are handholding your camera, try to keep the shutter speed roughly 1/the focal length, or shorter. For example, if you are shooting with a 300mm lens you need a shutter speed of at least 1/300 sec to ensure sharp results, so try to shoot at 1/500 sec or faster.

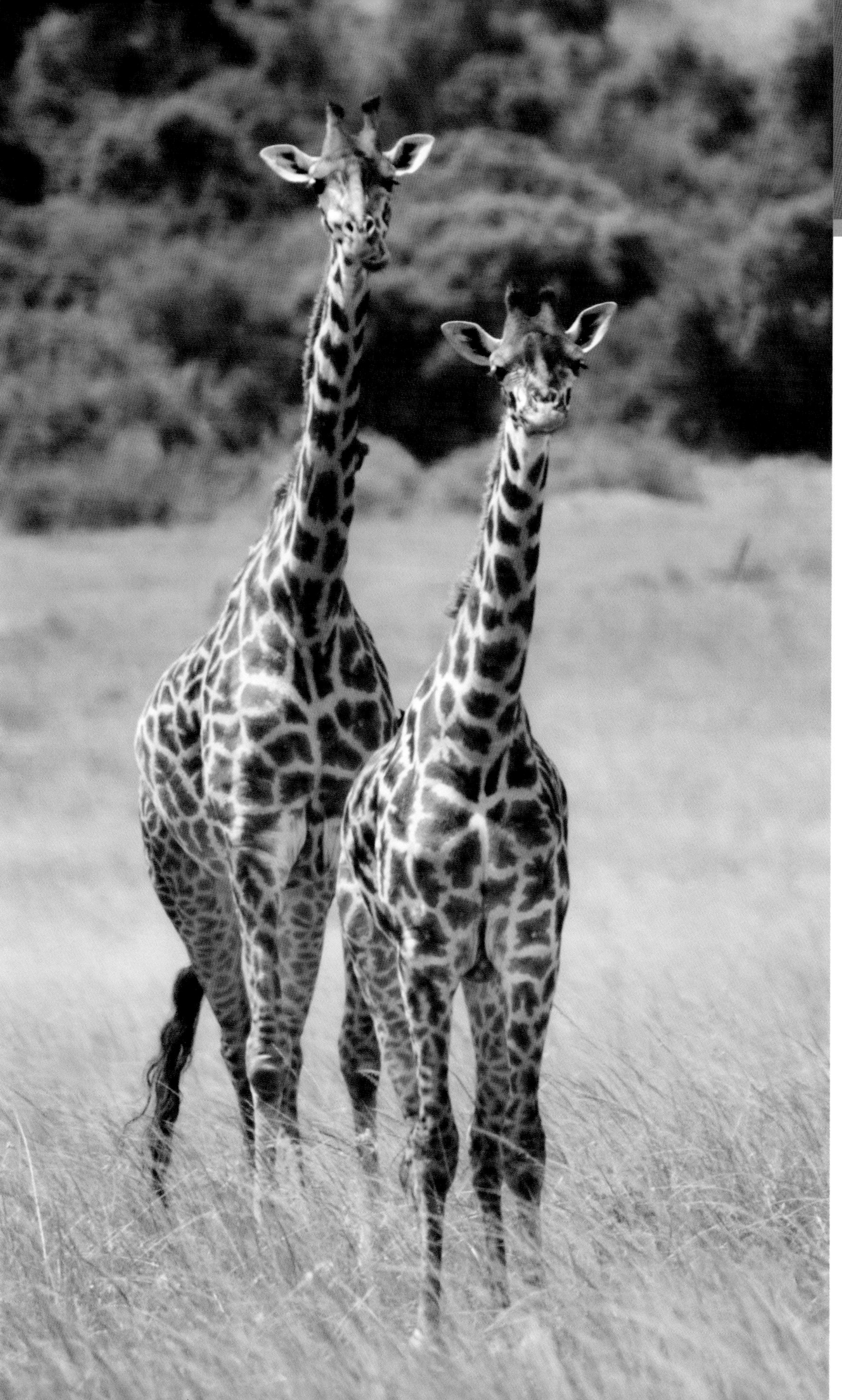

MACRO LENSES

Although many lenses are given the name "macro" by manufacturers, this is usually nothing more than marketing speak for the ability to focus reasonably close. Technically, a macro lens is one that allows you to focus close enough to give what is known as life-size or 1:1 reproduction (see panel below right).

Most dedicated macro lenses have a fixed focal length between 50 and 300mm, to allow you to achieve life-size reproduction at a reasonable distance from the subject. The longer the focal length, the farther away you will be from the subject, so it's worth thinking about this before you buy a macro lens.

Insect and wildlife photographers will find the greater working distance of a 150mm or 180mm macro lens means that they can get better shots of timid wildlife. The most common focal length for macro lenses is around 90 to 105mm. On a full-frame DSLR these focal lengths are also great for portraits, although they can be a little too long on a small-sensor model. To overcome this, some manufacturers have introduced 60 or 70mm macro lenses that give just the right field of view for portraits on these cameras.

Using other lenses for close-ups
You can shoot close-ups with many different types of lenses, although the effect of the focal length and viewpoint will give very different results. With wide-angle lenses you'll need to get extremely close to the subject to achieve a close-up, giving a very different perspective to a telephoto lens where you will be much farther away for the same magnification. We'll look in more depth at how you can use these lenses for close-ups in Section 6.

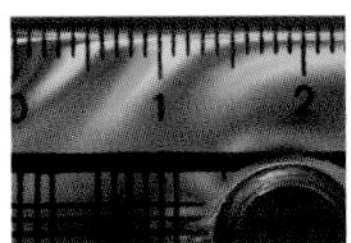

BELOW
This shot was taken using a macro lens at life-size reproduction, hence the frame is filled by a subject exactly the same size as the sensor inside the camera, which is 23x16mm.

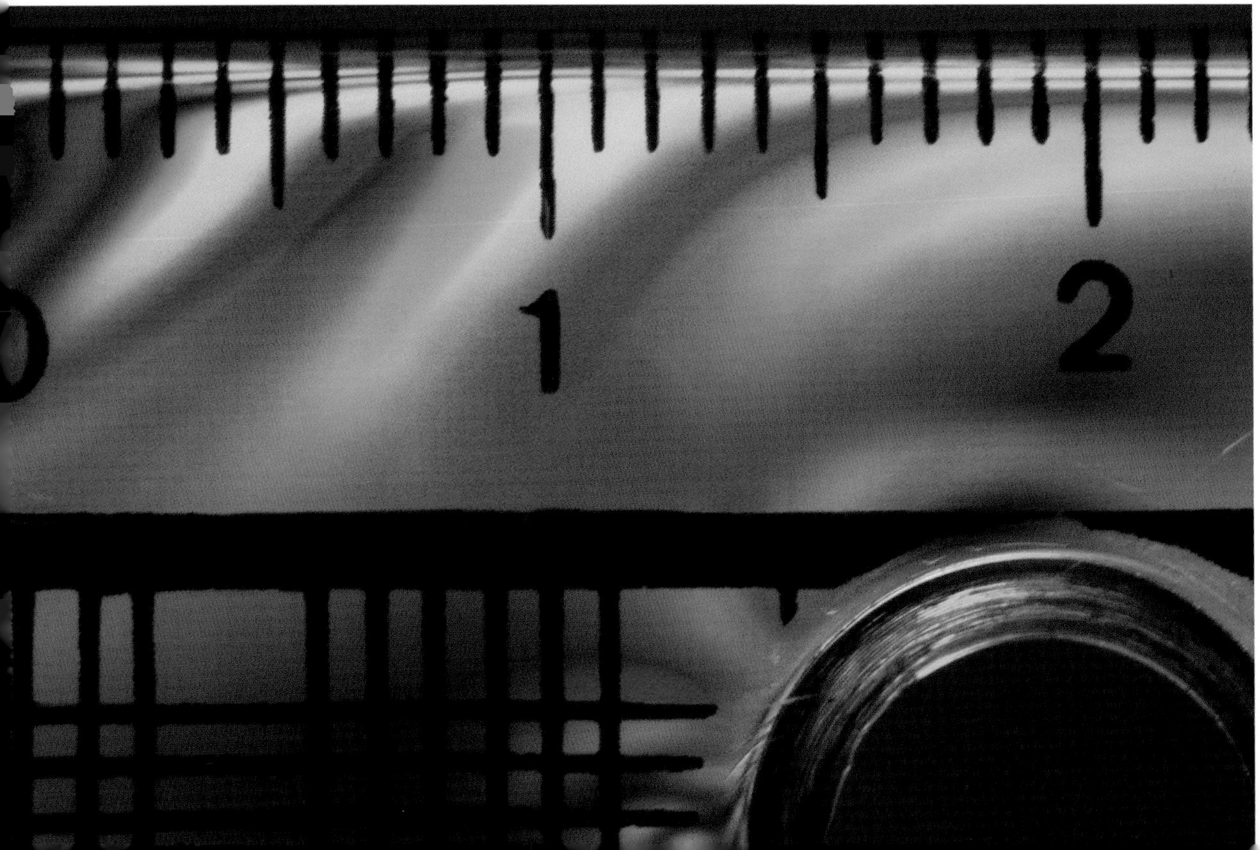

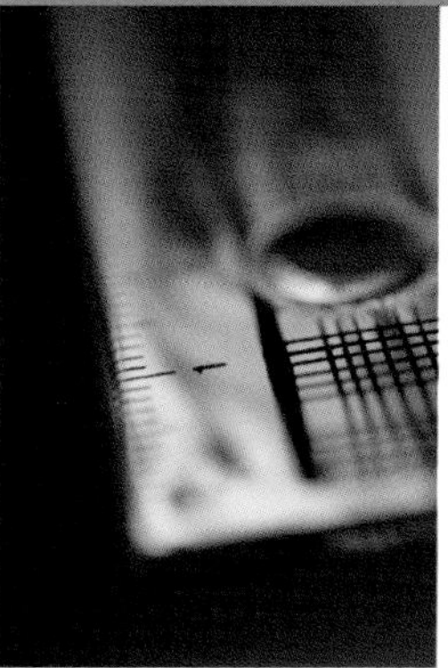

f/2.8

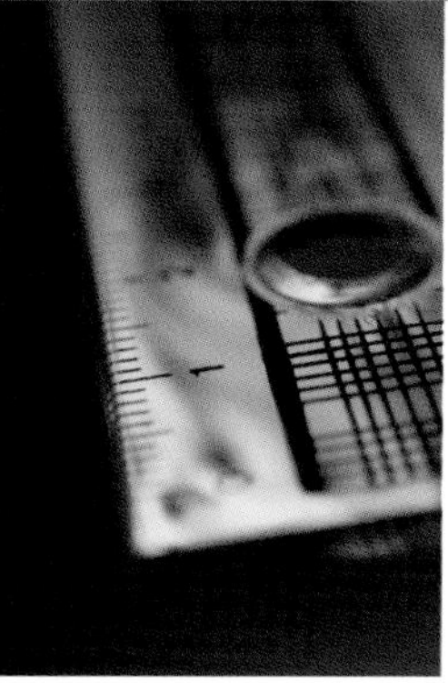

f/5.6

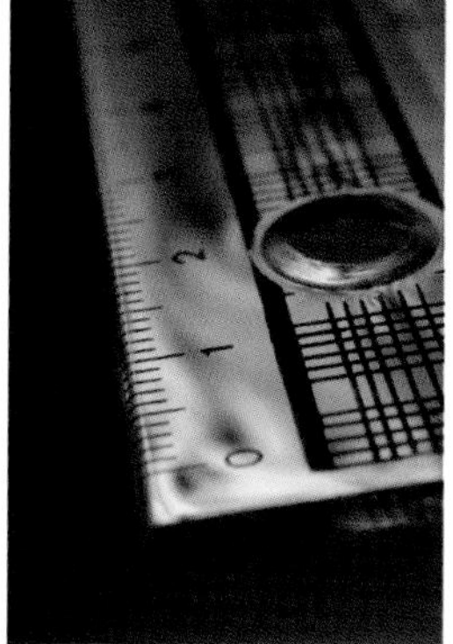

f/11

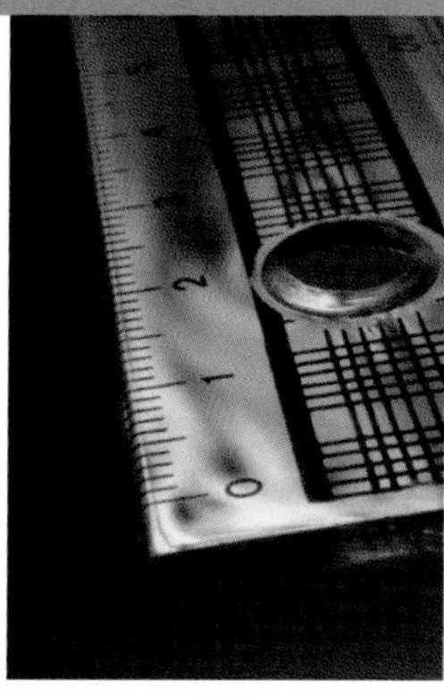

f/32

ABOVE
The depth of field available in macro shots can be extremely small. These four shots were taken at half life-size at different aperture settings with the lens focused on the 1cm marking. At f/2.8 the sharp area doesn't even cover the distance from 1mm in front of the main point of focus and 2mm behind it. As the lens is stopped down, this area increases in size until at f/32 it covers almost 10mm in front and 15mm behind the focus point.

BELOW
The narrow depth of field can be used to concentrate attention on a single part of the image, such as the stamen of the main flower in this shot.

Reproduction ratio

This term describes the magnification that you can achieve with a macro lens. It tells you the smallest object that you can focus on so that it will fill the frame of your image, giving you an idea of the type of subject that you'll be able to shoot. This relates the size to the size of the sensor (or film) so, although the reproduction ratio doesn't change when a lens is used on cameras with different sized sensors, the size of the object that will fill the frame will be different.

Most digital cameras have a sensor that is approximately 23x16mm in size, so that at 1:1 or life-size reproduction you'll fill the frame with an object that is this size. On a full-frame camera, the same reproduction ratio will fill the frame with an object 36x24mm.

Reproduction ratios only apply to the sensor size—so as soon as you use the image larger, the reproduction ratio no longer applies.

TYPICAL DISTANCES NEEDED TO ACHIEVE 1:1 REPRODUCTION

Focal length	Subject to camera distance
50mm	7½ in (19cm)
70mm	9¾ in (25cm)
105mm	12¼ in (31cm)
180mm	18 in (46cm)

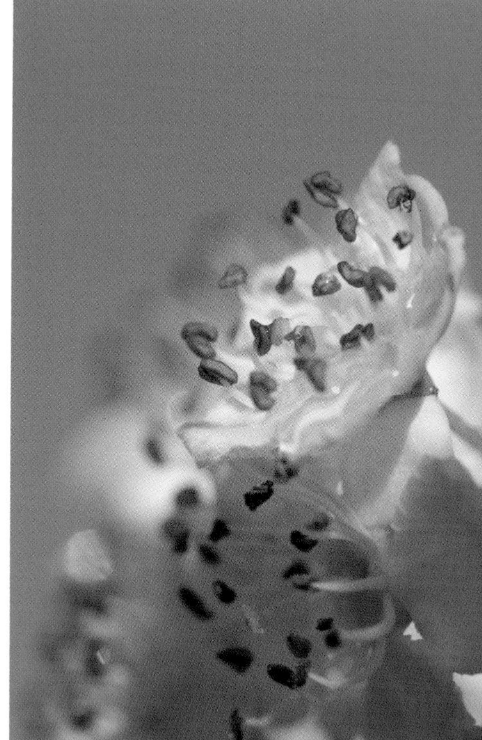

While the previous pages dealt with the sort of lenses you'll find in most photographers' bags, there are some more specialized options available for your DSLR.

Prime lenses

Prime lenses offer only a single focal length, rather than the more common zoom. You will find prime lens options at most focal lengths, although they are becoming less popular thanks to the greater versatility offered by zoom lenses. When it comes to composition, prime lenses force you to search for different viewpoints, rather than simply zooming in or out to achieve the framing you want. Also, prime lenses offer wider maximum apertures than zooms, allowing you to use shallower depth of field in your composition.

Fisheye

Most wide-angle lenses are designed to give as little distortion as possible, athough there is a tendency for straight lines at the edge of the frame to bend outward in the middle. Fisheye lenses, however, are designed to produce either a circular or a very distorted image at the edge of the frame.

Fisheye lenses tend to be at the very wide end of the focal length range from around 7 to 14mm. To get the full circular fisheye effect, you'll need to use a full-frame DSLR, although even on a camera with a smaller sensor many will still produce extremely distorted images.

Because of the extremely short focal lengths, you need to get close to the subject for them to appear at any size in the frame, so they also tend to produce very distorted perspectives. While this can be effective when used sparingly, the distortion can soon become more of a curiosity than a valid photographic technique, so think carefully before buying one.

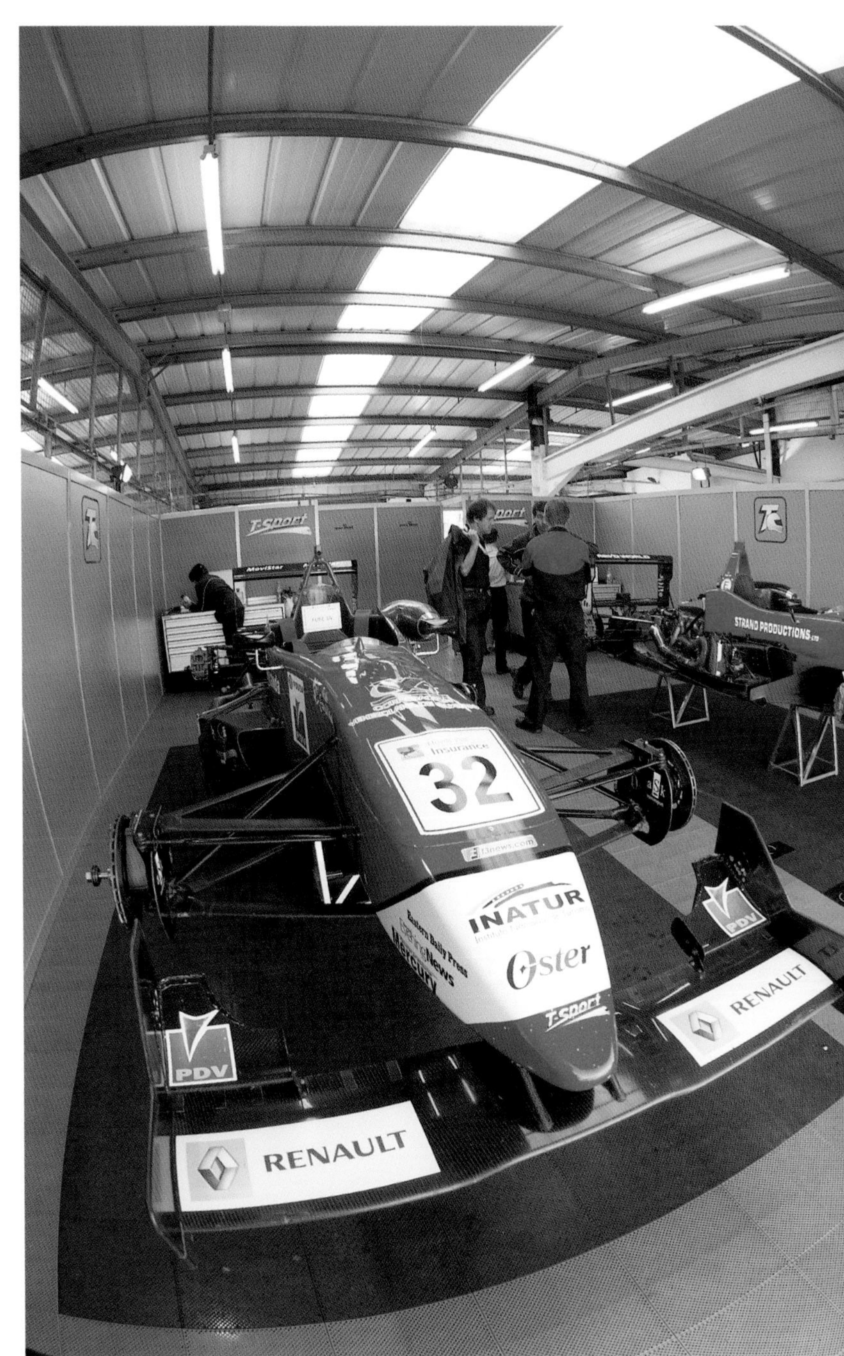

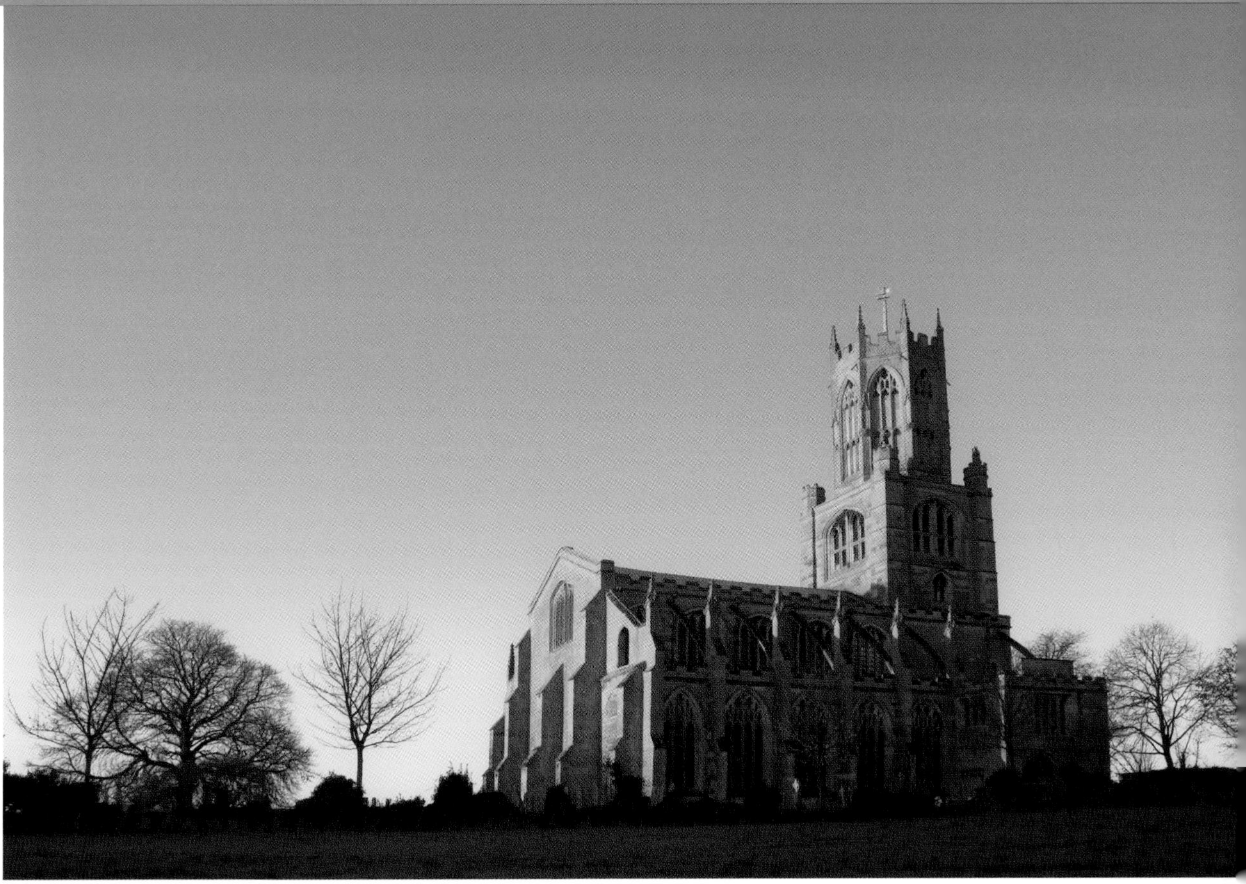

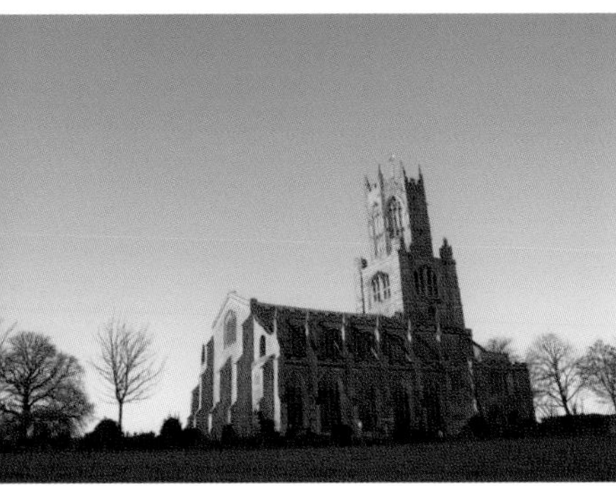

OPPOSITE
Notice how the straight lines at the top of this shot have been curved by the extreme wide-angle view of the lens.

Perspective control (or shift) lenses
While the focal length of a lens doesn't affect the perspective of your images, this specialized lens can offer some control over it. It does this by moving the body of the lens up and down, or from side to side, in relation to the sensor.

The main use for perspective control lenses is in architectural photography. You would normally have to tilt the camera upward to include the whole of a building, resulting in the building appearing to fall over backward. With a perspective control lens you can keep the camera level, then move the body of the lens upward to include the building.

The high price of these lenses means that they are a rare sight, and with digital images you can achieve similar results in many cases in your imaging software. (See page 168 for how to achieve this effect in Photoshop.)

ABOVE AND LEFT
A shift or perspective control lens allows you to avoid the problem of converging vertical lines. You can keep the camera level because elements of the lens move instead to alter the area of the scene captured by the lens.

Section 3

Cropping and Composition

THE BASIC RULES OF COMPOSITION

The basic theories of composition have been around for centuries. Ever since people first started drawing and painting, they have tried to come up with ways of translating the three-dimensional world into two-dimensional images.

Over the years these ideas have become what we now think of as the "rules" of composition. They should perhaps be called conventions rather than rules, as they are simply techniques that can make your photography more successful; they do not necessarily need to be strictly adhered to.

The rules of composition fall into two main categories: first, those that are designed to make the arrangement of objects in your images appear more pleasing, and second, those that give the impression of depth to the photograph. Rules such as using lead-in lines and adding foreground interest add depth to your images, while those that deal with the simple placing of objects—like the rule of thirds—are more about making the composition appear pleasing and balanced. When you're planning the composition of your image, try to visualize the effect that you want to achieve. Do you want the viewer to be drawn into the image, or do you want to ensure that the main subject is in the best position? Once you've answered this question you can start to use the rules to help you to achieve your goal.

In the real world, subjects don't always fall neatly into these two categories, and you'll eventually find yourself applying two or more rules to a single image. But you need to gain an understanding of the individual rules before you can start to weave them seamlessly together. Over the following pages we will be dealing with the main rules that you should learn, along with ways to break them successfully.

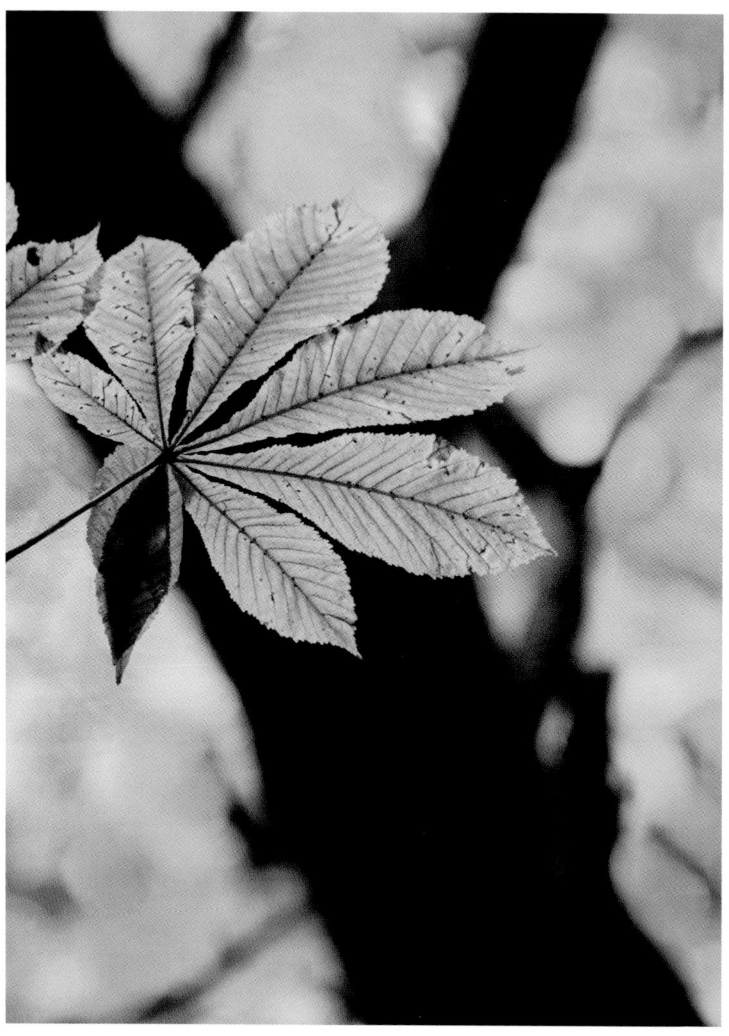

LEFT
Using the basic rules of composition can add impact and order to your images. Simply positioning the single leaf in the correct area of the frame, and using the diagonal lines formed by the branches behind it to lead the eye toward it, makes the most of this shot.

WHICH RULE FOR WHICH EFFECT?

Adding depth
Lead-in lines
Foreground interest
Perspective

Arranging objects
Rule of thirds
Subject positioning

It is not enough to simply follow (or even deliberately break) rules blindly. Successful composition is all about seeing the potential in your subject, trying different viewpoints, and above all, pinpointing what you are trying to show in your picture. Although the rules are great for making this possible, you should always try to see beyond them, rather than forcing your subject to conform to them. The best way to learn composition is to experiment with your treatment and positioning of the subject, and that's one great advantage of digital—you can experiment without having to go to the expense of buying film or having your pictures processed and printed. That's not to say that you should fire off shots indiscriminately, hoping some of them will work, but you should always be on the lookout for new ways of composing your images.

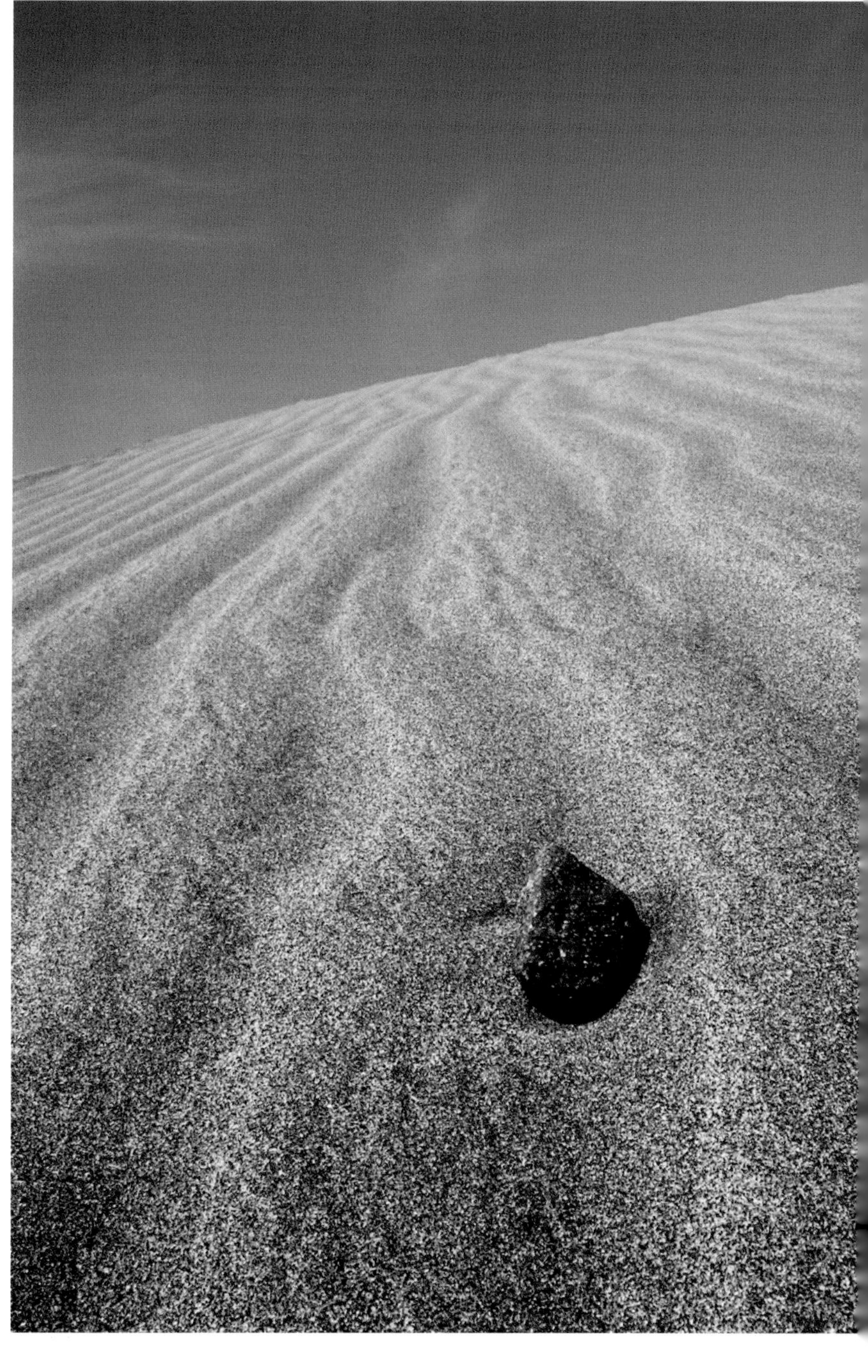

RIGHT
Even with just a simple scene, you can still produce effective shots by looking for unusual angles. Getting down low, using the ripples in the sand, and finding a solitary rock to use as foreground interest, has made a striking composition from almost nothing.

A digital camera doesn't see the world like we do. This may seem like an obvious statement, but this fact lies at the heart of successful composition. The camera is simply a tool that allows us to record the scene in front of us. It can't compose the picture, or decide when to fire the shutter. Photography is all about translating the scene in front of you into a two-dimensional image, and this is down to you.

Before we learn the rules of composition, let's look at the terms we will be using to describe the elements of photographic images.

Foreground
The area of the image closest to you. We naturally pay the most attention to things that are closest to us, because they are the most likely to interact with us.

Focal point
The most dominant object in the image. Learning how to use compositional techniques, such as limited depth of field and selective focus, will allow you to maximize the impact of the focal point.

Horizon
Usually the intersection between the sky and either the land or sea. Its position in the frame is a major factor in the composition of any scenic image.

Viewpoint
The place from which you take the image. It is tempting to take every photograph from eye-level when you are standing, but never be satisfied with just one viewpoint. Simply moving your position can dramatically alter the composition and impact of your images and is one of the most important aspects of successful composition.

Perspective
This is an expression used for all of the elements that fool you into accepting that a two-dimensional image has depth. The most common elements you'll find are diagonal lines that converge from front to back and objects that get smaller in the frame. Perspective also describes the view

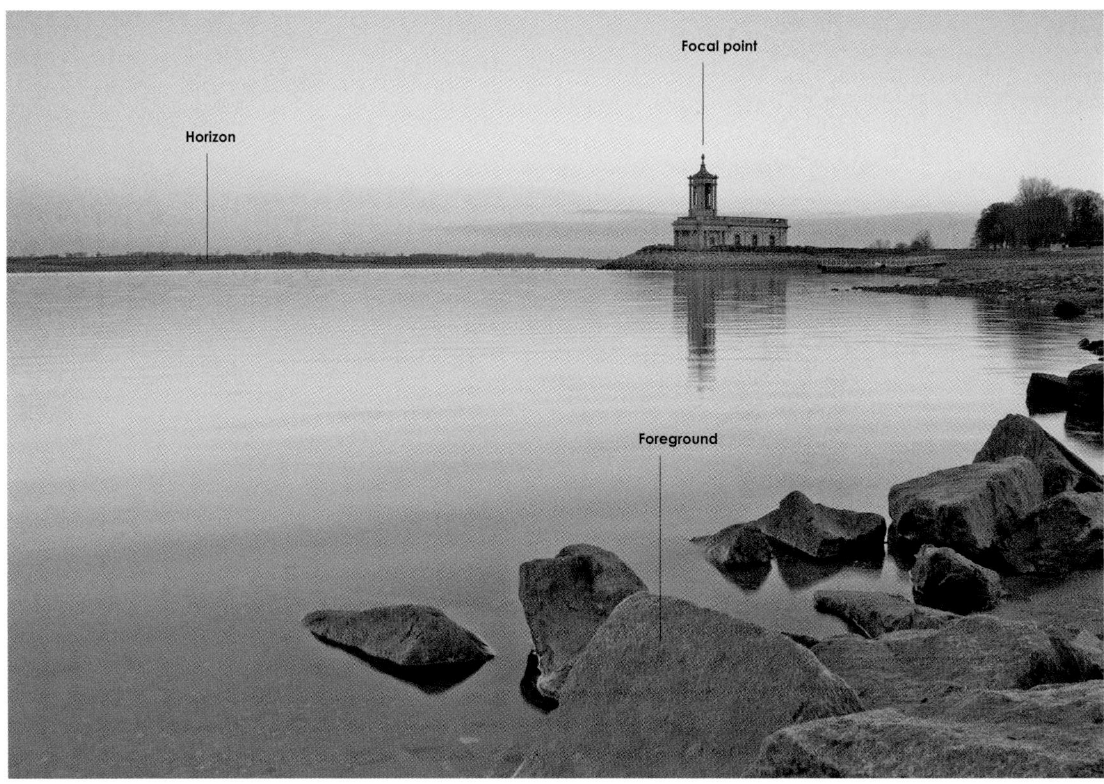

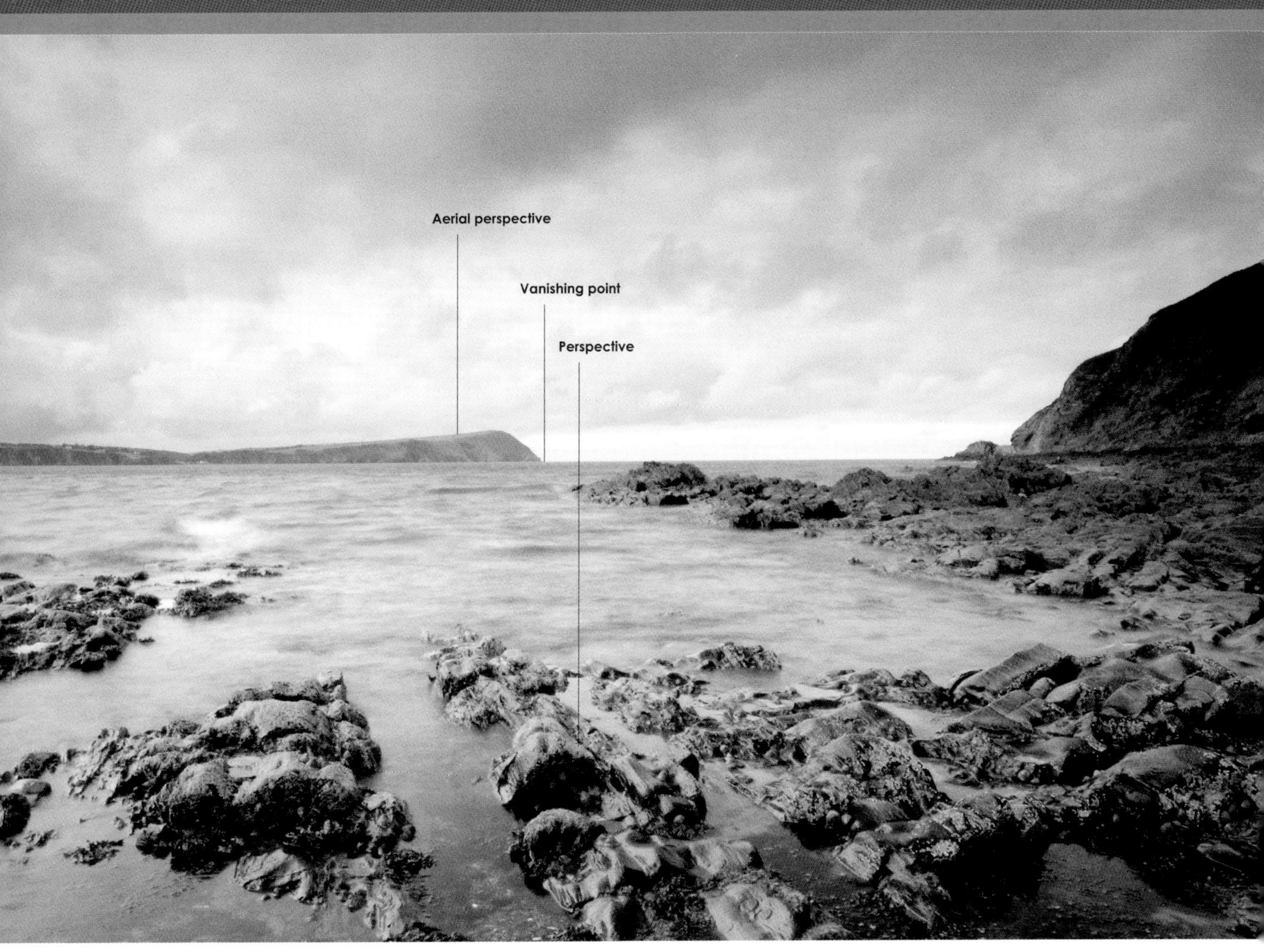

that you get from a particular viewpoint, since perspective is determined by the viewpoint from which the image is taken.

Vanishing point
An imaginary point where straight lines in an image converge that is used to convey a sense of depth in two-dimensional images. This is one of the building blocks of rendering perspective in a picture.

Aerial perspective
This describes the effect of viewing objects through the atmosphere. Tones and colors appear lighter and less saturated the farther away they are because we view them through the atmosphere. This effect is most noticeable in landscapes when there is fog or mist in the air making background objects appear less distinct than those in the foreground.

OPPOSITE
A strong focal point and foreground interest have been used to capture this classic composition.

ABOVE
The converging lines of the rocks give this image a sense of depth, which is emphasized by the lighter tones of the background.

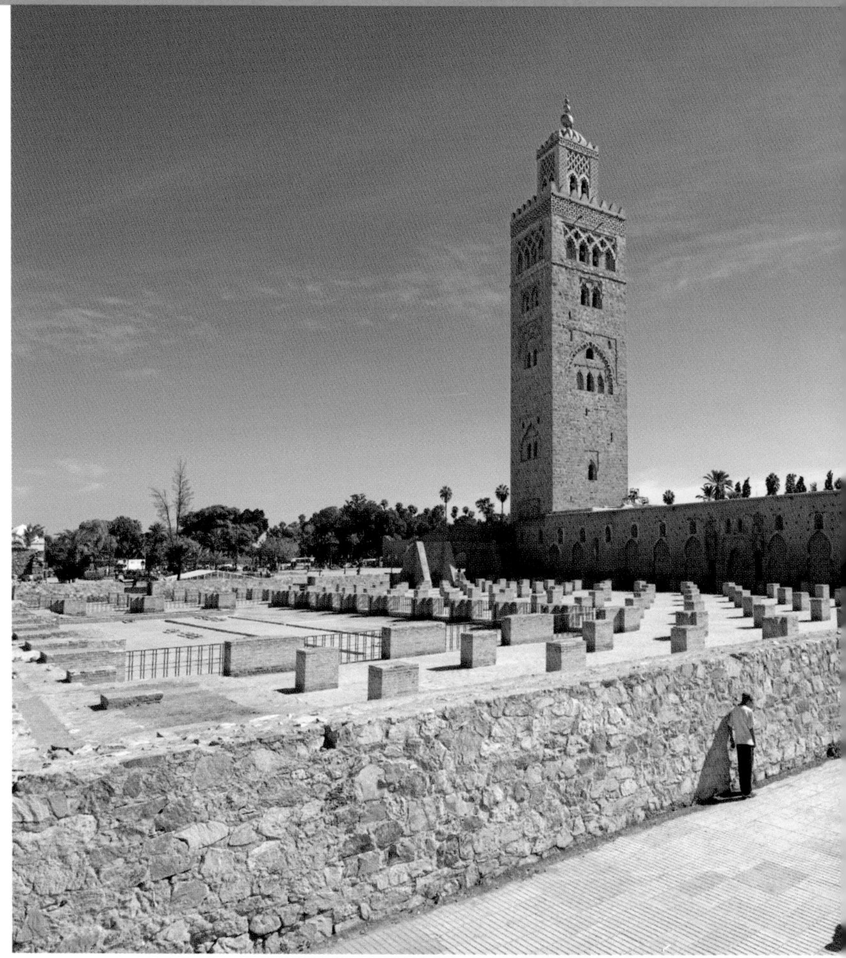

Seeing the picture

We see the world very differently to how an image is captured by your camera. Learning how to see a photographic image within a real-life scene is the key to successful composition. Although our eyes have a relatively narrow field of view, we can constantly scan the scene in front of us. This information is processed by our brain to give us an impression of a wide area.

The first decision to make is where to point the camera. This is very much a personal choice based on your feelings about the scene, what it is that you want to record, and the type of image that you're looking to create. Place two photographers next to each other and it's likely that they will produce very different images. But the important thing is recognizing the element or elements of the scene that you want to shoot, then concentrating your attention on this area. At this stage many people find it easier to look through the camera to get an idea of how the image will look, but with practice you'll be able to visualize the image even before you put the camera to your eye.

One of the most important aspects is deciding what to leave out, rather than what to include in the picture. Decide which areas or objects detract from, rather than complement, the image. For example, if you're shooting a portrait, should you include some of the background to give a sense of where you took the shot, or get a closer view and concentrate your attention on the person themselves? There are no simple answers to these kinds of questions, but asking them before firing the shutter will help you to take more successful images.

TAKE INSPIRATION FROM OTHER IMAGES

While you don't want to slavishly copy the work of others, there is a host of images available to you for inspiration. When you look at photographs, paintings, and drawings that you admire, try to determine why they work and what it is that you like about them. Try to spot how the artist has positioned elements in the frame and see if they've used any of the rules to help the composition. You'll be surprised at how often the basic rules are used to create great images.

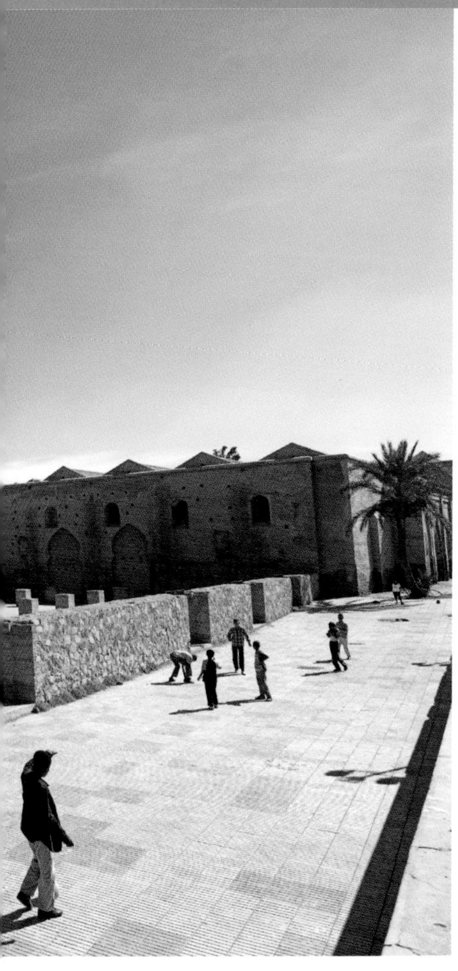

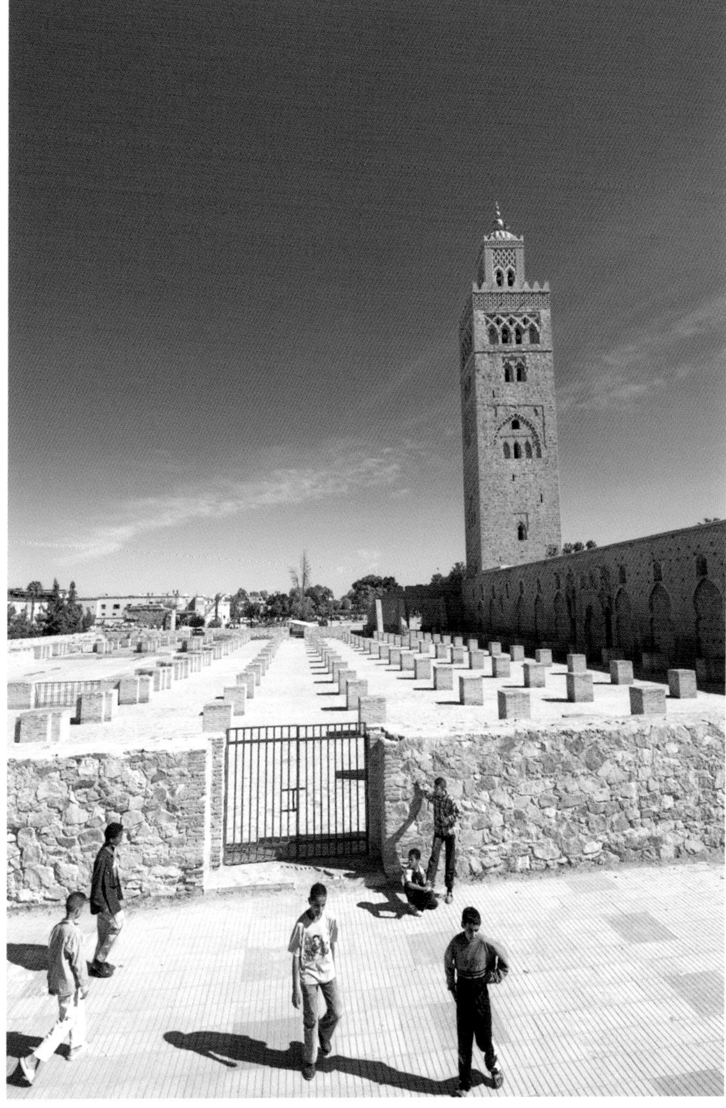

ABOVE AND RIGHT
Choosing your viewpoint and how you frame the subject makes a huge difference to the end result. These two shots, taken just moments apart, show that by simply walking around the subject to try alternative angles, you can create very different images. In the landscape-format shot above, the main focal point is the tower, and it is only after looking at the picture for some time that you notice the children playing in the bottom right. For the upright-format shot, I moved closer to the children, making them more prominent in the frame. The children then become the focal point, with the tower now secondary.

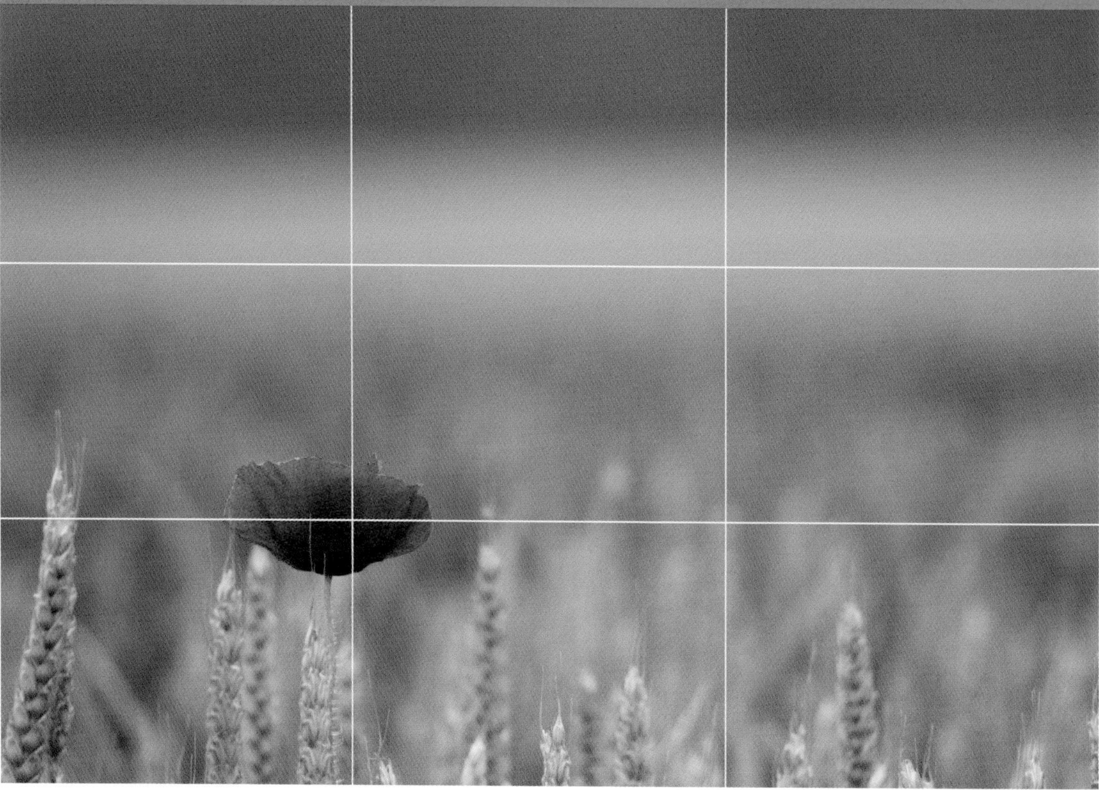

The position and placement of elements within a picture play a crucial part in the composition. Many images contain a main subject that acts as the focal point, drawing the viewer's attention. The placement of this subject is one of the most important decisions to make when composing your images.

The main focusing point of most DSLRs is in the center of the frame, so this would seem to be the most logical place to put the main subject. However, using this position often produces a very static composition, so the center of the frame is rarely the most effective place for your focal point.

The rule of thirds is one of the most effective devices for producing a balanced and dynamic composition. This technique has been used by painters for centuries and is one of the simplest compositional rules that you can use. It's called the rule of thirds because you divide the image into thirds using two imaginary, equally spaced, horizontal and vertical lines. These form a grid over the image indicating the ideal placement for objects.

Where to place the subject

Deciding which of the lines to use varies with the subject. For subjects such as portraits or anything that has a recognizable front and back, it's best to leave the largest area facing the front of the subject. This leaves space for the subject to engage with the picture. If the front of the subject is close to the edge of the picture it looks like the subject is leaving the frame, giving an unnerving feel to the image.

The ideal positioning

The points where the horizontal and vertical lines that make up the thirds meet are the most powerful and effective places to put your subject. Because they are positioned on the third of both planes, they act like anchor points that can hold the whole composition together. This is especially useful when the subject is small in the frame, so needs to be placed carefully to give the most balanced composition.

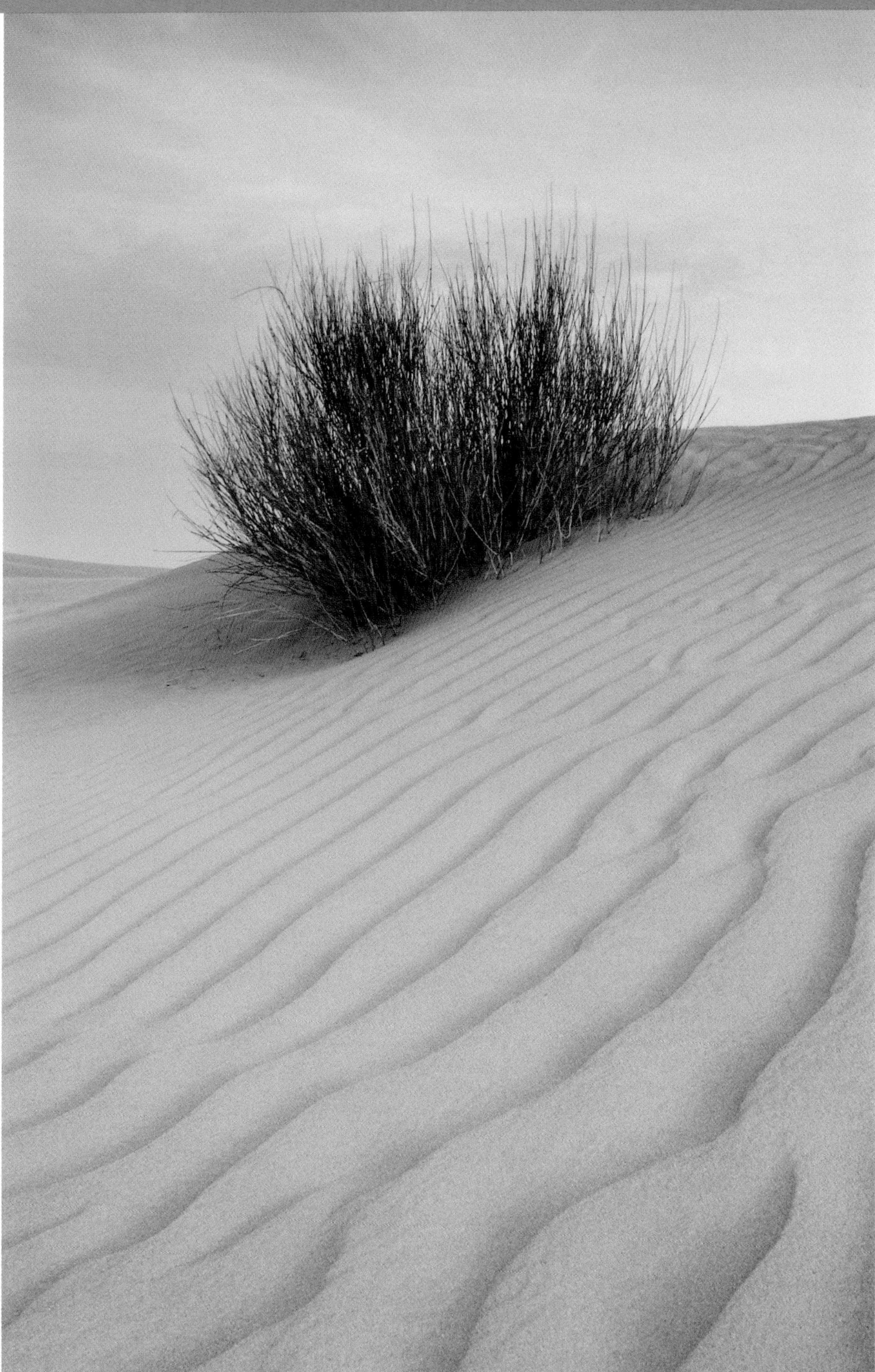

LEFT
Placing the subject on the intersection of the horizontal and vertical lines that divide the image into thirds produces the most balanced composition.

RIGHT
Placing this clump of grass in the top third of the image, with the ripples in the sand below it, gives the right balance in the vertical plane. In addition, placing the grass in the middle of the horizon creates a pleasingly symmetrical composition.

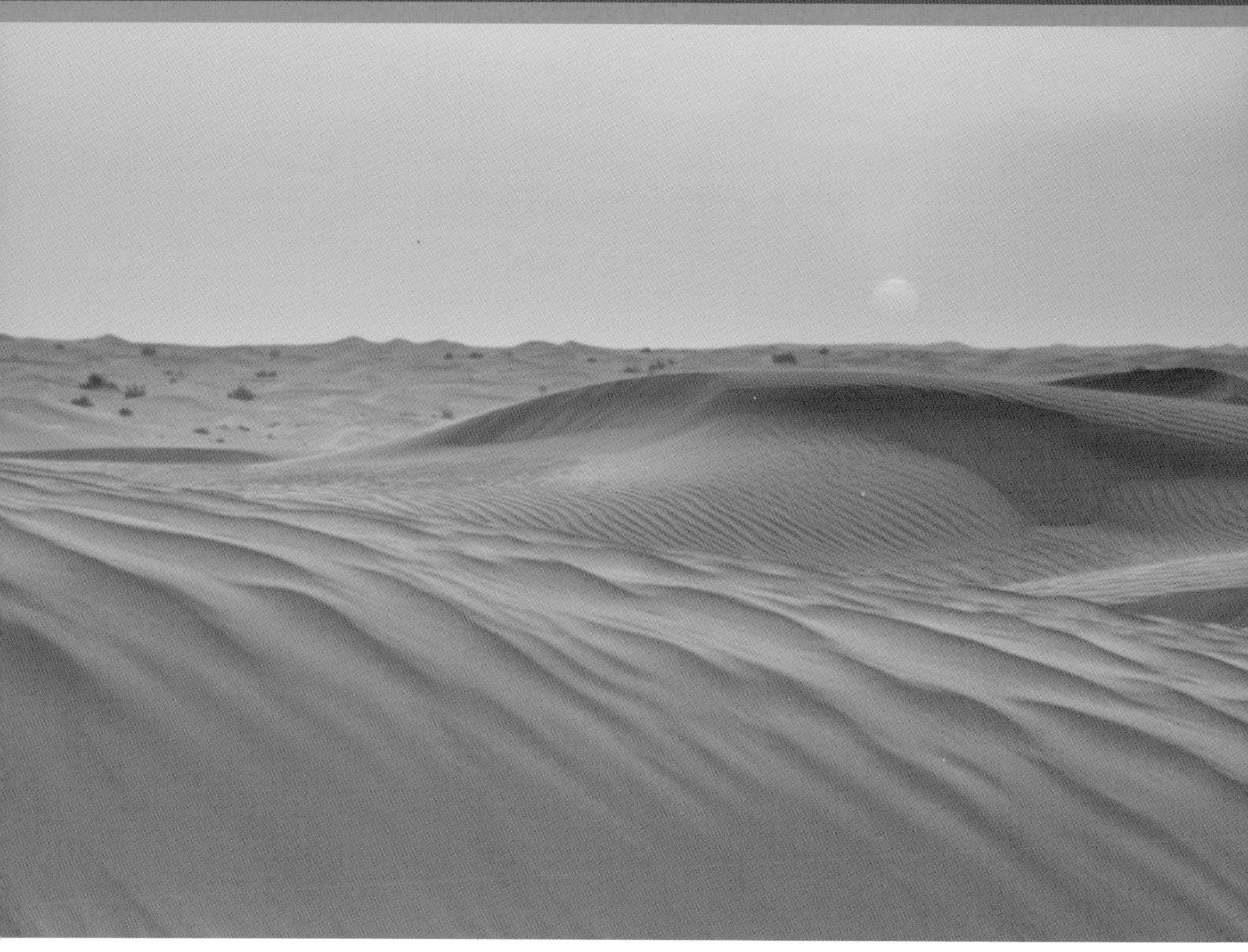

Placing the horizon

The rule of thirds is extremely useful when dealing with strong horizontal or vertical lines. Placing strong lines in the middle of the frame divides a picture into two equal halves, giving a very static and disjointed feel to most images. Placing these lines on one of the thirds gives a much better balance. Place the line so that the most important area takes up the greatest part of the image. For example, if you're shooting a landscape where the scenery is important, place the horizon on the top imaginary line, not at the bottom.

ABOVE
When your image has a strong horizon, the ideal place to put it to create a balanced composition is the line across the top third of the image.

RIGHT
When using autofocus with off-center subjects, you need to ensure that the camera does not focus using the middle of the frame. For this shot I used the left-hand focus point to ensure that the leopard's eyes were in focus.

Using autofocus
Because the main autofocus (AF) point on most DSLRs is in the center of the frame, you can run into problems when trying to focus on subjects placed using the rule of thirds. If you frame up the subject off-center you will find that the camera will focus on whatever is in the middle of the image, not on the subject you want.

One way around this is to select manual focus mode and adjust the focus yourself. You can also use the focus lock facility available on most DSLRs by placing the subject in the middle of the frame, automatically focusing on it, then locking this focus using a button on the camera before reframing your image.

Both of these methods are fine for static subjects, but are less suitable for shooting moving subjects. Most cameras have a number of focus points positioned across the frame to allow you to focus on off-center subjects. Take a look in the viewfinder of your camera to see where these points are. Unfortunately, few cameras offer focus points on the intersections of the imaginary rule of third lines, but by selecting the point closest to where you want to place the subject you can minimize the amount of time you'll spend adjusting the focus.

DON'T ALWAYS FOLLOW THE RULES

Although the rule of thirds is one of the most useful devices in composition, don't feel that you have to force every image to conform to it. There are times when placing the subject in the center of the frame, or even at the edge, works best. As a general rule, putting the subject in the middle of the picture will produce a very static result. However, this can be useful when you want to emphasize a sense of loneliness or boredom in a picture. Placing the subject at the edge of the frame will give it less prominence in the scene, which can give your image a sense of mystery or intrigue, especially if the subject is facing out of the picture.

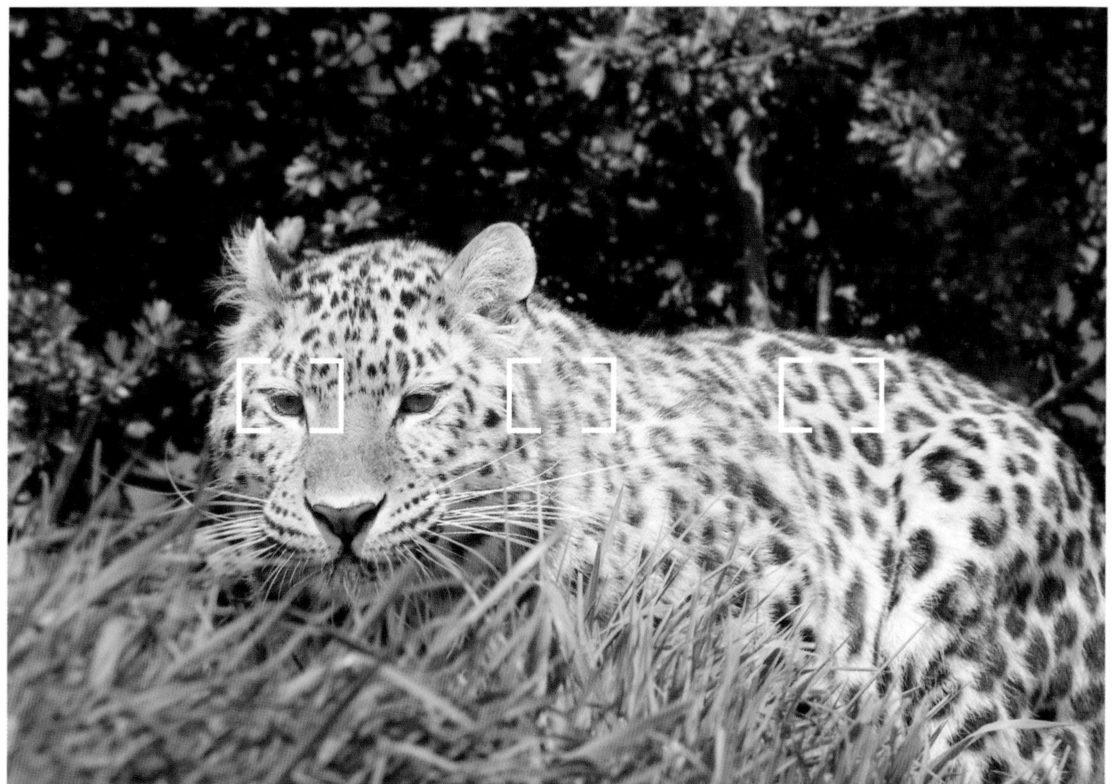

LEAD-IN LINES

When we see a line, we want to follow it to see where it leads because we are naturally very inquisitive. This instinct means that lines are a hugely influential part of composition. When viewing a line in isolation we find it difficult to judge its direction, but in a photograph we can refer to the straight edges of the frame. So it is the relationship between the line and the frame that really lies at the heart of using lines effectively in your images.

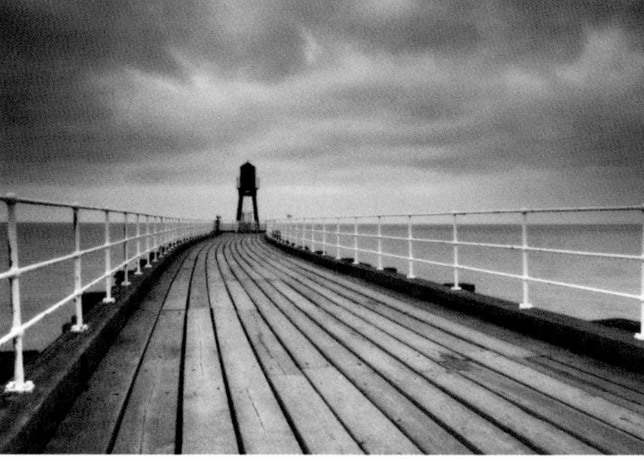

LEFT
The lines formed by the planks of wood on this pier make perfect lead-in lines to draw the eye toward the lighthouse.

Direction
When using lines in compositions, their position and direction plays a major part in how we react to images.

Horizontal
Lines that cross the frame horizontally are generally considered to be quite passive. We are so used to seeing the line of the horizon in our daily lives that horizontal lines give a sense of solidity and calm to an image. Scanning a picture from left to right (or right to left) is the most restful and natural way of looking at an image, and horizontal lines help this action.

Vertical
Lines that cross the picture vertically are more dynamic than horizontal lines. Because they break up the comfortable horizontals, they can make an image appear much more uncomfortable and mysterious. Using vertical lines forces the viewer to scan the image from the bottom to the top, which is a less comfortable action than looking across the horizontal axis.

Diagonal
Lines that pass diagonally across an image create a number of effects. They are more dynamic than either horizontal or vertical lines, so they add energy and a sense of depth to an image.

Converging
Two or more lines converging give the greatest sense of depth to your image. They are a classic way of adding a sense of perspective to two-dimensional images because we recognize that objects diminish in size as they get farther away.

Using lead-in lines
This is a classic composition technique that uses diagonal or converging lines in the image to lead the viewer in. The most obvious lines to use are usually man-made because they tend to stand out from their surroundings and are more regular in appearance. Objects such as tracks, fences, roads, and walls create strong lines in a landscape, whereas natural features such as rivers and rock formations are a more subtle alternative. Lead-in lines can be used to direct the viewer toward the focal point of an image, or can even be used on their own to create a more enigmatic or graphic composition.

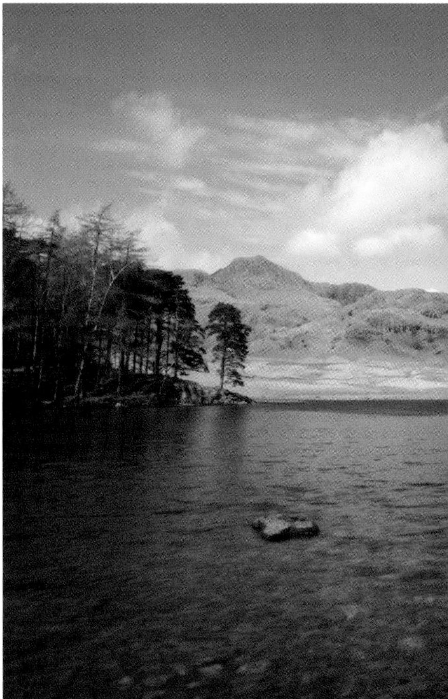

BELOW
The small fence on the right is a subtle, but effective lead-in line to give a sense of depth to this landscape. The diagonal line of the fence also echoes the lines of the mountains in the distance. Without it, the composition of this image would be much weaker.

RIGHT
Lead-in lines can become the subject themselves if you don't include a focal point or other elements. This produces a simple, graphic image emphasizing patterns.

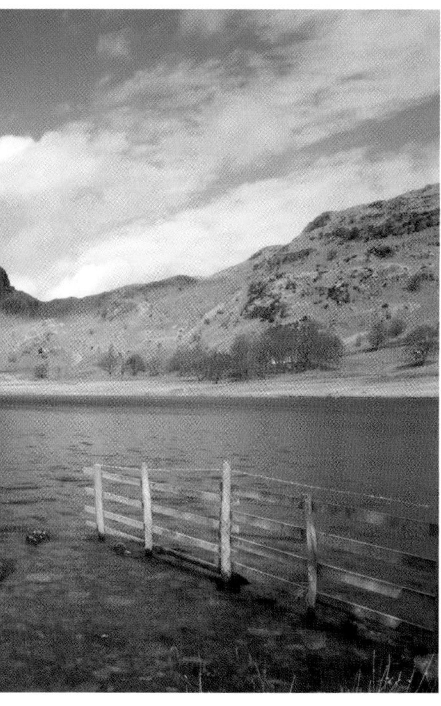

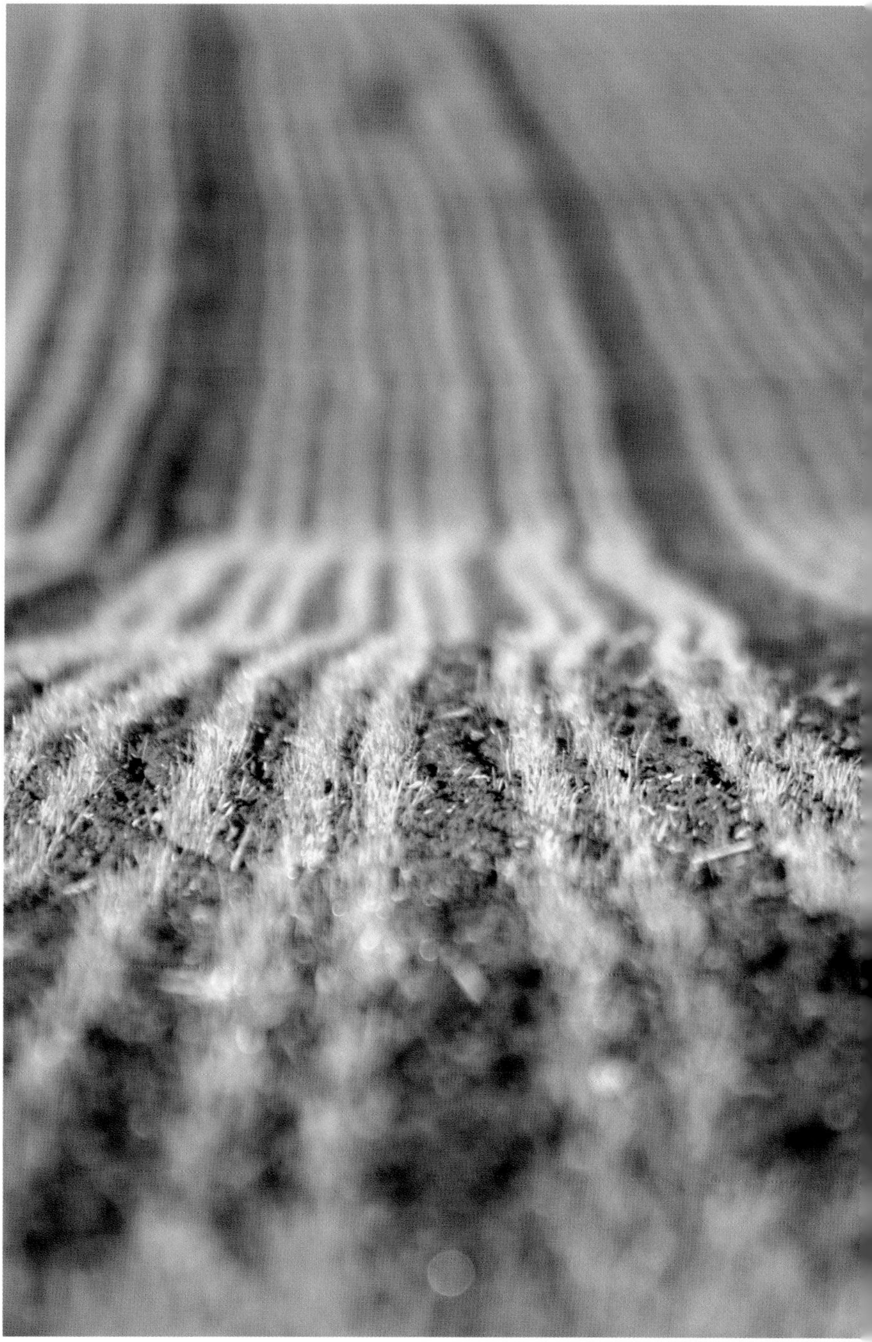

FOREGROUND INTEREST

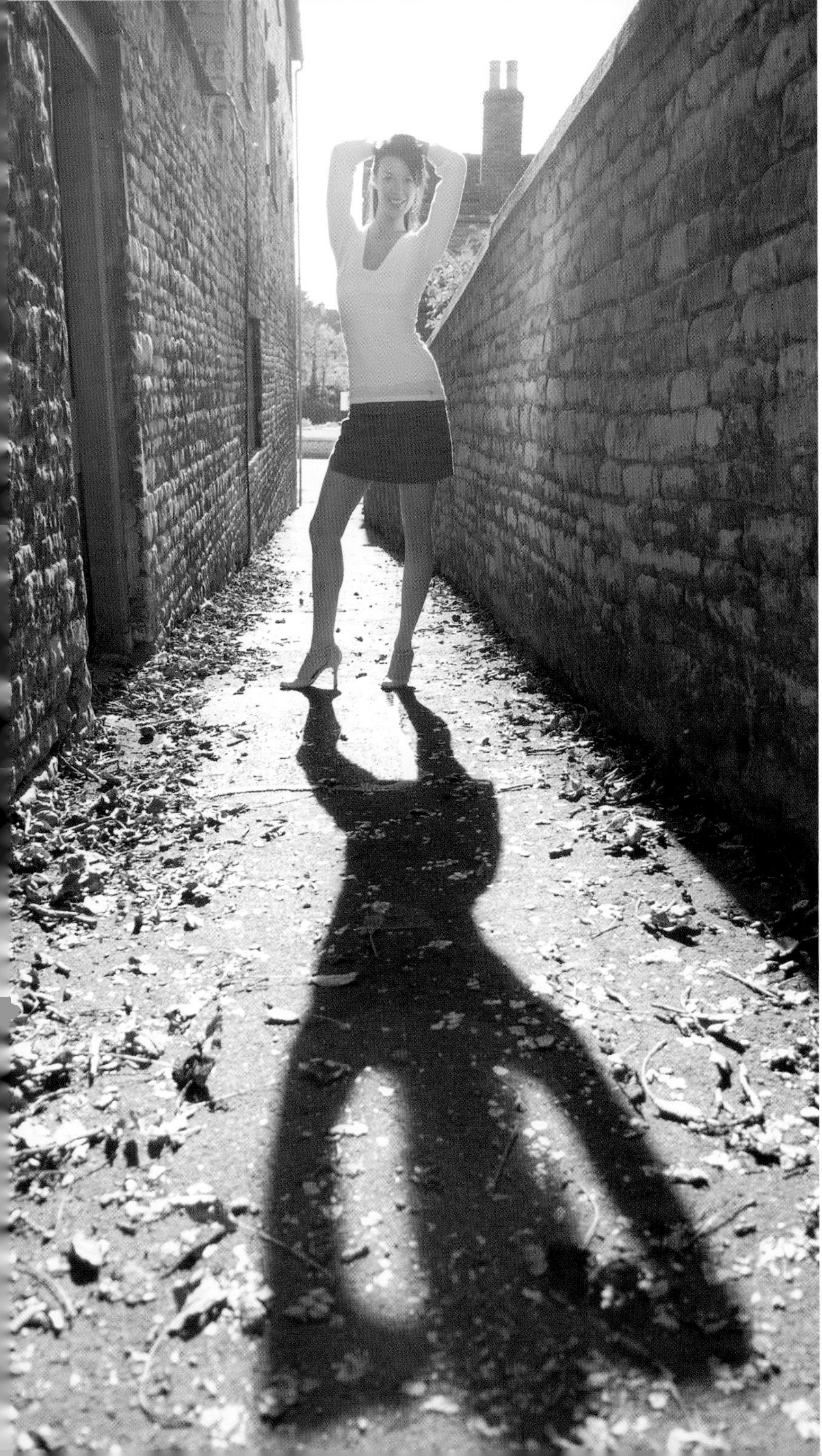

When shooting wide views it is easy to focus all your attention on the beautiful scenery or fantastic light, and forget to think about what's right in front of you. But the foreground is one of the most important elements of a successful composition, so you need to pay close attention to what is almost under your feet. Learning how to use the objects in the foreground helps to add a sense of depth, particularly in wide-angle shots, and also gives your images a sense of scale.

You can use almost anything as the foreground of your shots, from a simple rock or interesting plant to a person or animal. Try to find an object that says something about the subject that you are trying to capture. For example, if you are shooting a coastal village look out for fishing paraphernalia, the boats themselves, or even a local fisherman to include in the foreground.

The foreground is also useful for leading the eye into the image. Using an object such as a fence or rock formation as both foreground interest and lead-in line is one of the most powerful ways of adding depth to your images.

With a wide-angle lens you can include the greatest amount of the foreground. These lenses allow you to get very close to the foreground object without it becoming too large in the frame, emphasizing the perspective between it and the background. Without including something in the foreground, wide-angle shots can look very empty, as everything appears too small in the frame.

LEFT
The strong shape of the shadow adds a sense of depth to this portrait. This was maximized by using a wide-angle lens and shooting from a low angle.

How to use foreground interest

To make the most of the foreground you need to think carefully about your viewpoint, as well as the lens that you use. By getting close to the foreground you will emphasize the perspective between it and the background, while shooting from farther back will make the difference less exaggerated.

Using a low viewpoint makes foreground objects appear higher in the frame, giving them greater prominence. Shooting from a high viewpoint and tilting the camera down will have the effect of "stretching" the foreground. The viewpoint that you choose will also influence the type of lens that you need. An extreme wide-angle lens will allow you to shoot objects literally at your feet from a standing position. In fact, it can be difficult to avoid including your feet in the shot. Shooting from a low viewpoint is often more effective with a moderate wide-angle lens of around 18 to 28mm on most DSLRs. With a wider lens you'll include objects a few inches from the lens that will be impossible to keep in focus if you want the background to be sharp as well.

FOCUSING THE FOREGROUND AND BACKGROUND

If you want to keep both the foreground and background in focus you need to ensure that you maximize the depth of field. Use the smallest aperture available on your lens (usually f/16 or f/22) and focus around a third into the scene. Because you are using a small aperture you may find that you need to use a tripod, as the shutter speeds can become too slow to hold the camera by hand.

BELOW
The rocks and boulders in the foreground would work on their own, but including the flowing water draws the viewer into this picture. This works like a lead-in line to link the foreground and background together.

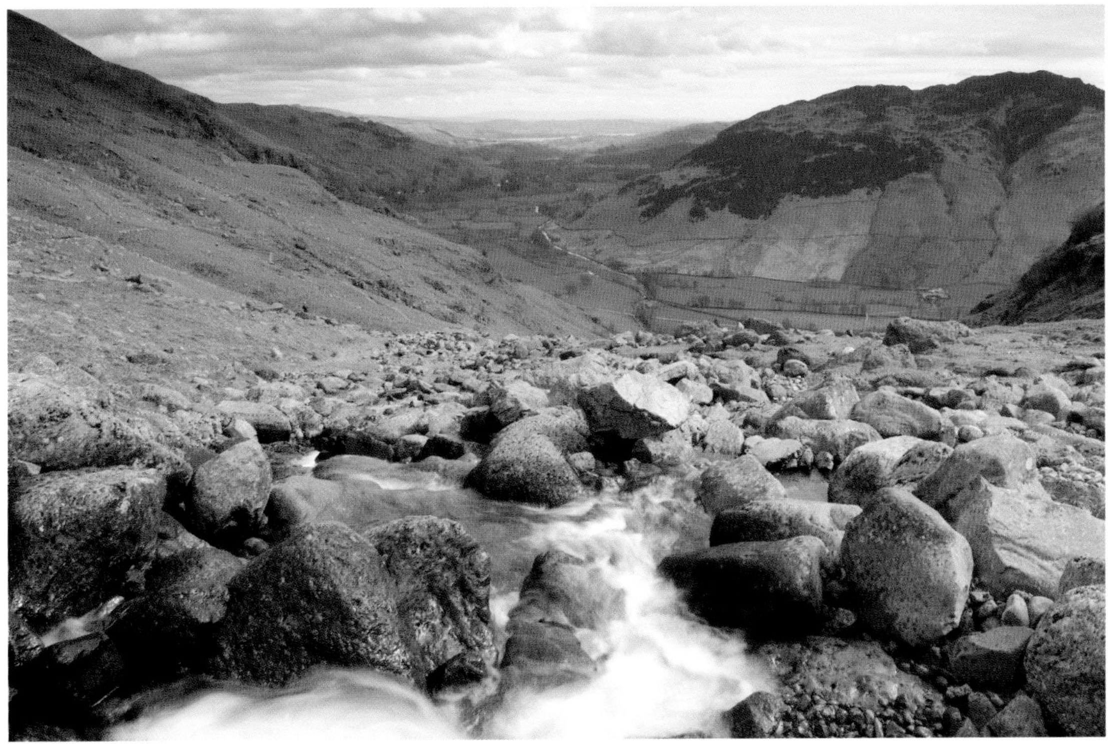

Natural frames

We are used to putting a frame around a print before hanging it on a wall to draw attention to the image and make it stand out. We can use natural frames to do a similar job for the subjects in a photograph. By using an element in the scene to frame the subject, you focus the viewer's attention on this, rather than on the surrounding area, creating a very strong composition. It can also give the effect of looking through a window, and we all know how difficult it is *not* to look through a window. This technique can look false if you don't choose your frame carefully, so use it sparingly.

RIGHT
Using the foliage to frame the spires of this cathedral isolates it from the surrounding buildings. In this case, there were also several cranes and scaffold towers around the cathedral that could be hidden by the trees.

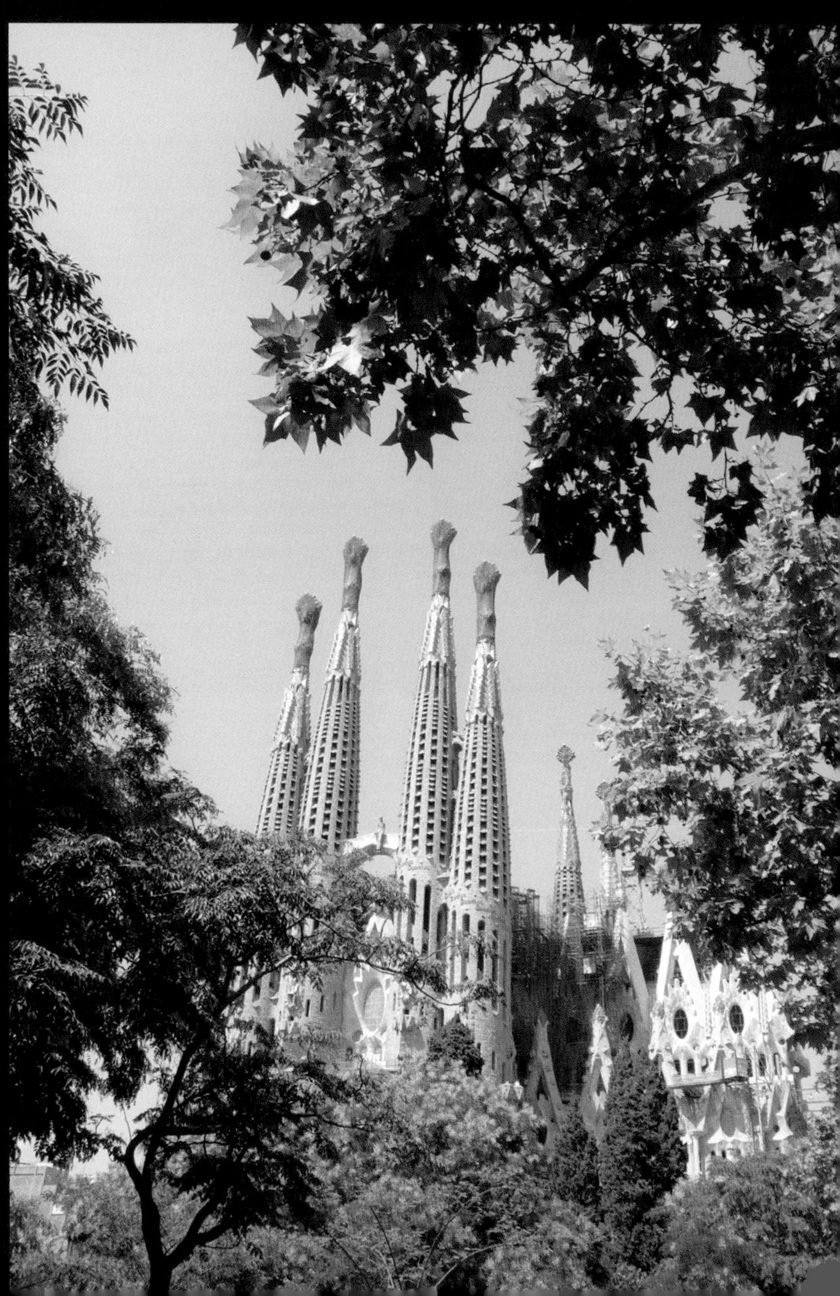

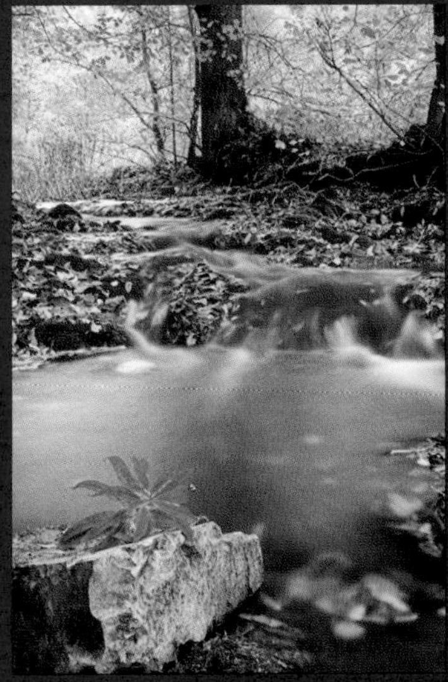

ABOVE
The red plant in the foreground of this shot draws the viewer's attention. Without it, the eye tends to wander around the image looking for a focal point.

Color

Color and brightness play a key role in how we react to a subject and also how much attention we pay to it. Colors like red and yellow tend to appear brighter than blue or green, and also grab our attention. You can use these effects in your composition to draw the attention to a particular point, or to create drama or atmosphere. For example, placing a red flower against a blue background makes the flower stand out much more than if it were set against another bright color, or even against a white background.

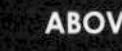

ABOVE
By using a wide aperture to give a narrow depth of field you can concentrate the viewer's attention on a single point of the image. We instinctively look at the sharpest area of an image because it contains the most definite information.

Depth of field

The amount of the picture that is sharp can make a massive difference to how the various elements work together. Using shallow depth of field can draw attention to the sharp areas of an image. By carefully selecting the point of focus and using a wide aperture, you can blur the background of an image so that it doesn't detract from the main subject.

Using this technique, along with careful placement of the subject, you can create a composition that is even more powerful than using just a single compositional technique, such as the rule of thirds.

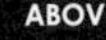

ABOVE
By excluding the background you force the viewer to pay attention to the subject as there is nothing else to distract them.

Get in close

Even when following the rules, it is easy to make the mistake of leaving too much room around the subject. This often stems from a lack of confidence in your compositional skills, and allows for some cropping of the image later on. But you will find that simply by taking a few steps closer to the subject your composition will improve, along with the impact of your pictures.

Whenever you start to compose a picture look for any wasted space around the subject. If the space is not there for a reason—to give a sense of place or to show the subject in context, for example—the shot could probably be improved by removing it.

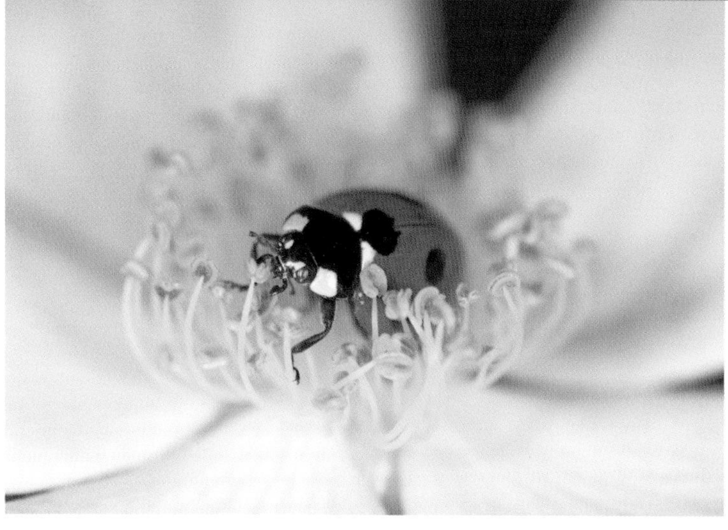

LEFT
Sometimes the center of the image is the best place for the main subject. In this image the bright red color of the ladybug is strong enough to ensure that it draws the eye very well. The central composition complements the symmetry of the flower, giving a balanced feel.

BELOW
By tilting the camera, what would normally be a static subject is made much more dramatic. Because we know that the columns should be upright, the image has a slightly unnerving feel.

While all of the rules and techniques of composition can help you to produce great images, you do not have to use them for every picture. To successfully break the rules it helps to know the rules themselves, so once you have practiced using the composition techniques in your images, why not try something different?

Breaking the rules can often produce more challenging images than simply following convention. These types of image rely much more on your personal taste than conventional compositions, so you may find that they won't appeal to all. But go with your instincts and you might surprise yourself at how successful they can be.

If you want to find some inspiration for your rule-breaking, take a look at the images used in cutting-edge fashion, advertising, and lifestyle magazines. Because many of these are designed to challenge your expectations, you will find that they often try to shock by using unconventional compositional and photographic techniques.

Here are some examples of how to push your composition. The only limit on this type of photography is your own imagination.

Place the subject in the center of the picture
Although placing the subject right in the center of the picture would normally create a very static image, there are times when it is the best place. You can use this static feel to your advantage for some subjects, while it is also a great way of creating a symmetrical image.

Try different angles
You don't always want to shoot from eye-level at standing height. Try pointing the camera upward or downward for a more dynamic feel. You can also use the camera at an angle for an even more dramatic effect. Although you normally want to keep your camera straight and level, shooting at an angle will create unconventional and eye-catching shots. The trick to successful use of this technique is to be bold. Don't angle the camera slightly, or it will give the impression that you wanted to shoot it level, but didn't quite get it right. Making the viewpoint extreme will leave the viewer in no doubt that this was the effect that you were trying to achieve.

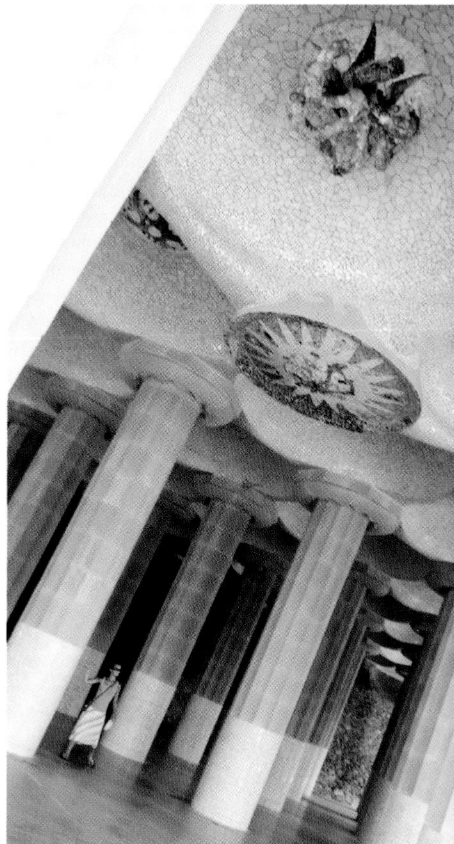

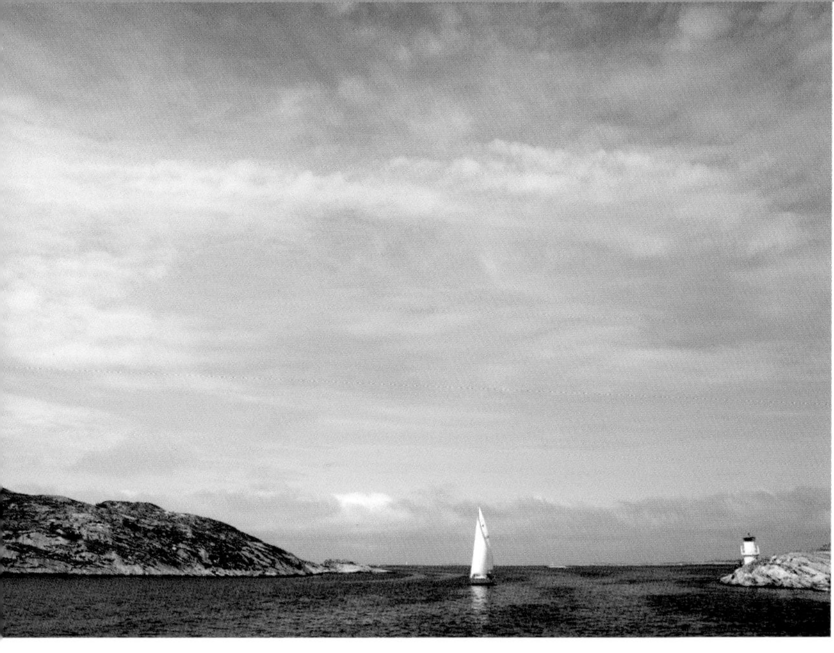

Place the subject at the edge of the frame
We naturally look toward the central portion of the image for the main subject, but that does not mean that this is where you have to put it. By placing the subject at the edge of the frame, you create unsettling shots, because you pose the viewer more questions than answers. The viewer will want to know why the subject is there and what is just outside of the frame.

LEFT
Placing the horizon right at the bottom of the frame gives this image a feel of freedom and space. It also leaves more to the imagination of the viewer by not showing them the rest of the landscape.

No obvious focal point
Do not assume that you need an obvious focal point. You can create abstract images by simply working with blocks of color and tone in your shots. This technique is all about inspiring a feeling or emotion in the viewer rather than simply recording a scene.

BELOW
Framing this seascape so that there are no recognizable features produces a strong, abstract image. This composition works because of the flowing horizontal lines and strong colors, similar to an abstract painting.

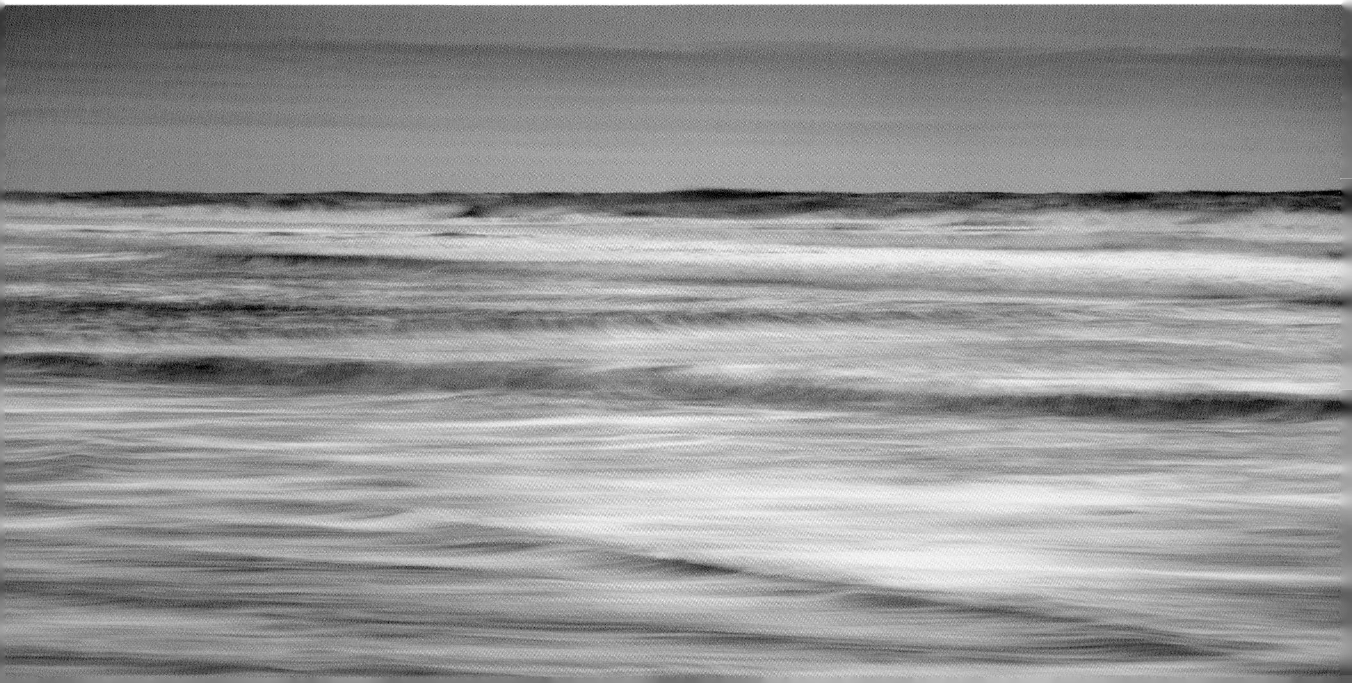

RADICAL CROPS FOR PORTRAITS

In portrait photography you would normally include the subject's face as this is how we engage with people. By excluding the face, especially the eyes, you lose much of the information that the viewer would normally expect. Without this information the viewer asks more questions about the subject than a straight portrait, forcing them to try to find out the information from what *is* included in the image.

Another way of breaking with convention is to try cropping your images, whether in-camera or later on in your image-editing software. Leaving out elements or information that you would normally include can create a feeling of tension or add a sense of mystery because you are not giving the viewer the whole story.

Using radical techniques like this is very much a question of personal taste. You will find that shots that don't conform to the accepted conventions will be more controversial than those that follow easily identifiable compositional rules. Don't expect everyone to love these unconventional shots. They will challenge the viewer by contradicting their accepted view of the world. You have to go with your own instinct; if a shot works for you, then it's a success.

Because these techniques are much more subjective than other compositions it is almost impossible to learn them. Every subject is different, and needs to be treated in a new way. It's a good idea to try the conventional shot first, then look for new ways of recording the subject. Even more than any other type of composition this is all about being able to see the result before you fire the shutter. Decide beforehand whether you're deliberately not going to show the eyes in a portrait or not show the sky or horizon in a landscape. Like any experimentation you will probably find that many of your early shots don't work, but persevere and you will find that a whole new world of images will open up.

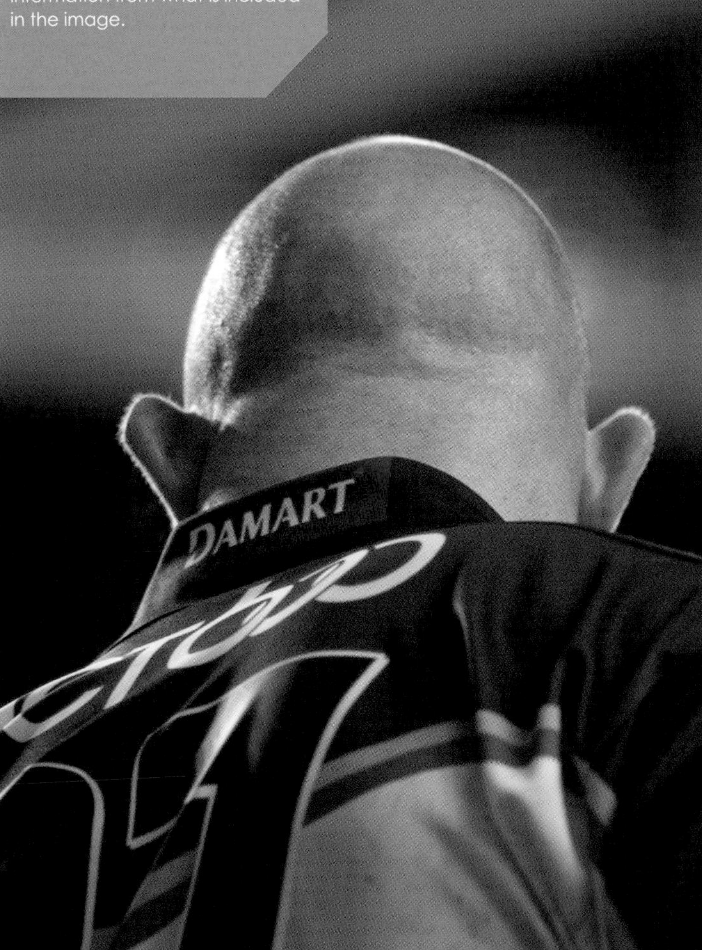

LEFT
The eyes are our natural point of contact with people, so shooting a portrait where the eyes are not visible can add a sense of mystery to your pictures. In this shot, you cannot tell whether the sportsman is happy or angry. Cropping in tight also excludes any other points of reference, such as his surroundings or teammates, so the viewer has to make up their mind from just the limited information available.

RIGHT
Cropping out part of the subject creates an unsettling feeling in the viewer. In this shot, cropping the front sunflower in half makes it much more dramatic, almost as if the flower is trying to force its way into the image.

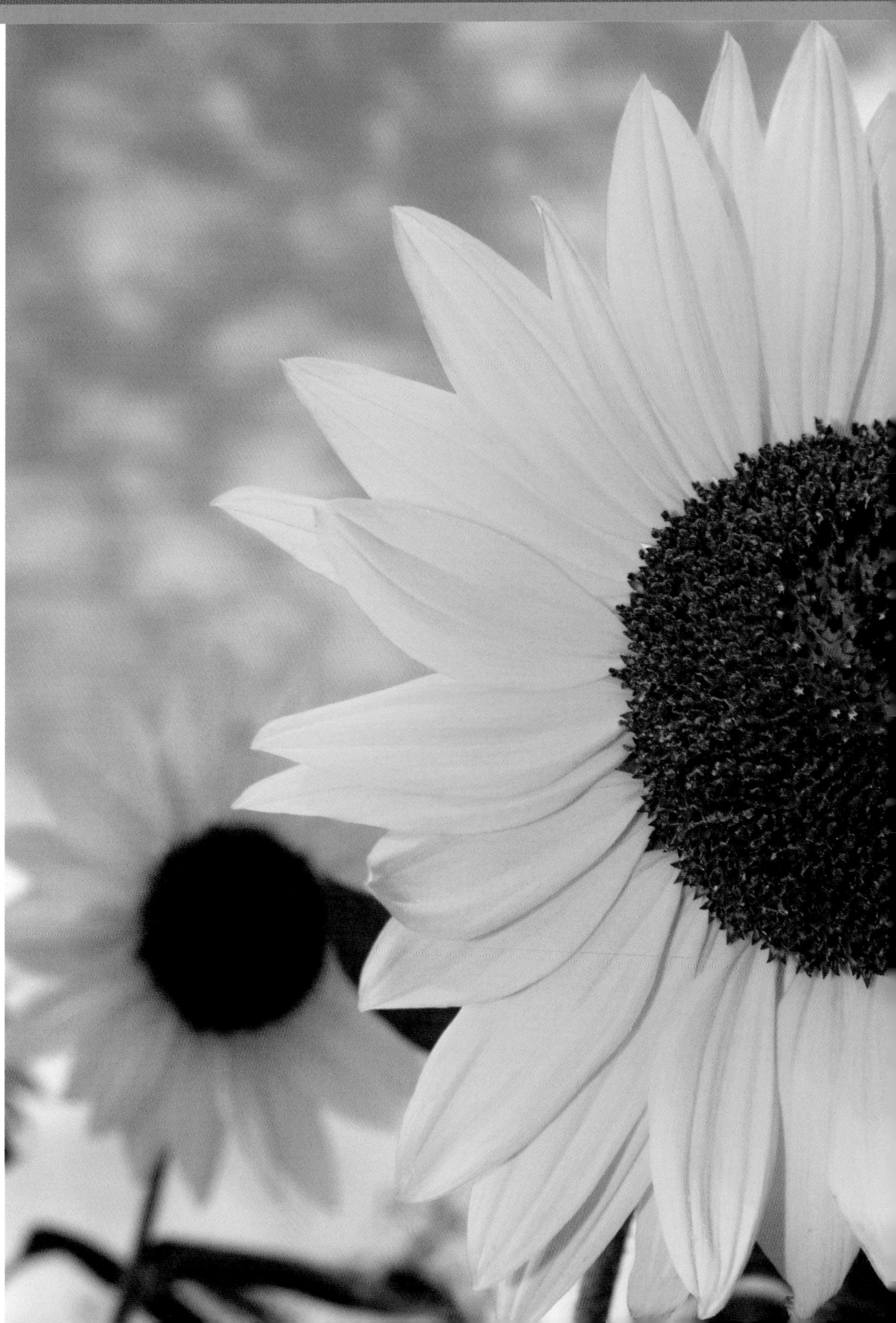

Section 4

Landscapes

Landscapes are ideal for honing your composition skills, and the DSLR—with its versatility, control, and quality—is the perfect camera for the job.

Capturing the beauty and drama of a landscape may seem simple; you have time to select the right lens and viewpoint, and there's an unlimited number of viewpoints to choose from. However, it is the sheer amount of choice available to the photographer that creates much of the challenge of landscape photography—where do you take the shot from, when do you fire the shutter, and how much of the scene do you include? While there are no simple answers to these questions, learning the basics of composition and visualizing how you want the final image to look can help you to make the most of your landscape photography.

How to approach different landscapes
While the basic rules such as lead-in lines and foreground interest that we outlined in Section 3 are useful for all, your approach and expectations should revolve around the landscape that you are faced with, not a set of strict rules. Let the features of the landscape dictate the compositional techniques that you use. For example, a stream, shoreline, or track can form perfect lead-in lines, but these need to lead the eye to the main subject for them to work well. Similarly, choose foreground subjects that will complement and add to the landscape, rather than just choosing the first thing that you come across.

BELOW LEFT
When out shooting landscapes, look for strong elements such as the lead-in lines formed by the trees in this image. The key is to use and recognize the many patterns and elements present in the landscape to make the strongest composition.

BELOW
Even a simple element, such as the single tree in this shot, can be used to strengthen your composition.

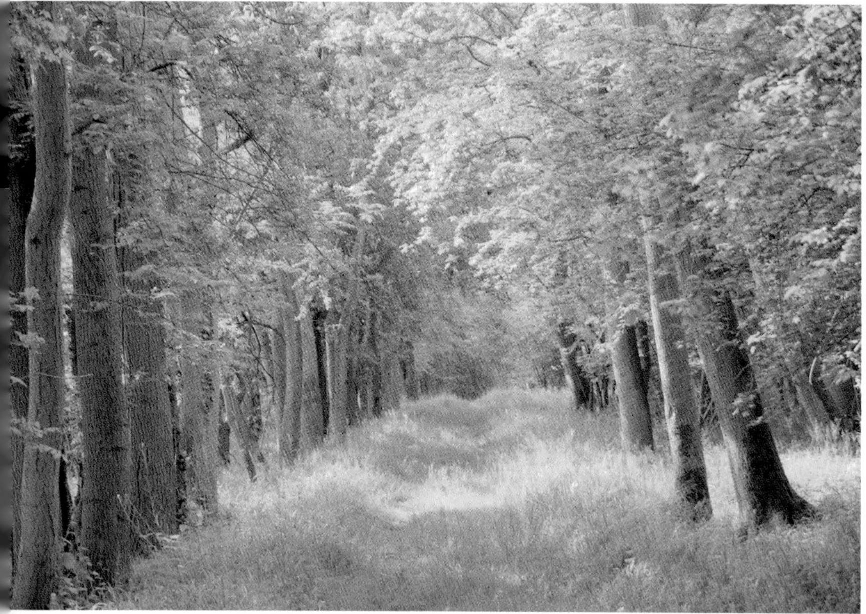

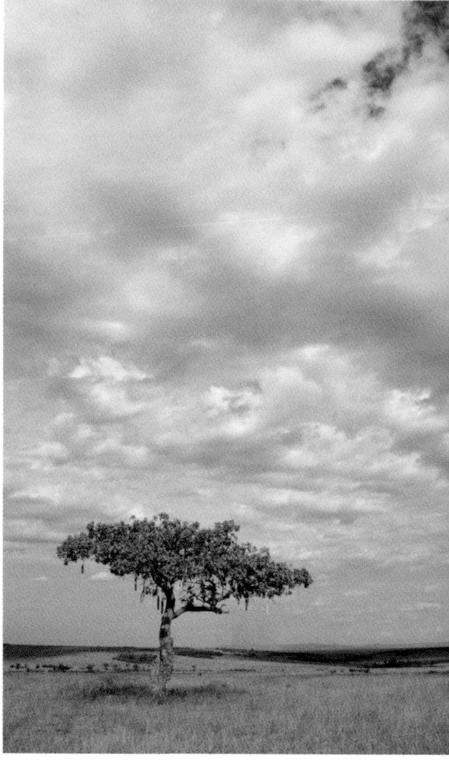

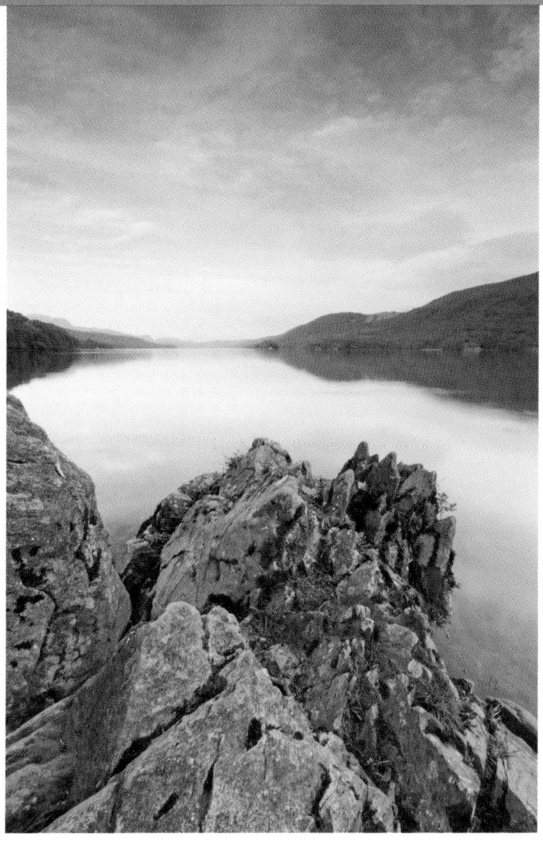

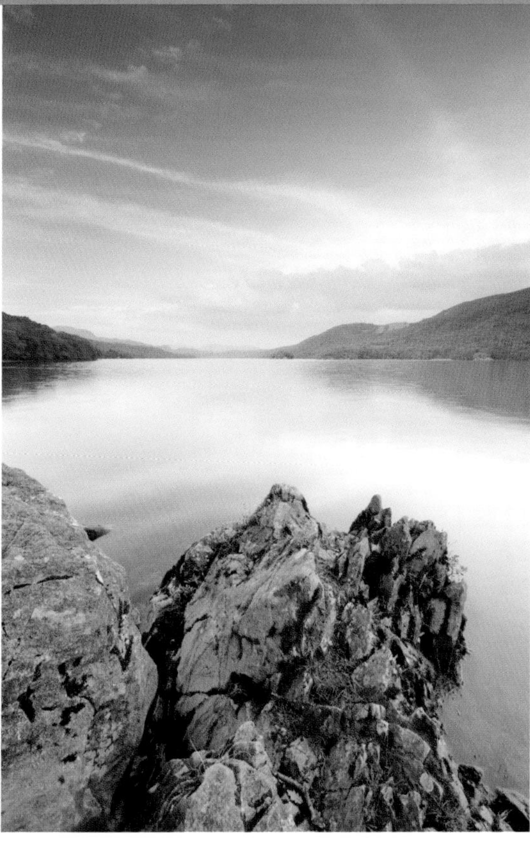

ABOVE
The time of day and the quality of the light have a huge effect on the look of your landscapes. The strong, warm colors of a sunset or sunrise can distract attention away from the landscape, so your composition has to be as strong as possible to compensate.

How lighting affects composition
The color, quality, and direction of the natural light plays a huge part in the appearance of a landscape, and also how you compose your images. In addition, the white balance facility on your DSLR can fine-tune the color balance of your images to give different effects. Bright areas and strong colors grab more attention than darker areas and recessive colors, so ensure that these are used to their maximum effect by positioning them in the strongest points of the frame.

A colorful sky can be so intense that it becomes a subject in itself, taking attention away from the landscape. For the landscape to stay an integral part of the scene, you need to use all of your composition skills to make sure that it is strong enough to hold the viewer's attention.

FORMAT

Don't think that just because your camera is a particular format that you have to force the image to fit it. One of the major benefits of using a DSLR is the ease with which you can crop the image to suit the subject. Try shooting a landscape with the intention of cropping it to a panoramic or square format if that suits the image.

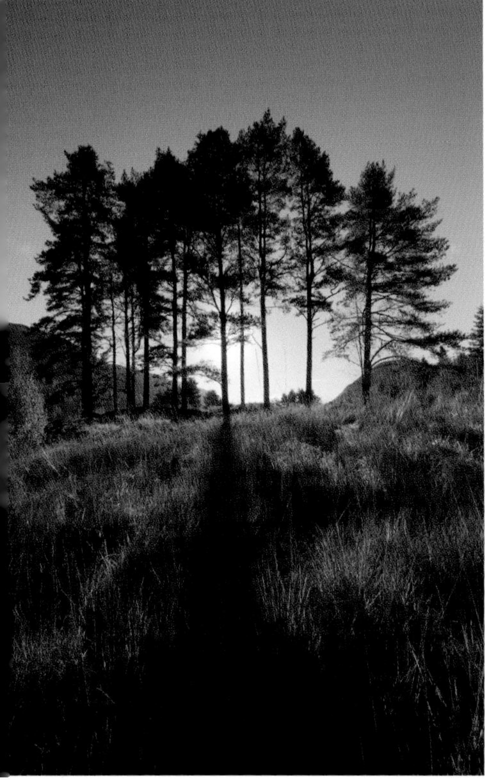

Wide-angle lenses are the classic choice for landscape images. Their ability to capture as much of the scene as possible thanks to their wide field of view means that you can take in sweeping vistas in a single shot.

The standard zoom supplied with your DSLR is a great starting point for shooting landscapes. The shorter focal lengths of around 17 or 18mm of these lenses give a view equivalent to around 28mm on a 35mm camera. This gives a reasonable wide-angle view. They also offer the versatility of using the longer focal lengths to shoot smaller areas of the scene.

LEFT
Using an extreme wide-angle lens allows you to get very close to the foreground to emphasize the distance between it and the background. Here, the shadow formed by the trees is only a few feet from the camera.

BELOW LEFT
The widest setting on the standard zoom supplied with most DSLRs is perfect for general landscape images. The moderate wide-angle allows you to encompass plenty of the scene, including foreground interest.

While the widest setting on a standard zoom will cope with many landscapes, there are times when you will not be able to get the whole scene in your shot. There are plenty of shorter focal length options on the market for those wanting a wider view. On 35mm or full-frame, any lens shorter than 24mm is considered a super wide-angle, and these are great for making the most of your landscape compositions. On a small-sensor DSLR, look for focal lengths of around 10 to 15mm to offer the same extreme wide-angle view.

The precise choice of focal length will be determined by the type of scene you are shooting and the effect that you want to convey. Remember that if you shoot a distant landscape with a wide-angle lens, the features farther away from you will be smaller in the frame than they appear when you look at the scene. For example, mountains will appear less imposing if shot from a distance than if shot from close to. In other words, the choice of viewpoint is actually more important than the lens. The choice of which focal length to use is simply down to how much of the scene you want to include.

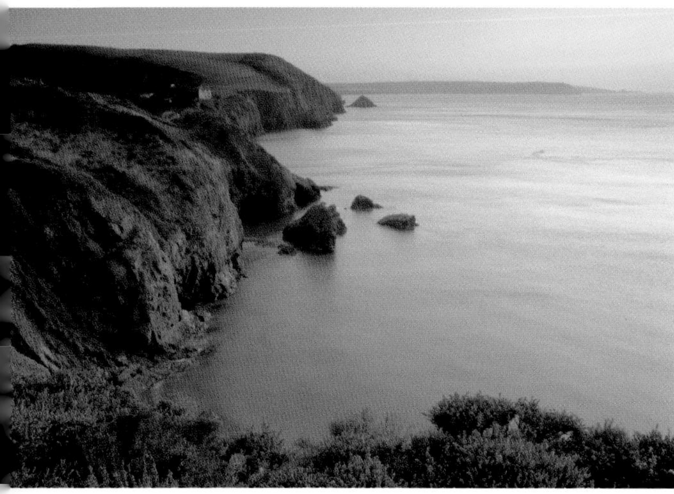

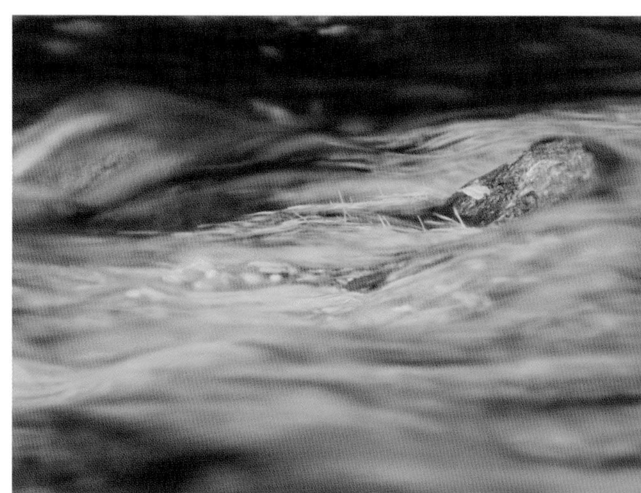

Having said this, the visual effect of using different lenses is still an important factor in the end result. Even from the same viewpoint, a shot taken with a wide-angle lens will give a very different look and feel to one taken with a telephoto lens.

Alternative lenses

Don't discount the possibilities of shooting landscapes with telephoto lenses. They are ideal for isolating small details in a scene, and, because you will generally have to be a long way from the subject to use a telephoto lens, they give the impression of compressed perspective. This effect makes objects appear very close together. For example, if you shoot a series of hills on the horizon from a distance they look almost "stacked" on top of one another.

TYPICAL USES FOR DIFFERENT LENSES

Extreme wide-angle

- Focal length is 10 to 15mm.
- When shooting wide scenes, you can include as much of the scene as possible.
- You can get very close to foreground detail, giving it more prominence in the scene.
- Shorter focal length lenses give greater depth of field, allowing you to keep as much of the scene in focus as possible.

Wide-angle

- Focal length is 15 to 30mm.
- Great for general landscapes allowing you to include a wide view without distant objects appearing too small in the frame.
- You can still include foreground interest, but, because you are farther away from the subject than with an extreme wide-angle lens, the perspective is more natural and the object tends not to dominate the image as much.
- Give good depth of field for front-to-back sharpness at small apertures.

Standard or short telephoto

- Focal length is 30 to 100mm.
- Ideal for picking out details and features in the middle distance to isolate them from the wider scene.
- Good for using shallower depth of field, especially at wide apertures for producing more abstract landscapes.

Long telephoto

- Focal length is 100mm and over.
- These are perfect for picking out distant details and making them appear much larger in the image than shorter lenses.
- The distant viewpoint needed with these lenses also allows you to achieve a compressed perspective effect.

OPPOSITE
A short telephoto of around 70 to 135mm allows you to isolate details in the landscape. This is a common focal length for many macro lenses, so it is always worth taking one along when you are shooting landscapes.

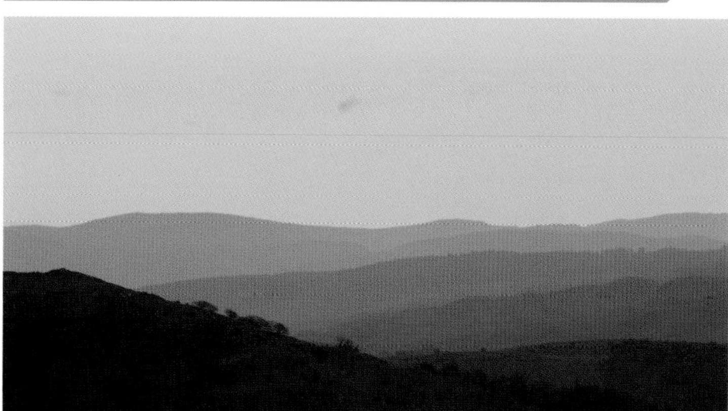

RIGHT
Rather than shoot the wider landscape, a telephoto lens allows you to shoot distant details. The distant viewpoint gives a compressed perspective, making objects appear close together.

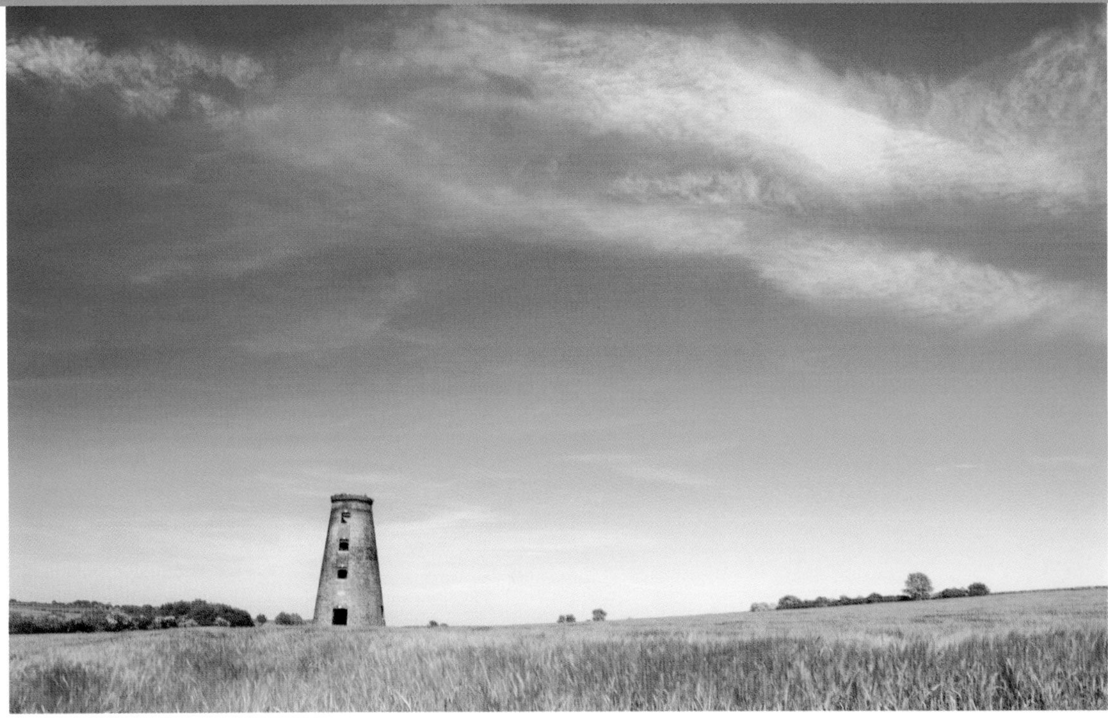

The most common problem with many landscape images is that they lack a sense of focus. This has nothing to do with the sharpness of the image—although this is important—it is simply that they don't give the viewer anything other than a pretty scene to look at. When shooting landscapes it is too easy to simply arrive at a picturesque location and take a photograph without really knowing why you took it.

To make the most of the composition of your landscapes you need to go a little deeper into what aspects you want to convey. Ask yourself why you want to record the scene. Is it a particular feature or landmark, the quality of the light or striking colors, or even the bleakness of a wild and foreboding location? Once you have decided what it is in the scene that you want to record, the task of composition becomes a whole lot easier. You can concentrate your attention on this aspect of the scene and work the image around it. The DSLR's viewfinder will help with this, as it gives a view closer to how the final image will appear. If your subject is a single feature or landmark, think about how you will place it in the frame, how much of the scene you want to include, and the best viewpoint to make the most of the subject. If your subject is something less tangible, like the color or light, then you can hone in on this to make it become the main subject by excluding other elements of the scene that don't complement the effect. The playback facility on the rear LCD of your DSLR is useful for checking your composition as you shoot and making any necessary adjustments.

You'll soon find that it is your emotional responses to a landscape that often throw up the most compelling reasons that you are photographing the scene. These are just as valid as the more concrete objects in the scene as subjects. If it's the imposing size and splendor of a mountain that you find important, try to find a viewpoint that makes the most of this. Use the composition skills and techniques that we have discussed elsewhere in this book to help you to make the most of every landscape.

Don't be satisfied with simply taking a wide view of a beautiful scene; get inside the landscape itself to find out why you are photographing it.
Be prepared to experiment with different viewpoints, lenses, and crops to produce an image that says more about the beauty, remoteness, or emotion of the location.

ABOVE
Always try to use your composition to say something about the subject, rather than simply following the rules. I placed this derelict windmill at the bottom of the frame to emphasize the remoteness of the location.

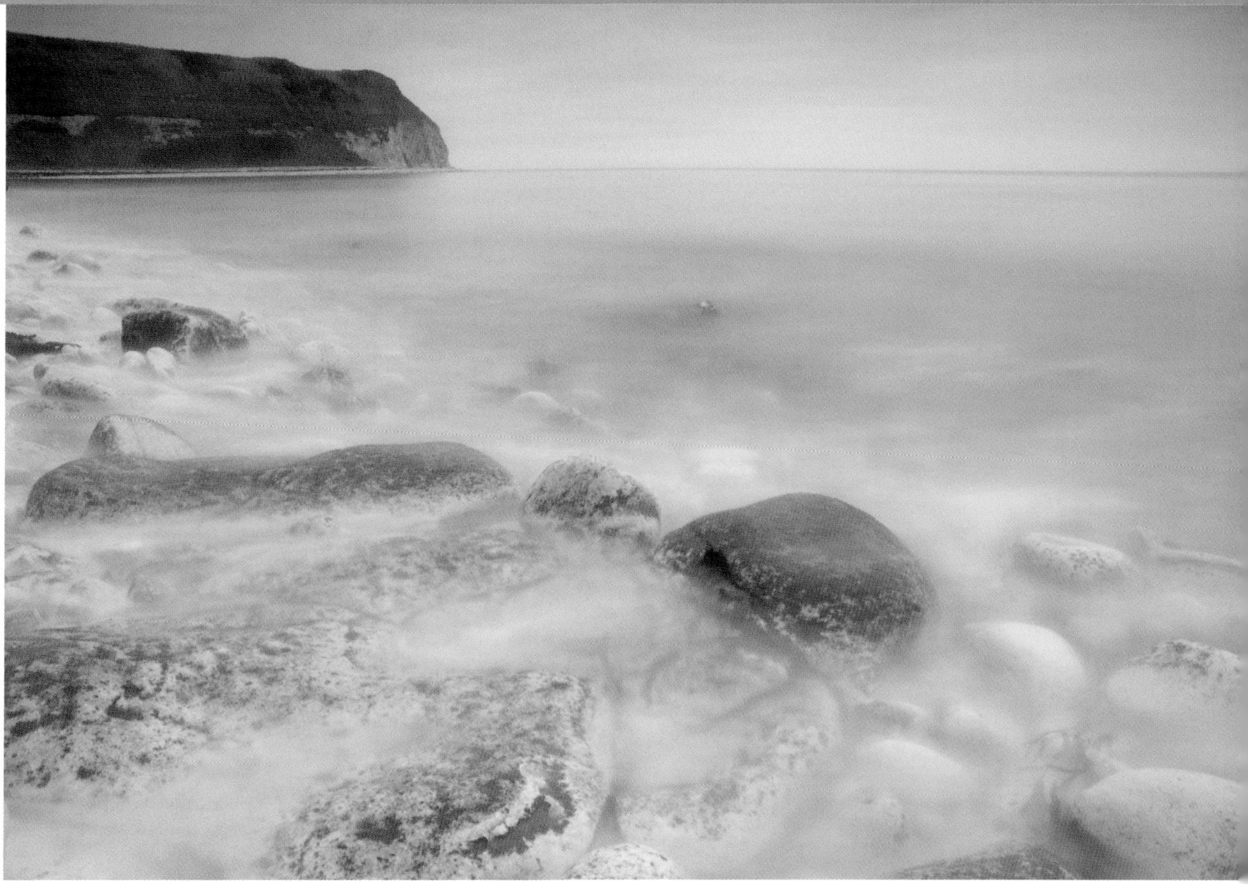

ABOVE
The shape, texture, and tone of the rocks along this shore were the strongest element in this coastal location. I framed this shot so that they took up almost the entire frame, and used the single darker rock on the lower right third to balance the dark cliffs on the top left.

RIGHT
It was the symmetry of these trees that drew me to them, so I used this in the composition to draw the eye right into the center of the picture.

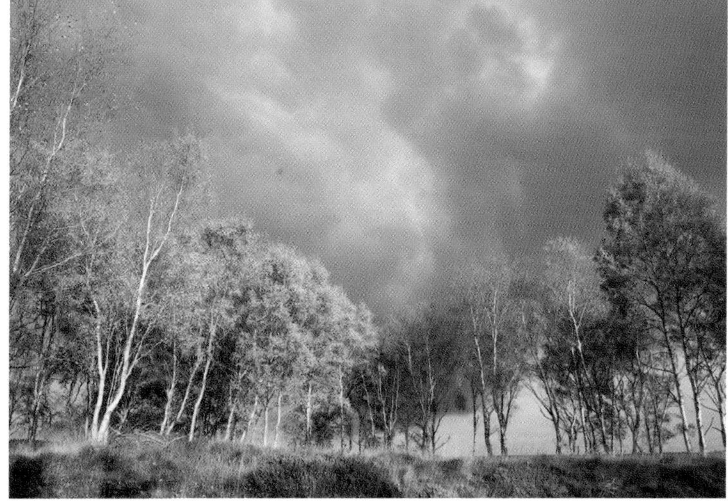

Many landscape photographers go to great lengths to find locations that are free from the signs of human existence. However, that doesn't mean that these scenes don't have a story to tell. All landscapes have been shaped over the years by a variety of influences. From the forces of the elements, the passage of time, to the actions of people, all of these influences can be included in your images to help to tell the story of what makes up the landscape.

BELOW
Including a man-made element in your landscapes helps to give them a new meaning. This tells the story of how man has shaped and used the landscape, rather than simply shooting the scene itself.

Choosing the elements that you include and how you place these in the image can help you to convey this story to the viewer. The importance of this feature to the landscape can be implied by the prominence that you give it in the frame. If you place the object in the foreground so that it takes up a large area of the frame, it becomes dominant over the scene, whereas if it is small or in the background it takes on a less important role in the landscape.

Time also has a place to play in how the landscape appears, and this can be captured in your images. Any moving elements, such as water and clouds, can convey a sense of the passage of time. To capture these elements in action you can use a long shutter speed so that they are blurred, implying that time has passed.

You can also use man-made features to give a sense of time. Buildings, bridges, and even people themselves will place the landscape in a particular period. By including modern features you can place the landscape very much in the present, or you can juxtapose them against something more ancient to convey the sense of time passing. It is also possible to include a historical feature to give the impression that the image harks back to a previous age.

Here are some simple ways in which you can compose your images to add to the story of the scene.

The force of the elements
Rain, wind, and running water all play an integral part in the appearance of landscapes, so by placing one or more of these elements prominently in the frame, you give the viewer a sense of the forces at work in the environment.

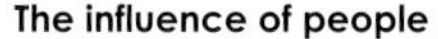

The influence of people
The buildings, monuments, and structures in the landscape can tell the viewer how the land has been (or is still being) used. By placing a single building small in the frame against a magnificent landscape, you imply that the people play a less significant role there than if it was the dominant subject in the image. Think carefully about how the object "sits" in the landscape. Does it almost blend in and become part of a much greater force, or has someone tried to impose their own will on the landscape and become its master? Answering these questions will help you to decide where to place the structure in the image.

The passage of time

Time can be one of the most difficult things to capture, as the nature of photography means that it can usually only show how the subject appeared when you fired the shutter. This "snapshot" of time can be expanded by what you include in the frame and how you compose the image. By showing items that obviously show the passage of time, such as derelict buildings, you can give a sense of age to the landscape.

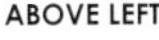

ABOVE LEFT
Buildings can help to tell the whole story of the landscape. This lighthouse was almost the only point of interest on this rocky island, so I used it as the main focal point for this image.

RIGHT
Although it can be difficult to show in a single image, I wanted this shot to convey a sense of the passage of time. I achieved this by making the derelict house among the trees the focal point, and used a five-second exposure to blur the movement of both the grasses in the foreground and the clouds.

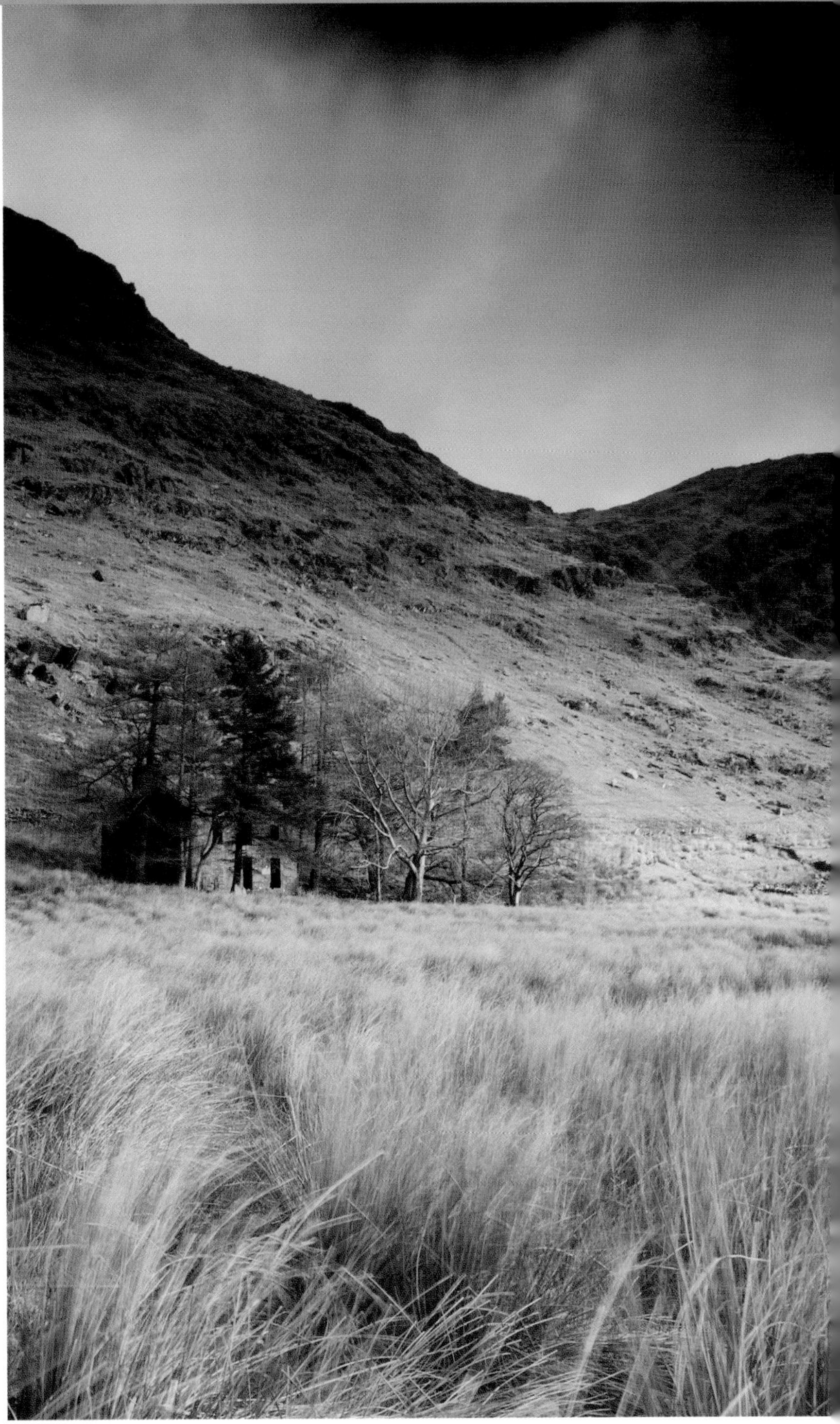

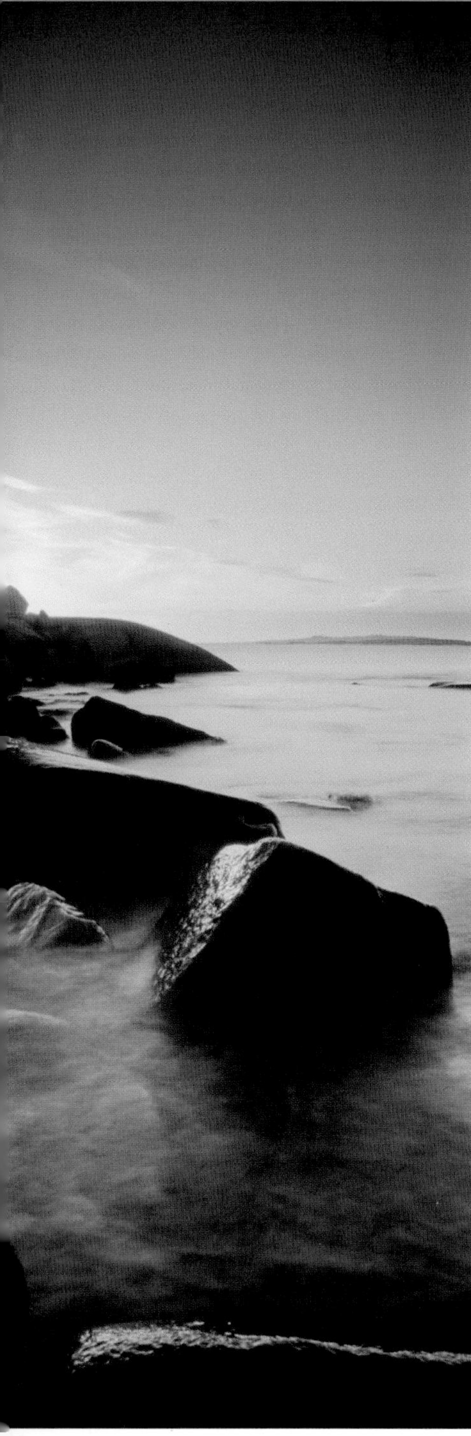

The potential subjects and treatments available in the landscape and from the versatility of your DSLR are limited only by your imagination. The trick is to think beyond the traditional view of the wide, scenic landscape and look at the scene in a new way.

Don't always shoot in horizontal format
Let's start with one of the simpler techniques available for spicing up your landscapes. Most landscapes you'll see are taken in the horizontal format, hence why it's also known as "landscape." But that is not always the best format for many landscapes, as an upright format often brings a more dynamic and energetic feel to the image. This is especially effective when you want to include foreground detail, as the upright format gives the maximum scope for including this along with the landscape or sky above it.

You can take this one step further by shooting an upright panoramic. Because of the quality of the images from most DSLRs, this can be done simply by cropping a normal image without too great a loss in quality. Alternatively, you can stitch together a number of images to give an even wider view.

Minimalist landscapes
Strip any landscape image down to its component parts and it is simply a composition of shapes, colors, and textures. However, when you go out to deliberately shoot minimal landscapes, you have to actively look for these simplified forms in the scenery.

Seascapes and coastal areas are an excellent source of minimal landscapes, as the water can be used to form an almost uniform background to contrast with the features you include in the shot. It can take time before you start to see how to isolate these features from the wider scene, but one great way to learn is to use a telephoto lens to narrow the area that you view.

LEFT
The upright panoramic format can produce a much more dynamic composition than conventional horizontal framing.

BELOW
Landscapes don't have to include many elements to be successful. This shot is all about the color of the field and sky, but is completed by including the single tree on the right-hand third line.

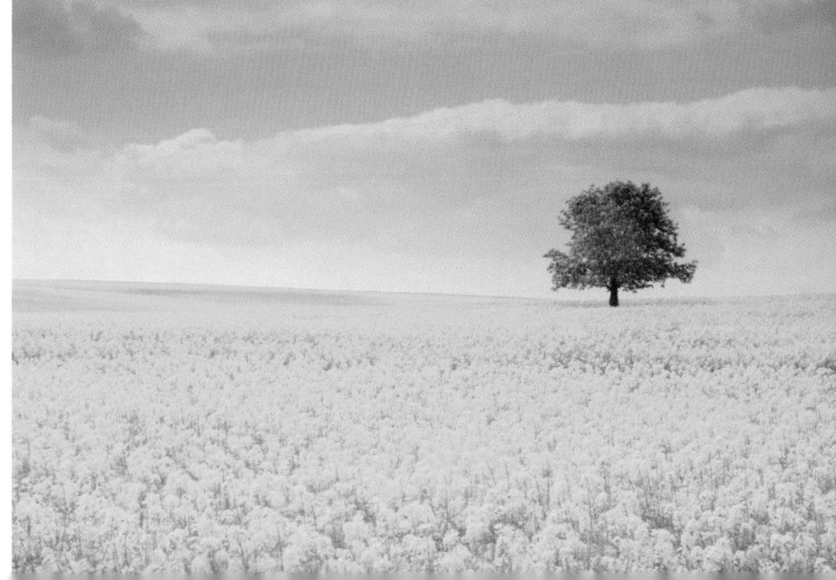

Use limited depth of field

Most landscape shots are taken with the maximum depth of field to ensure maximum front-to-back sharpness. However, using a more limited depth of field to deliberately blur parts of the scene will keep the viewer guessing and will also draw attention to a particular feature in the landscape. It is easiest to achieve this type of image using a short telephoto lens at a wide aperture, rather than a wide-angle lens, although a wide-angle lens focused on a subject very close to the lens can also give good results. The lenses available for DSLRs make this type of image easy to achieve by using a short telephoto lens at a wide aperture, rather than a wide-angle lens.

COMPOSING THE SKY

Here are two perspectives that are particularly good when you are faced with a scene with great potential but either the sky or the landscape itself does not produce the image that you want.

Maximize the sky

The sky plays an integral part in how we react to scenery and the world around us, so why not make it the main subject of your landscape? You can shoot just the sky—although whether this is then a landscape image is debatable—but you can usually include a piece of land at the bottom of the image to give the sky a sense of scale and place. Look for dramatic patterns, colors, and textures in the clouds to make the most of this type of shot, and you can even use these patterns and lines to draw the eye of the viewer just like in traditional landscapes.

Exclude the sky

There are times when the sky itself is either too overcast or even too devoid of clouds to add any interest to the scene. In these conditions you can always exclude it entirely from the image. By removing the sky as a point of reference, you can either look for abstract details in the landscape to photograph, or simply work with the subject as you would any other landscape image using the same composition techniques to maximize the impact of the scene.

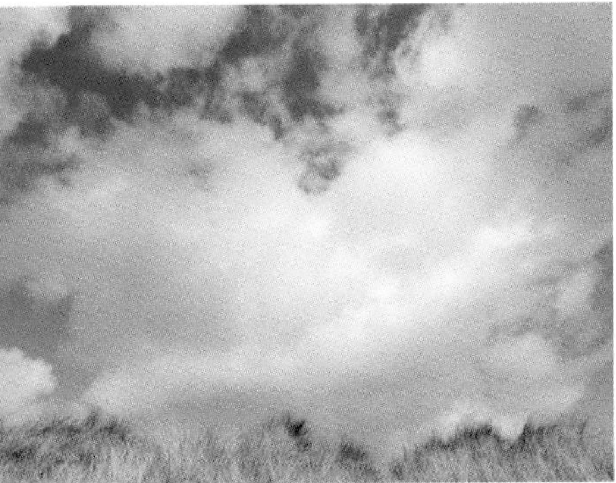

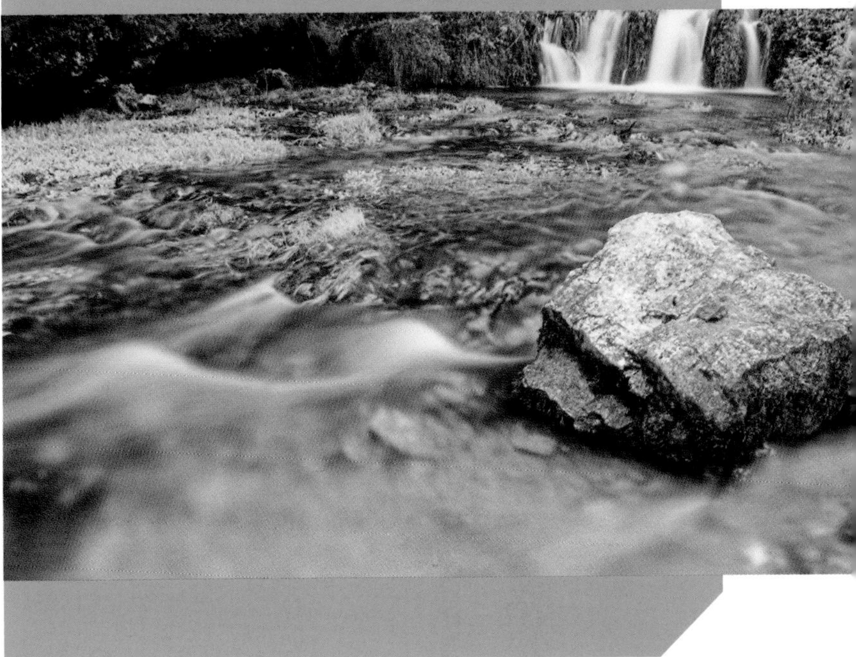

ABOVE
Dramatic skies are just as much a part of the landscape as the ground or water. Make the most of the shapes and textures in the clouds by either just shooting the sky, or including only a small strip of land at the bottom of the frame.

RIGHT
You don't always need to include the sky in your landscapes. Excluding the sky is particularly useful when shooting in dull, overcast conditions.

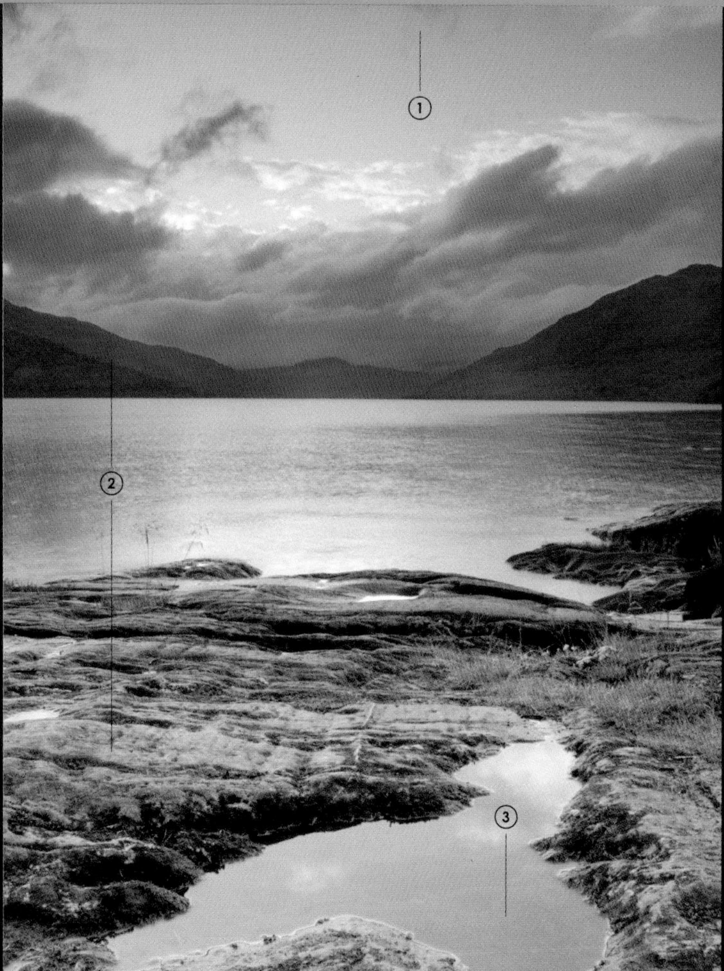

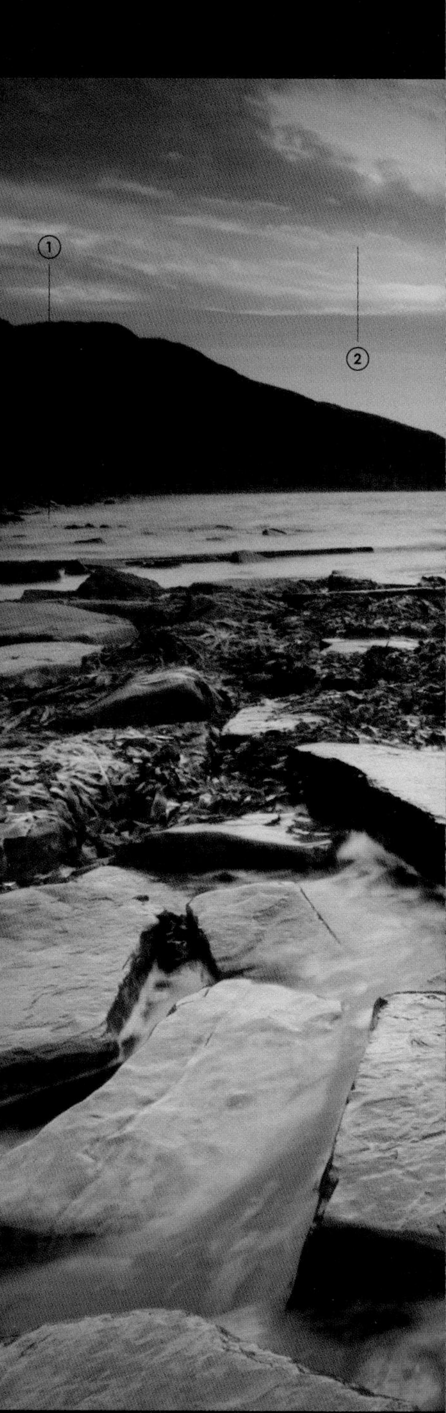

ABOVE

1. The upright format gives the image a stronger, more dynamic feel.

2. Using a low viewpoint and a wide-angle lens increases the sense of distance between the foreground and the mountains.

3. Strong foreground interest is created by the reflection of the sky in the pool.

RIGHT

1. The curved line of the shore gives a strong, dynamic composition.

2. The lines of the clouds lead the eye into the landscape.

3. Placing the horizon in the top third of the frame maximizes the amount of the shore and the sea included in the image.

4. The diagonal lines created by the waves, shot using a long exposure, lead the eye into the image.

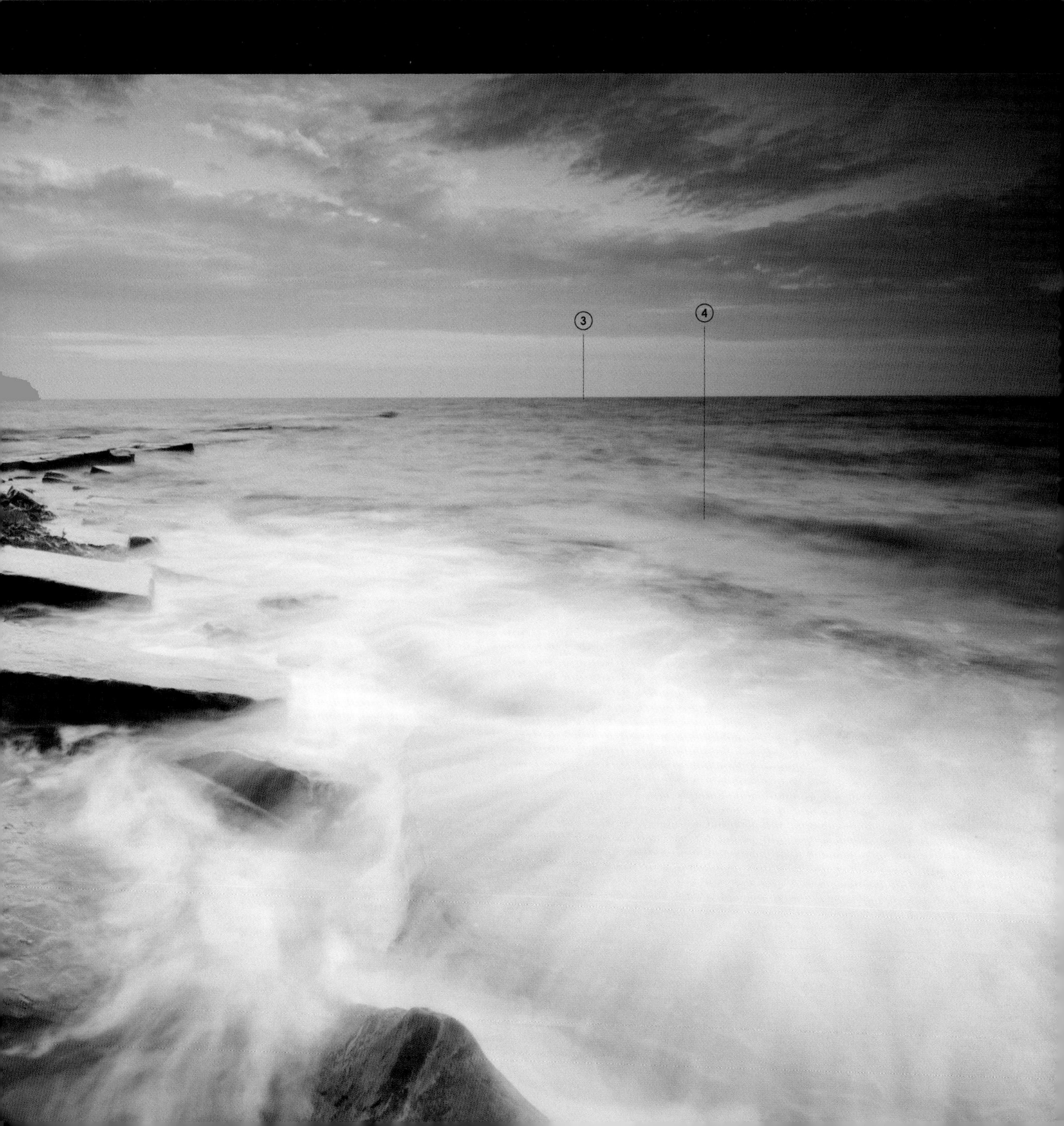
3
4

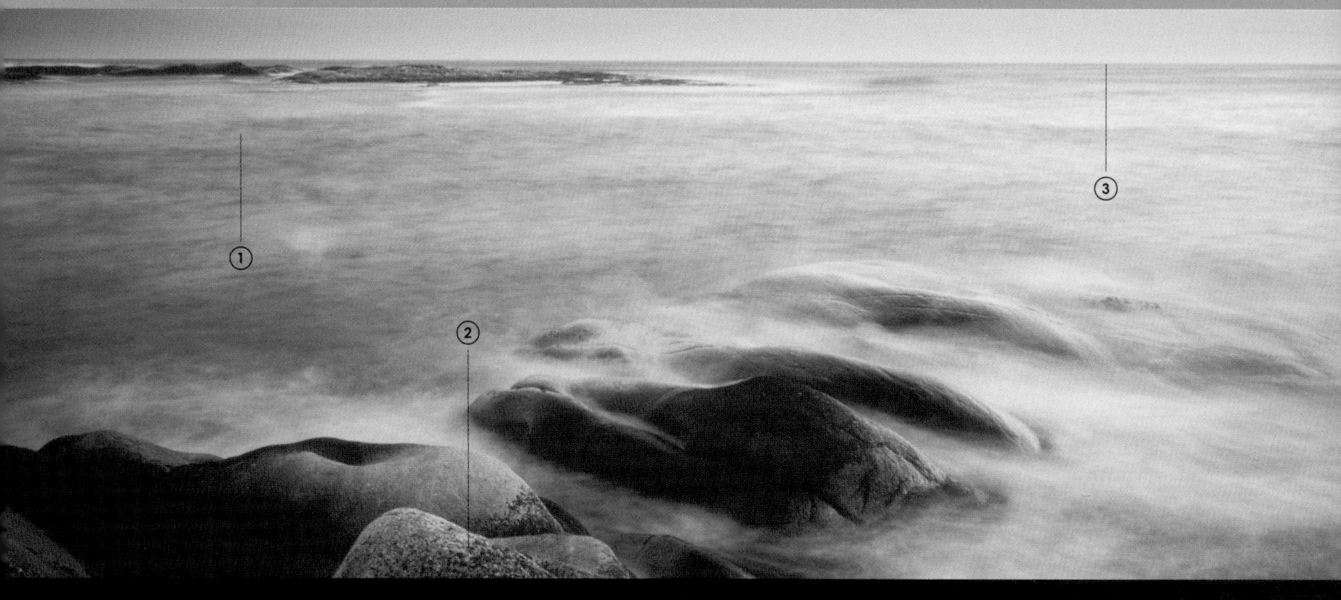
1
2
3

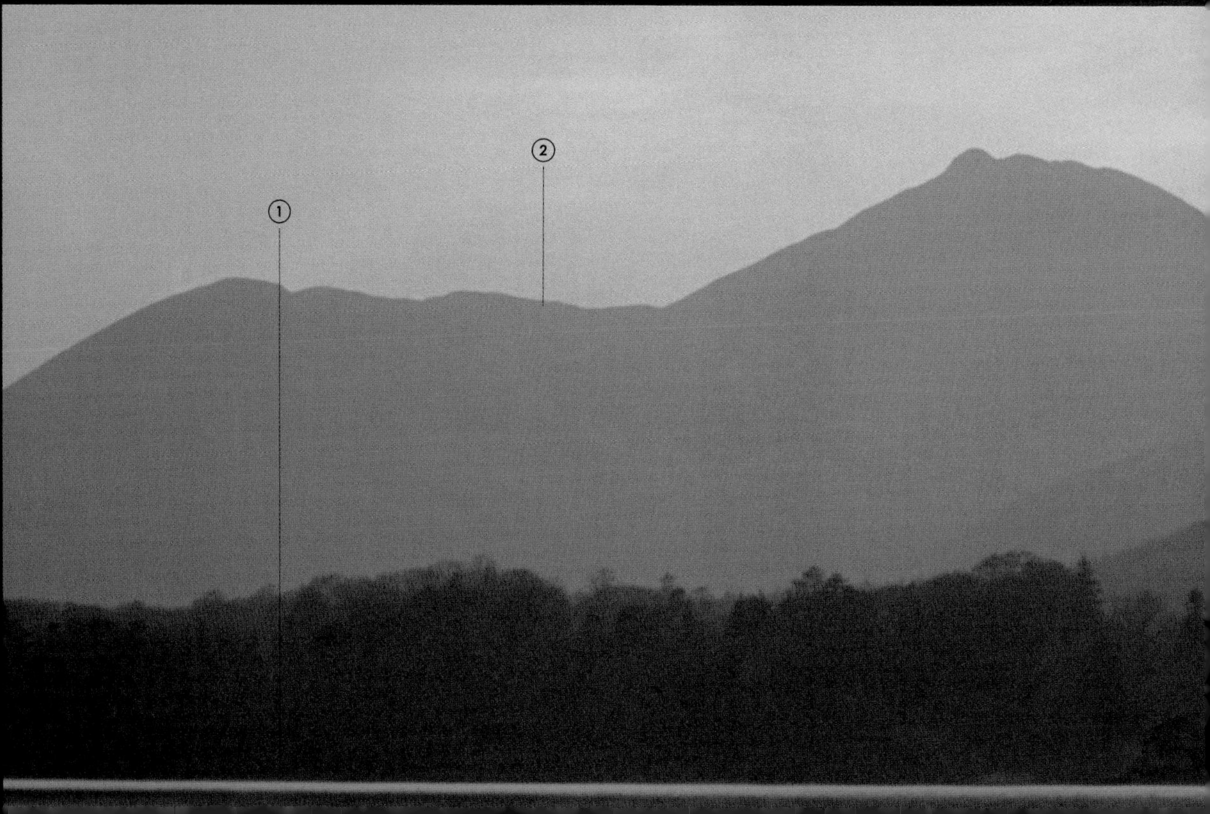

LEFT

1. The panoramic format and blue colors give the image a peaceful feel.

2. The rocks in the foreground lead the viewer in and give the image a strong base.

3. Placing the horizon near the top of the image allows the sea to dominate.

BELOW

1. Using a distant viewpoint and a short telephoto lens makes the mountains appear very close to each other.

2. The smooth curves and general horizontal direction of most of the lines give the image a restful feel.

3. The receding tones of the mountains gives a strong aerial perspective.

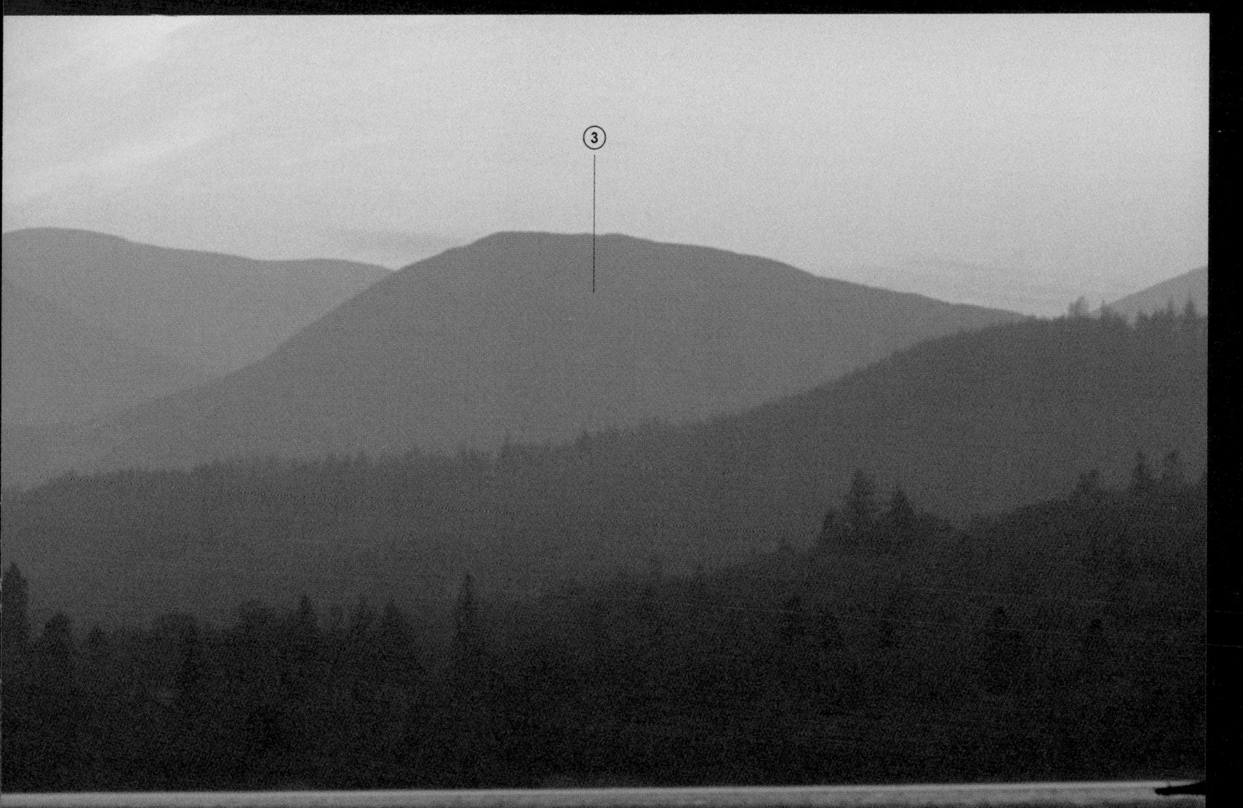

Section 5

Nature

The challenges facing the nature photographer are vast. The first problem is finding the subject, but then you have to get close enough to photograph it. The huge range of telephoto lenses available for DSLRs make it easier to get close-ups, but it still pays to get as close as possible to the animal. In most cases you do not have the luxury of being able to pick your ideal viewpoint, and, even in captivity, animals have a habit of doing exactly the opposite of what you expect. Despite these challenges, it is still possible to take some stunning images. A combination of fieldcraft, knowledge of the subject, planning, patience, and a little luck will help to get you in a position to go beyond simply recording the animal. You can then start to use your composition skills to produce the best pictures possible. Because you need to react quickly when photographing wildlife, these skills need to be almost instinctive, rather than the considered approach that can be adopted when shooting static subjects. You need to be able to see the shot and take it almost without thinking, and it is this ability that makes the difference between simple record shots and those that say something more about the subject. Shooting in either shutter speed or aperture priority mode on your DSLR means the camera will deal with most of the exposure, allowing you to concentrate on the subject and the composition.

The best way to learn these skills is through practice, but this can be difficult to do out in the field. As an alternative, try subjects that are closer to home. Don't overlook the animals in your own garden, as photographing them is a great way to practice your skills. Even just spending time observing these creatures can help you to understand animal behavior. Set up a feeding station in your garden, try to attract as many different species as possible, and find a location for a hide that allows you to both observe and photograph the wildlife.

Wildlife parks, zoos, and nature reserves are also good places to find subjects. Try to find zoos and parks where the

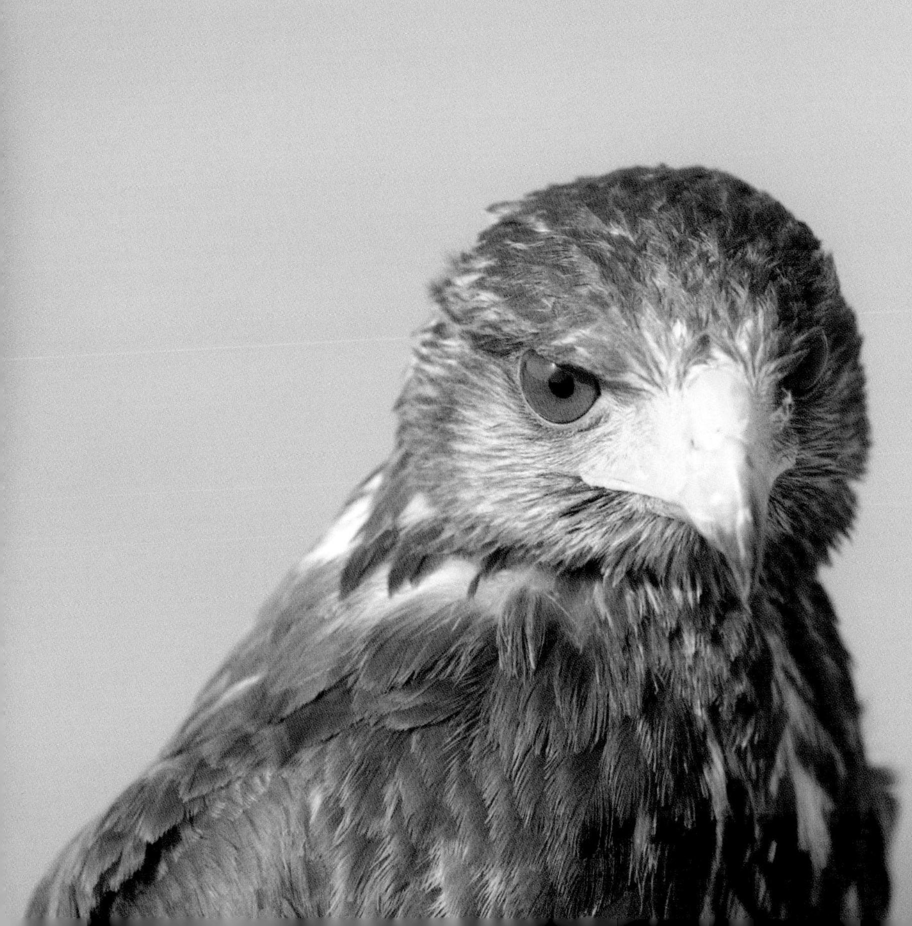

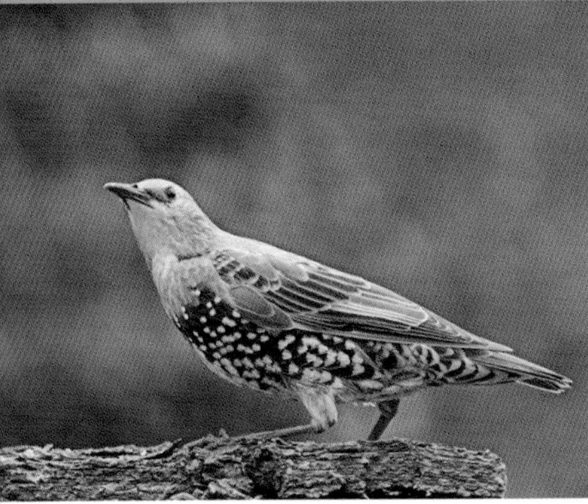

enclosures look natural and the animals have room to behave as they would in the wild. Fences and barriers can pose their own problems, but even if you don't take a single shot, you will still get a feel for how animals behave, how they move, and how they interact with each other. These skills will be invaluable when you come to photograph animals in the wild. Being able to predict how and where the creature will move will give you extra time to consider the composition of your nature shots.

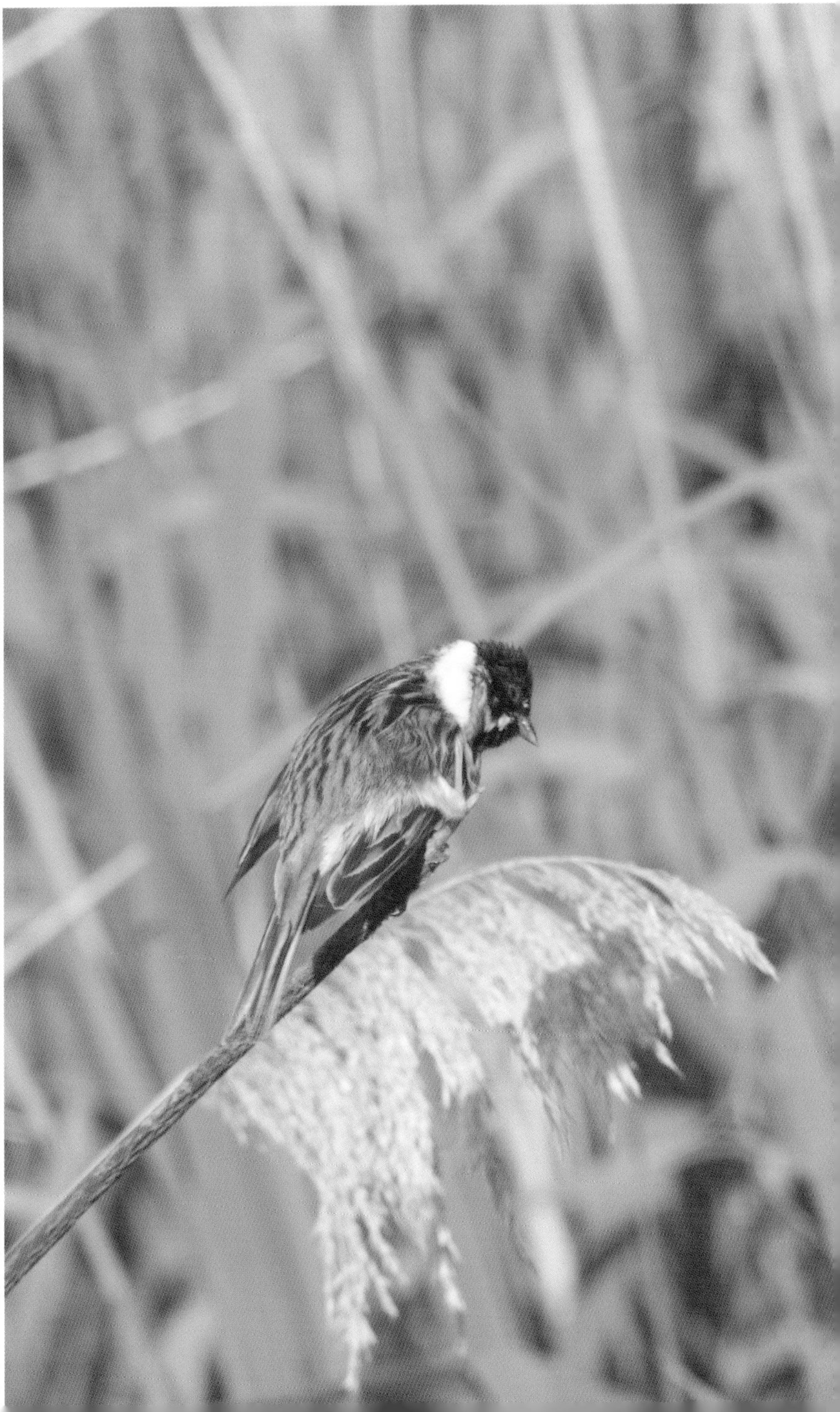

ABOVE
Setting up a wildlife-friendly area in your garden can produce great results. Make feeding areas look as natural as possible by using logs and foliage. This will allow you to choose a variety of compositions, including wider shots.

RIGHT
Shooting from a hide will give you the opportunity to get close to your subject, although it can take time and patience to get the exact shot that you want.

LEFT
Animals in zoos and wildlife parks are excellent subjects for practicing your wildlife photography. Compositions are often limited by the enclosures, as you can struggle to find a background that does not include fences or other distracting elements.

Many people assume that you need super-long telephoto lenses to shoot wildlife, but this is not always true. The choice of lens is governed by how close you can get to the subject, and often the closer you are the better your shot will be. There are some occasions, and indeed animals, when it is either impossible or even dangerous to get too close to the subject without either putting yourself in danger or, more importantly, causing the animal distress.

The distance between you and the animal will affect the perspective of your image along with the focal length of lens that you need to get the shot you want. The farther you are from the animal the more "compressed" the perspective will appear. This makes objects in front of and behind the subject appear closer together than if the subject is closer to you. The greater the distance from the subject, the longer the focal length of lens that you need to record it the same size in the frame, giving rise to the common misconception that longer lenses compress perspective. So the distance from your subject and the resulting lens choice has a massive effect on the appearance and composition of your images.

It is also common to assume that to take a successful nature shot you have to fill the frame with the subject by using the longest lens possible. This can produce great images, but don't dismiss the possibility of shooting with a wider lens to give a sense of the animal's environment and surroundings. We will explore the creative possibilities of this approach over the following pages.

There are also plenty of natural subjects that are so small that you will need to use a macro lens to capture them successfully. In general for wildlife macrophotography, a longer focal length macro lens is the best option because it allows you to get a good magnification without getting too close to the subject. As we discussed above, shooting from a greater distance will affect the perspective of your images.

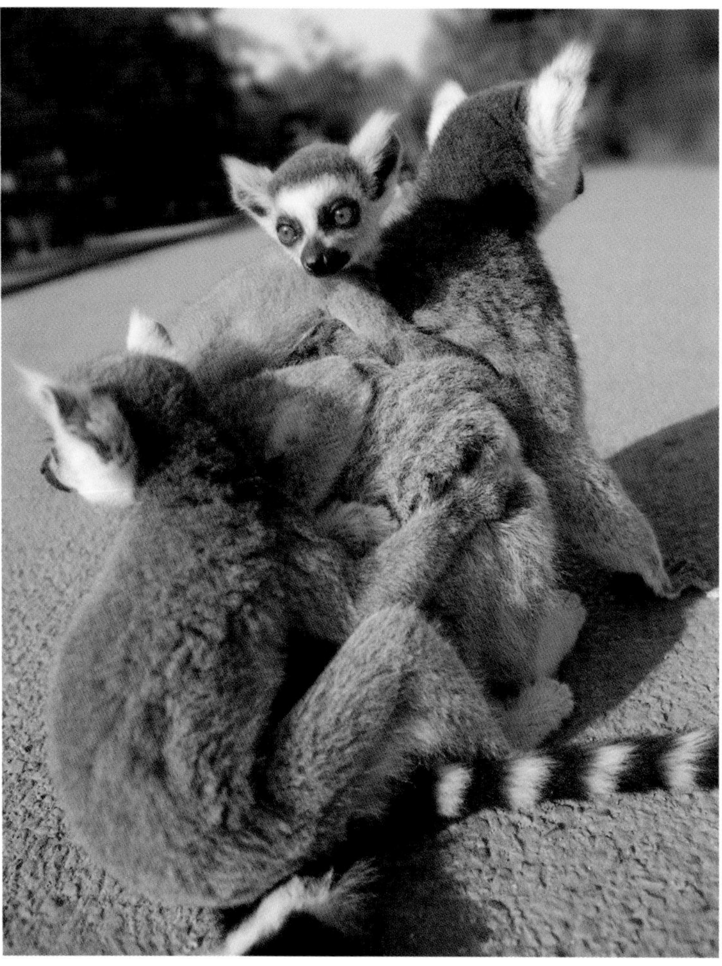

LEFT

Some animals will allow you to get very close to them. Using this kind of viewpoint and a wide-angle lens gives an intimate feel to your shots. The effect here is that the lemurs appear much closer as the background seems farther away than it would using a more distant viewpoint.

TYPICAL USES FOR DIFFERENT LENSES

Wide-angle and standard lenses

- Focal length is 18 to 35mm.
- Allows you to get very close to the subject, so they are ideal for photographing pets or park wildlife, such as squirrels. The wide field of view allows you to include a lot of the animal's environment, and, because you are close to the subject it appears much more dominant in the frame than shooting from a distance.
- It is also possible to use the same lens when the camera is set up on location and fired remotely from a distance. This technique is useful for producing incredibly dramatic shots of animals that would appear to be impossible in normal conditions.

Short telephoto

- Focal length is 100 to 200mm.
- Great for shooting garden wildlife, captive animals, and animals that you can get close to in the wild.
- They are also useful for including the environment when shooting from a distance.
- This is the most common range of focal lengths for dedicated macro lenses for shooting close-ups.

Long telephoto

- Focal length is 200 to 400mm.
- Probably the most common focal length for capturing animals in the field. They allow you to fill the frame, while keeping a reasonable distance between you and the subject. For larger species the distance will be greater than for smaller ones, giving the appearance of compressed perspective.
- They are also ideal for photographing garden birds and details of captive animals.

Super telephoto

- Focal length is above 400mm.
- These more specialized optics allow you to shoot from a greater distance from your subject, giving the appearance of compressed perspective.

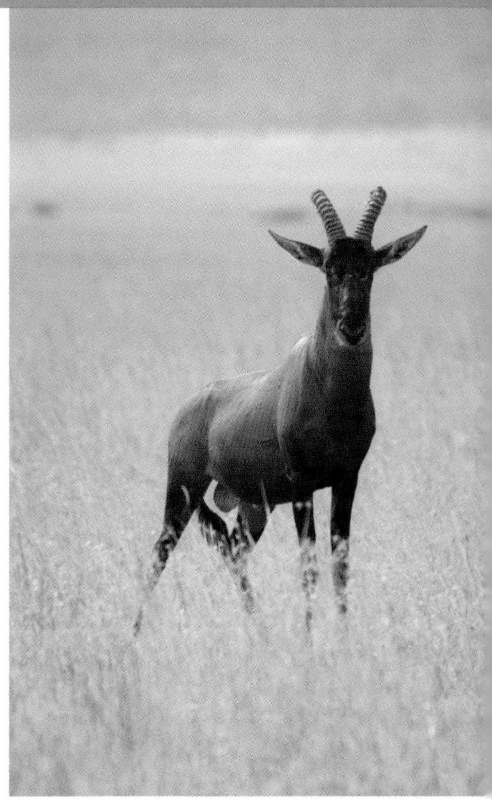

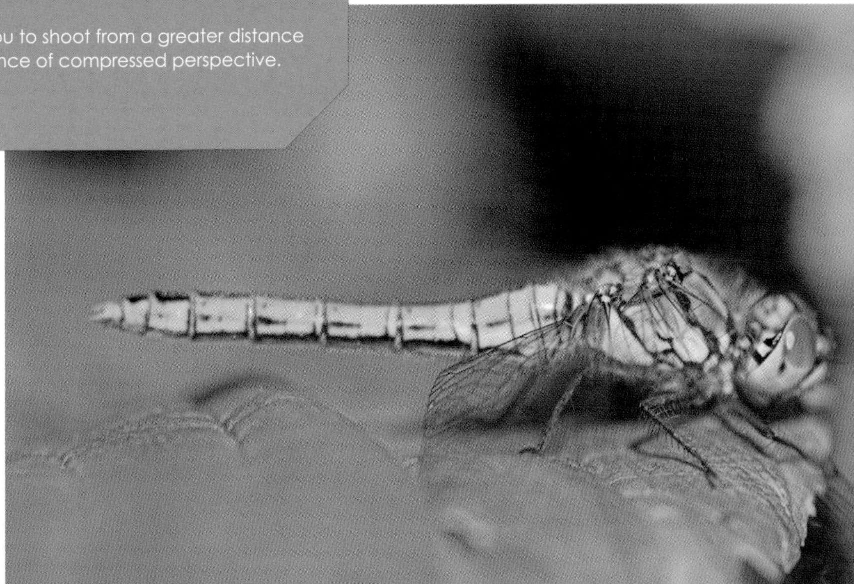

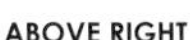

ABOVE RIGHT
The telephoto is the most common lens choice for wildlife photography. Here, shooting from a distant viewpoint with a 400mm lens means that the animal appears quite close to the background.

RIGHT
Many nature subjects are so small that you will need a macro lens to capture them successfully.

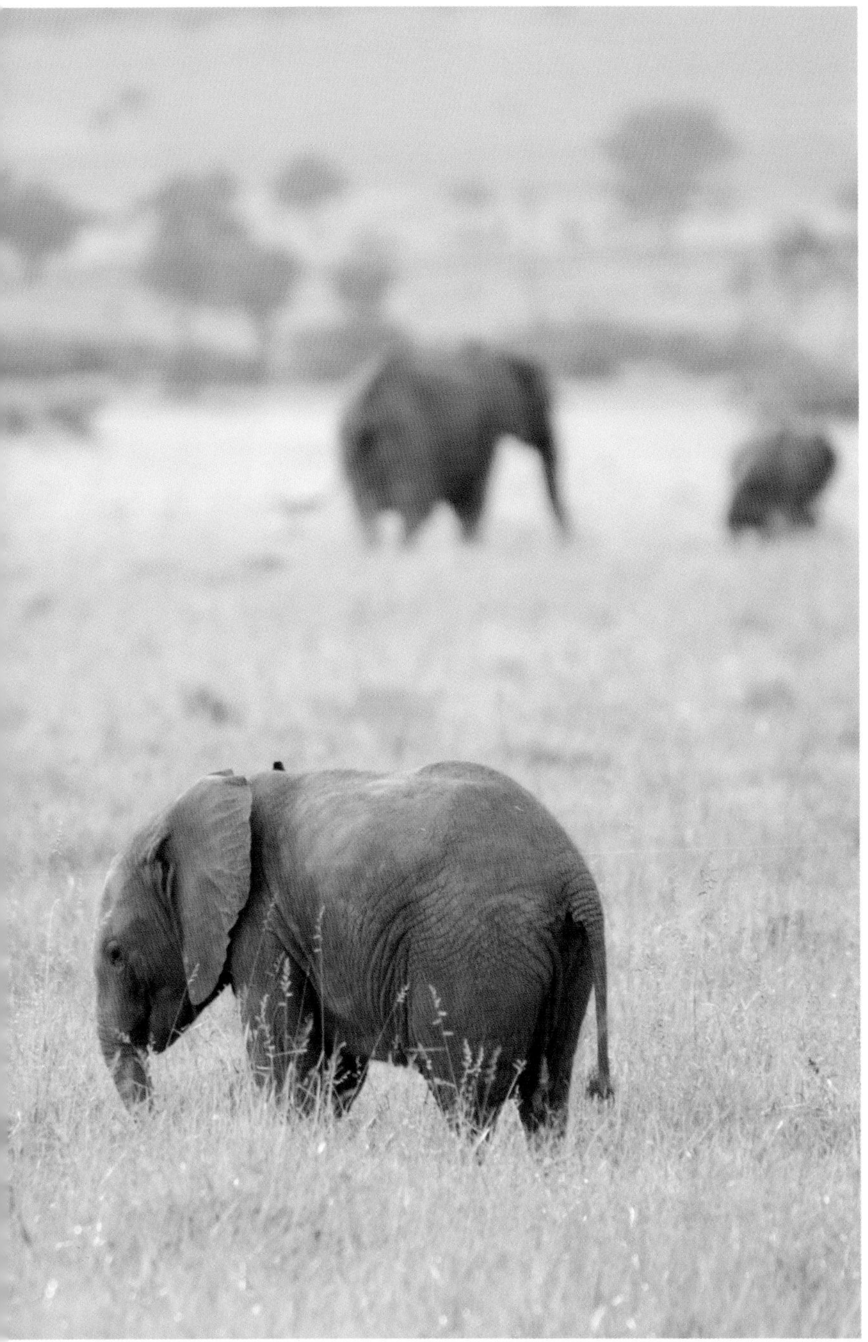

In the wild, locating the subject can often be the most difficult part of nature photography. As we discussed earlier, you do not have to go on safari or spend days in the wilderness to find potential subjects, as the local zoo, park, or even your own garden can provide plenty of wildlife to photograph.

Whichever location you choose, one of the most important aspects of composing your nature images is the background. The clearer the background the more the animal will stand out in the frame, whereas a cluttered and messy background will focus the viewer's attention on this rather than on the subject itself. The key to making the most of your wildlife compositions is learning to quickly check around the DSLR's viewfinder for distracting elements before you fire the shutter. There are also a number of techniques that can help to ensure that the background is as clear as possible.

Viewpoint

Although sometimes you will not have much choice in the viewpoint, you can move your position so that the background is free from distractions. This can mean that you have to wait until the animal moves into a more suitable position for your new viewpoint. It is always worth taking a few initial shots just in case the animal doesn't move into the right area, but patience is the real key to successful nature shots.

Depth of field

Controlling the amount of the image that is in focus is one of your most powerful tools in nature photography. With medium to long telephoto lenses, try to shoot at around f/5.6 to f/8 to blur the background.

LEFT

By selecting a wide aperture such as f/5.6 you can blur the background of your shot to help the main subject stand out in the frame.

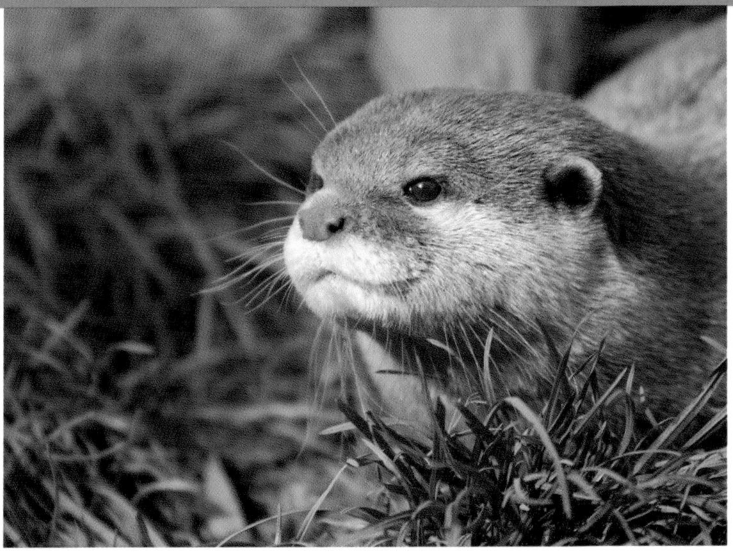

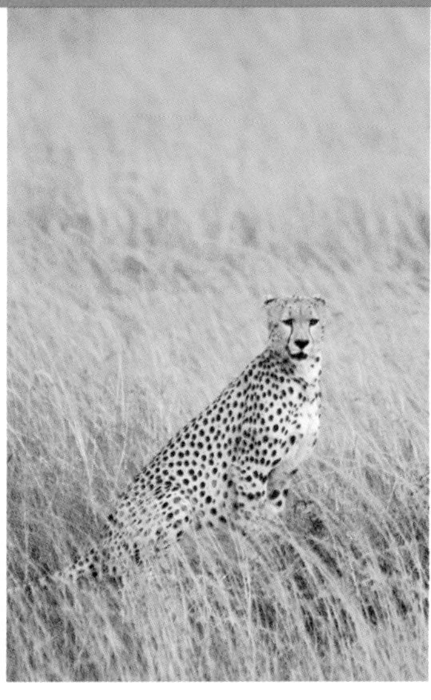

Crop in tight

If you can't adjust either the viewpoint or the depth of field, cropping in tight on the animal will eliminate the background altogether. This can be done using a longer lens or zoom setting, but one of the great advantages of DSLRs is the ability to crop images quickly and easily post-capture to fine-tune the composition.

ABOVE LEFT
Adjusting your viewpoint to the same level as your subject makes it appear more dominant in the frame. Looking down on an animal makes it appear less important in the image.

ABOVE RIGHT
When you can't get close enough to fill the frame with the subject, position it on one of the lines used by the rule of thirds for a successful composition.

BELOW
If the animal is looking out of the frame, leave space for it to move into. Here, the bird is facing the right of the frame, so I left more space on that side to give balance.

Photographing captive animals

While zoos and parks mean that you don't have to trek through the wilds to find the subject, they do present some unique difficulties to the photographer. Shooting through wire mesh or glass can cause problems for the autofocus, so it is best to switch to manual focus. To ensure that the wire is invisible in the final image, get as close to it as you are allowed and use the widest aperture available on your lens. This will give a very narrow depth of field. This is also great for throwing the background out of focus, as having bars, fences, or other people clearly visible in your shots is not usually the effect that you want.

Animal portraits

As with human portraits, the first point of contact with an animal shot will be the eyes. We naturally try to make eye contact as it is the best way of communicating, so the first step to successful animal shots is to ensure that the eye is sharp.

If the head of the animal is angled to one side, or you are shooting from the side, try to leave some space for the animal to "move" into. Psychologically, we expect an animal to move in the direction that it is facing, so leaving a gap between the head and the edge of the frame produces a more balanced image.

Applying the rule of thirds will also help you to create successful portraits. Try to place the head of the animal on one of the lines used to divide the image, or even better, use one of the intersections of the horizontal and vertical lines. If the animal is small in the frame, use these same places to position the whole of the animal's body.

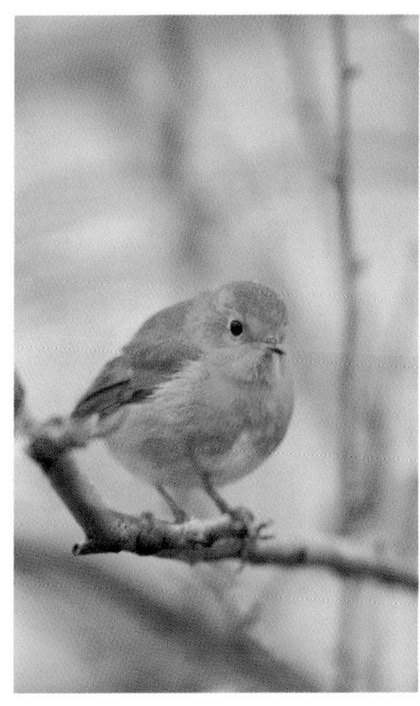

With practice you will find it much easier to find your subjects, but then it's time for a new challenge. Animals do not exist in isolation, they are part of a wider environment of other animals and plants that they interact with. This wider picture can tell the viewer more about the animal than a simple portrait shot. You won't want to waste time changing lenses on your DSLR when switching between portraits and wider shots. The ideal solution is to carry two camera bodies, one with a standard zoom and the other with a long telephoto lens. But for those with only one camera, a "superzoom" lens that covers focal lengths from around 18 to 200mm will help you to cover the widest range possible.

Behavior
The activities of feeding, playing, fighting, and mating define an animal's character and where they fit into the world. So it makes sense to include these in your nature images. The composition of these shots depends very much on the specific behavior being recorded, but there are some basic rules to give you a start.

If the behavior involves several animals, try to include the whole group, as one animal's reaction seen in isolation won't tell the whole story. For individual actions it's worth cropping right in; for example, a close-up of a lion eating, showing the scene in gory detail, has more impact than a wider shot.

Interaction
How animals interact with each other makes a fascinating study. Look for young animals with their mothers, playing and learning. Try to include at least two animals in a scene, although you do not need to include all of the animals in a group.

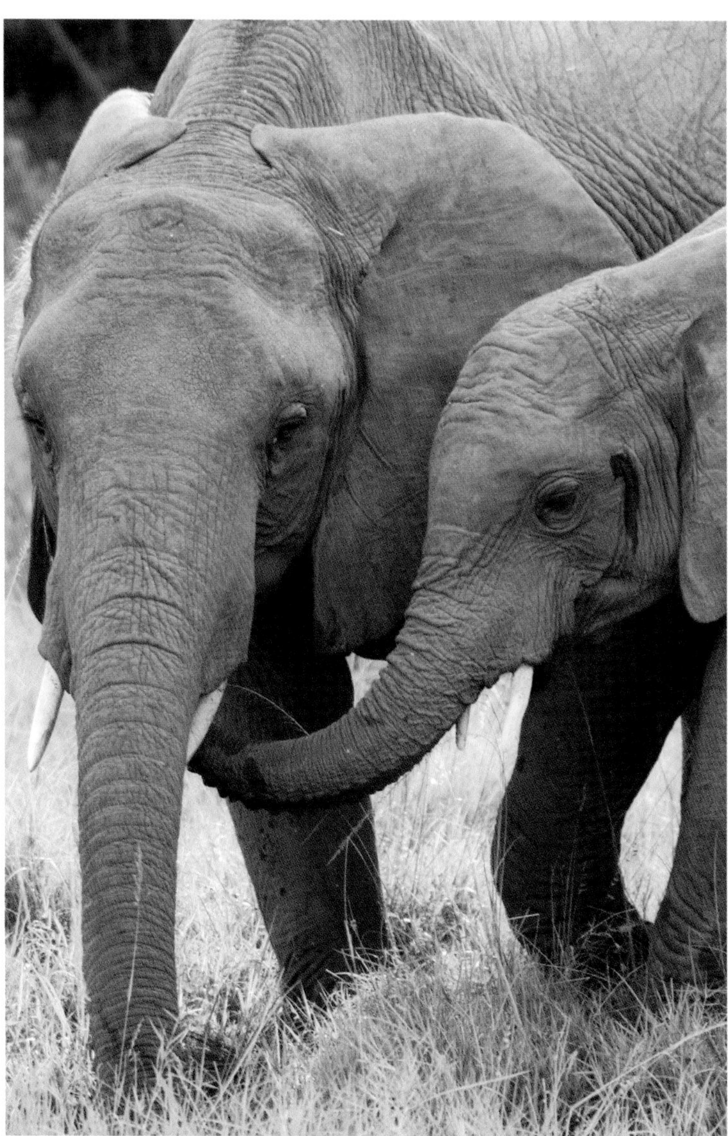

ABOVE
Photographing a mother and her young can produce powerful and emotive images.

Try to crop in close to emphasize the interaction between the two animals for maximum impact.

RIGHT
Although not a classic wildlife picture, this shot of water buffalo sheltering from the sun says more about their lives than a straight portrait.

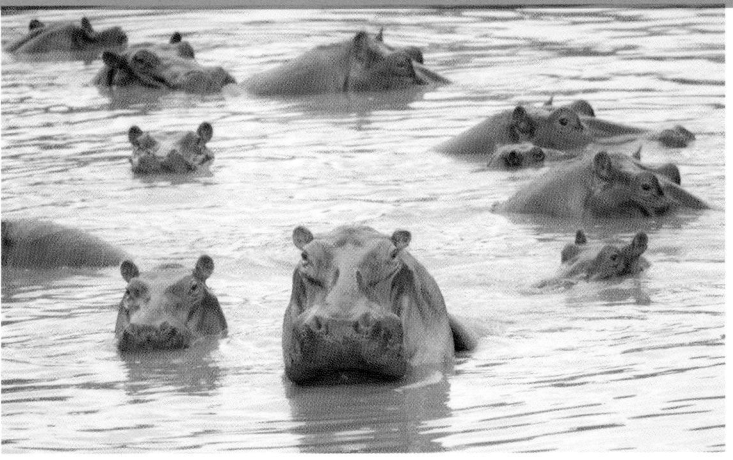

ABOVE
Rather than capturing just a single animal, including this whole group of hippos all looking toward the camera gives a much greater sense of the overall scene.

BELOW RIGHT
This lone giraffe was wandering across the landscape having just lost its offspring to some lions. I placed the giraffe at the bottom of the frame to make it appear more isolated and alone in the scene.

Large groups of animals

Many animals are naturally very social or live in large groups for safety, so by showing the whole group you can put the animal in context. When shooting groups, look for natural patterns or focus the attention on an individual animal by placing it in a dominant part of the frame. Look for an animal with unusual markings or some other feature that makes it stand out from the rest. The intersection used for the rule of thirds is a great place to position this animal as it is a point that naturally draws the viewer's eye.

Environment

It is tempting to try to fill the frame with the animal every time you shoot wildlife. If you're lucky enough to go on a safari, why come home with a set of pictures that you could have got in the local zoo? Including at least some aspects of the animal's environment can give your images a greater sense of place.

The animal in the landscape

The next step from this is to include the animal in the wider landscape to give it an even greater sense of space and environment. As with general landscape photography, where you place the animal in the frame will affect how dominant it is in the scene. If capturing the landscape is more important to you than the animal, try to place it near the edge of the frame. If you want the animal to be more visible, put it in a more eye-catching location such as on one of the lines used to denote the rule of thirds.

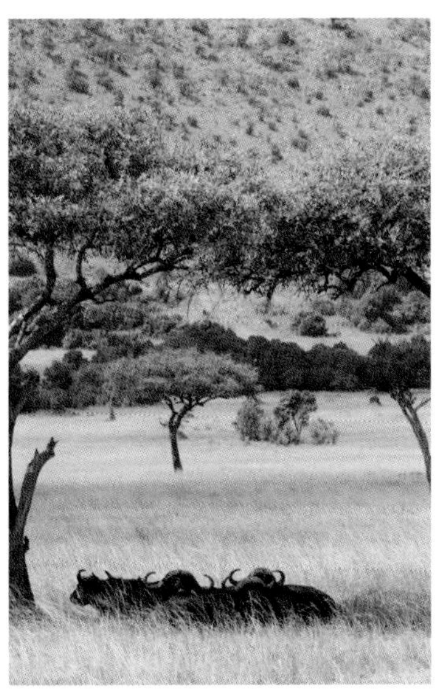

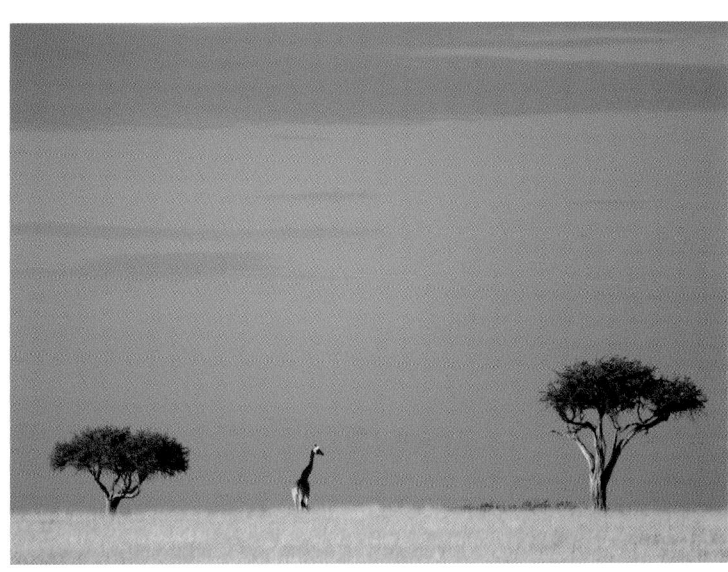

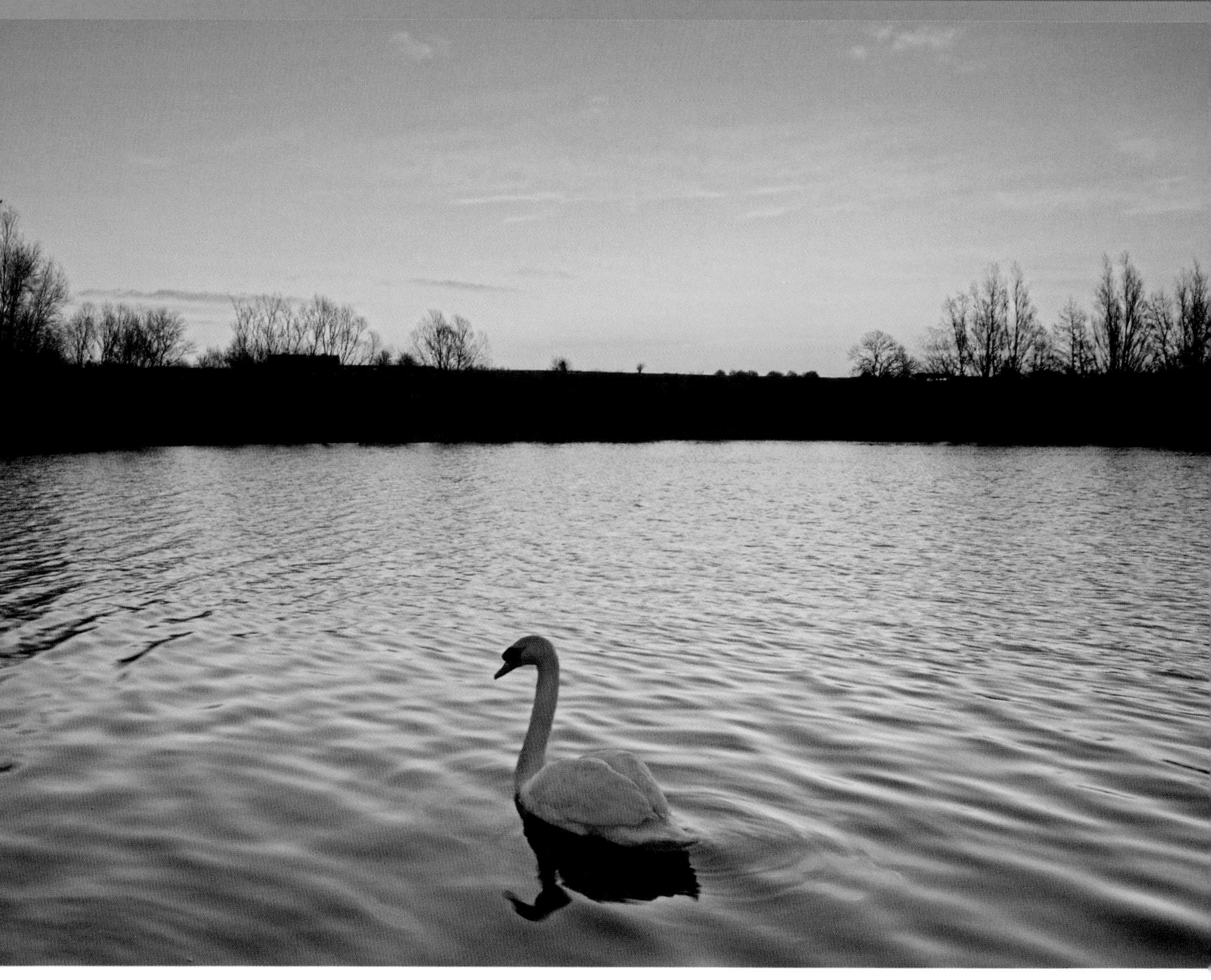

Nature photography offers plenty of scope for creative compositions. We've just seen how you can record behavior and environment, but the range of long focal length lenses available for DSLRs also makes it possible to record animals in terms of shape and form by cropping in on details. This can open up a whole new world of pattern, texture, and design. Also, the ability to control the shutter speed on your DSLR means you can use the animal's movement to create blurred, almost abstract, shots.

Using wide-angle lenses

Getting in close to the animal and using a wide-angle lens on your DSLR gives your nature shots a different perspective to shooting from a distance with a telephoto lens. When you are close to the subject, the distance between it and the background looks much greater than if you are farther away from it. This means that shots taken with a wide-angle lens appear more intimate and give the impression that the animal is almost coming out of the image.

ABOVE
Using a wide-angle lens to show the animal in its environment is a great way to put it in context.

OPPOSITE
You do not always have to include the whole animal in your images. Look out for details and textures to shoot in isolation, such as eyes, skin, or fur.

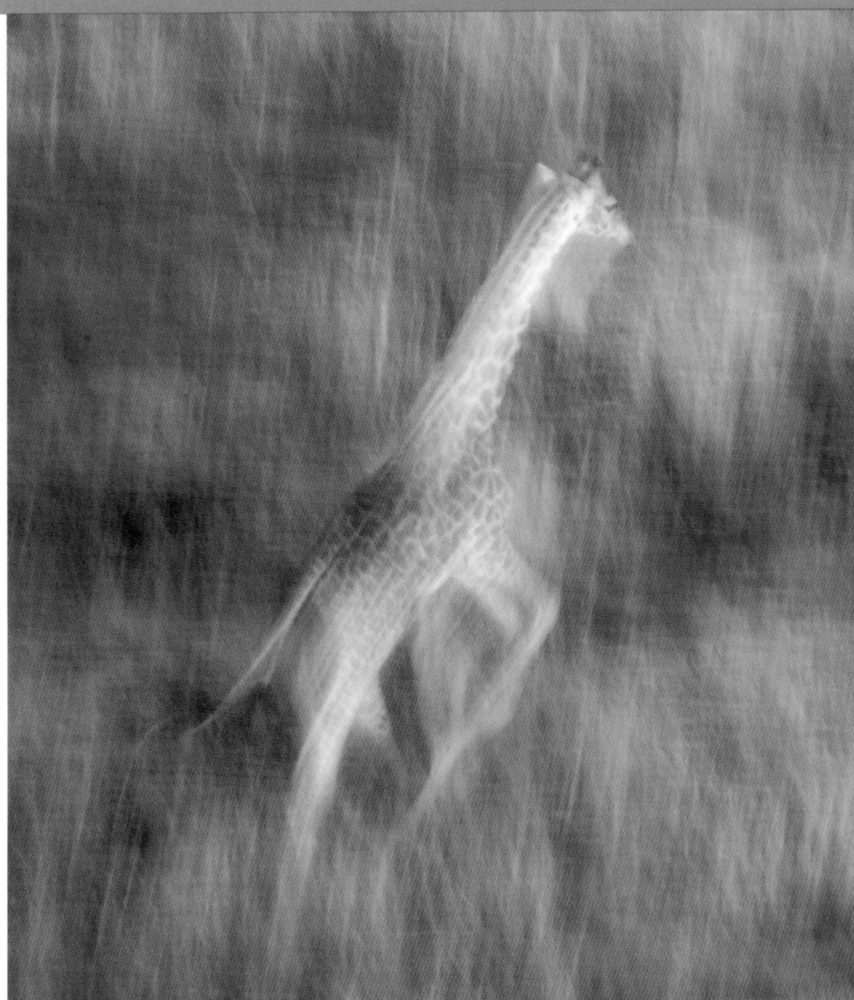

RIGHT
A slower shutter speed will allow you to show the animal in motion, producing a more abstract image.

Details
Rather than just shooting a straight portrait of an animal, try to capture the beauty of the patterns and textures in their skin, feathers, or fur. Although it's possible to get this type of shot in the wild using extreme telephoto lenses on your DSLR, you'll often find it easier when shooting captive animals. Many zoos and wildlife parks allow you to get close enough to the animals to use a 300mm lens, and many even offer special photography days where you will get even better opportunities.

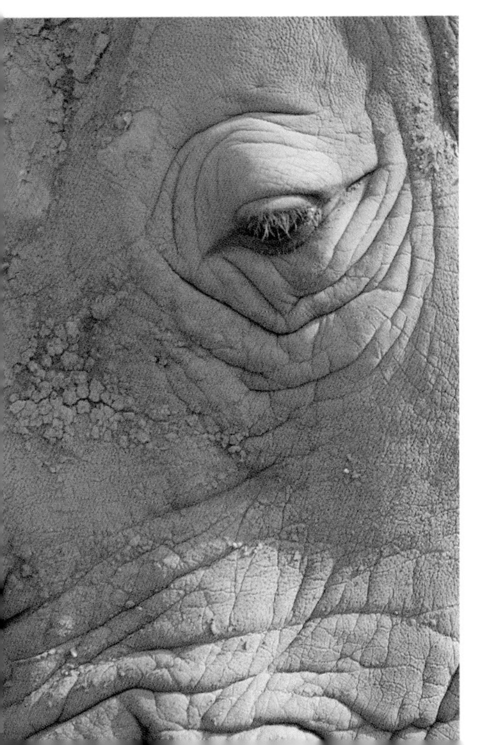

Capturing movement
There are many techniques that you can use to emphasize movement in your shots, although trying to keep up with a speeding cheetah or bird of prey can test even the most experienced nature photographer. All of these techniques take practice, so don't get too disheartened if your first attempts don't work out.

The easiest technique is to freeze the movement by using a fast shutter speed. Although this can sometimes appear to diminish the appearance of the movement, especially if there is no obvious effort from the animal, it can be effective when the animal is straining to move as fast as it can. Try cropping in tightly on the animal's expression and limbs to give the maximum effect.

Rather than freeze the action, you can also use a slow shutter speed to blur elements of the image to give a sense of speed. You can do this by either holding the camera steady so only the animal is blurred, or you can try to follow the movement so the animal is sharper and the background is blurred.

BELOW
1. The largest elephant is positioned on the left third of the image.

2. The group creates a strong diagonal line which adds energy to the composition.

3. The baby elephant is positioned on the opposite third line to the mother to give balance.

RIGHT
1. This tree on the left balances the composition and adds a vertical line.

2. The giraffe is positioned approximately on the right third line.

3. The wide framing shows the giraffe's environment.

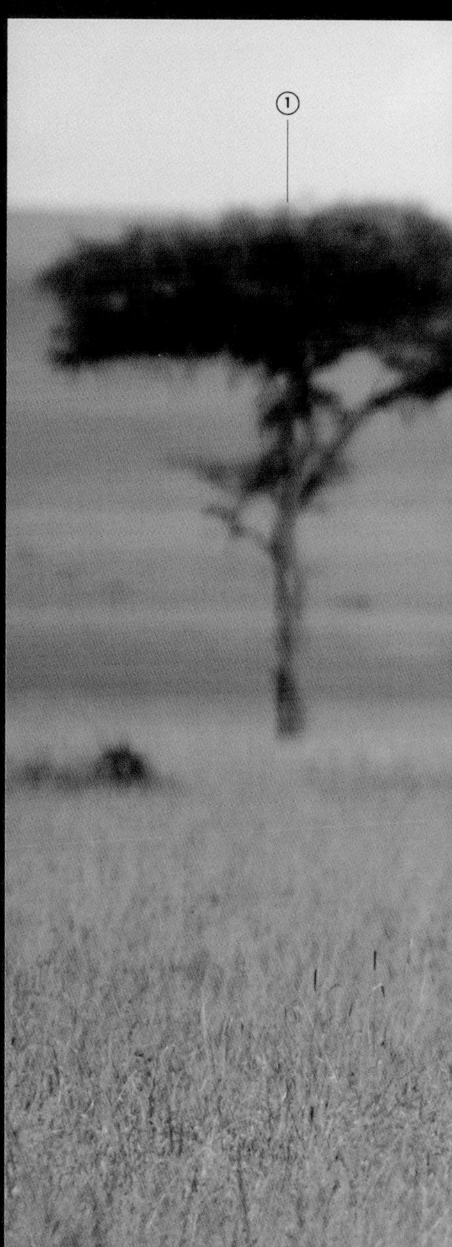

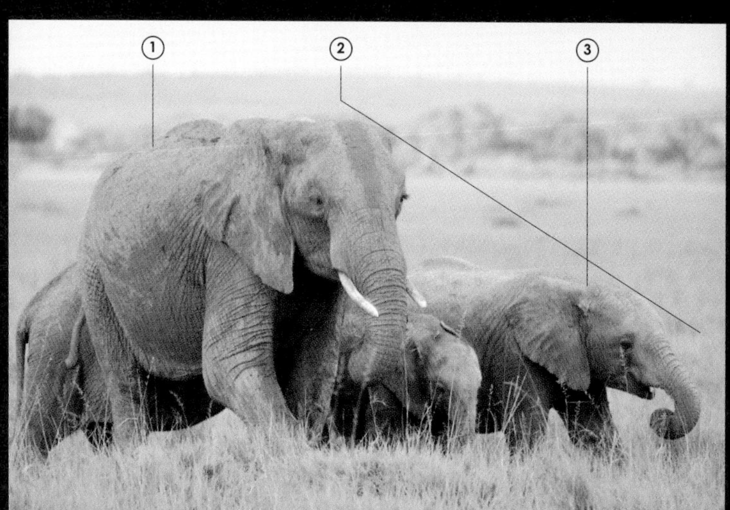

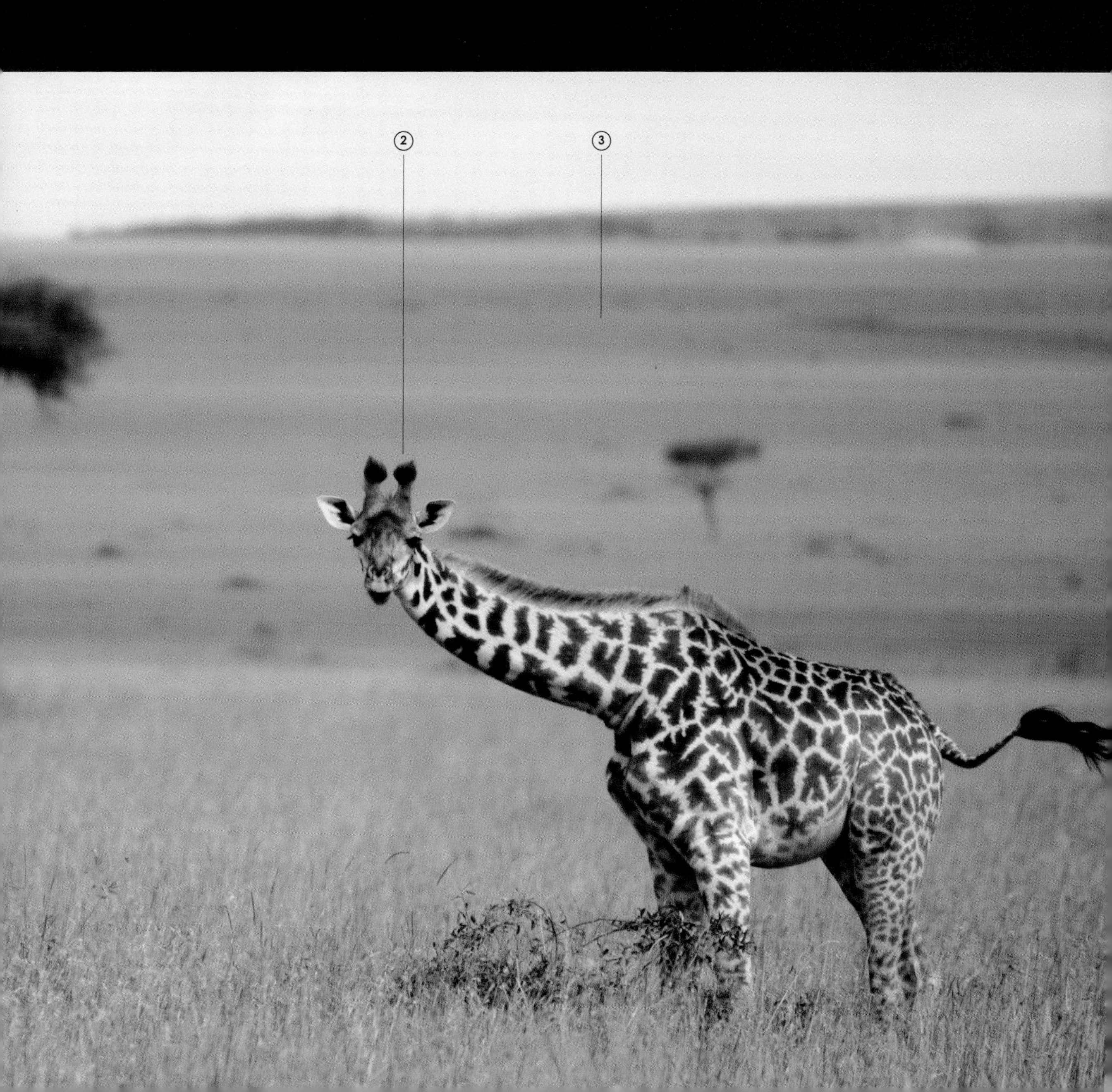
2
3

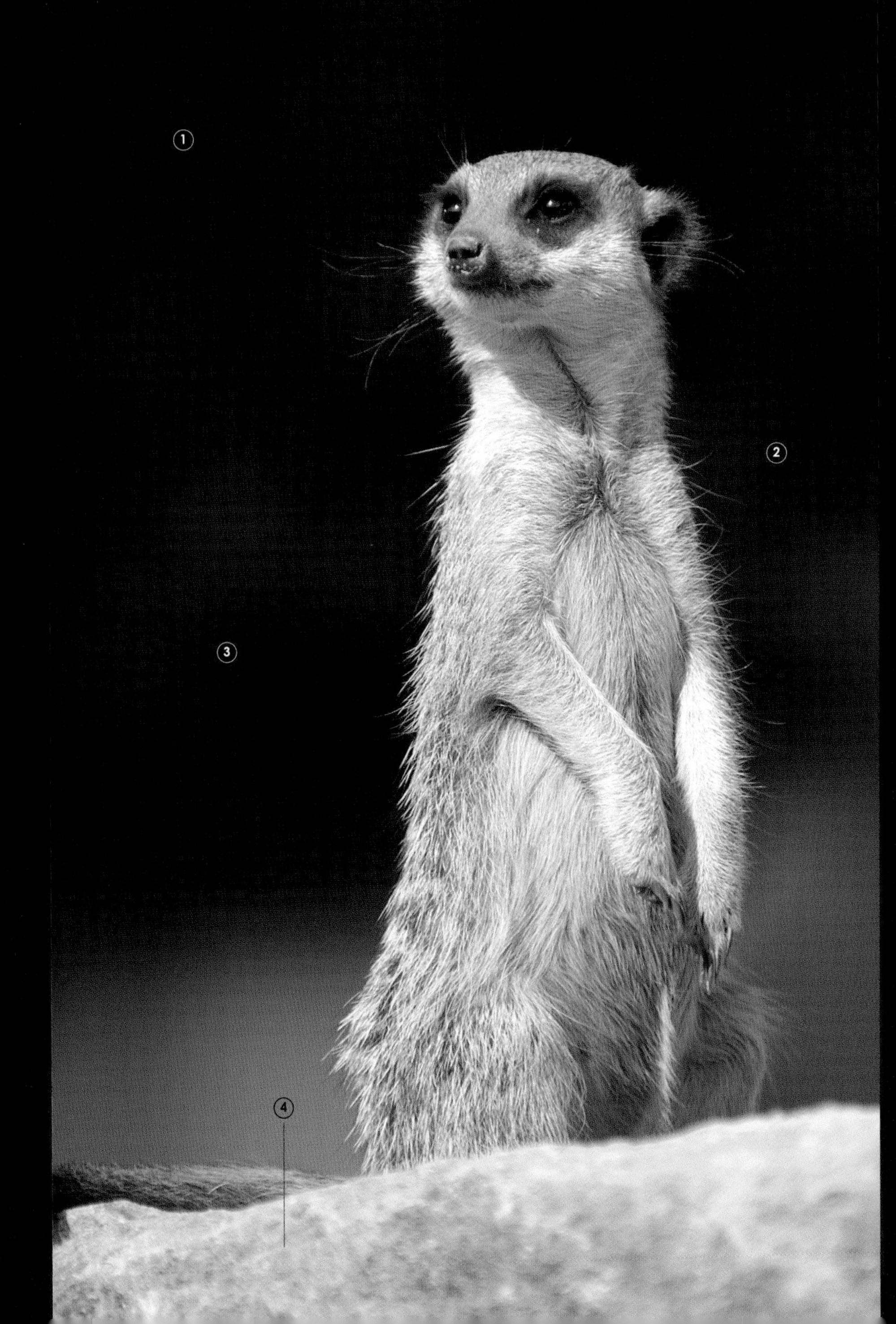
1
2
3
4

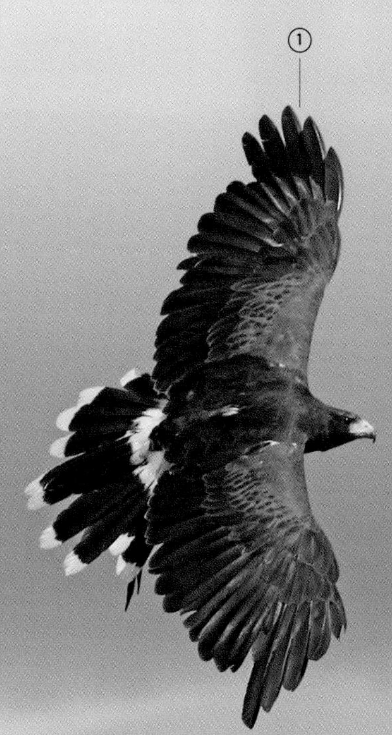
1
2
3

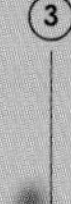

Section 6

Close-up and Macro

The results from close-up and macrophotography can be incredibly difficult to visualize before shooting. However, with practice and experience you will be able to get a good idea of how your shot will appear before you fire the shutter.

The best, and often the only way to explore the composition of your macro subjects is through the DSLR's viewfinder. This shows you the image "seen" by the lens that takes the shot, so gives an excellent idea of how your shot will look. The clarity and large size of the viewfinder on most DSLRs also helps to reveal detail and patterns that you'll miss with the naked eye. For many of the best compositions of macro shots you need to get down to the same level as your subject, rather than looking down on it, to give your shots a new perspective. While this can sometimes be easy, often it means getting down to ground level. You will find it easier and cleaner if you take a ground sheet, unless you enjoy getting covered in dirt!

With macrophotography the effects of camera shake are magnified, so it's best to support the camera on a tripod or beanbag. Because you are so close to the subject, even small movements in the position of the camera can alter the perspective dramatically. The support you use must allow you to position the camera close to the ground in a full range of positions.

Depth of field

Compared with normal photography, the depth of field in macro is very narrow. This means it is easier to use selective focus to make certain areas of the subject stand out, but can prove to be a problem if you want to keep the whole subject in focus. It's worth using the depth of field preview facility if it's available on your DSLR. The normal image in the viewfinder is shown with the lens at its maximum aperture, which makes it as bright as possible, but it doesn't show you how much of the image will be in focus at smaller apertures. By pressing the depth of field preview, the lens will be stopped down to the aperture you have set on the lens allowing you to see the depth of field.

BELOW

Taking the time to explore the various views and settings in macrophotography makes it possible to achieve a range of different results from a single subject. The view of this mushroom from above (A) produces a very poor result, but a lower viewpoint produces better images.

The appearance can also be greatly influenced by the depth of field. Using a wide aperture such as f/4 (B) isolates the subject from the background, while using a small aperture of f/16 (C) makes the background clearer.

A B C

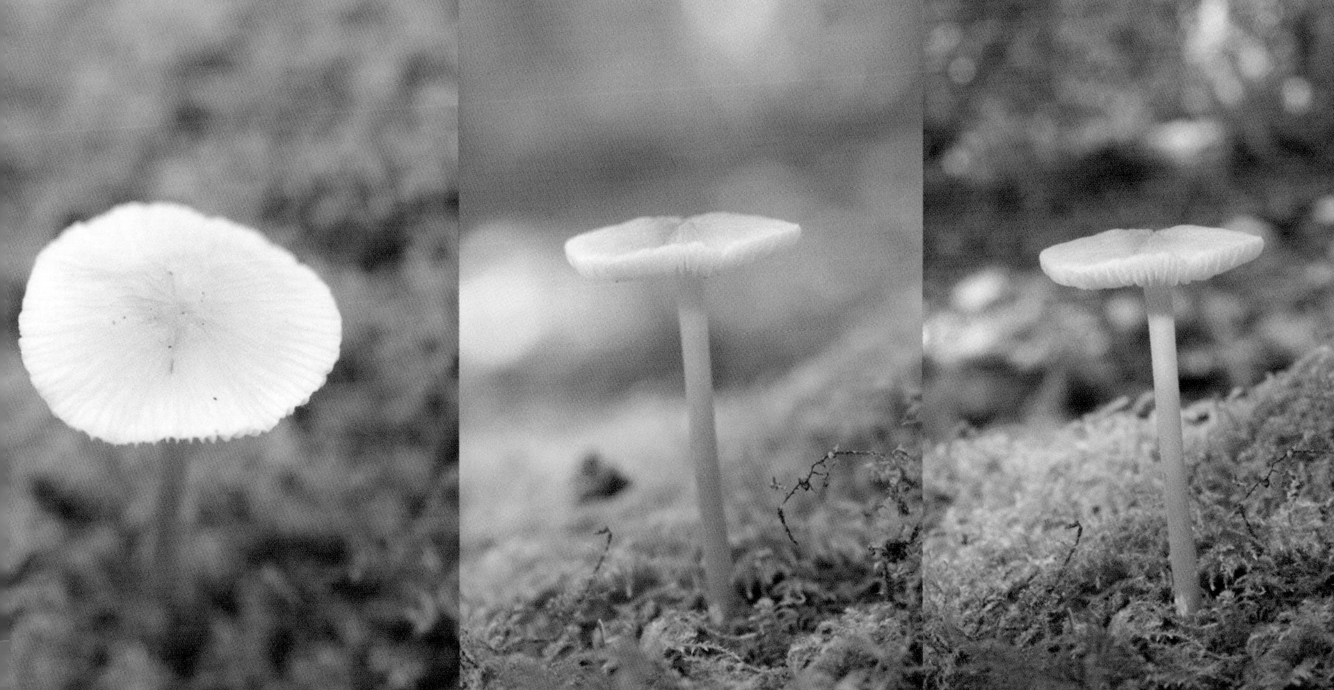

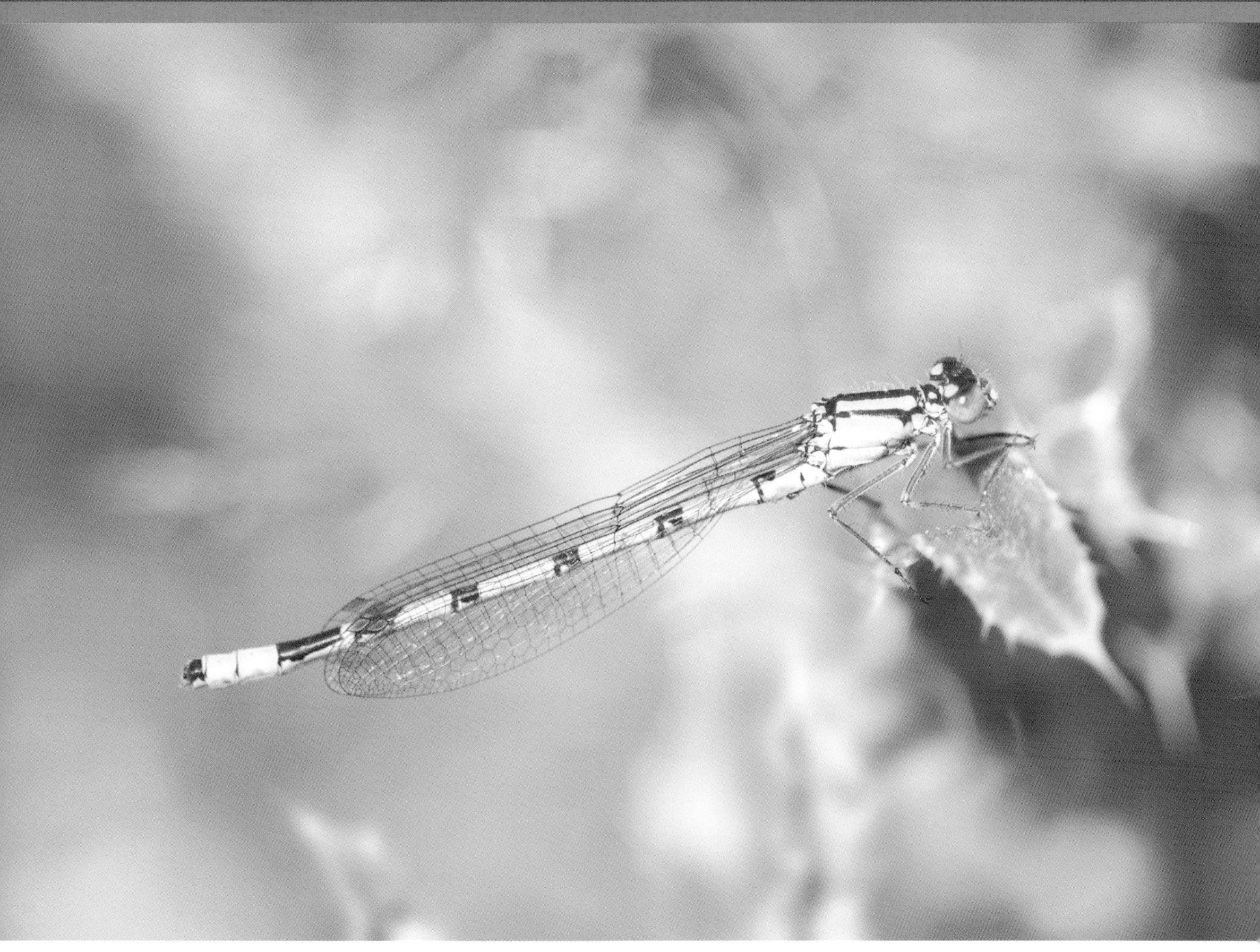

ABOVE
Locating and shooting insects requires plenty of patience and a little knowledge of when and where you will find likely subjects.

Lighting
Successful composition often relies on the main subject being the brightest part of the scene, as brighter areas grab our attention. At normal shooting distances it is relatively easy to add light using flash or reflectors, but getting light onto your subject without unwanted shadows can be a problem in macrophotography. The front of your lens is sometimes barely inches away from the subject, meaning that with either the on-camera flash available on most DSLRs or even with natural daylight, it is difficult to avoid the camera or lens causing shadows. You can get good results by using a small reflector to bounce light back onto static subjects. However, many insect photographers prefer to use flash as they need to work quickly before the subject moves. There are a couple of solutions among the range of accessories available for DSLRs. You can use an off-camera flash using a bracket or a device known as a ring flash. With a ring flash, the flash tube is positioned around the lens rather than on top of the camera. The light is directed straight at the subject, so you get even, almost shadowless, lighting.

BELOW
The focal length of your macro lens determines how far away you need to be from the subject to achieve your shot. This will affect the perspective in your images, with the closer viewpoint needed with a short focal length lens giving a greater sense of distance between the subject and the background (A). The more distant viewpoint of a longer lens makes the distance between subject and background appear shorter (B). In each of these shots, the main subject is the same size and the same aperture was used, but the backgrounds appear very different. Image A was taken using a 50mm lens and image B with a 200mm lens.

Many standard lenses supplied with DSLRs offer a macro or close-focus facility. What sets true macro lenses apart is their ability to focus close enough to produce an image of a subject at the same size as the sensor. This ability—known as life-size or 1:1 reproduction—means you can take shots much closer than you can with normal lenses, which at best offer only half life-size or 1:2 reproduction.

True macro lenses come in a range of focal lengths from 50mm up to around 200mm. The focal length of these lenses doesn't affect their reproduction ratio, but does make a difference to the composition and perspective of your macro shots.

The effect of focal length
Even macro lenses that offer the same reproduction ratio can produce very different results. The reason for this is the effect of the focal length, as the longer the focal length the farther away you are from the subject for the same image size.

This difference in the camera-to-subject distance affects the perspective of your images. The greater the distance you are from the subject, the closer objects will appear in front of or behind the subject.

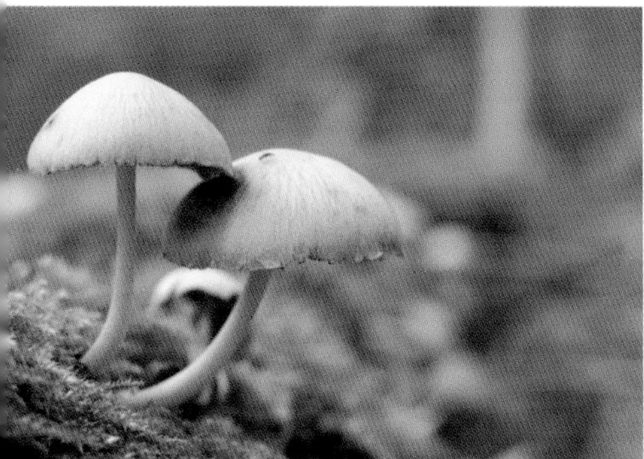

A

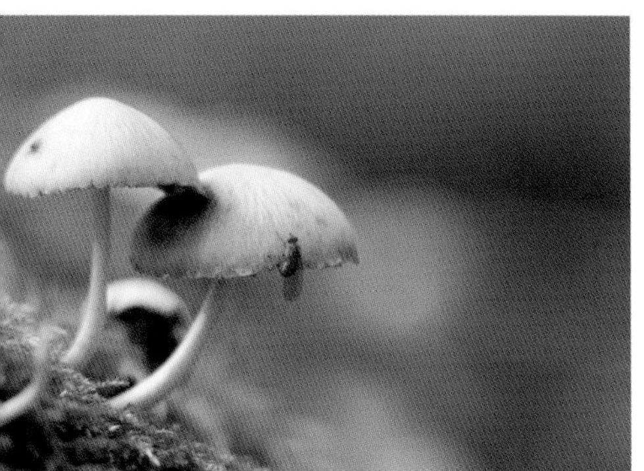

B

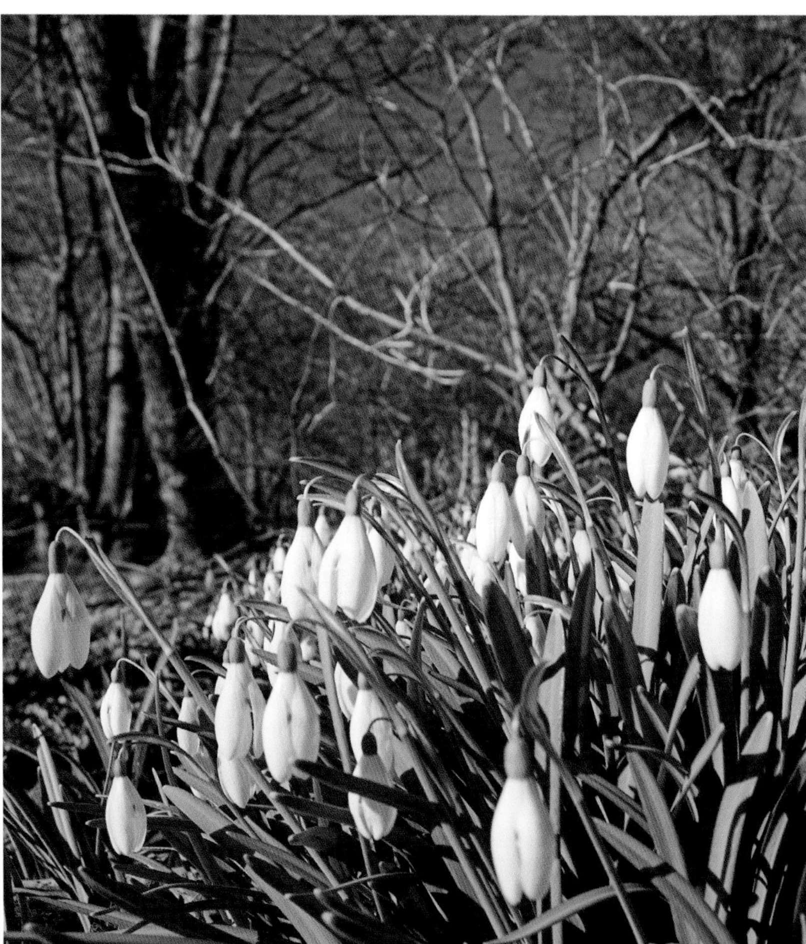

BELOW
Getting very close to the subject and using a wide-angle lens for close-up shots gives a very different perspective to using a telephoto lens.

RIGHT
A telephoto lens with a close-focus facility will allow you to get macro shots of timid creatures without having to get too close to them.

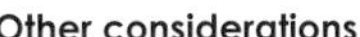

Other considerations

While the focal length affects the perspective and composition of your shots, there are some other reasons for choosing different focal length macro lenses. On most DSLRs, the smaller sensor compared with a 35mm camera means you can use a shorter focal length lens to fill the frame at a given distance. So you can get good close-ups of insects and other wildlife using a 105mm macro lens. But the greater working distance given by longer lenses can still be extremely useful. I often use a 300mm telephoto lens on a DSLR with a 1:2 close-up facility when shooting particularly timid subjects, such as dragonflies and damselflies, allowing me to keep my distance and still get good close-ups. Shorter focal length macro lenses are more useful for general close-up photography, and the 70mm to 105mm versions make great lenses for head and shoulders portraits thanks to both their focal length and their wide f/2.8 maximum apertures.

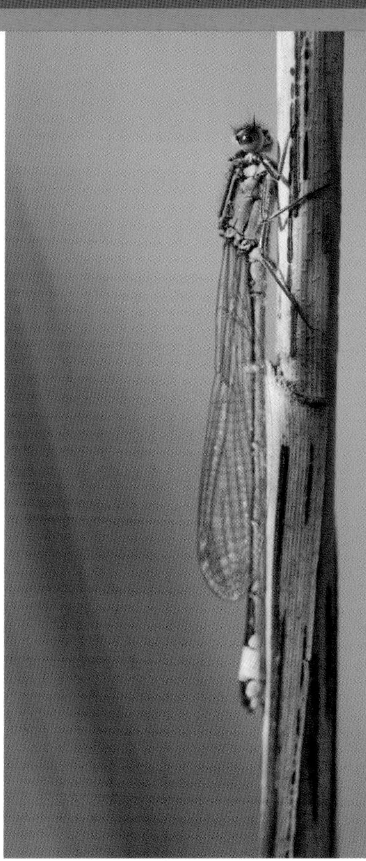

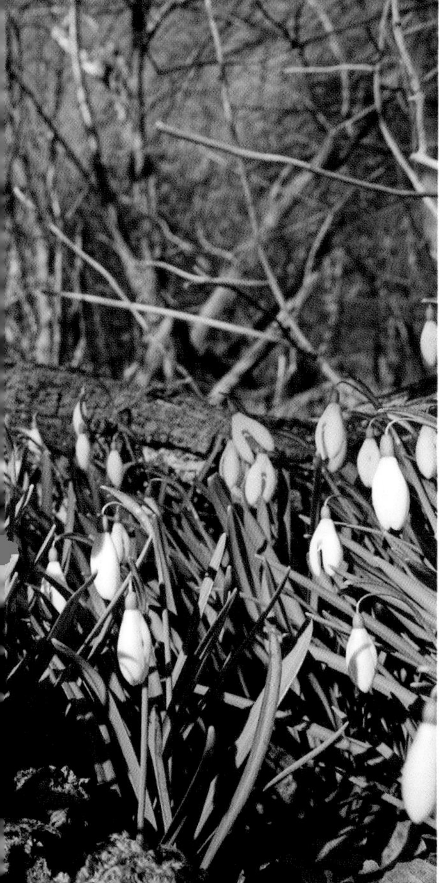

OTHER WAYS OF GETTING CLOSE-UPS

While true macro lenses are great for close-up shots, you can achieve similar results by using add-on accessories with your existing lenses. There are two main accessories available, with the cheapest being screw-in close-up lenses. Although they are known as lenses, these actually fit onto the front of your existing lens like a filter, allowing it to focus closer. They come in a range of strengths, known as diopters. The higher the number, the closer it allows you to focus.

The second accessory is a device known as an extension tube. This is a hollow tube that fits between the lens and the camera. The larger the tube, the closer you can focus. When buying extension tubes, make sure they are the right lens fitting for your DSLR, and that they retain all of the metering functions available on your camera.

Both of these solutions are less convenient than a true macro lens as you often have to swap them over to achieve different distances, but they are a cheaper route to getting close-ups.

CLOSE-UP AND MACRO: FINDING THE SUBJECT

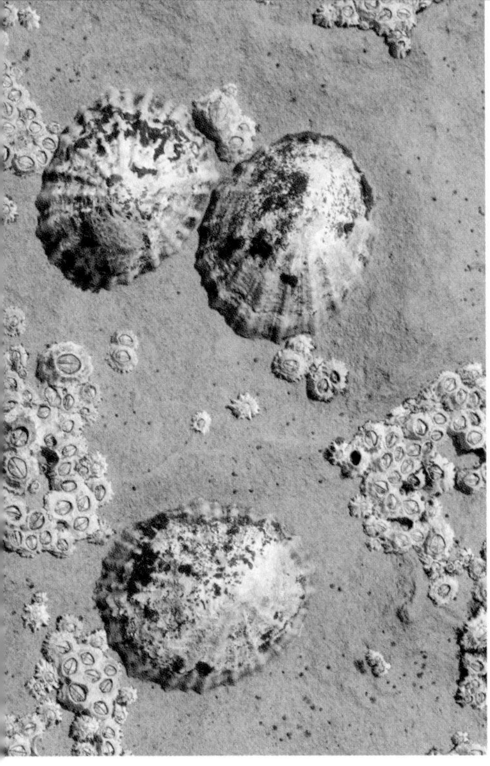

There are thousands of macro subjects all around us, but recognizing their potential is the key to successful close-up work. Once you start looking, you can find beautiful shapes, patterns, and textures in almost any location.

When you start to work with a macro lens, it can take some time to get the right macro "mind-set" for making the most of your subjects. The first thing to do is to put the macro lens on the camera and start looking around the subject through the viewfinder. Don't be too disappointed if you don't get great macro shots straight away, as the limited depth of field and new perspective on the world can take some getting used to. Reviewing your images on the DSLR's rear LCD screen will give you a better idea of how your shots can be improved. I often find that seeing the results on the screen gives a better idea of the composition than the image in the viewfinder, especially when working at awkward camera heights.

Because you are working on such a small scale, it is easier to manipulate the elements of the scene to help your composition. When shooting outdoors you can easily move grasses, leaves, or flowers to achieve the perfect composition. Remember that you probably won't have to move objects very far to make a huge difference to their positions in the frame. With an object as small as a leaf, for example, even moving it just an inch can mean that it's no longer in your shot.

ABOVE
Photographing static subjects gives you the opportunity to try almost every possible angle and composition. Shooting from above gives a very flat, static composition, but by careful framing, these three shells form a strong triangular shape.

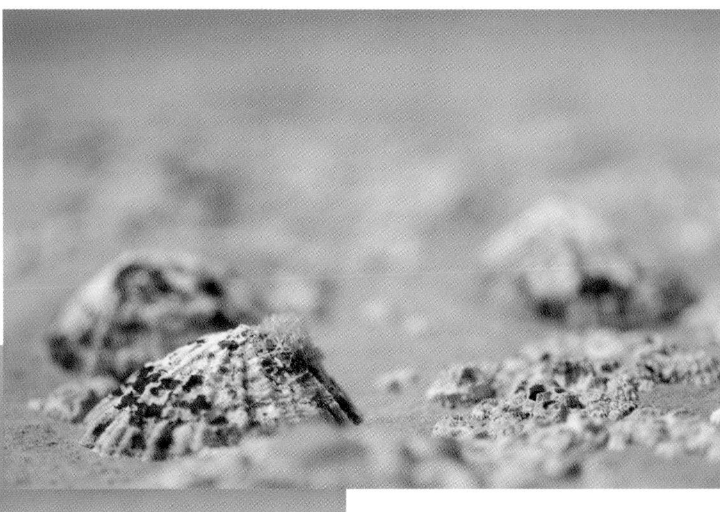

LEFT
Getting level with the shells gives a very different composition and allows me to include the blue of the sea as a background to give a sense of the location. However, the shells are now too small in the frame.

ABOVE
Getting in closer in a horizontal format makes the shells appear larger, but cuts out most of the background.

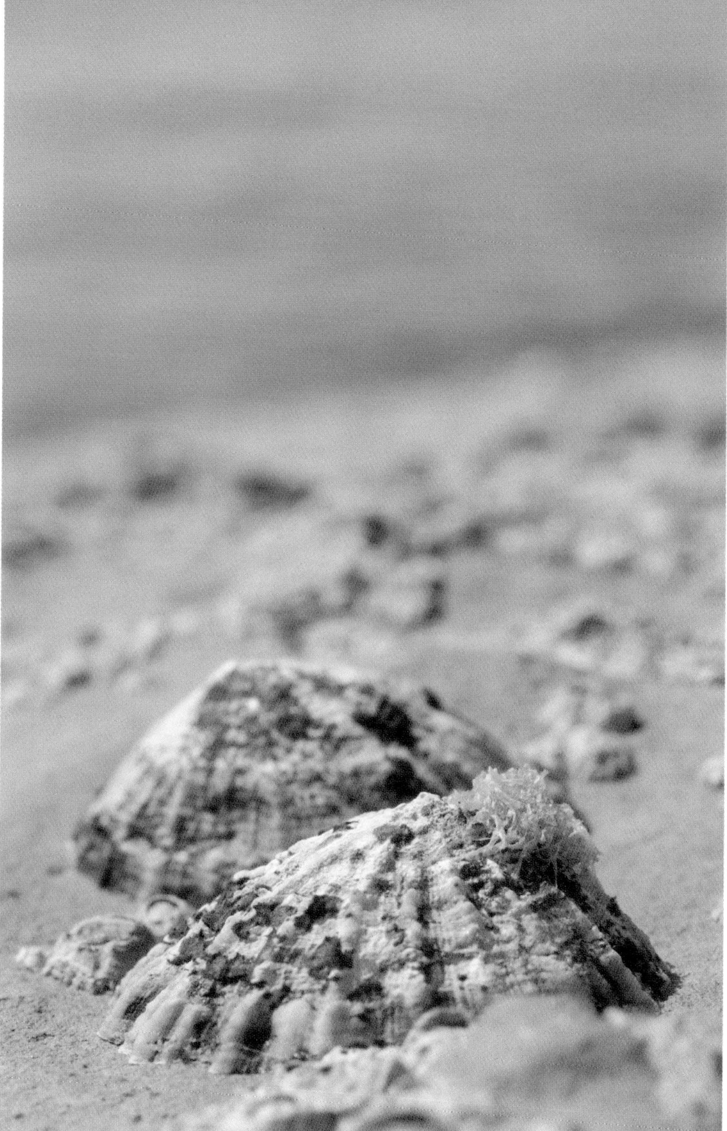

LEFT
I finally settled on an upright framing, with the shells placed in the bottom third of the shot and the sea in the top third. This allowed me to get a great close-up of the shells along with the background.

Viewpoint

Your viewpoint is probably the single most important aspect of composing macro images because it makes such a difference to the final result. Get into the habit of looking at the whole frame, especially the background, to see how it works with your main subject. Watch out for distracting highlights or bright colors that take attention away from the subject. You won't have to shift your viewpoint far to change the background completely, so try moving just a few inches to either side, or up and down, to get your shot just right.

INSECT PHOTOGRAPHY

While most macrophotography is best tackled at a slow, leisurely pace, insects and other small animals often need to be photographed quickly before the creature takes flight or runs away. One of the best ways to minimize this problem is to go out early or late in the day when the temperature is low enough to make insects less active. Out in the field you need some basic knowledge of where you are likely to find your subjects, but even more important is to take the time to search closely through the likely habitat. Although the photography may need to be done quickly, you cannot hurry the search for your subject. Pay attention to where your shadow is falling, both when you are searching for the subject and when you are trying to get your shots. If your shadow falls across the insect, it will notice your presence. Many insects are also extremely sensitive to movement, so once you have found the subject you will need to move slowly into position or you will scare it away.

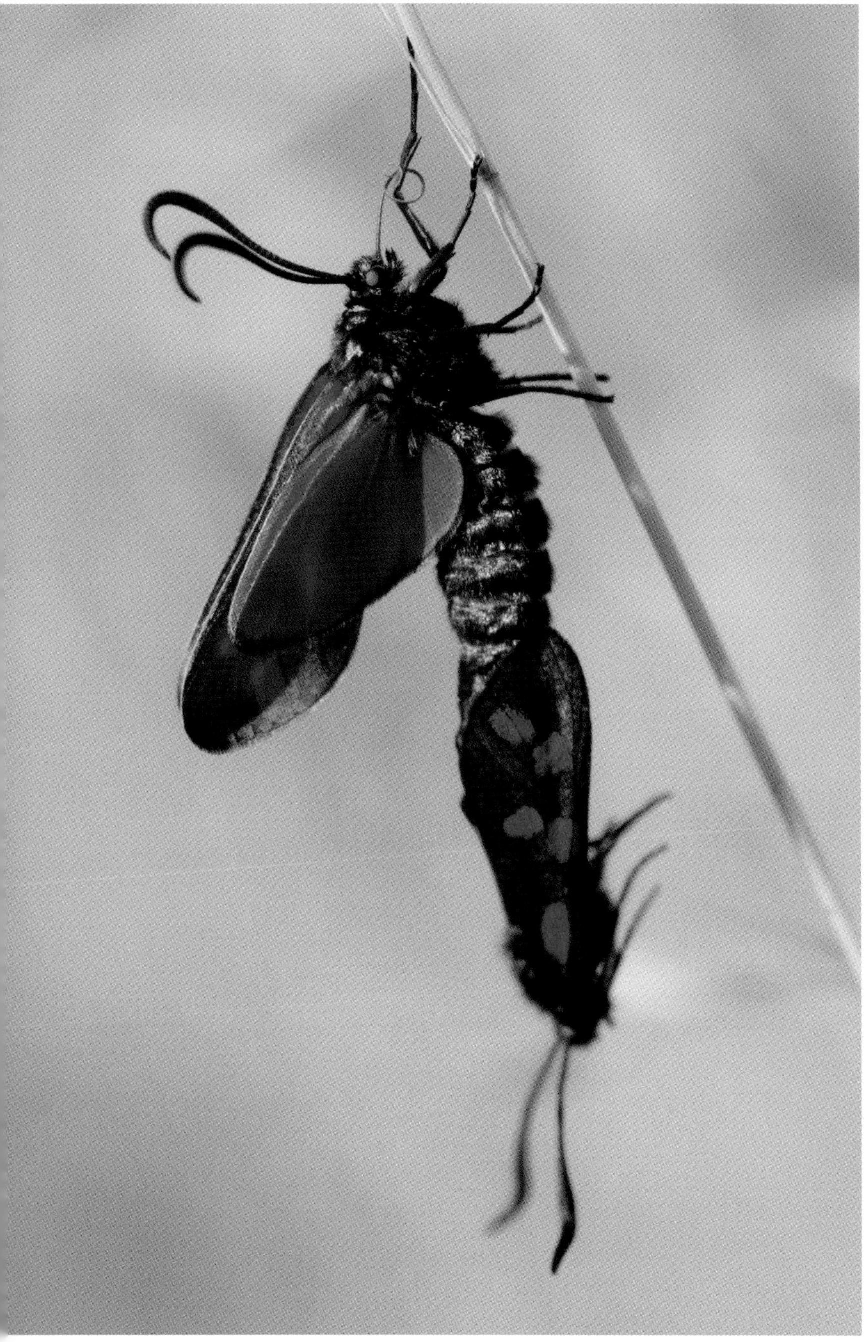

Compared with most other subjects, it is not easy to tell a story with macrophotography. The subjects are so small that it is often a struggle to include any additional objects in the frame, but it is not impossible. When shooting close-ups on location you can try to include the background to give a greater sense of the environment and surroundings. You will find this task easier with a shorter focal length macro lens on your DSLR, such as a 50mm, rather than a longer one, as the closer viewpoint often allows you to get a better view of the background.

Because of the limited depth of field in close-up photography, even at the smallest aperture the background can still be blurred. So you need to make sure that the scene is strong enough to give a sense of the location even if it's not in focus. Look for features such as trees, people, and buildings that can be easily recognized to use as a background.

Insect close-ups

Insects are perhaps the easiest subjects for showing the story behind the picture. With animals you can always record their behavior to give your pictures this extra element. Whether it's feeding, mating, or simply surviving what can be a very short and dangerous life, nature is full of stories that you can convey in your close-up nature shots.

LEFT
Shooting the behavior of insects in macro images tells the viewer much more about their lifestyle than straight portraits.

RIGHT
By positioning the subject to one side of the image, you can include more of the background. Here, I used a wide aperture to blur the other flowers, but I could still use their color to complement the main subject.

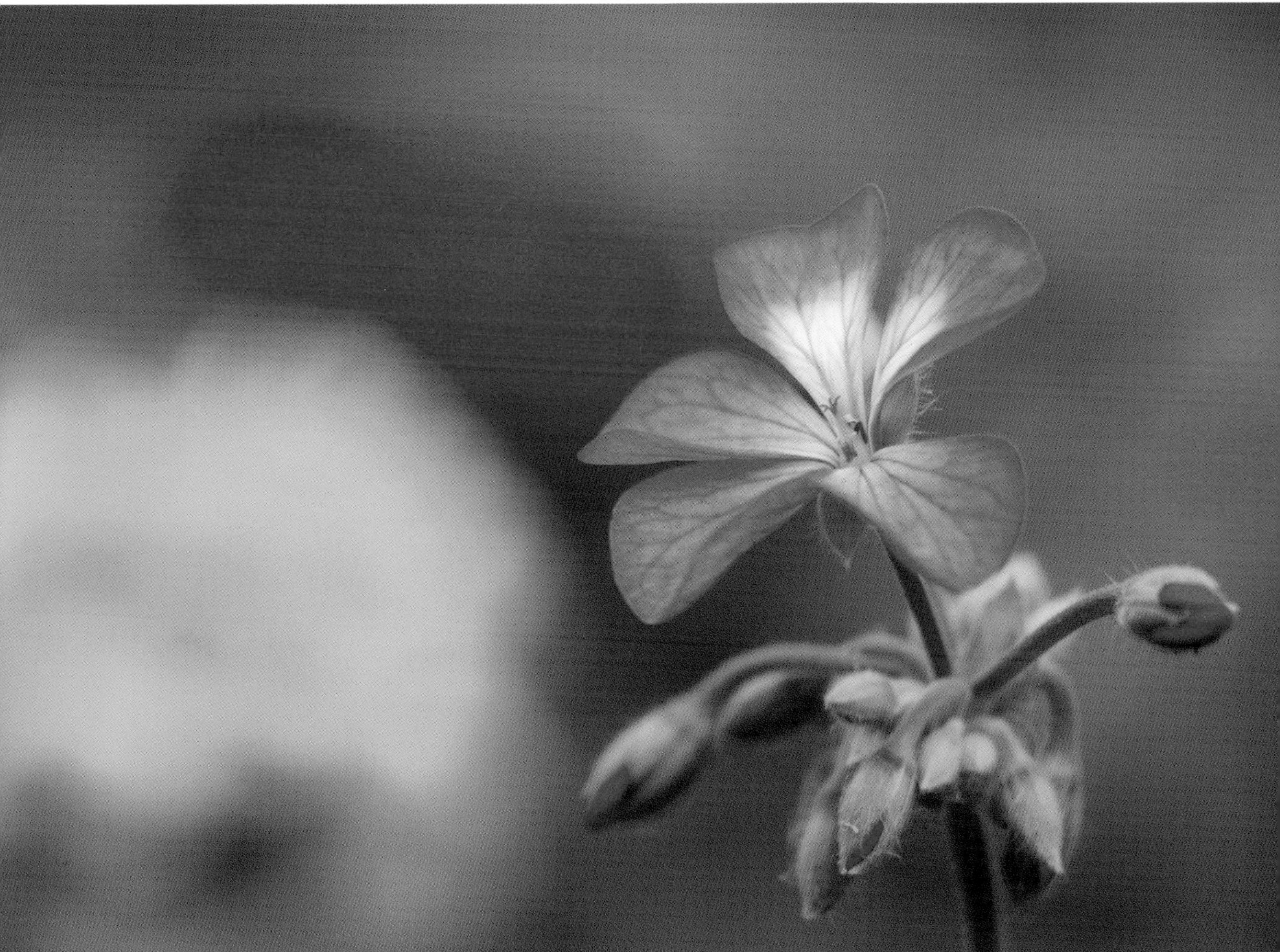

Depth of field
The amount of depth of field in close-up photography is often extremely limited. The greater the magnification, the less depth of field you will get in your images. You can use this limited depth of field to concentrate all of the attention on the main subject in your close-ups, or try to maximize the depth of field to allow other areas of the frame to be in focus to show the wider scene.

Including the background
Although most close-ups and macro shots concentrate on the main subject, it is worth including the environment around the subject. You will find this easiest if you use a shorter (50mm) focal length macro lens, or even a wide-angle lens with larger subjects, as this will allow you to include a wider view of the background than a longer focal length lens.

Try positioning the main subject to one side or at the bottom of the frame to maximize the amount of the background that you can include. Placing the main subject on one of the third lines makes it more prominent in the frame.

Macrophotography is all about getting a new perspective on the world. The freedom of seeing a subject from a viewpoint that you don't normally see and noticing detail that is invisible to the naked eye means it is almost impossible not to discover new ways of shooting close-ups every time you shoot them. But even though it's a world that we can't see with our own eyes, it's easy to fall into the habit of simply shooting the standard macro shots that photographers have been taking for years.

Traditionally, close-up photographers have tried to maximize the depth of field by using small apertures. This is fine for scientific or technical images where you want to show as much of the subject as possible, but it's not necessarily the most effective. Using wide apertures produces more limited depth of field, which can give abstract or impressionistic results.

Although not technically macrophotography, you can also use wide-angle lenses on your DSLR for close-up images. This doesn't give the same sort of magnifications available with a macro lens, but allows you to include more of the surroundings and environment to put the subject into context. Many wide-angle lenses offer a good close-focus facility, but you can get even closer by adding a screw-in close-up lens to the front of the lens or by using extension tubes.

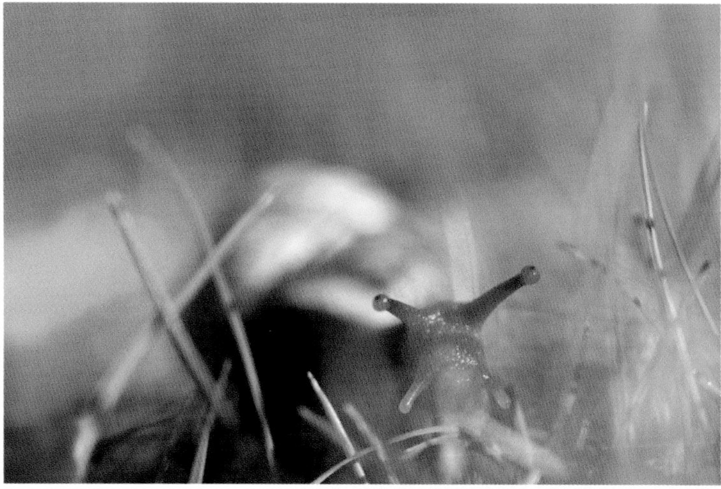

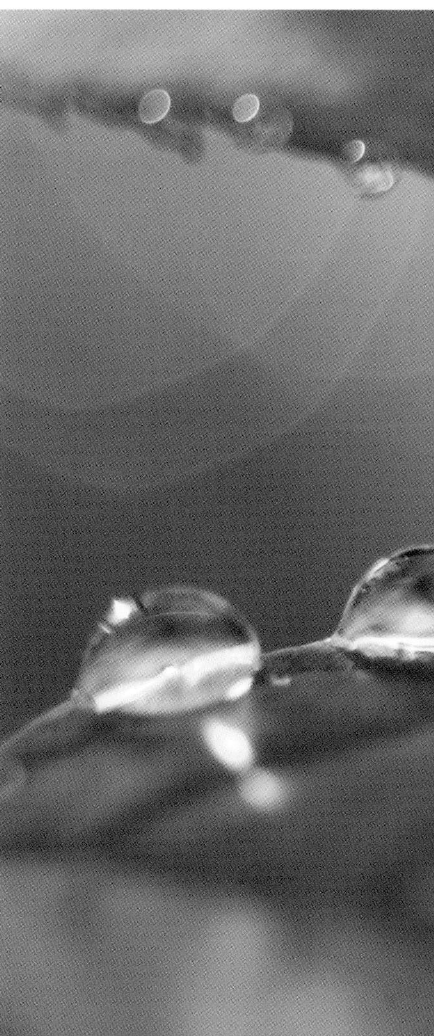

ABOVE
Using a wide aperture can make even familiar subjects appear unusual in macrophotography. By carefully focusing on the eyes of this snail and blurring the rest of the animal, it takes on a whole new look.

RIGHT
Unconventional compositions and framing can often be used effectively in macrophotography. Leaving a blank area in the center of this image and focusing on the edges of these two leaves rather than the background produces an abstract and interesting result.

TOP RIGHT
When shooting abstract macro images, look for strong compositions such as the diagonal lines in this leaf.

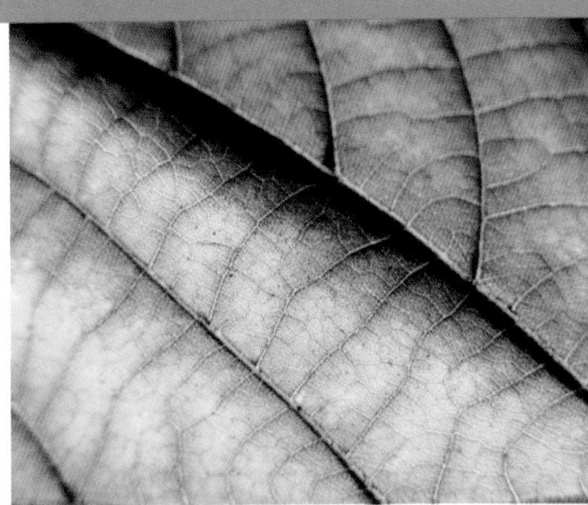

Another way to compose your macro shots is to look for abstract shapes, colors, and textures. When shooting abstracts rather than trying to show the whole subject, you still need to apply the same compositional techniques that you would in normal photography. Look for strong diagonal lines to create more dynamic images, while horizontal lines will give a calmer, more relaxed result. If the image has an obvious focal point you should also try to position this in the best area of the frame. As with any focal point, you can maximize its impact by positioning it on one of the intersections of the lines denoting the rule of thirds. However, placing the focal point away from the more conventional positions can produce eye-catching results. Experiment with different positioning for abstract shots, as the center or the edge of the frame can emphasize the abstract nature of the image.

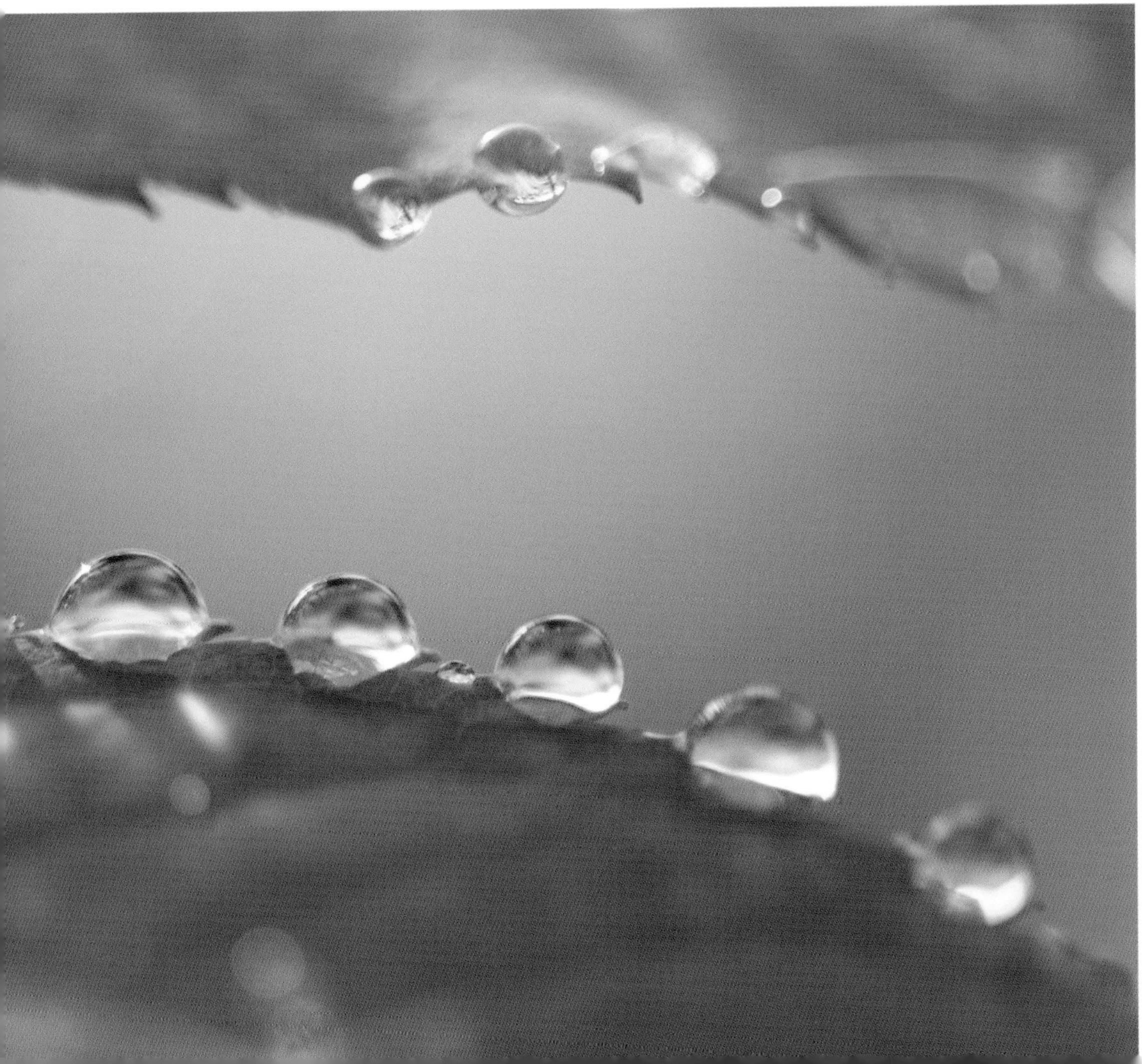

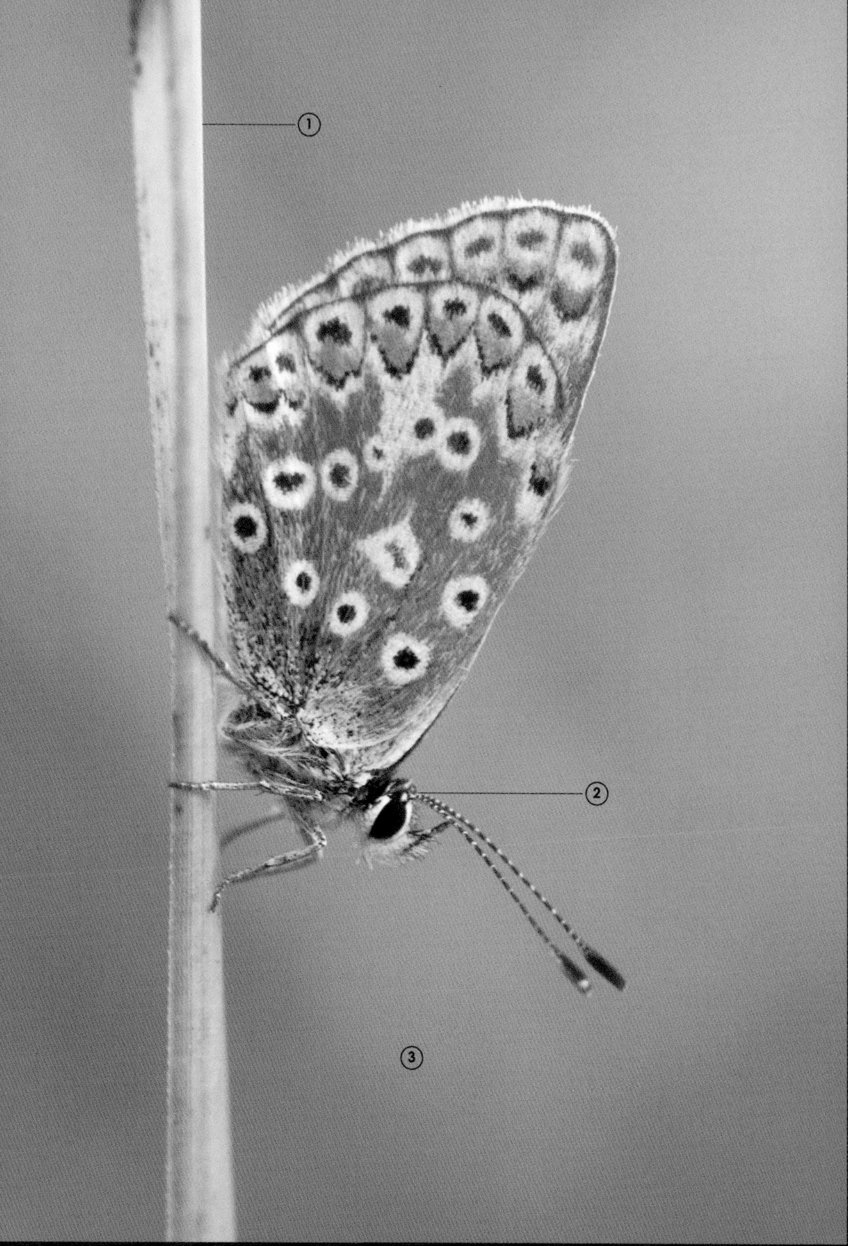

LEFT

1. Placing the grass stem on the left-hand third line produces a balanced composition, leaving the right two thirds of the picture free for the main subject.

2. The head of the butterfly is on the bottom third line giving it space below to "look" into.

3. Selecting an aperture of f/8 means that the background is blurred to concentrate all of the attention on the main subject.

RIGHT

1. The flower is positioned in the top third of the image, giving a feeling of space to the water below it.

2. Keeping the surroundings free of detail emphasizes the isolation of the main subject.

3. Including the reflection of the flower at the bottom of the frame helps to balance the picture and adds a sense of depth to the water.

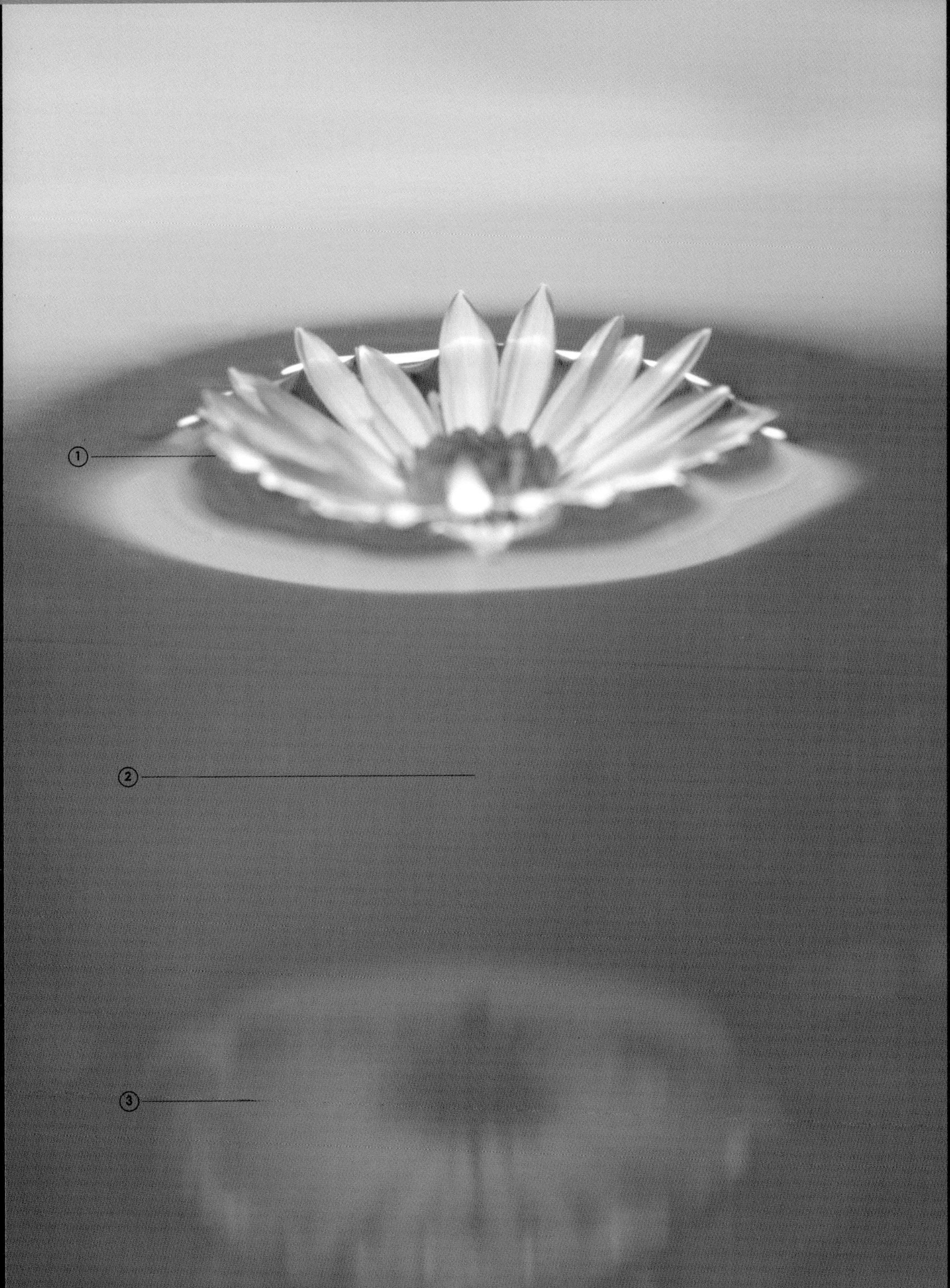
1
2
3

Section 7

People and Portraits

People are among the most fascinating and rewarding subjects that you can tackle with your DSLR, but they can also be one of the most challenging. They are the only subjects that will comment on the pictures you take, and this puts a unique pressure on you and the way you compose your images. Keeping the model happy with the results can go a long way to making them feel at ease, which is where the instant review facility on your DSLR can come into its own. During the shoot you can show your subject the results and even discuss possible changes.

We all have an idea of our own self-image, but how we see ourselves isn't always the same as the reality. As a photographer, you are often faced with a tough decision: do you portray somebody exactly as you see them, or do you try to produce an image that they will be most happy with? Although sometimes you can achieve both, the answer to this question will usually determine the type of composition that you use.

One of the first choices you have is the framing. From a tight shot of the face to a wider view of a person in their environment, there are almost unlimited approaches to shooting portraits. Your decision will often be determined by the sitter themselves, or by the type of portrait that you are shooting, but the focal length of the lens that you fit to your DSLR will also influence the composition. Before we go into detail about how you can use the various composition and framing options, here's a brief summary of three of the most common types of portraits and their basic composition.

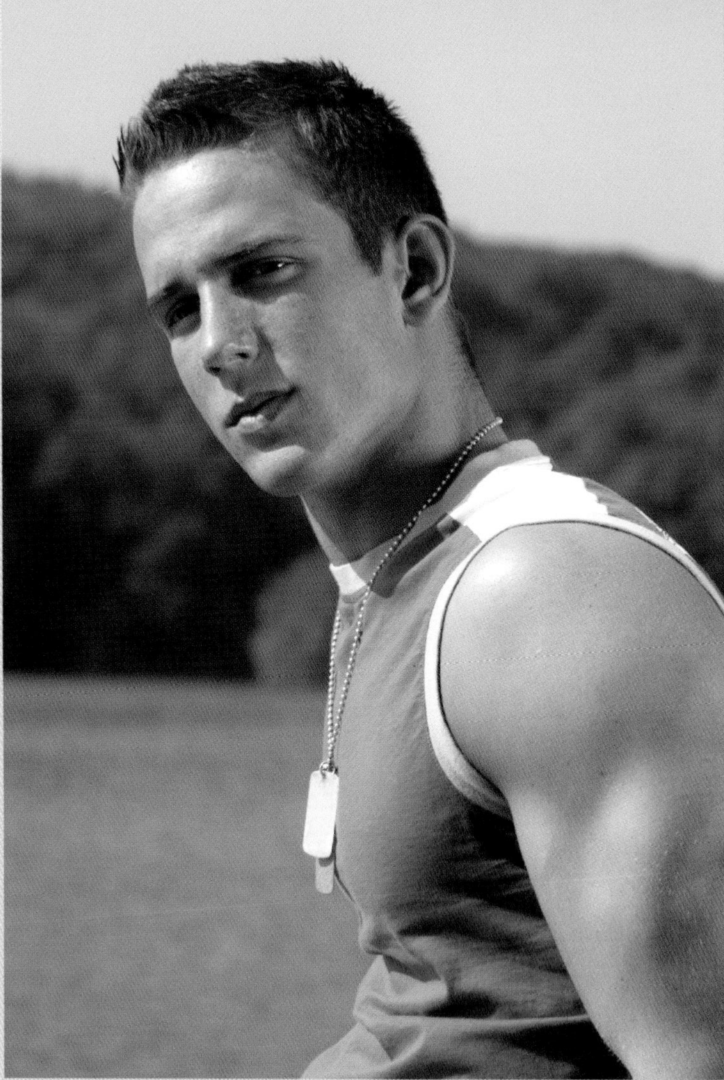

Head and shoulders
This classic portrait framing has been used by painters and photographers for centuries. Because you exclude much of the sitter's body, you focus all the attention on their face, and particularly on the eyes. Positioning the eyes on the top third line of the frame will emphasize their importance.

ABOVE
A head and shoulders framing allows you to concentrate most of the attention on the face, especially if you position the subject's eyes in the top third of the frame.

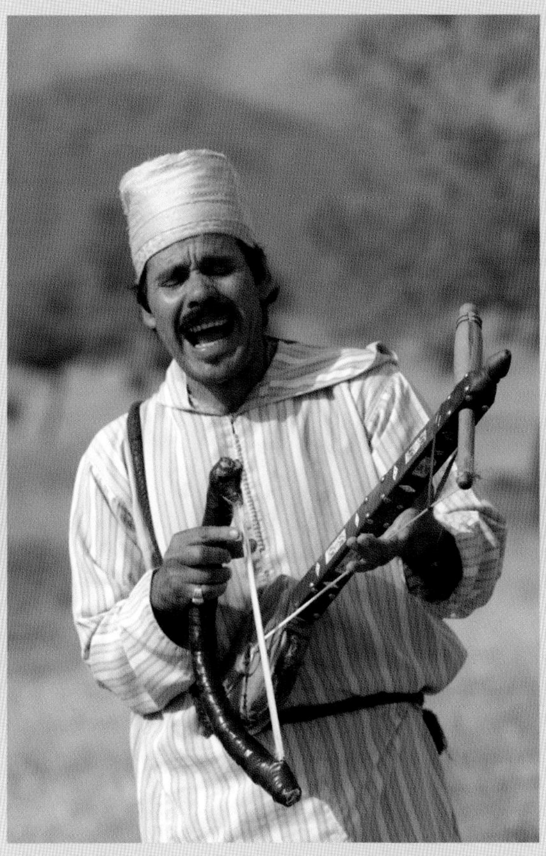

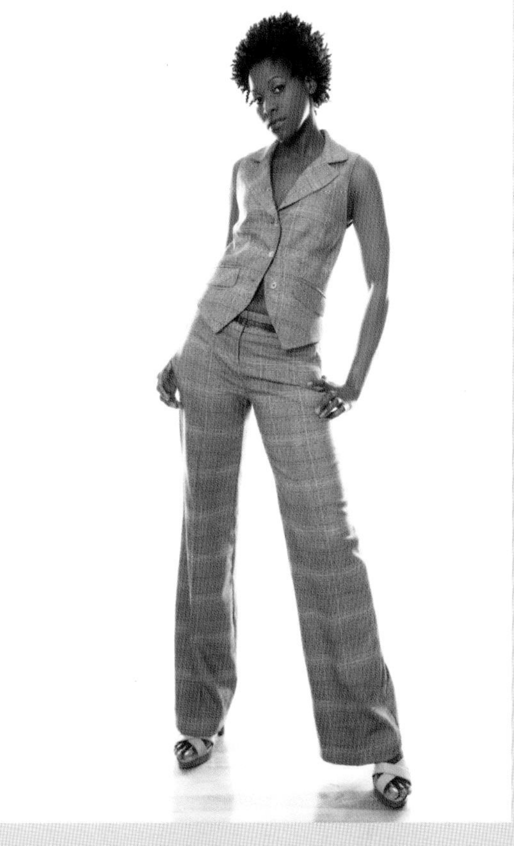

Half length

By including the top half of the body you put less emphasis on the face and eyes of the subject, but they still play an important part in this type of portrait. Placing the face in the top third of the image helps to keep the viewer's attention on this, rather than the rest of the image. With half-length portraits you also start to include the arms and hands, which can be one of the most difficult aspects of portraits to position successfully. Try to use natural hand positions, or give the sitter something to hold to make them more comfortable.

ABOVE LEFT
Shooting a half-length portrait allows you to include more of the surroundings. However, most of the viewer's attention is still concentrated on the face and expression.

ABOVE RIGHT
A full-length shot means that the face takes up less of the frame, so these portraits often have less impact than tighter compositions.

Full length

With full-length portraits you need to ensure that you have enough space to use a lens of at least 35mm on a small-sensor DSLR (50mm on a full-frame or 35mm model). This will ensure that you don't distort the proportions of the body by getting too close. Also, make sure that there is a little space above the head of the subject.

A short telephoto lens is a classic choice for shooting portraits, but why? The answer is down to perspective and composition. The angle of view of a short telephoto lens is perfect for filling the frame with a head and shoulders portrait while keeping a good working distance between you and the model. This working distance means that the perspective is the most flattering. Use a shorter lens and you'll have to get very close to the model, giving an unflattering, distorted perspective that makes the nose appear larger and the head smaller—not a look that many people will thank you for! A longer telephoto lens forces you to shoot from a greater distance, flattening the facial features: also not the most flattering portrayal.

On a full-frame DSLR you'll find that a lens between 90 to 105mm is perfect for portraits, while for smaller sized sensor models a lens between 60 and 70mm will give the same result. These focal lengths are commonly found at the long end of most standard zooms supplied with DSLRs—making them ideal for this type of shot—as well as many other lenses, including those designed for macrophotography.

Although these focal lengths are perfect for head and shoulders shots, this doesn't mean that they are the only lenses suitable for portraits. There are plenty of others that you can use to create different compositions.

BELOW
A short telephoto lens, such as the 100mm lens used here, means that you can fill the frame from a distance. The perspective this gives is perfect for flattering portraits.

OPPOSITE
Wide-angle lenses can be used for indoor portraits where space is limited. To avoid distorted perspective, keep your distance from the subject, shoot full-length portraits, and include plenty of the background.

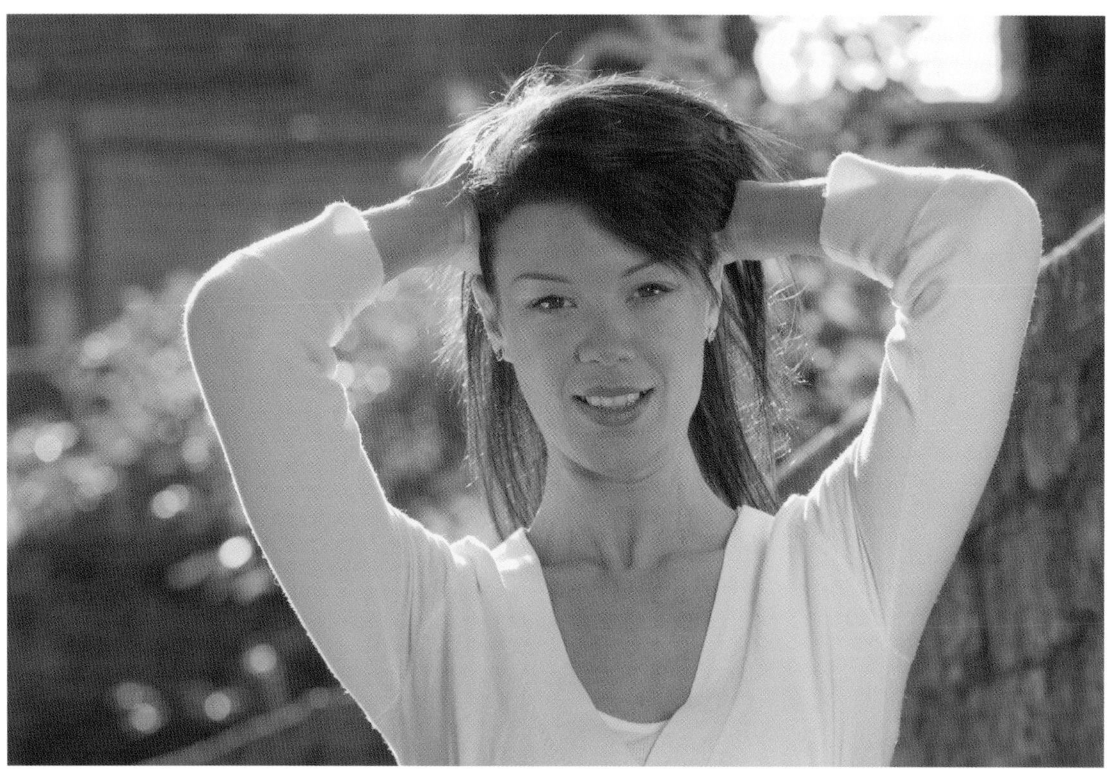

Wide-angle lenses
Using a lens shorter than 35mm on a small-sensor DSLR may not give the most flattering head and shoulders shots (although you can use the effects creatively as we will see later) they are a great choice for shooting environmental portraits or group shots. Something to watch out for when using wide-angle lenses is that, if you shoot from above or below the subject when you are close to them, you can distort the proportions of their body. Shoot from eye-level or above, and the head will appear much larger in relation to the body, while from below the head will appear smaller. The shorter the focal length and the closer you are to the subject, the more pronounced these distortions will become.

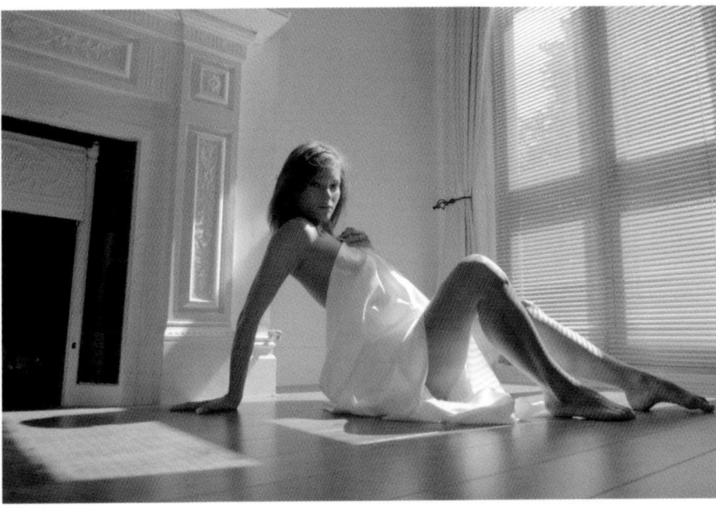

Long telephoto lenses
The narrow field of view of lenses of 100mm and longer on a DSLR means that you'll need plenty of room to shoot portraits. They are most useful when shooting outdoors, where a large working distance makes the gap between the subject and the background appear shorter.

Both wide-angle and telephoto lenses are widely used by fashion and advertising photographers to produce dynamic and eye-catching portraits. Professional models won't mind this more artistic approach, but those shooting commercial portraits will find that their clients won't be so forgiving. If you are shooting a commissioned portrait, think about what the sitter will expect before trying some of the more extreme lenses.

BELOW
The focal length of the lens that you use has a huge influence on the appearance of your portraits. This is due to the distance you need to be from the subject to fill the frame. With a wide-angle lens you need to be very close to the subject, which can distort features and limbs. Longer focal length lenses allow you to shoot from a greater distance, flattening the perspective for more flattering results.

20mm

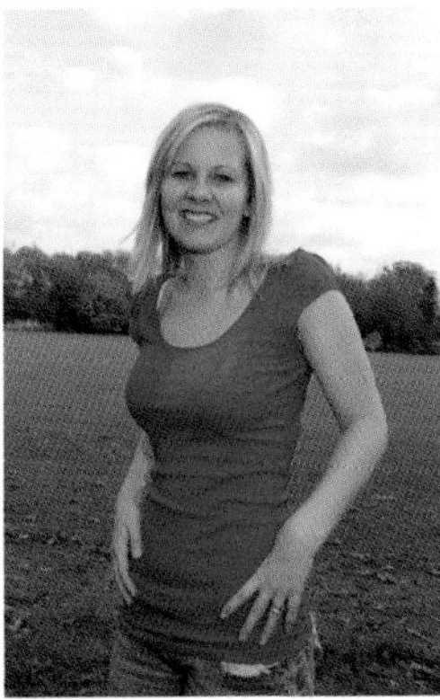

35mm

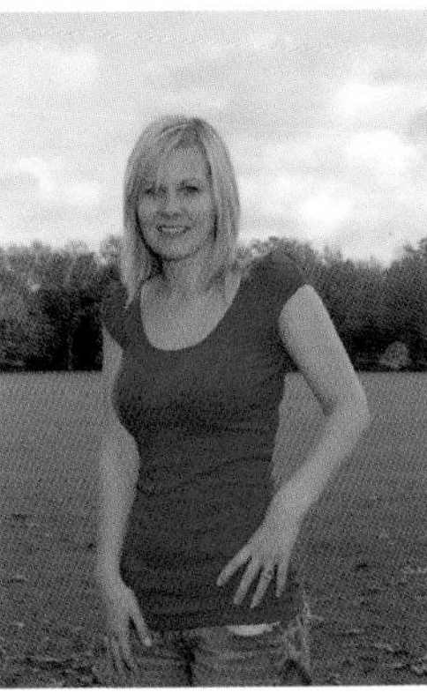

70mm

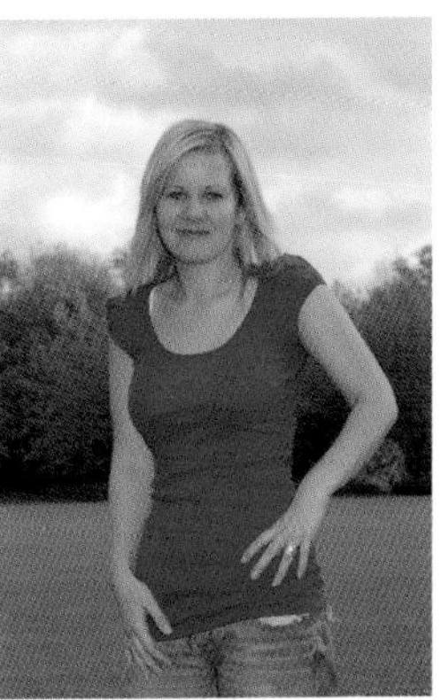

100mm

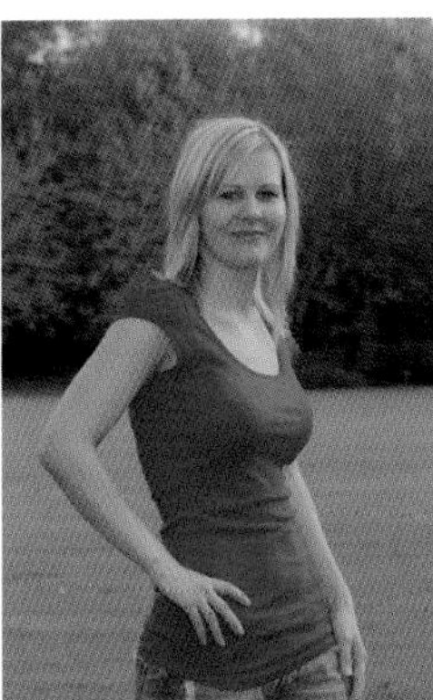

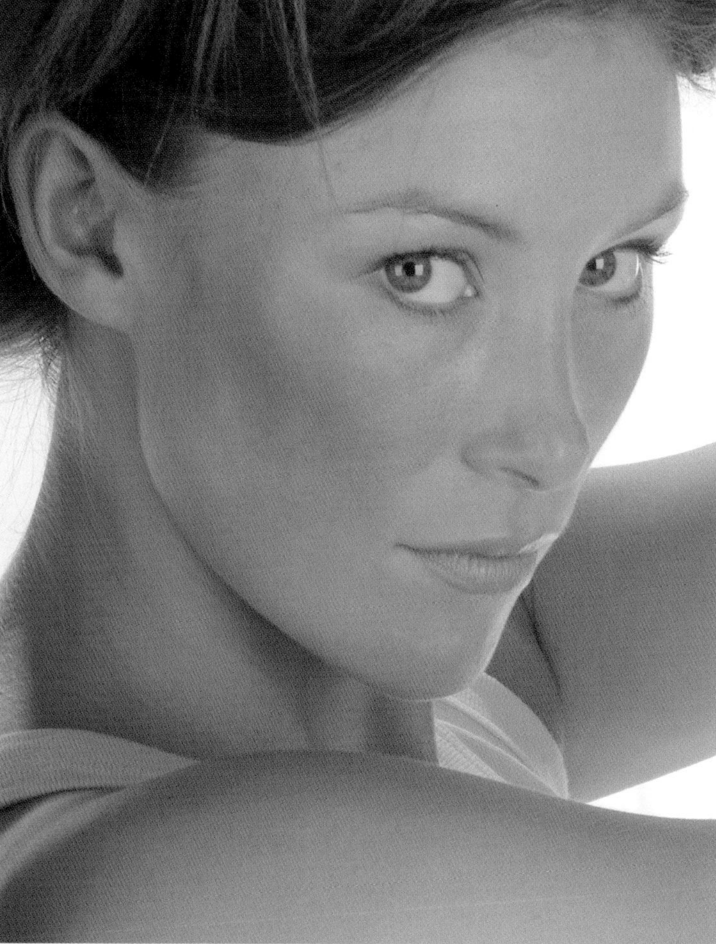

RIGHT
Simplicity is often the key to the most powerful portraits. By filling the frame you concentrate all the attention on the subject. This can be enhanced by getting direct eye contact with your subject.

With portraits it's not so much about finding the subject, but rather how you want to portray them. This will be determined by a number of factors, but in terms of the composition it's largely down to where you position the person in the frame and how much of the image they occupy.

Deciding on your framing and pose

Getting in close and filling the frame with just the face will make the most of the expression, beauty, or character of your subject. For the most flattering perspective, use a telephoto lens of around 80 to 100mm on a small-sensor DSLR, or 120 to 150mm on a full-frame camera. This means that you can shoot from a distance so that there is no distortion of the subject's features. Like most portraits, when shooting this type of image the most important feature is the eyes. Position these on the third line at the top of the frame for maximum impact.

When shooting wider portraits, you need to think about the shape and position of the body. Unless you want a stiff, uncomfortable appearance, avoid having the subject standing straight ahead of you. You'll get a more natural pose if they stand with their body at a slight angle, then turn their face to look into the camera. You also need to position their hands and legs so that they look comfortable. For portraits that include the environment, use the rule of thirds to position your subject. Unlike many other images, portraits can work well with the person positioned in the middle of the frame. The static composition that this would normally produce can be overcome because of the way we tend to look at people. The head, and particularly the eyes, are the most important part of most portraits. So even if the model's body is positioned in the middle of the frame, this isn't where our attention is drawn. Placing the face in the top third of the frame produces a more dynamic and interesting composition. Angling the body and positioning the hands away from the middle of the frame helps to offset the central positioning of the subject.

Clothing

When you are shooting full length or even wider, you need to consider the color of the clothes worn by the subject. A bright color will help the subject stand out in the frame, but can take attention away from their face, while more recessive colors such as green and blue can make the figure blend into the background.

OPPOSITE TOP
Where you place the subject in the frame has a huge effect on the look of your portraits. Here, moving the model from the center to the left of the shot has created a more dynamic shot.

RIGHT
You don't always have to position the subject in the middle of the image. Try to place them to one side on the third line and ask them to look into the frame.

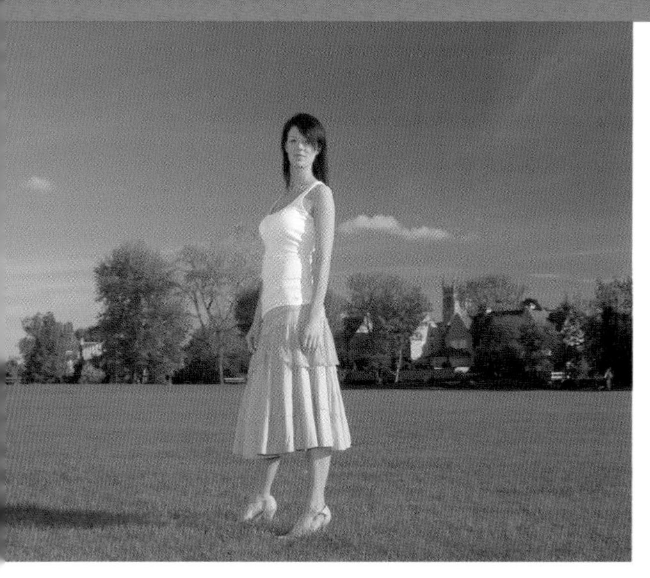

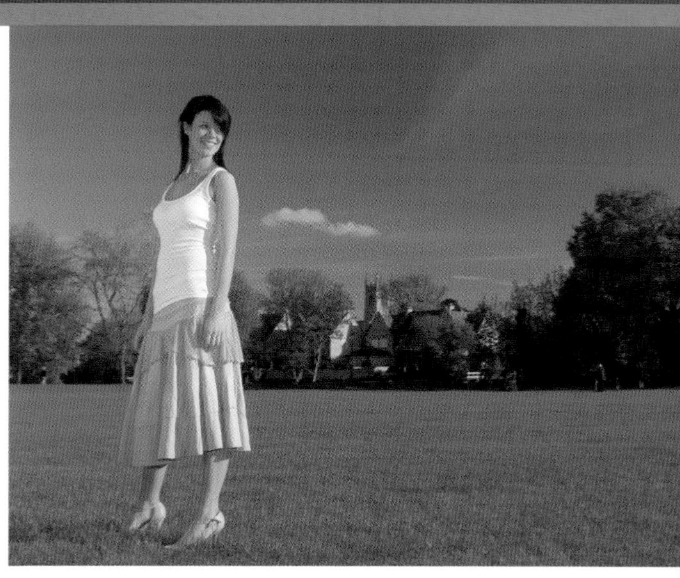

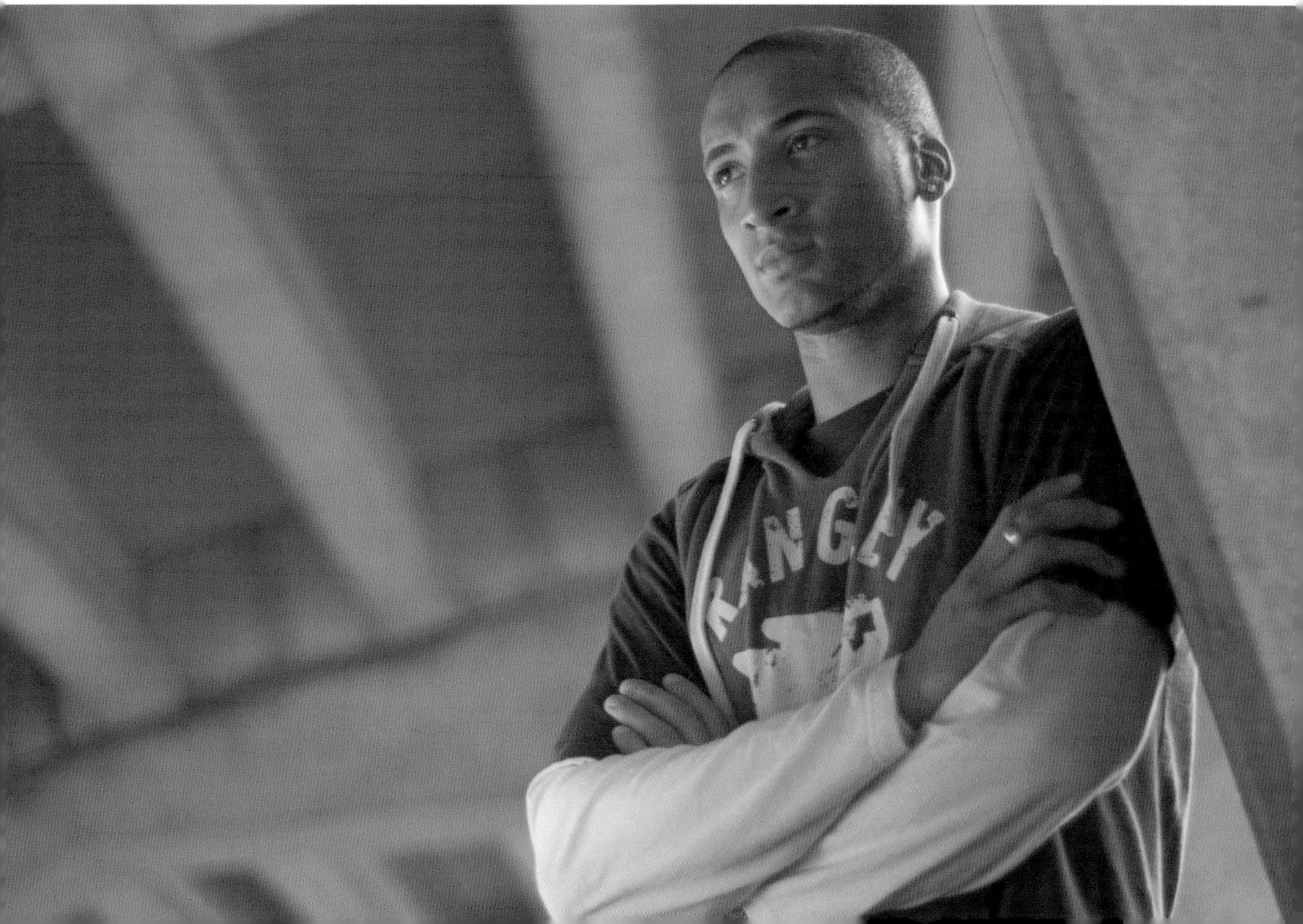

Although each person has many stories to tell, your composition, framing, and approach will determine what your portraits tell the viewer. How you frame the image—along with props, clothes, and surroundings—will help to give a sense of the person in the picture almost as much as the subject themselves. Here are the main composition techniques that you can use to tell the viewer more about the subject.

Position and size in the image
Where you place the person in the frame and how much of the image they take up determines how much attention we pay to each part of the image. If the person is small in the frame they will appear to be secondary to the background, so the viewer will look at this to learn more about the subject. Placing the subject toward the edge of the frame will also make them appear unimportant. This type of composition is great for giving a sense of isolation and insignificance to the person. Alternatively, you can make them more dominant in the frame by positioning them on one of the intersections of the lines used to divide the image into thirds. This produces a more balanced composition and draws attention to the person. When using this framing, remember that the DLSR's viewfinder shows you the image at the maximum aperture, so with the minimum depth of field. The preview facility available on many DSLRs allows you to check how much of the background will be in focus at the aperture at which you take the shot.

The environment and props
We may not always like to admit it, but we tend to judge people by their clothes, possessions, and surroundings. While this may not always tell us the whole story, it still plays an important part in how we view a person. So you need to think about what the items and surroundings that you include in your portraits say about the subject. Including expensive jewelry, cars, or clothes will give the viewer a very different message to shooting your portrait in a thrift store, for example. Where you place these objects, and how prominent they are in the frame, also affects the viewer's reaction to the portrait.

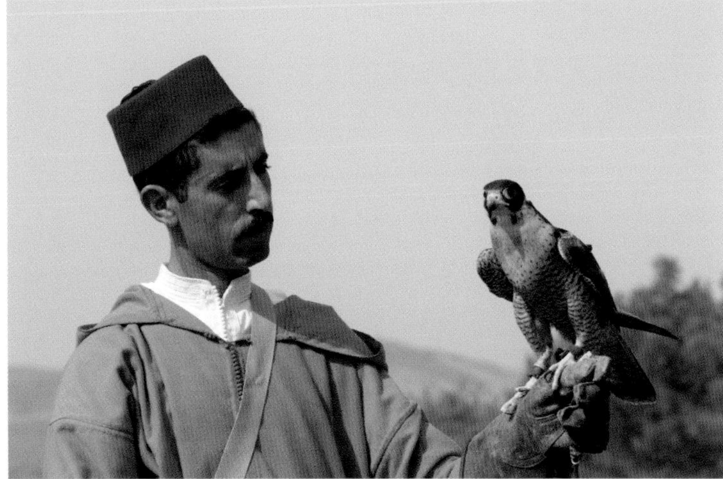

LEFT
It's much easier to tell a story about your subject if you frame your shots to include objects and props.

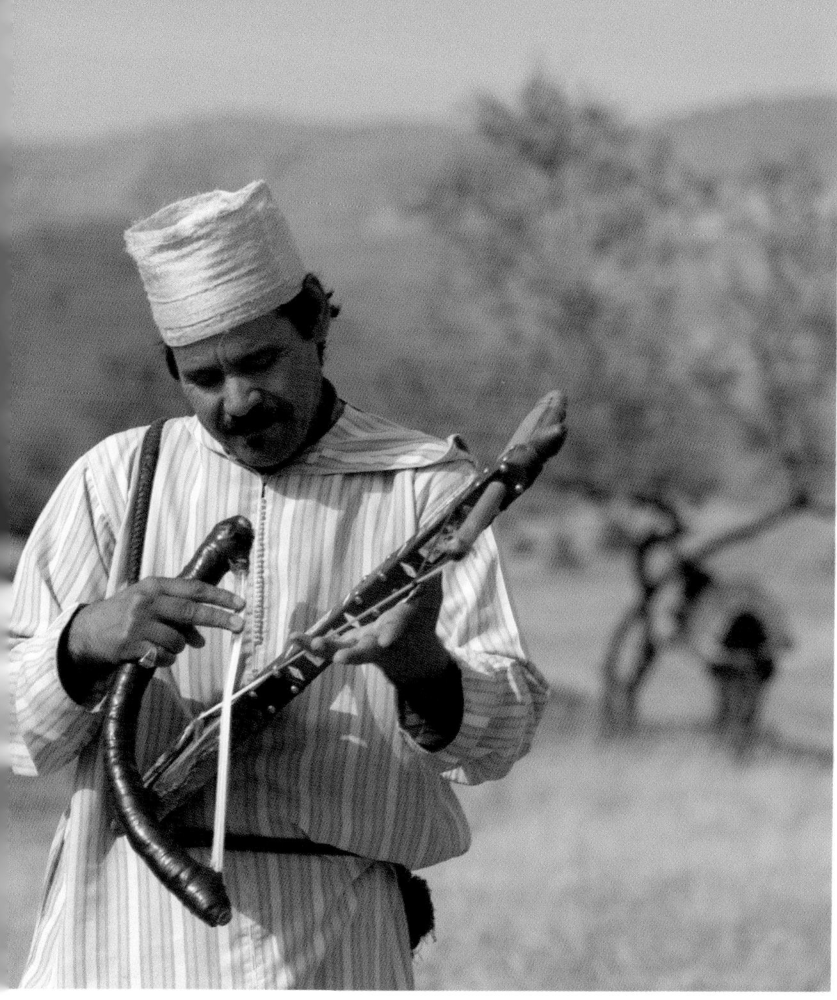

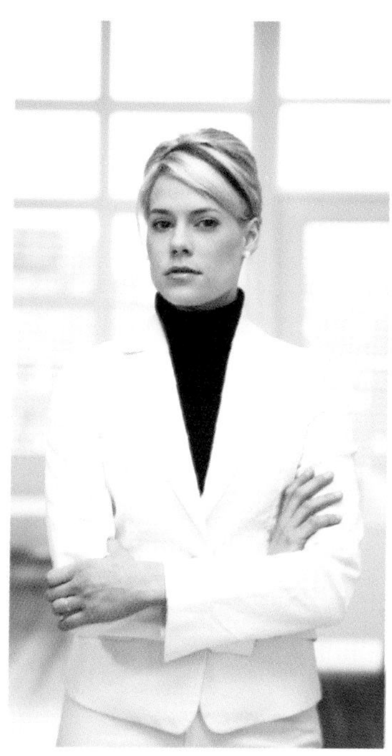

Using contrasts

While most of the time you will want your props and surroundings to complement the portrait, you can use something that seems at odds with the main subject to create a sense of tension. Contrasts always grab our attention, whether it's colors or objects that don't appear to go together. They make us ask more questions about the image than a harmonious setting. This technique is often used by advertising and editorial photographers by placing subjects in an environment that you wouldn't normally associate them with. For example, if you shoot a glamorous model in expensive clothes in a run-down setting it creates a sense of unease that can say something about your attitude toward the subject. Put the same person in an expensive apartment, and you won't get the same sense of unease and wonder.

ABOVE LEFT
Including the environment of your subject can tell the viewer much more about them.

ABOVE
The background and clothes of your subject tell the viewer more about the idea behind the image than a close-up portrait, so try to use both when composing your portraits.

There are several techniques you can use to liven up your portraits, especially if your subject is happy to work in a more "artistic" style. With no film and processing costs to worry about, a DSLR is perfect for trying out new viewpionts and techniques. Many of these techniques are now commonly used in advertising, fashion, and even lifestyle portraits, so people are becoming more comfortable with portraits that step away from the standard studio shot with the subject facing straight at the camera. Discuss your ideas with the model, show them the results during the shoot on the DSLR's LCD screen, and don't be afraid to experiment with your portraits.

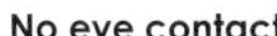

No eye contact
Most portraits rely on eye contact to get the viewer to connect with the subject, but you can produce enigmatic results if the subject is looking away from the camera. Without this focal point to give a connection with the subject, we tend to pay more attention to the composition of other aspects of the image.

Use unusual viewpoints
Although shooting from the eye level of the model usually gives the most flattering portrait, shooting from above or below will give more dramatic results. Looking up at the subject makes them appear more dominant in the image, whereas looking down on the model makes them seem subservient to the viewer. These techniques can be used subtly by positioning yourself just above or below the subject. For more dramatic results, try using extremely high or low viewpoints.

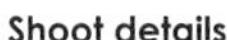

Shoot details
Rather than shoot the whole face, you can crop in tight and shoot details, such as the eyes. This approach can produce abstract images, rather than conventional portraits, and you need to think carefully about the lighting to make the most of these shots.

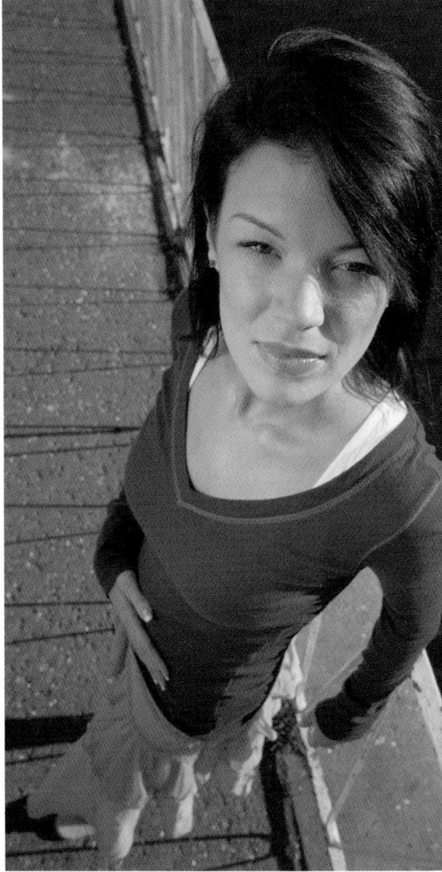

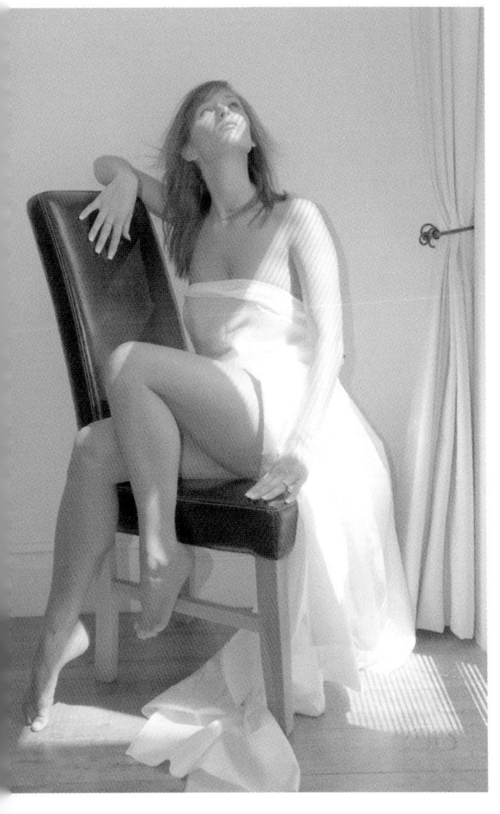

LEFT
Posing your model so they are looking away from the camera forces the viewer to look around the frame more than when there is direct eye contact.

ABOVE
A high viewpoint can create dramatic portraits, especially when combined with using a wide-angle lens.

BELOW RIGHT
Even when shooting head and shoulders portraits, you don't need to fill the frame for successful results. Try shooting in a horizontal format and position the subject toward the edge of the frame.

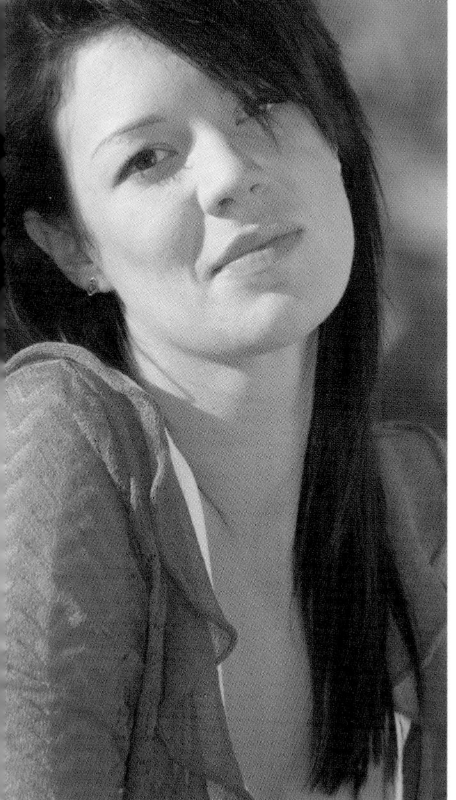

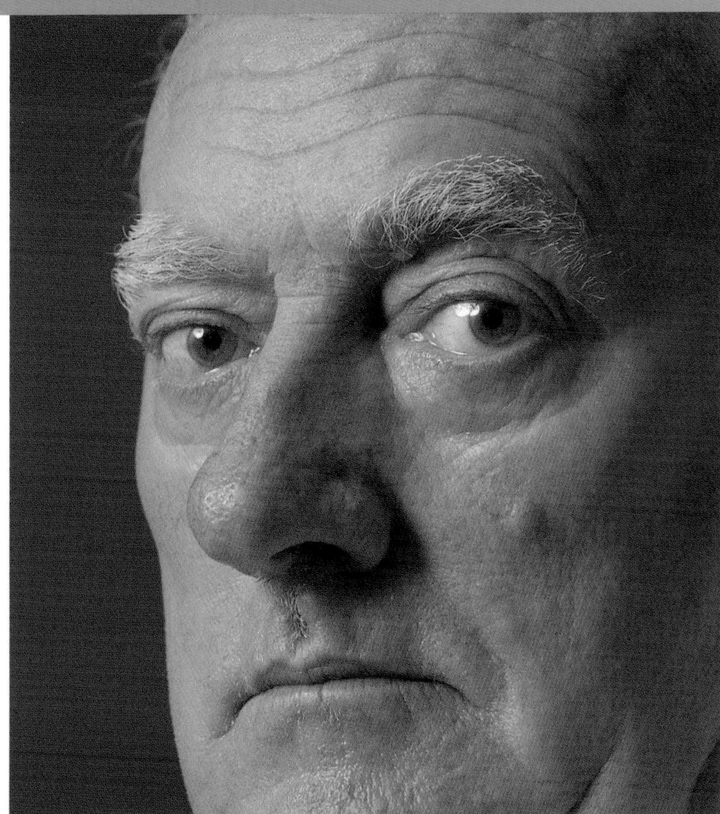

ABOVE LEFT AND RIGHT
For a more contemporary feel to your portraits, use unconventional crops, such as not including the whole head or getting in very close to the model's face.

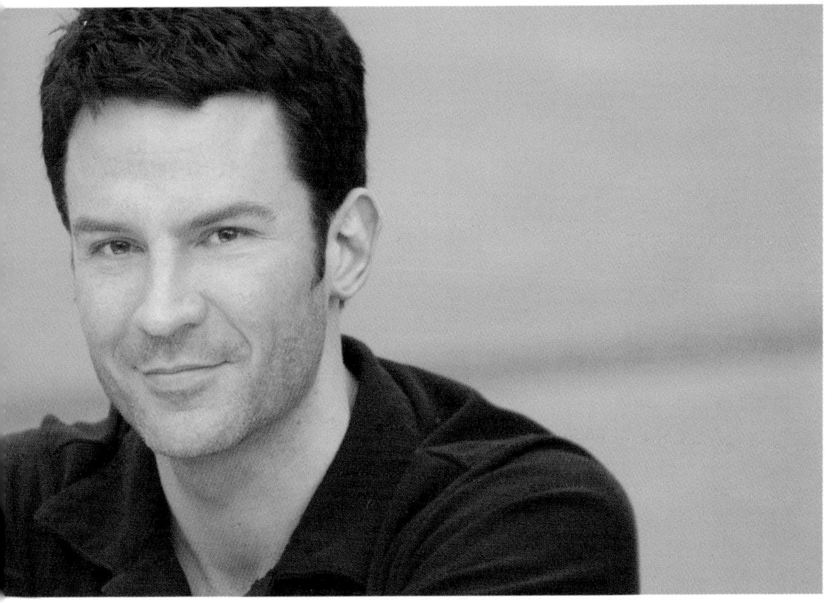

Unconventional framing and crops
Placing the model away from the more conventional areas of the frame produces edgy portraits. Positioning the model at the edge of the frame, or even cropping part of them out of the frame, makes the viewer ask more questions about the person, and about the image itself.

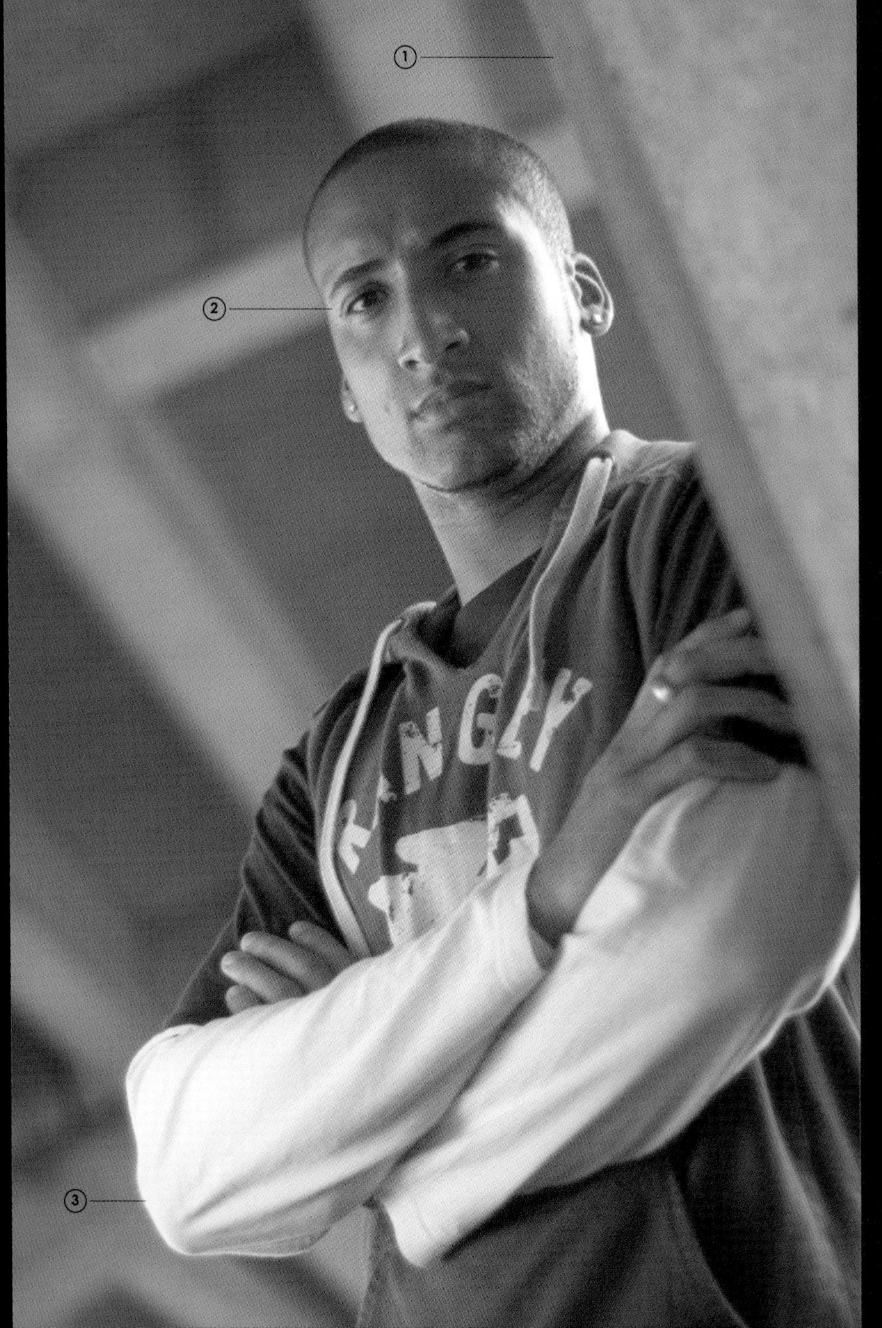

LEFT

1. Shooting at an angle rather than straight gives the image a more dynamic look.

2. Direct eye contact allows the viewer to connect with the subject.

3. The subject's folded arms add foreground interest and also give the image a more edgy feel.

OPPOSITE

1. Cropping in tight at the top of the frame concentrates all the attention on the subject's face.

2. Catchlights in the eyes and direct eye contact create a focal point for the image.

3. Including space at the bottom of the frame gives the image a more relaxed feel than simply cropping in on the face alone.

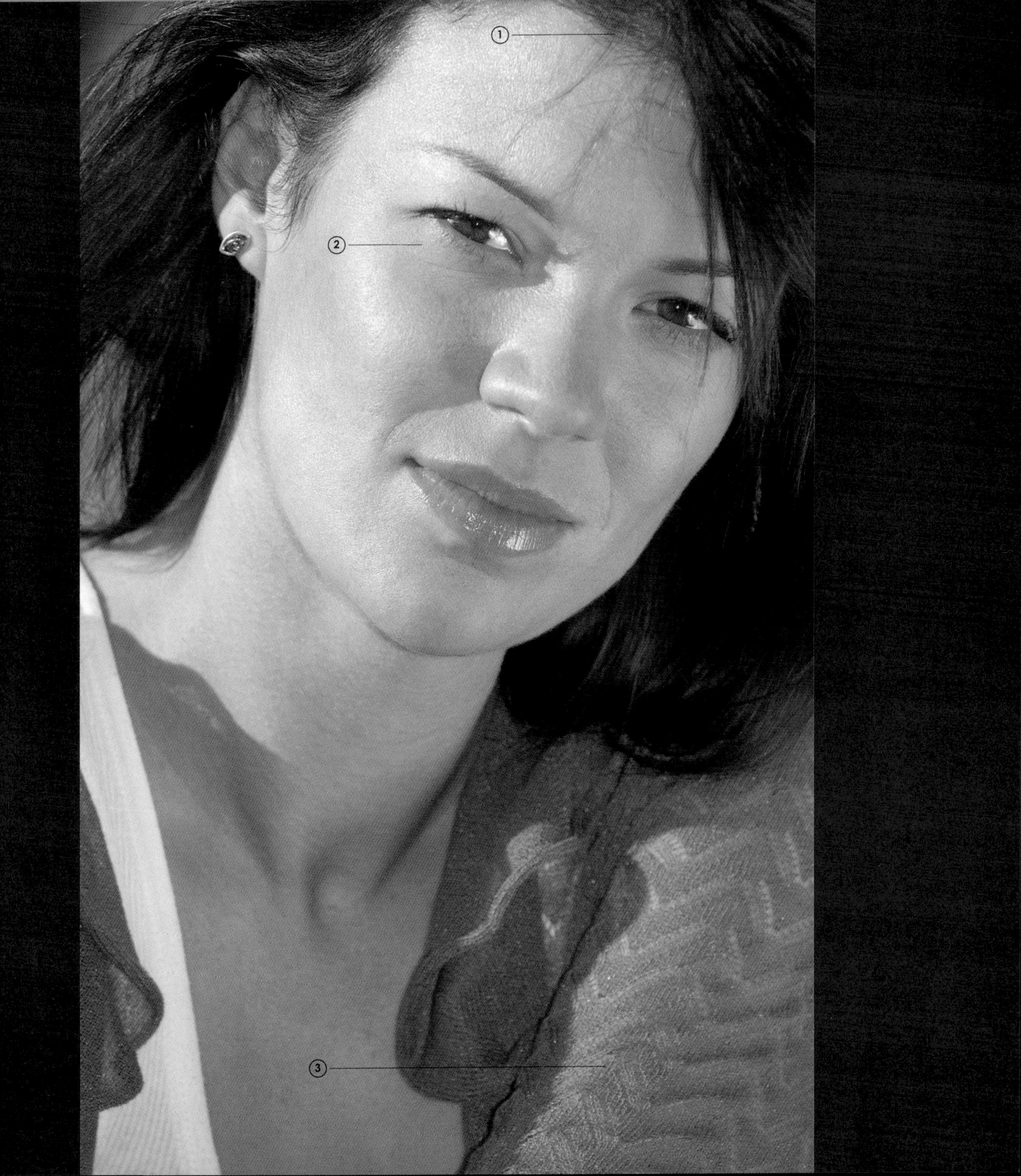
1
2
3

RIGHT
1. The model is looking out of the frame, giving the image a sense of mystery and asking the viewer to add their own interpretation to the story behind the image.

2. The line created by the raised arm leads your eye toward the model's face.

3. Including the model's legs adds foreground interest and also the line that they create leads the eye toward the face.

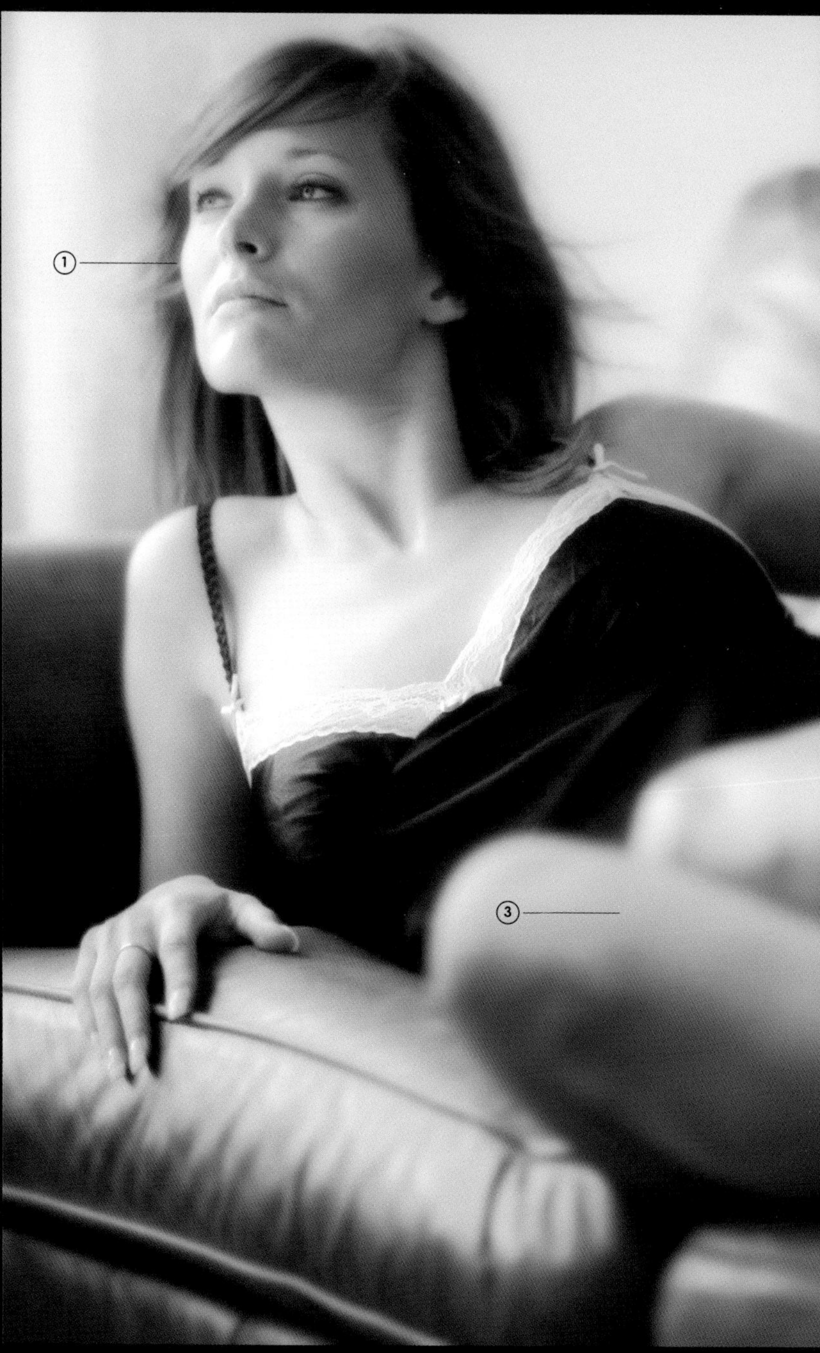

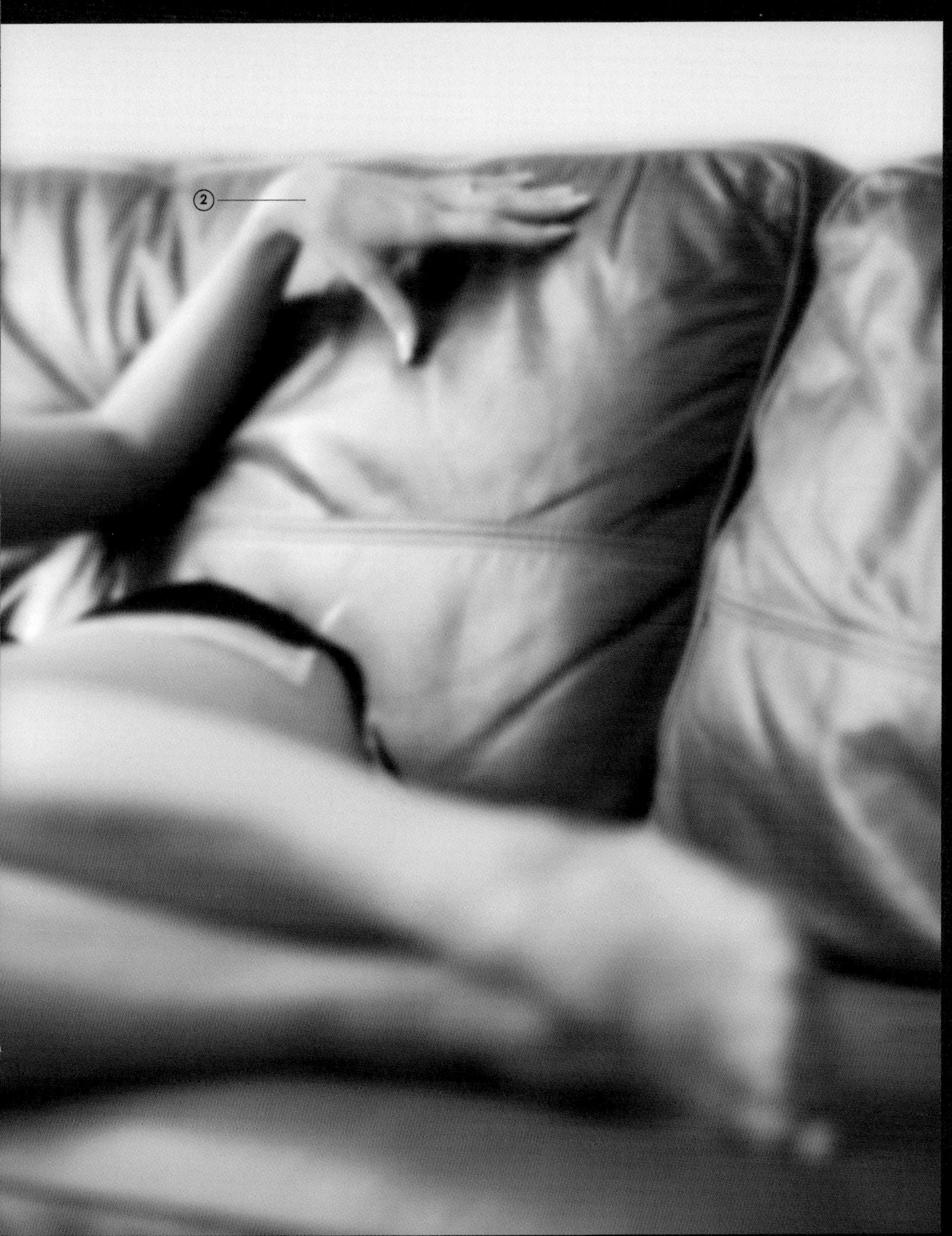
2

Section 8

Special Occasions

BELOW AND RIGHT
When capturing the wider landscape, look for interesting details and characters. While shooting this scene, I noticed a group of mules and riders in the bottom left corner, which made a great subject in itself.

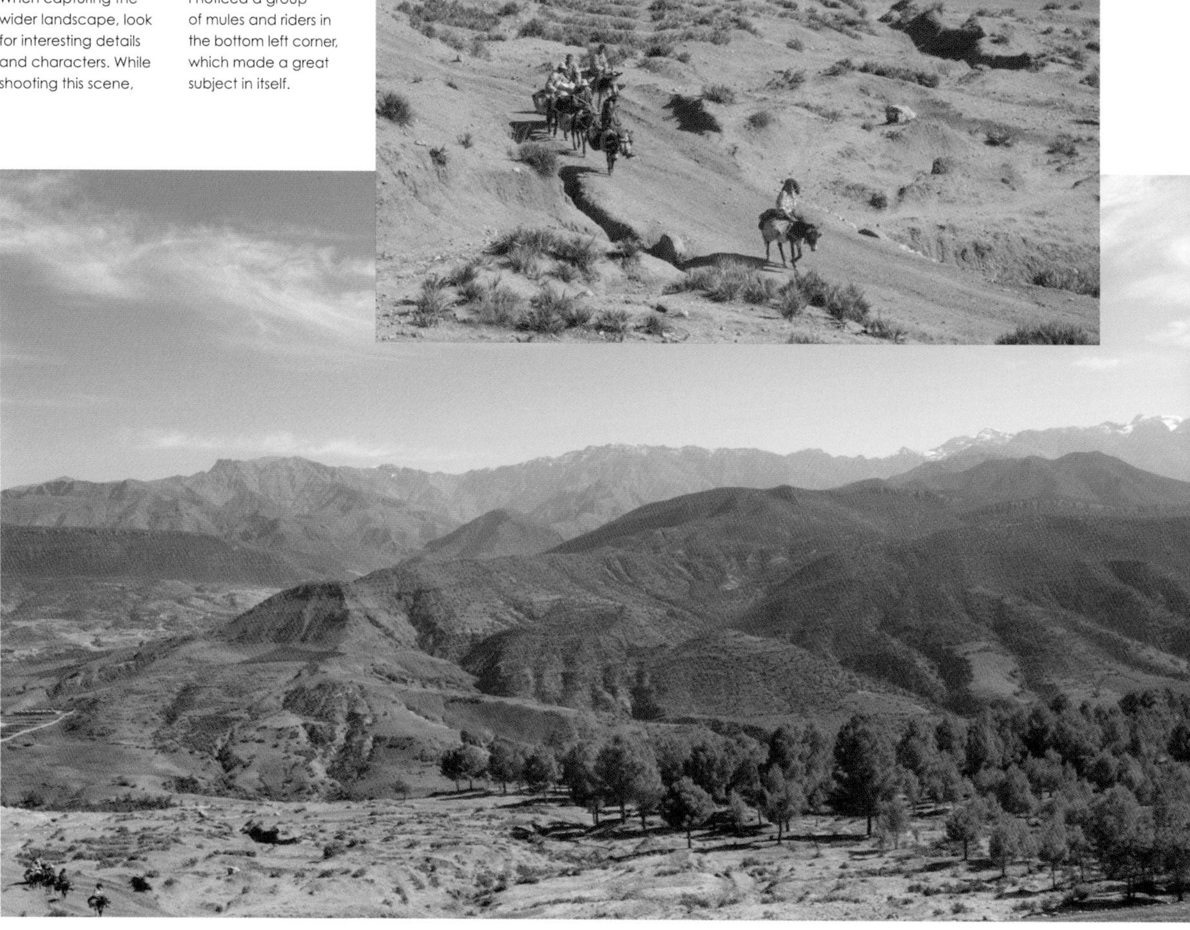

From vacations and day trips to weddings and parties, many of the photographs that we take are about capturing special days in our lives. Careful composition means you will produce images that capture more of the occasion, producing both better photographs and more memories in years to come.

In this section, we will concentrate on two of the most popular subjects: vacations and weddings. These pose their own compositional challenges, but the techniques employed can easily be transferred to many other occasions and events.

The main challenge is time: because these occasions will happen only once, you need to get your shots right on the first attempt, often with little time for composition. Because of this pressure, and the fact that you'll usually be shooting in unfamiliar locations, you need to be able to quickly assess the picture-taking opportunities. Practicing the composition rules and techniques well before the event will help, as they will soon become second nature to you. This will free you up to concentrate on capturing the atmosphere of the event, rather than having to think too much about your composition. While it's no excuse for poor composition, the high resolution and quality of DSLR images make it possible to shoot wider than normal, and make final adjustments by cropping later on.

Vacations
From landscapes and architecture to portraits and candids, the range of subjects you'll face on any vacation will be vast. The key to meeting these challenges is to try to spot the most important elements in the scene and make sure that they are positioned for maximum impact in the frame.

Being in an unfamiliar environment means that you will need to assess and compose the scene quickly. If you do have more time, it's useful to get a flavor of the location before even taking your camera out of its bag. Taking the time to absorb the atmosphere and the stories around you will help you to capture them more successfully in your pictures.

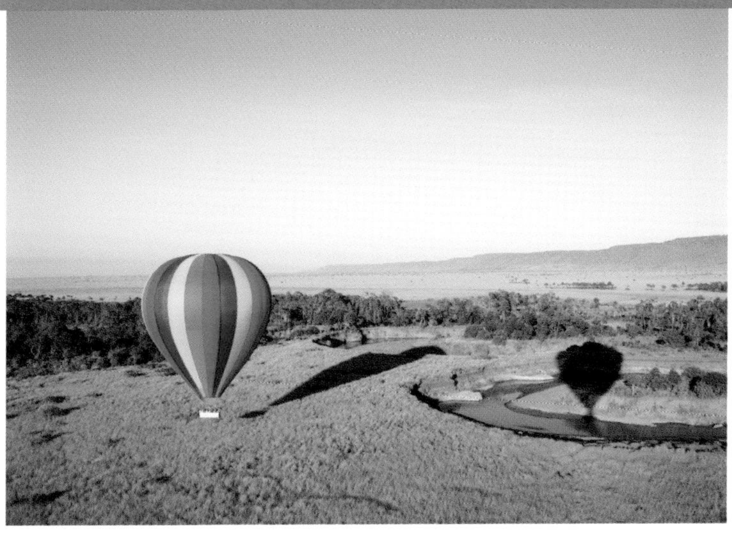

ABOVE
When you have more time to plan the composition, you can use techniques such as the rule of thirds to position the subject.

LEFT
Candid images of weddings require you to compose quickly and almost without thinking.

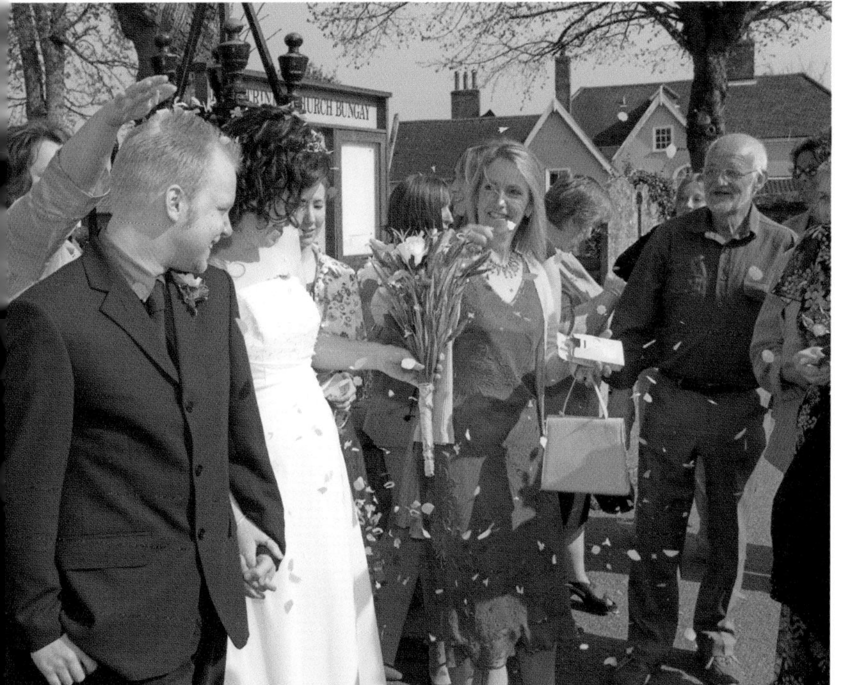

Weddings
Your approach to photographing weddings will depend on the type of shot that you are trying to achieve. For professional photographers, the greatest challenge is organizing the guests and ensuring that you get the shots that the bride and groom will be happy with. This is the key to getting formal and staged shots right, as no matter how well you compose your shots in the camera, if you can't communicate these ideas successfully to your subjects, you'll never get the shots you (and the subjects) want.

For candid shots you can have a more relaxed approach, but it's often difficult to achieve successful compositions. Because you can't organize your subjects, you need to think and shoot quickly. To compensate, you need to be able to compose your shots quickly through the viewfinder.

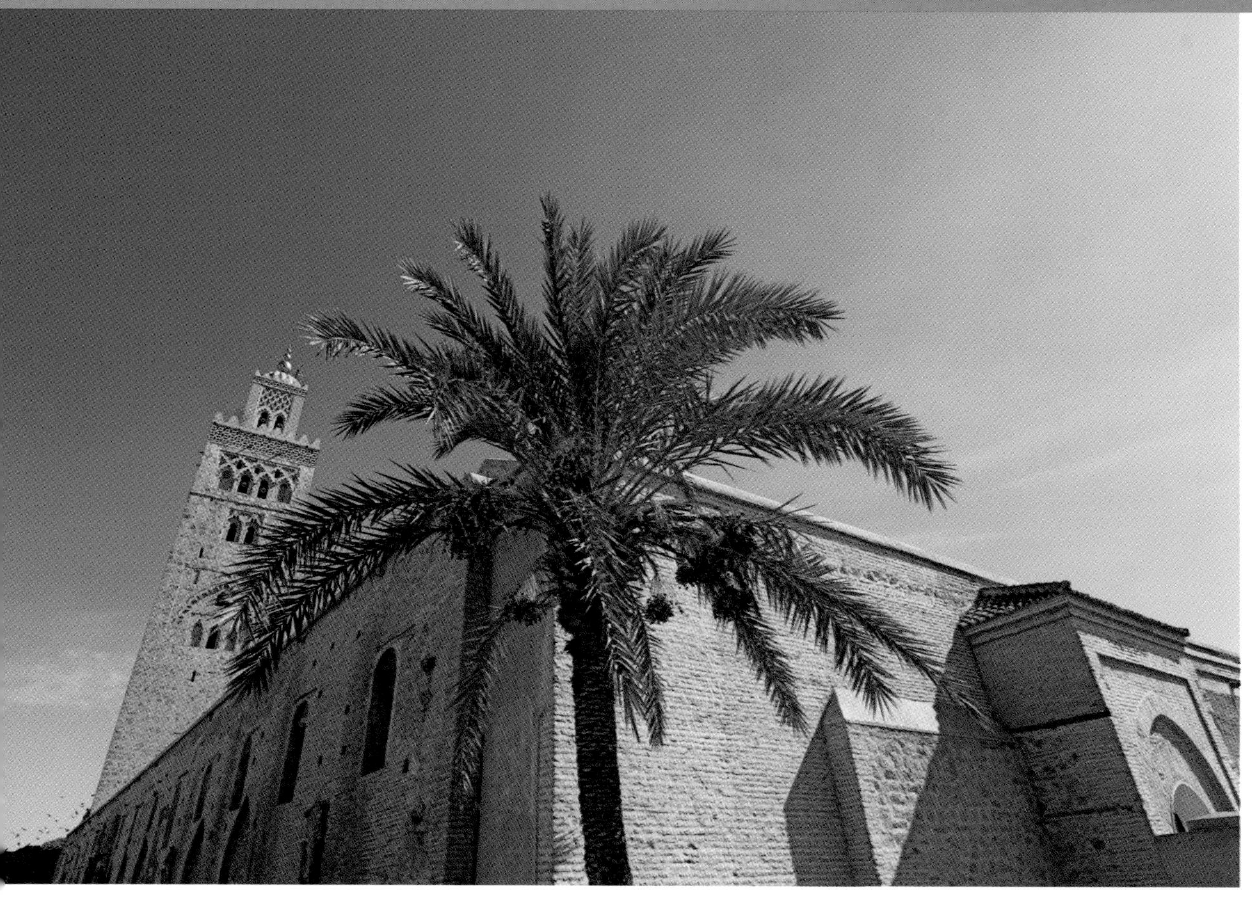

Choosing which lenses to use at special events can be difficult as you won't want to waste time changing lenses in case you miss the best shots. This is why you will often see professionals carrying two cameras. As well as offering the insurance of having a spare camera in case one breaks, they will usually have different lenses attached to each so that they can quickly swap from a wide to a long lens. This is a great option if you have the luxury of owning two cameras and don't mind carrying them both, but if you are at the event as a guest, or are on vacation, you won't want to be weighed down by lots of kit. Here are some suggestions for the best lens options.

Vacations

Be sensible about the number of lenses that you pack, taking account of the type of location that you'll be visiting. If you are going to shoot mainly landscapes, it's worth taking a wide-angle lens as well as your standard zoom. Even so, it's amazing how versatile the humble standard zoom can be. An 18 to 70mm lens on a small-sensor DSLR, or 28 to 105mm on a full-frame or 35mm camera, will cover most landscape and architecture shots, and can even be used for close-ups. A more versatile option is one of the many super-zoom lenses available that have an even greater zoom range. These usually start at around the same focal length as your standard zoom, but give a 200 to 300mm telephoto at the maximum zoom.

ABOVE
An ultra-wide lens will allow you to get in close to your subject for a dramatic perspective.

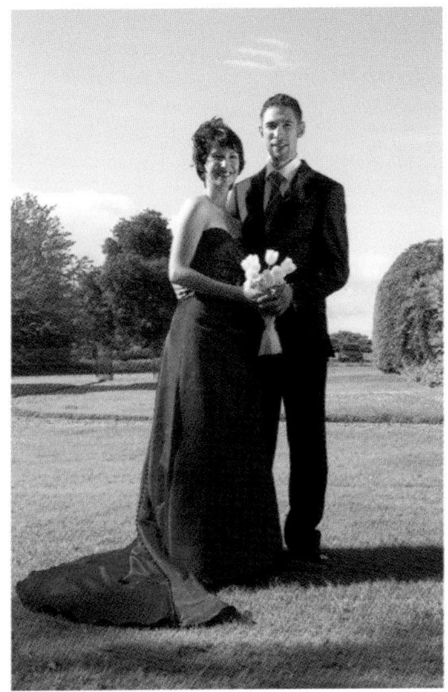

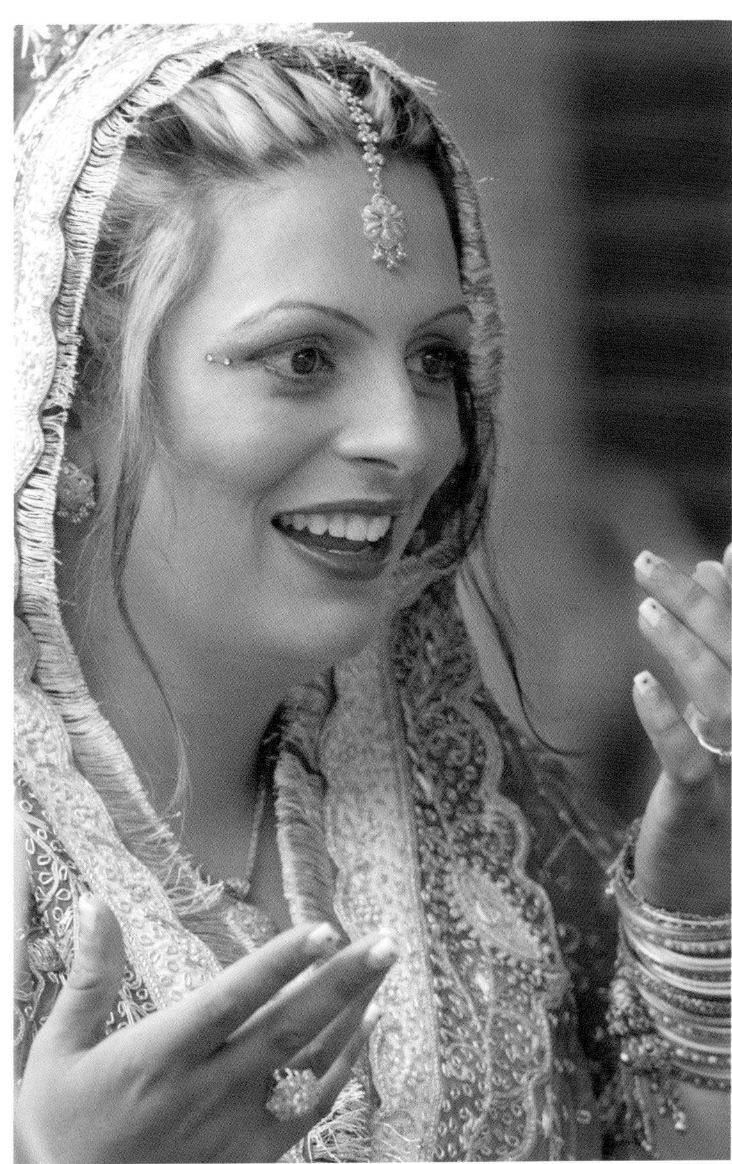

Weddings and other events
Before you pack your gear, you really need to decide what sort of shots you want. For general shots and groups of people, a standard zoom will be sufficient. But there are other options that will be useful for different kinds of images. Candid and reportage-style pictures are increasingly popular, so it's worth taking a short telephoto lens to capture these images without having to get too close to the subject. This is particularly true if you are not the "official" photographer for the event. The professional won't thank you—and nor will the bride and groom—if you get in their way. A telephoto lens of around 100 to 200mm is also ideal for taking individual portraits.

When you can get close to the subject, or if you simply want to shoot wider scenes, you can use a lens of around 18 to 24mm on a small-sensor DSLR for most shots. Any wider, and you'll run the risk of getting too much distortion in your shots.

TOP LEFT
For formal shots, you'll find a standard zoom is ideal for most situations. Try to shoot at a distance and use a focal length of around 35 to 50mm to give the most flattering perspective.

ABOVE
A telephoto lens is great for capturing candid moments during an event or special occasion.

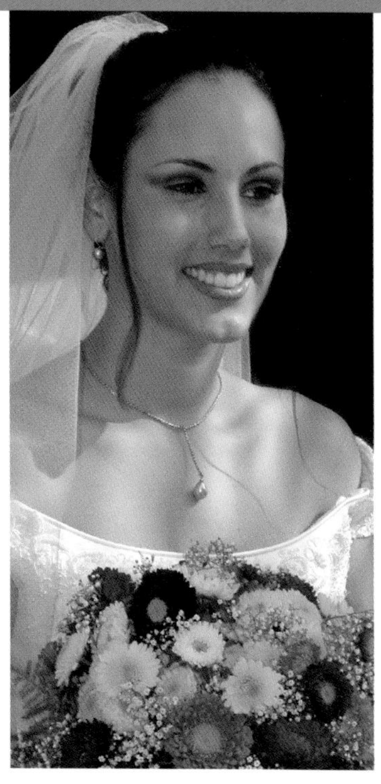

At many special events there is so much happening at once that your composition is as much about deciding what to leave out of the frame as what to include. This decision will depend on the event and the type of image that you are trying to create, but there are some techniques that will help you to produce the best results.

LEFT
Getting in close and capturing expressions and emotions is one of the best ways to capture the essence of the day.

BELOW
It's often the local people who make a vacation special. Here, I focused on the eyes of the closest person, placing them on the intersection of the two third lines for maximum impact.

Capturing expressions and characters
By cropping in close on individuals, you will capture expressions and emotions that can be lost in wider shots. Speed is essential for this, so switching your DSLR to continuous shooting mode will help ensure that you get the shot that you want. You also need to quickly identify the best subjects and the right moment to fire the shutter. At events such as weddings, where one or two people are the main focal point of the celebration, this is relatively easy. By concentrating your attention on the bride, groom, and their immediate family you are almost sure to get some displays of emotion. At other events it can take longer to recognize the main characters, so spend the first few moments trying to get a feel for the location or group before you start shooting.

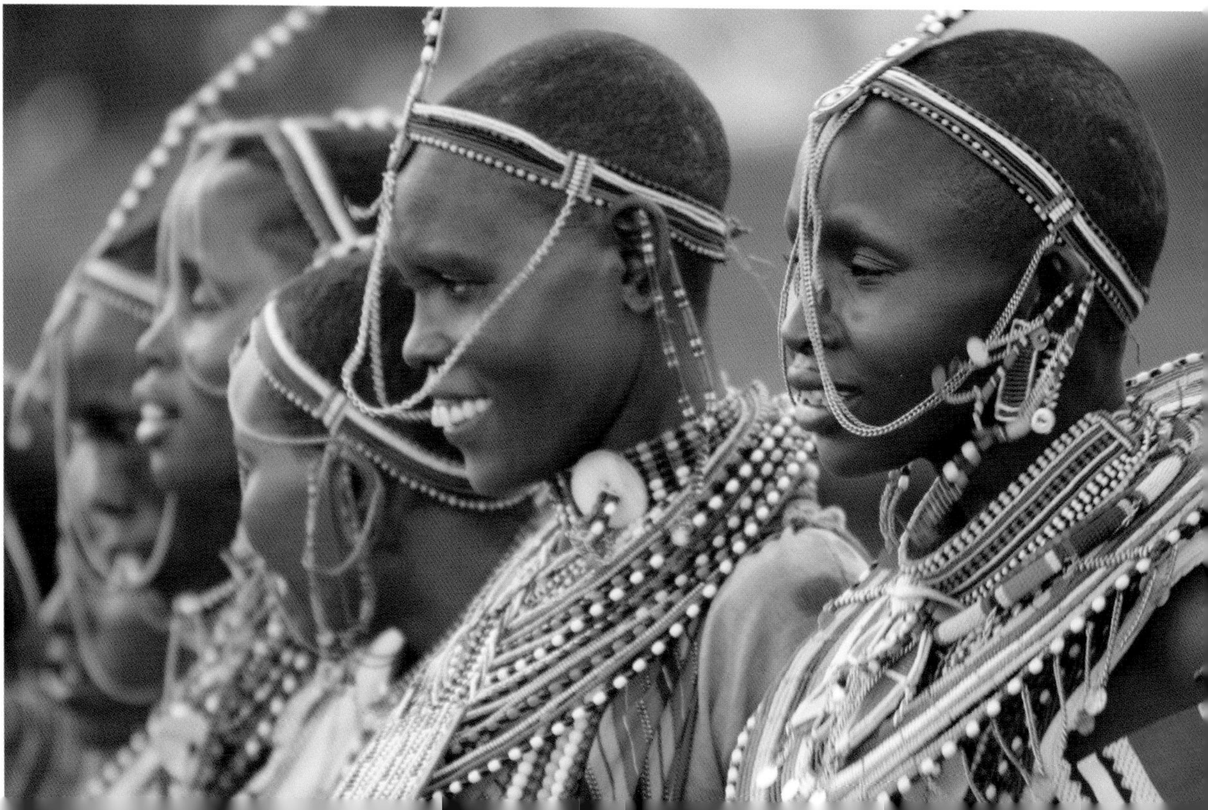

Once you've identified your subjects, there are two ways of approaching and composing this type of shot. The first is to shoot from a distance with a telephoto lens. This approach will help you to achieve more natural-looking results as your subjects may not even realize that you are taking pictures. However, some people may not appreciate being photographed unawares, so it is always best to check first, particularly when you are shooting in an unfamiliar culture.

The alternative option is to get in close with a wider lens. This viewpoint makes it easier to include the background to add atmosphere to your shots and also gives your images a more "intimate" look, as the viewer feels much more a part of the event. You will need to adopt an "in your face" approach to take shots of people at such close range, but the results can be worth the effort. With both approaches, setting your DSLR to auto focus and exposure allows you to concentrate fully on the composition.

Include a focal point in wider scenes
While an individual person or object can give a taste of an event or location, it's also worth shooting wider scenes that include one main subject as a focal point. If chosen carefully, this can give a sense of the character of the place or event.

Don't always shoot the most obvious person or object
It is very tempting to focus all your attention on the most obvious subjects, whether that's the bride and groom at a wedding, or the loudest person at an event. But it is often the less obvious characters who make the most intimate and interesting images. Take time to get to the heart of the event and discover the hidden gems and people that wouldn't normally get much attention. When shooting these subjects, you can emphasize their sense of being on the sidelines of the event by positioning them at the edge or bottom of the frame.

BELOW
When shooting landscapes, try to include a focal point to give a greater sense of the character of the location.

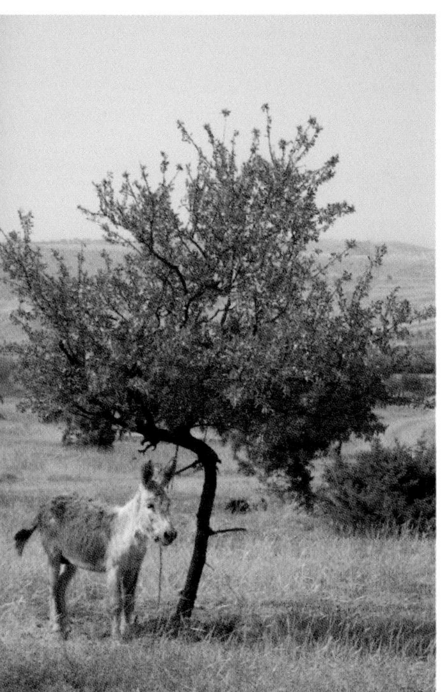

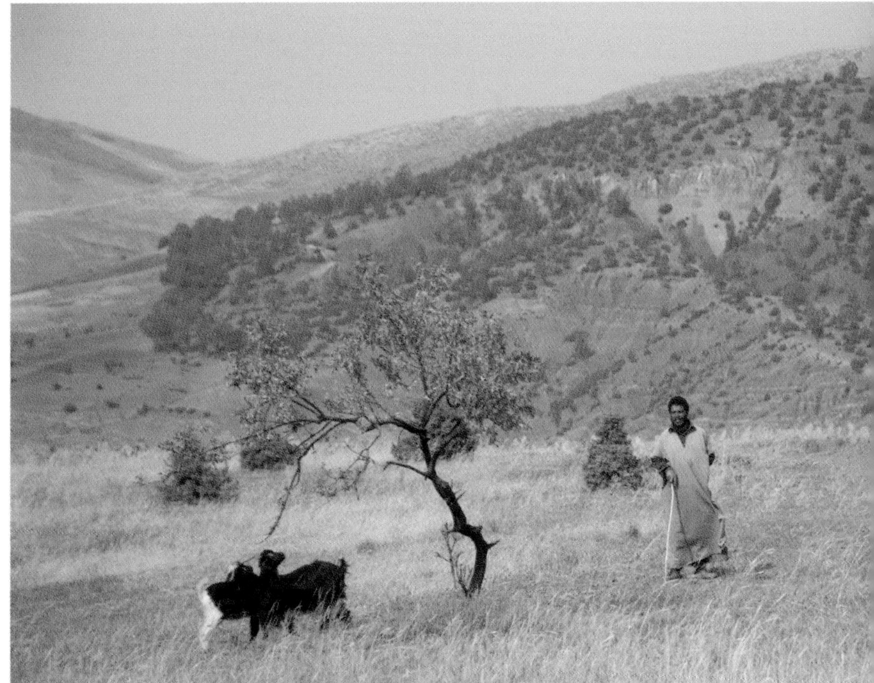

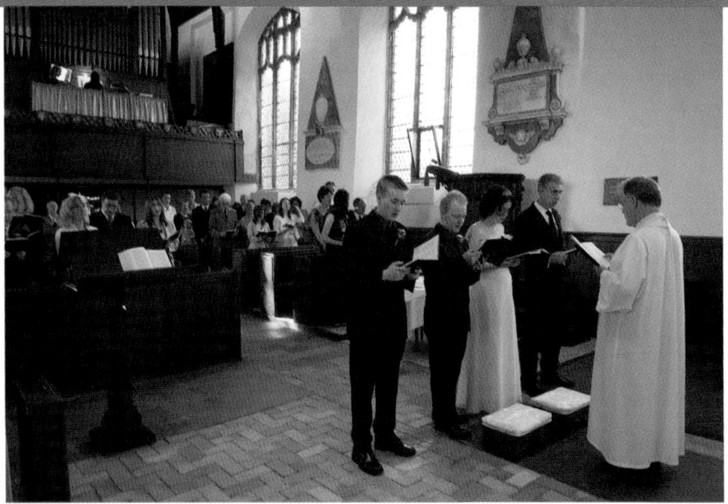

LEFT
Shooting wider scenes adds variety to your images. Here, I used the church interior and the congregation as the main subjects, positioning the wedding party in the right third of the image.

RIGHT
Even the smallest details can help you to capture the essence of an occasion.

FAR RIGHT
Getting in close to the people in your shots will make the viewer feel more a part of what is going on. Here, I used an 18mm lens on a small-sensor DSLR to capture as much of this scene as possible.

The story behind most special occasions lies at the heart of why you are there taking photographs. The way that you compose your shots will help you and the other people involved to remember the occasion years after the event.

While staged photographs can be the ones that many people value at the time, it's often the "off the cuff" images that capture the spirit of the occasion better, especially if you can include as many of the people or places involved as possible. These candid shots can be more difficult to achieve with a DSLR as the camera is more noticeable than a compact model. The benefits of the DLSR are the automatic exposure and focusing options that allow you to take images quickly and simply. At many events people will be too engrossed in what's going on to worry about you and your camera, especially if you use a longer lens so that you don't need to get close to them.

With any candid photography, you need to exercise some discretion, so get permission from the organizers of the event before you start shooting and make clear what you are trying to achieve. Always respect people's privacy: if they object to you taking their picture, don't try to take it without them knowing. If you are up-front and honest about what you are doing, you will usually find that people are willing to pose for you, and after a while they'll forget about the camera and you'll get more relaxed-looking shots. Often in these situations you won't get the best shots straight away, as some people will simply "play" to the camera, while others will be very self-conscious and look uncomfortable. It's often best to forget about taking pictures for a while and wait until people feel more relaxed before you start shooting again.

As well as trying to include the whole scene, there are often great stories to be found in people's expressions. When people are engaged in the atmosphere of an event, they'll often be at their most relaxed and expressive. So keep an eye out for situations where people are reacting to the events around them. Try to fill the frame with just one or two people to maximize the impact of their reactions.

RIGHT
One of the major advantages of DSLRs is their ability to easily crop your pictures to suit the subject. This shot benefited from cropping into a panoramic format to remove the area of bland blue sky at the top of the frame, concentrating all the attention on the main subject.

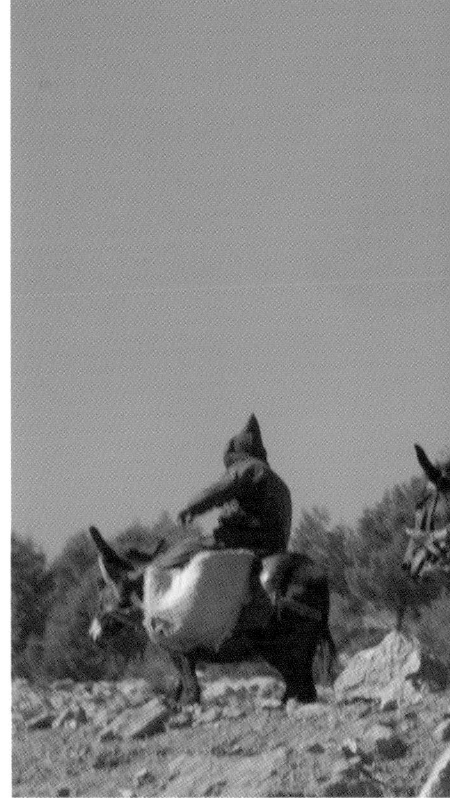

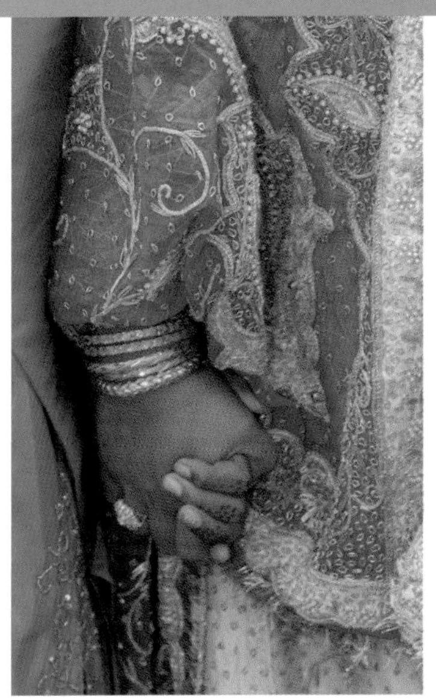

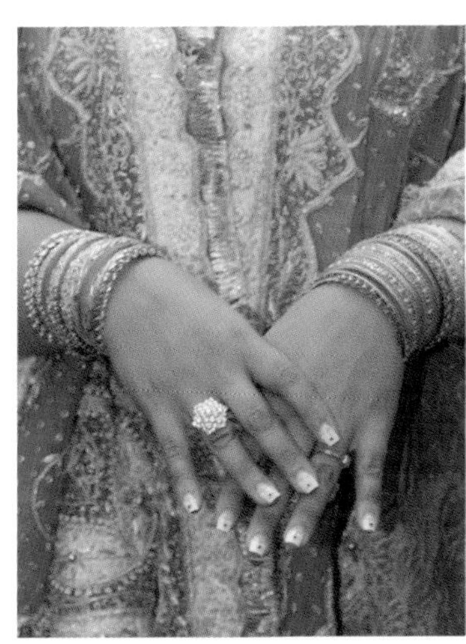

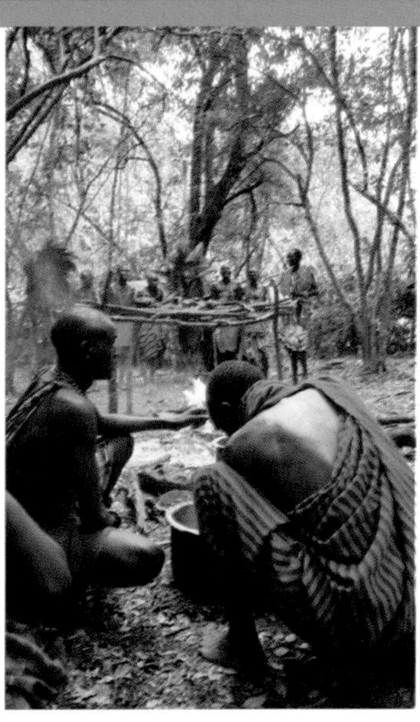

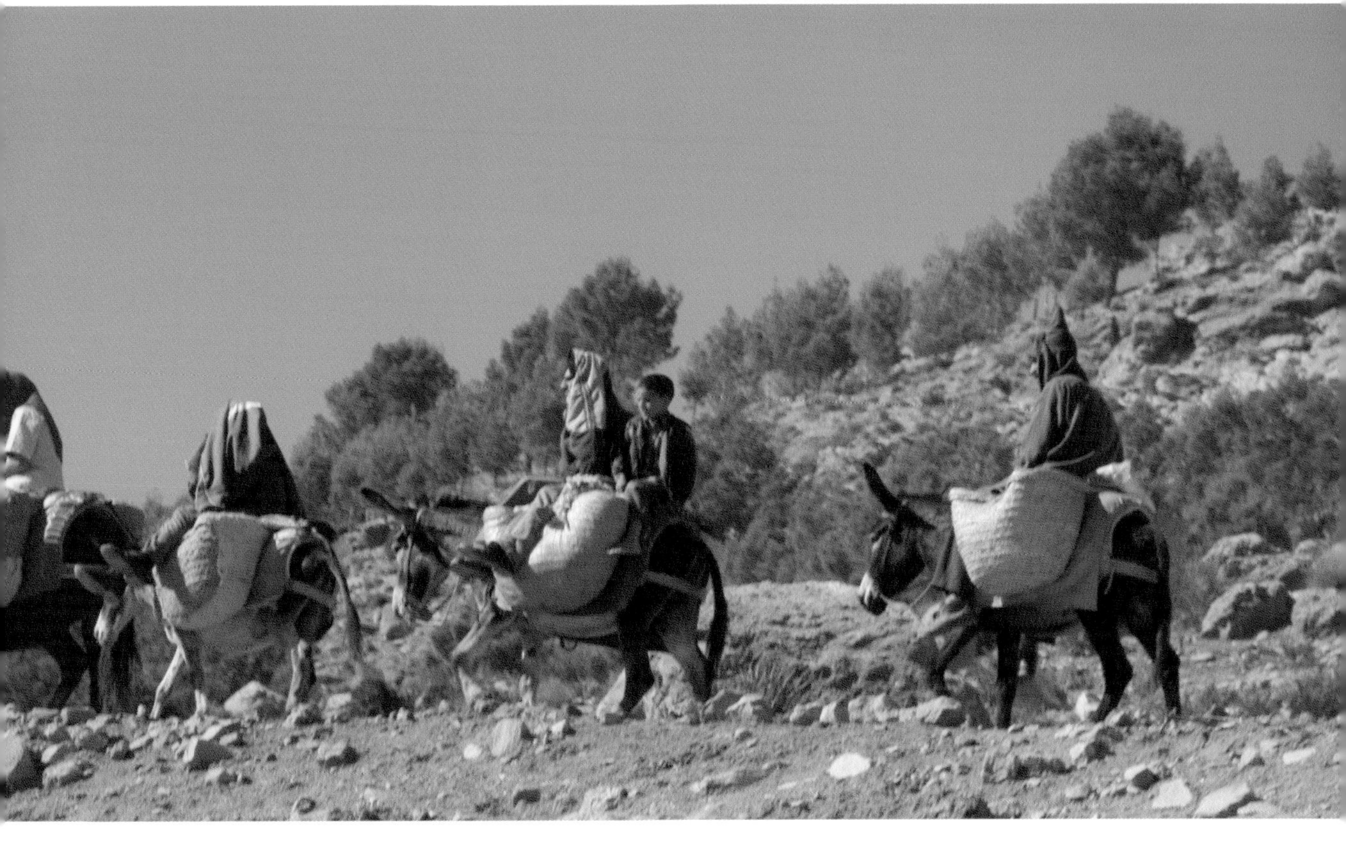

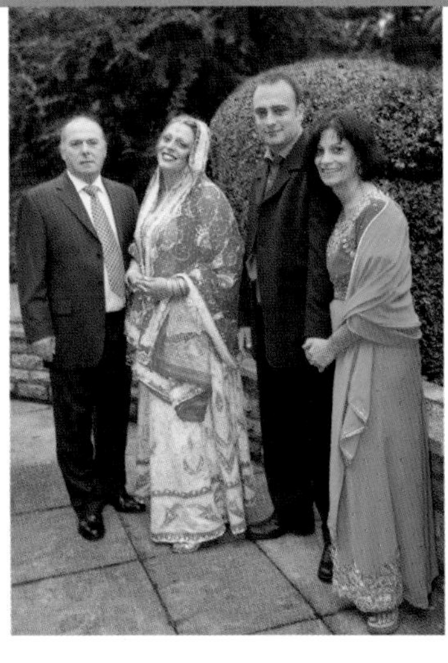

LEFT
Even smaller group shots can sometimes benefit from shooting from a slight angle to add a sense of depth.

RIGHT
The classic wedding group shot may appear simple, but getting a whole group of people to look straight at the camera can be surprisingly difficult to achieve.

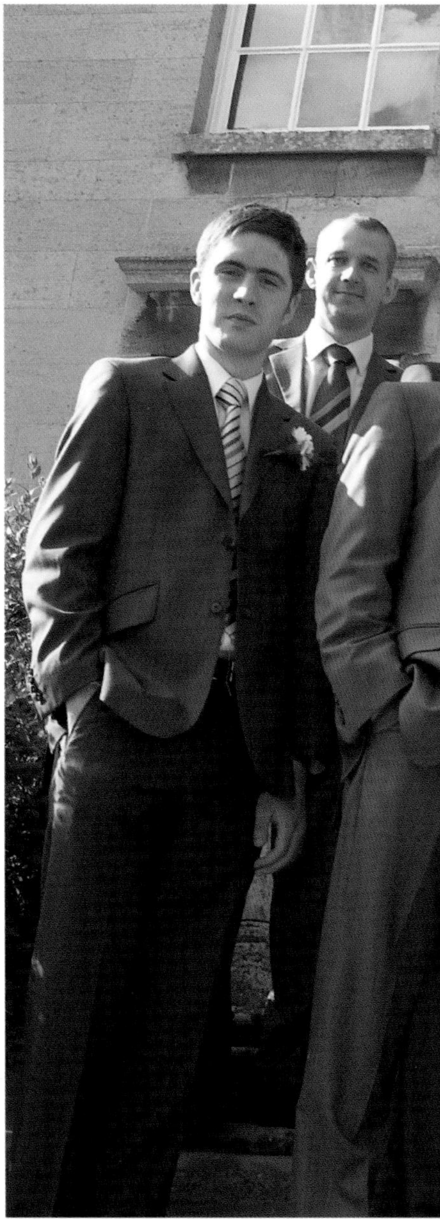

From ensuring that everyone is looking in the right direction to arranging them in the best order for your composition, group shots can be more challenging than almost any other type of people photography. They often require more organizational skills than photographic ones, so a loud voice and the ability to get everyone's attention play as much a part as your composition skills.

Using a DSLR and a tripod can help here, as people are more likely to take you seriously if you look the part, and an SLR looks more professional than a compact camera. But you still need to be able to communicate effectively with your subjects and work quickly to get the shot before anyone loses interest. There are some simple composition techniques that you can use to create the best arrangements.

Formal groups

When shooting formal group shots, you usually have the luxury of being able to arrange people in order to get the composition right, but always double-check in the viewfinder before firing the shutter. The most important aspects are people's heights and clothes. The viewer will look at people's faces first, so you need to ensure that the position of people in the group makes this as easy as possible. Avoid having the tallest people at the edge of the frame, or positioning the tallest and shortest people next to each other. What you are trying to achieve is to position the faces so that they form a flowing line in your shot, without any breaks or sudden changes in position that will spoil the effect. The color of the clothing can also influence where a person will look best in the frame. Brighter colors grab our attention more than darker ones, so avoid having a person in brightly colored clothes at the edge of the frame. If they are positioned in the middle or around a third into the group, they'll force the viewer to look into the frame, rather than take all the attention straight to the edge of the image.

For larger groups, you may need to create two or more lines to include everyone in the frame. This prevents the shot looking static and uninteresting. In these situations, make sure that you can clearly see everyone's face. It's often worth trying to get the front row to sit, or even kneel to add depth to the group. Even smaller groups can benefit from some of these techniques. Rather than simply lining the people up straight in front of you, shoot at a slight angle to add extra depth.

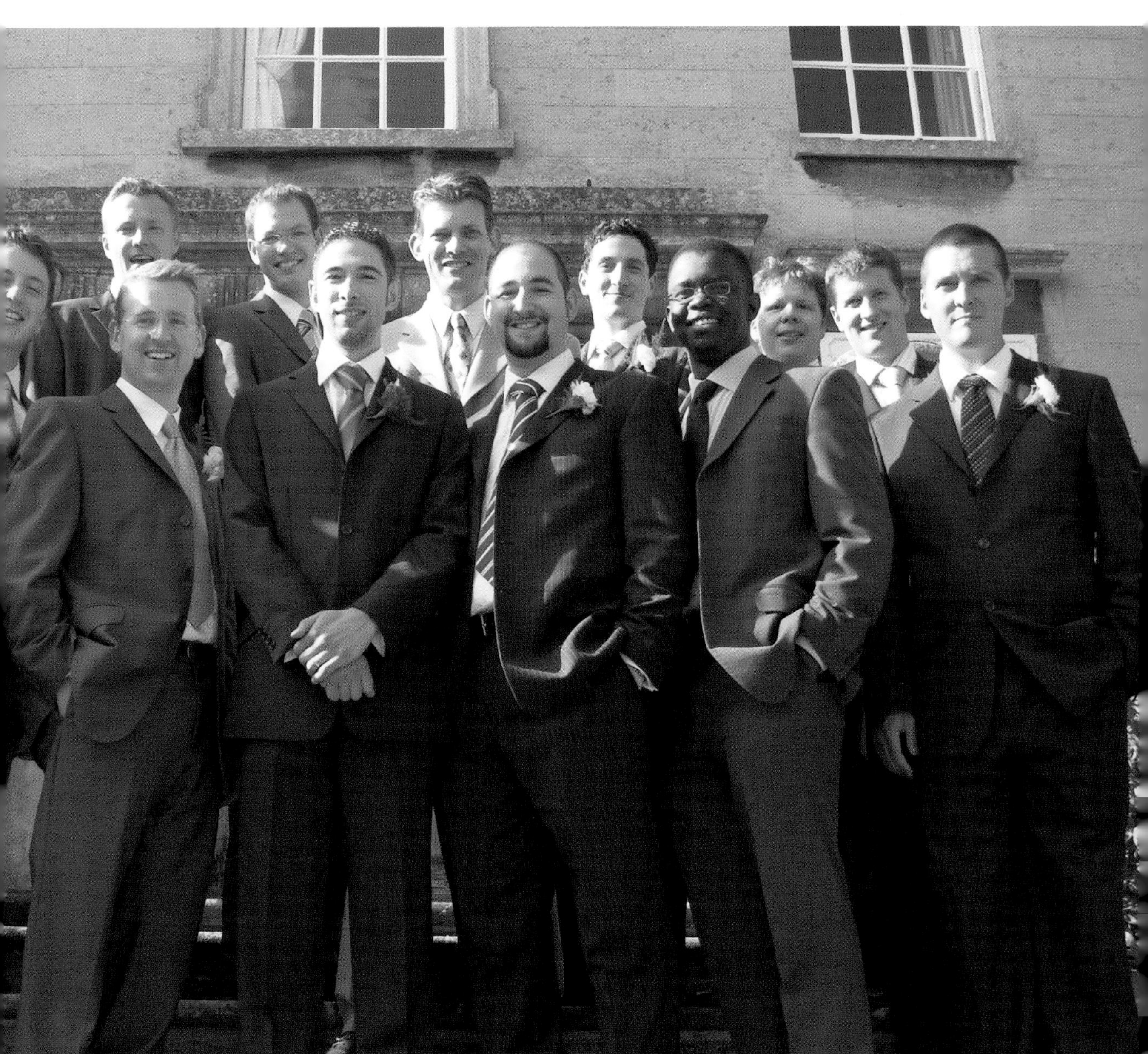

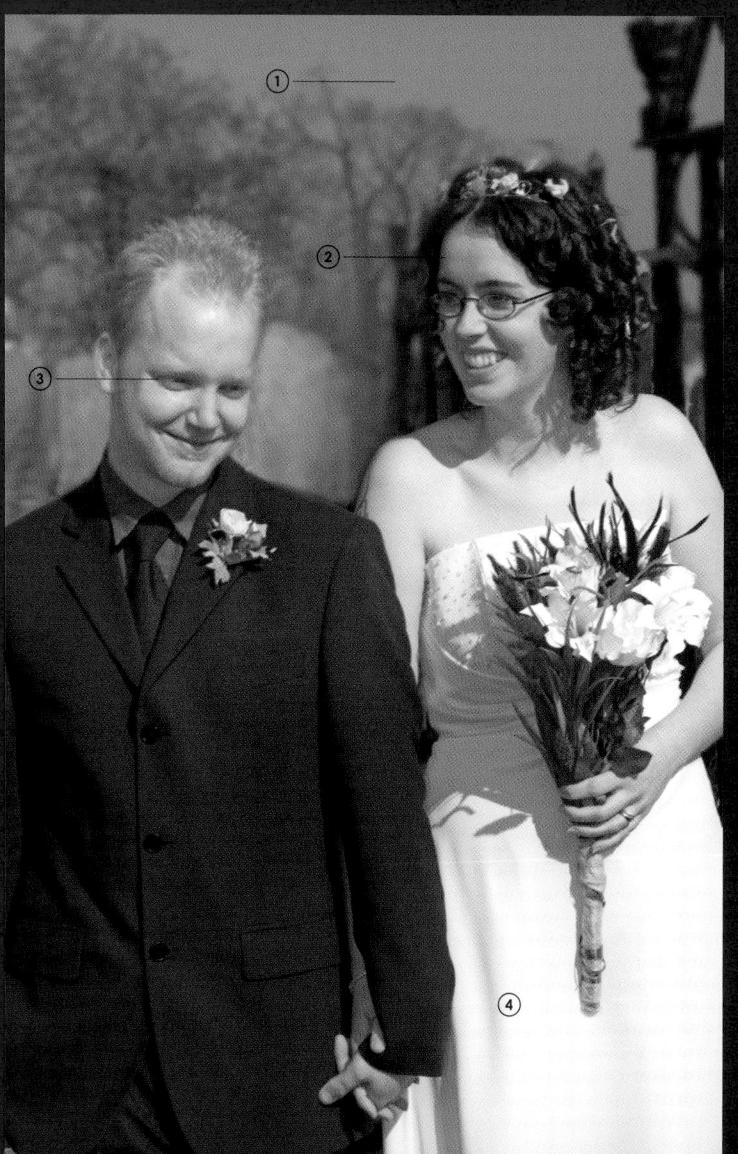

LEFT

1. Try to keep the background as simple and uncluttered as possible to concentrate the viewer's attention on the happy couple.

2. Getting close to the subjects helps when capturing the emotions of an event.

3. Frame your image so that the eyes of the subject fall on the top third line.

4. Converting to black and white helps to give the image a timeless quality and also emphasizes the tone and form of the composition.

OPPOSITE

1. Strong foreground colors hold the composition together by concentrating attention on the bottom of the frame.

2 and 4. Positioning the main elements on the intersections of the third lines helps to maintain this balance.

3. Placing the horizon on the top third line gives more emphasis to the foreground, but still produces a balanced composition.

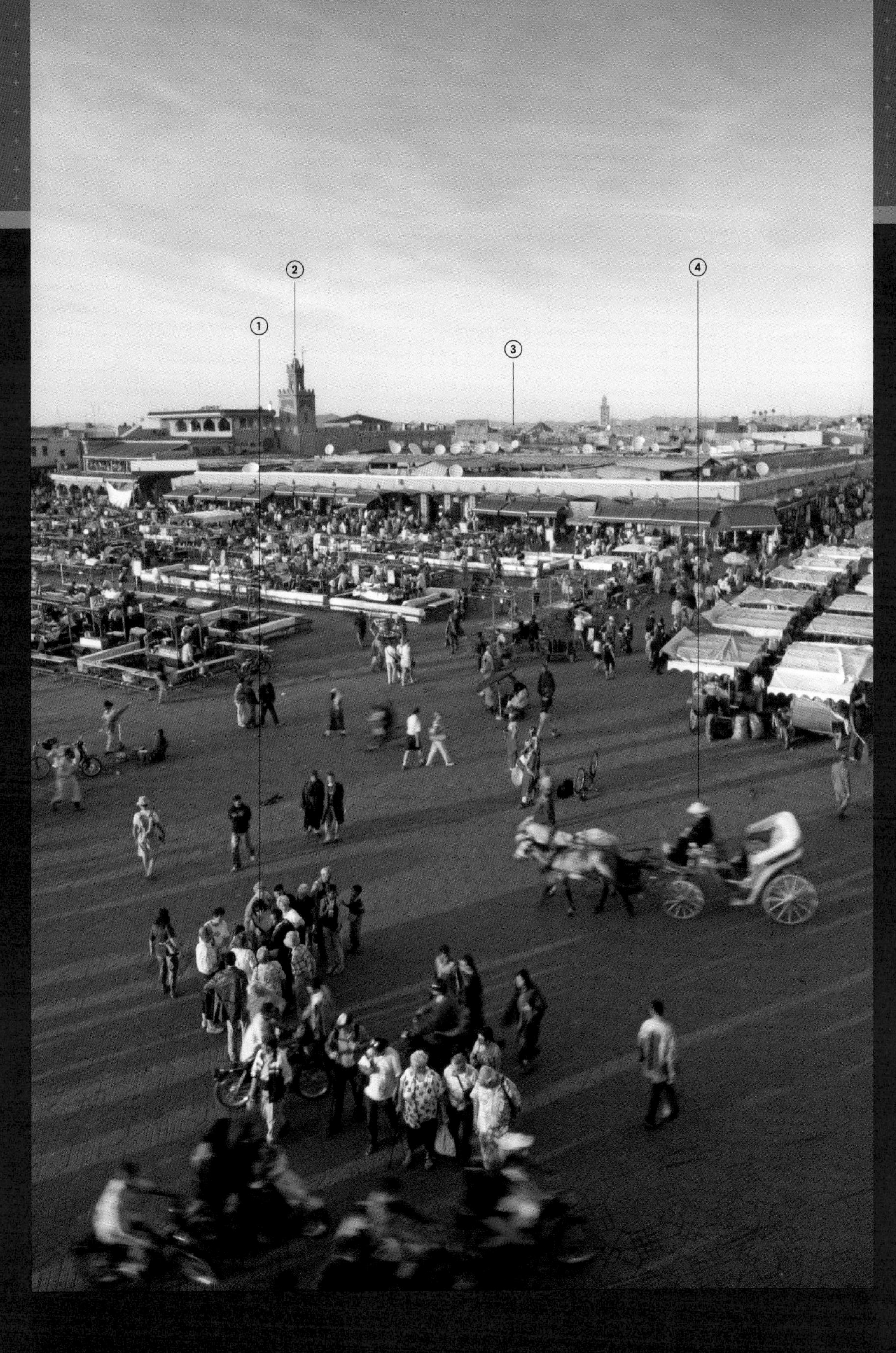
1
2
3
4

Section 9

Action

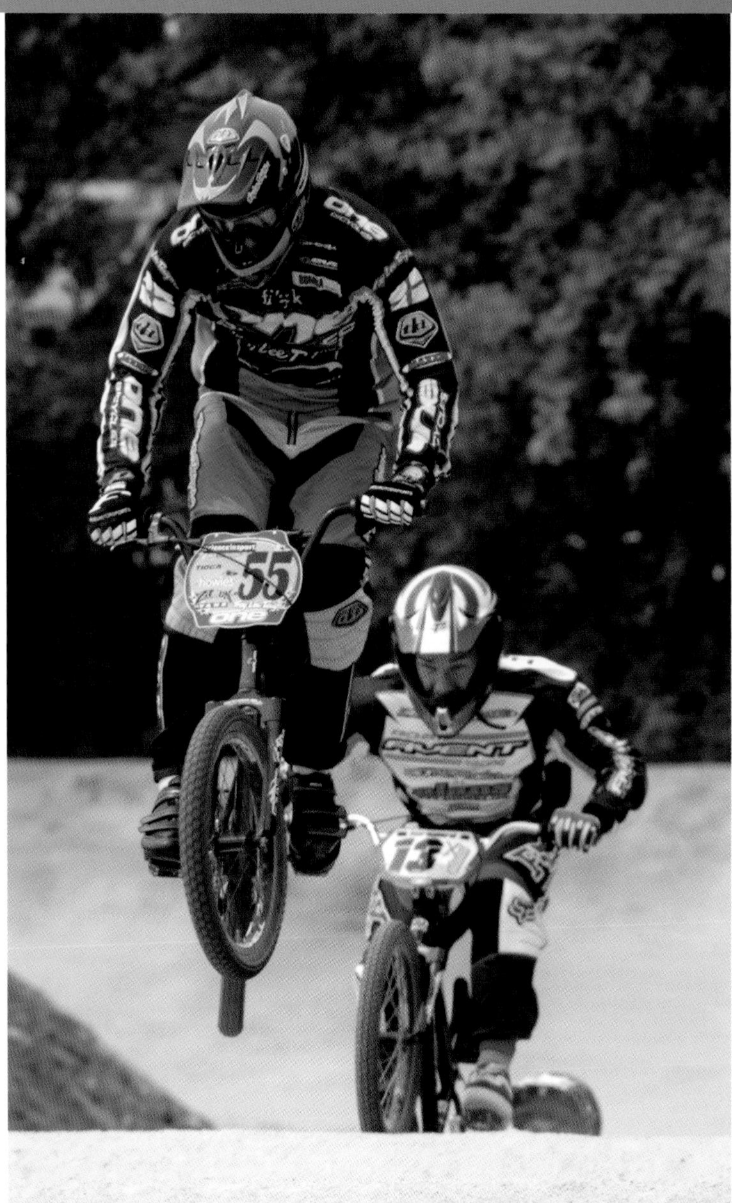

RIGHT
The fast-moving and erratic action of this bike race meant that the autofocus could not track the subject. I prefocused on a point where I knew the riders would jump, and only fired the shutter a fraction of a second before they reached this point.

Shooting moving subjects poses some unique problems when it comes to composition, as just getting the subject in the frame and in focus can prove difficult. However, that does not mean that you can ignore the composition in your action shots; in fact, producing well-composed shots of moving subjects can be one of the most rewarding photographic skills.

The greatest challenge of shooting action is predicting where the subject will be when you press the shutter. Becoming familiar with the type of subject helps enormously, but being able to react quickly is also key.

To shoot action successfully, you need to be able to concentrate on the subject, not on your camera settings or controls. Make sure that you are completely familiar with your camera, especially with the viewfinder.

Basic action techniques

Focusing
It can be difficult to focus on moving subjects. There are two main techniques for shooting action: continuous (or servo) focusing and prefocusing.

In the continuous mode, the camera will continually focus for as long as you hold the shutter release down. This is the best autofocus mode to use when shooting a moving subject. Keep the active focus point positioned on the subject for as long as possible before you take the shot to allow the camera a chance to follow the movement. To do this, you may need to select an off-center point if the subject isn't going to be in the middle of the frame.

Prefocusing is useful when you can predict where the subject will be when you fire the shutter, such as a car on a race track. Select manual focus and set the focus before the subject comes into the frame. Choose a point that is easily recognizable and wait until the subject almost reaches it before firing the shutter.

Shutter speeds

Unlike most subjects where camera shake is the main deciding factor for choosing shutter speed, with action photography, it also depends on how you want the moving subject to appear. Camera shake can still be a factor, but by moving the camera to keep the subject in the same position in the frame, you can also use different shutter speeds. A fast shutter speed such as 1/500 or 1/1000 sec will freeze the movement. In contrast, the blur created by using a slower shutter speed can add a sense of movement to your shots.

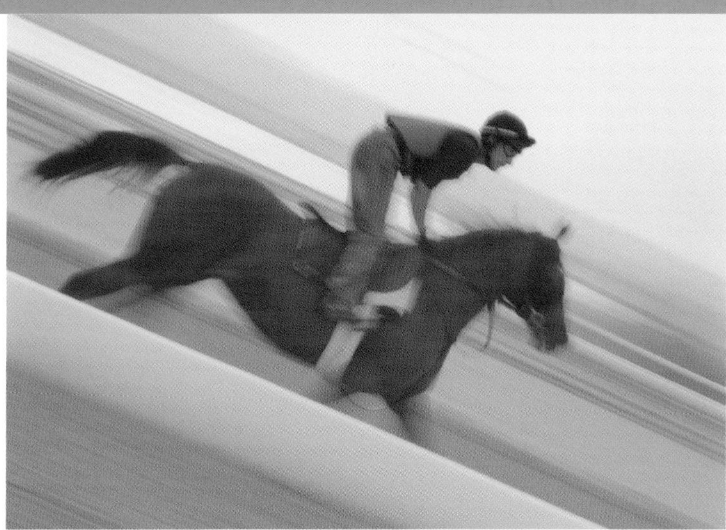

LEFT
When tracking the main subject, always look out for interesting compositions. Here, I waited until the boat in the background was perfectly aligned between the front two rowers before firing the shutter.

ABOVE
Panning is one of the most powerful ways of shooting action. Try to track the subject keeping a little more space ahead of it than behind to give the best result.

Panning

When the subject is moving across your view you can use a technique called panning to follow the action. You do this by following the subject as it passes you and firing the shutter only when it's in the best position for your shot. This allows you to capture moving subjects more successfully, and with slower shutter speeds, than waiting until it appears in the viewfinder.

Continuous shooting

All DSLRs offer the option of shooting a sequence of shots one after another. While this is extremely useful for taking several shots of the same subject as it moves, you will find that it's best to use this feature sparingly. Many cameras take time to process the images and write them to the card, meaning that the camera won't be able to take any more shots until it has cleared this backlog. This may mean that you miss the best moments, so be selective rather than just taking as many shots as possible in a single burst. Shooting large numbers of pictures also means that you'll have to change memory cards frequently, again running the risk of missing shots.

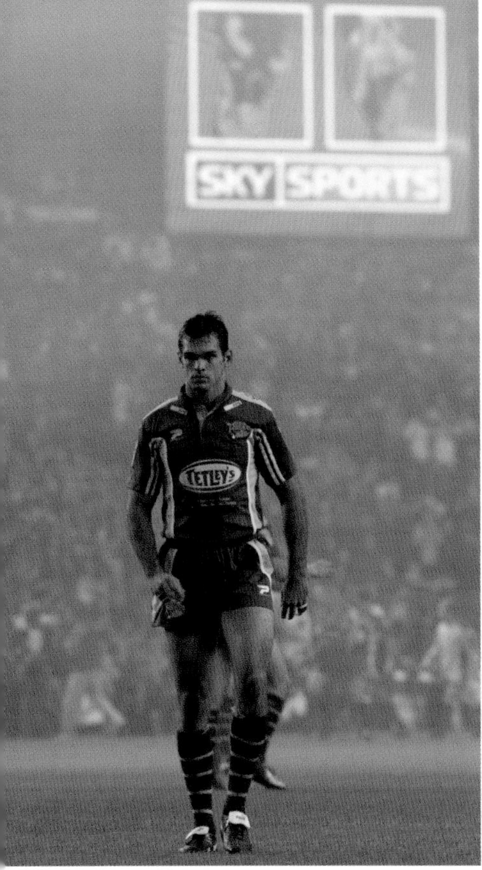

For your own safety, you often need to keep your distance from the action, this is why a telephoto is the most common lens for photographing action and sports. But this isn't always the only, or the best, option.

As we have seen, your viewpoint affects the composition of the final image. Shooting from a distant viewpoint and using a long telephoto lens to get close to the action will make the background appear very close to your subject. If you get close to the subject and use a wide-angle lens, the perspective will cause the subject to appear more dominant in the frame than from a more distant viewpoint. This is because a closer viewpoint makes the distance between the subject and the background appear greater than it does when seen from farther away.

Changing lenses

One of the most frustrating aspects of shooting fast-moving sports and action subjects is not having the right lens on

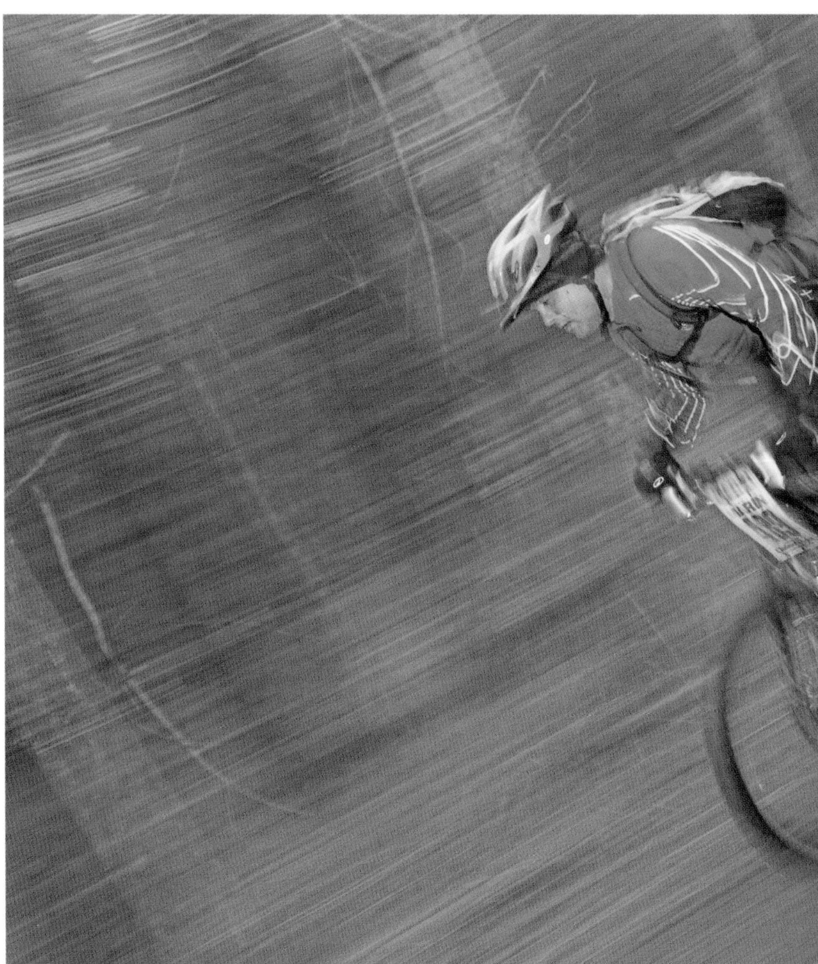

ABOVE
You will need a telephoto lens for many sports and action shots as you usually can't get close to the action.

RIGHT
When you can get closer, use a wide-angle lens, such as the 18mm used for this mountain bike shot.

your DSLR. Most professionals will use at least two cameras, one with a long telephoto lens and one with a wider lens for when the action moves closer to them. For amateurs, a zoom lens that covers the widest range of focal lengths is the best solution. This also minimizes problems of dust spots on your images caused by dirt entering the camera during lens changes.

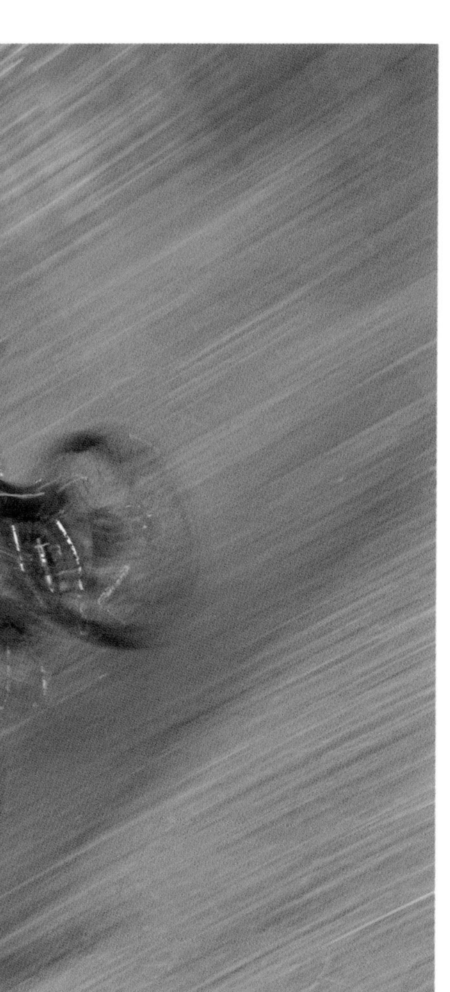

TYPICAL LENSES FOR ACTION

Choosing which lenses to take with you to an event can be difficult unless you are familiar with the subject, so here are some typical focal lengths for particular sports. These are based on wanting to fill the frame with the main subject from normal public viewing areas, so it's always worth packing some alternative focal lengths to allow you to vary your shots. Photographers with access to press areas may be able to use shorter focal lengths than those indicated here.

Sport	Focal length
Motor racing (cars)	200 to 600mm
Motor racing (bikes)	300 to 800mm
Cycling	18 to 200mm
Athletics (large venue)	50 to 400mm
Athletics, basketball (small venue)	18 to 300mm
Stadium sports (American football, soccer, hockey, rugby, etc.)	70 to 500mm
Large stadium sports (baseball and cricket)	200 to 800mm

When it comes to choosing the lens you need, don't just go for the obvious shot. Try a wider or longer lens for a completely different framing. By using a wide lens and keeping the main subject small in the frame, you can include much more of the surroundings to give a sense of place. Using a longer lens will allow you to capture small details, such as an athlete's expression or the wheel of a bike.

REMOTE SHOOTING

Professional sports photographers often use remote firing set-ups to allow them to position cameras closer to the action. Because you can't see precisely where the subject is when you fire the camera, these are usually fitted with extreme wide-angle lenses to capture as much of the action as possible. Check with the event organizers before you set up any such cameras, and be aware that they may get damaged in the heat of the action.

ZOOM LENSES

Because you can't always control precisely how far you will be from the subject, a zoom lens will allow you to fine-tune your framing. But even though it's tempting to zoom while you are shooting the action, try to predict which focal length you will need beforehand instead. Otherwise you could miss the best moments as you will be too busy trying to zoom your lens rather than watching the action.

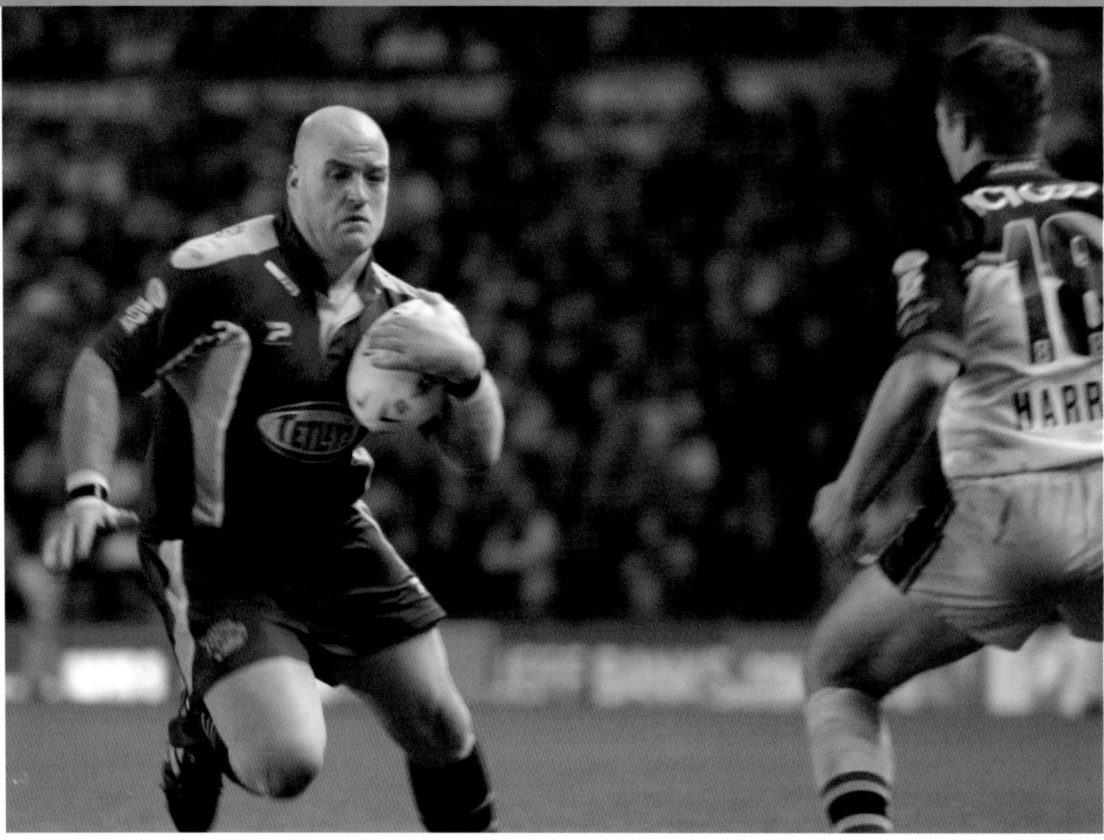

With many action shots it's not so much finding the subject that is difficult, but capturing the subject at the right moment. Some of this is down to luck and being able to react quickly to changing situations. But there are plenty of techniques that you can use to help you get successful action images.

ABOVE
Following the action in team sports can be difficult, so choose a single player to concentrate on to ensure that you get the best shots. Don't always place your subject in the middle of the frame; positioning them to one side allows you to include other players and gives a greater sense of movement to your images.

While fast reactions are helpful, much of the skill is in predicting where the subject will be and when to fire the shutter. So what have either of these got to do with composition? Well, being able to predict the movement of the subject gives you more time to think beyond simply getting the subject in the frame. While being selective about when you take the shot will ensure that the subject is in the right position for a successful composition. It can also help to overcome the very slight delay between pressing the shutter and the picture being taken, although DSLRs are much better in this respect than most compacts. One problem with using DSLRs for action is that the viewfinder goes black when you fire the shutter. This may be only for a fraction of a second, but it can make composing difficult. This makes it even more important to be able to predict the action and choose the right moment to fire the shutter.

Many of the events and sports that create the best action images involve multiple competitors. The techniques you use will depend on the event or activity taking place, but if you are shooting motor sport, for example, try to follow a single car as it passes you, almost ignoring the other competitors. When shooting ball games, you can try to follow the ball, but it's often easier to concentrate on a single player who's likely to receive the ball and try to get the best shot of them.

With so much to think about, action photography can be one of the most demanding, yet ultimately rewarding areas. Like all successful composition, it helps if you can previsualize how you want your shot to look. Don't be too disappointed if some shots fail—even the top professionals don't get it right every time. Be prepared for plenty of images where the subject is blurred or in the wrong position. One of the great benefits of digital is the ability to experiment and take shots at little or no cost. So when you are starting out shooting action, try to take as many shots as possible. As you get more experienced you'll find that you can be more selective about the images you shoot, but still be prepared to sort through plenty of images on your computer to find the best ones.

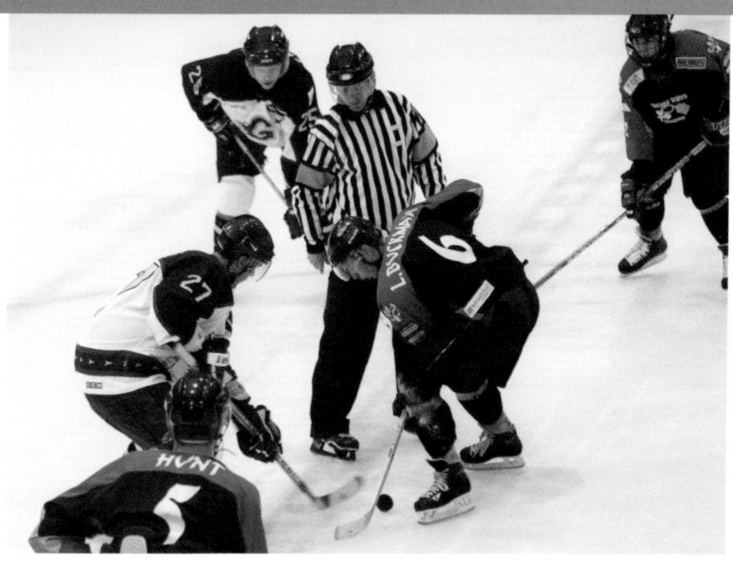

ABOVE
Identify predictable events, such as set-pieces that begin the action. You'll have a better chance to get your composition right, and these events give you a good starting point for following the rest of the action.

BELOW
You don't always have to shoot a single competitor, though, as a wider framing gives you a much greater chance of including other subjects in the image.

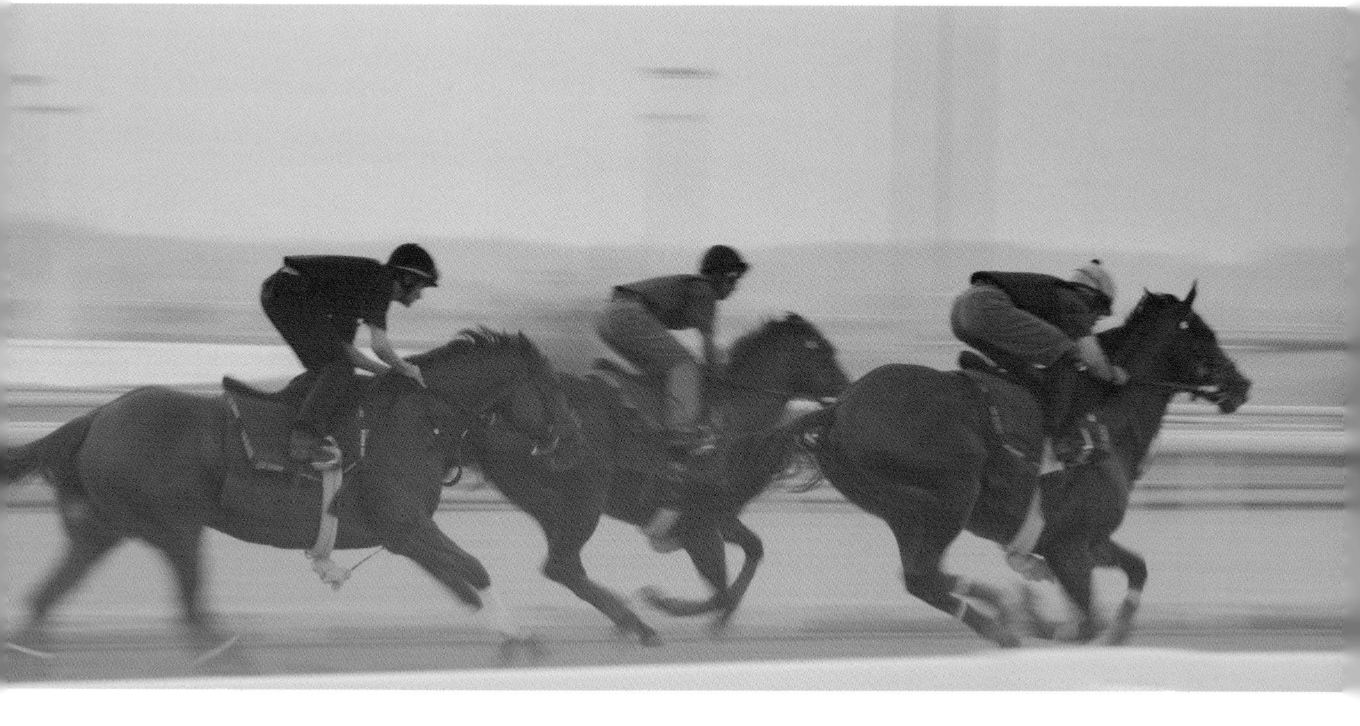

Most sports and action events have a host of stories to tell, so your task is to try to convey these in your pictures. The composition you use can help to tell more about the action. This can be achieved by either excluding other elements in the scene to make the main subject tell the story, or using the subject as part of the wider action to put it into context.

Expression

Much of the drama, strain, and emotion that action will cause can be captured by concentrating on the facial expressions of the people involved. This relies on being able to see their faces, but you can achieve similar results as long as you can at least see the eyes. To make the most of this technique, use a long focal length lens to maximize the impact of your shot. You can also use this technique on wider shots as long as you can clearly see the face. When composing these shots, try to place the eyes or the face on or near one of the third lines so that they are the dominant part of the frame.

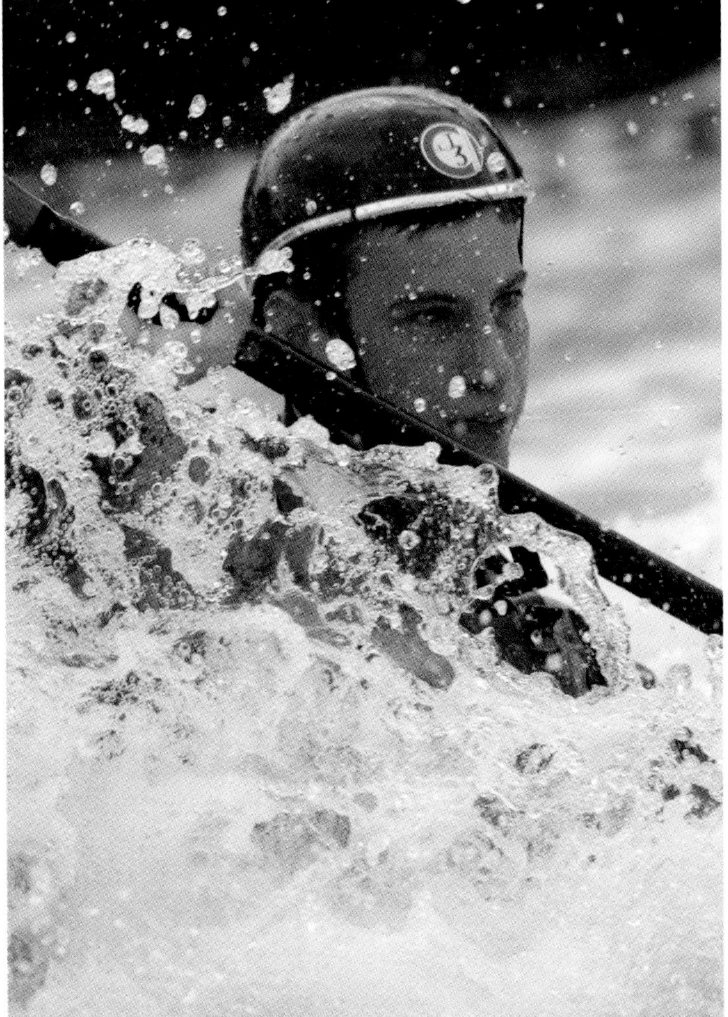

Include other subjects

While many action subjects can make dramatic images on their own, you can tell more about the event by including more than one subject. Many events involve two or more competitors, so by showing the interaction between them you will create a better sense of what is happening in your shots.

You will need to think carefully about the positioning of the various elements, while also reacting to rapid changes in the relationship between the different subjects. Shooting digitally means that you can easily crop the image later, so it's generally best to shoot a little wider than normal to ensure you get all of the subject in the frame.

Sequences

By shooting a number of frames in quick succession you can show how an event unfolds much more successfully than with a single shot. To use this technique, set your DSLR to continuous shooting and continuous (or servo) autofocus modes, then try to follow the subject. Most DSLRs offer a shooting speed of at least 2.5 frames per second, which is fast enough for most action. The number of shots you can take in a single burst will be limited by the buffer memory of the camera, the speed of the card, and the file type that you use. Most cameras will give a greater number of JPEG images than RAW files, so this is often the best option. Using the fastest type of cards possible will minimize the time you have to wait for your images to be written to the card.

LEFT

Much of the energy and emotion of action will be shown on the face of your subject. A tight crop will maximize the impact of their expression.

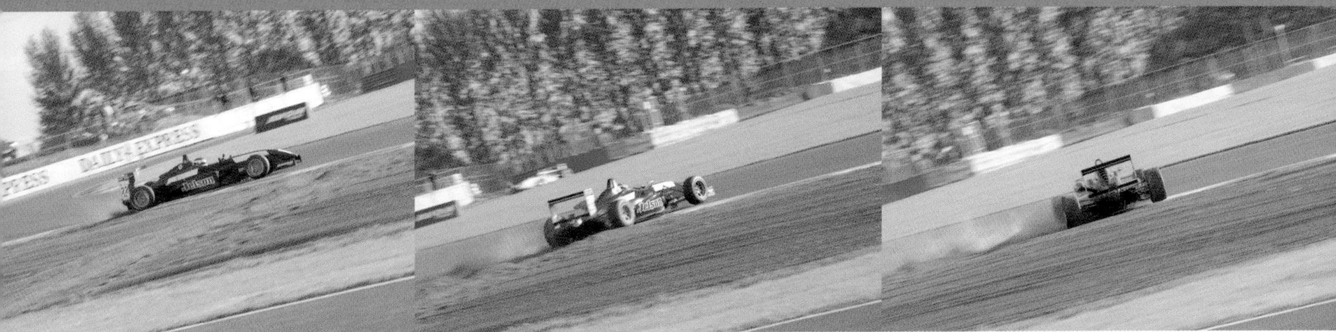

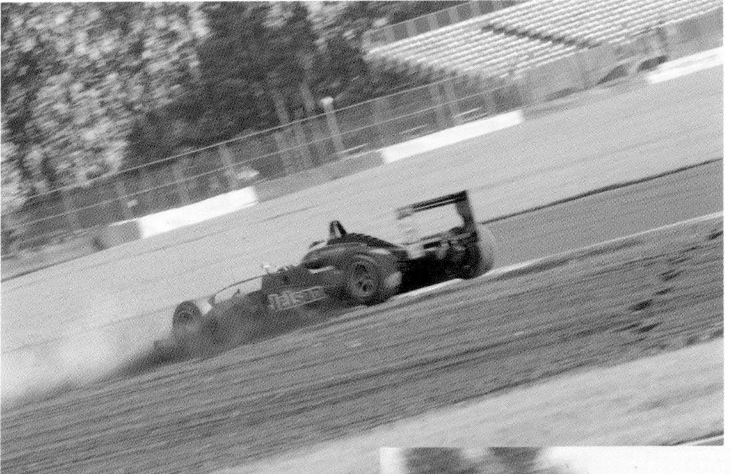

PRESENTING SEQUENCES

Shooting digitally gives you access to a whole range of quick and simple presentation options. If you've shot a sequence, you can create a montage of the results using your image-editing software. This can then be printed as a single image for a very powerful result.

ABOVE AND RIGHT
Shooting sequences of pictures allows you to show how the action progresses through time. Here, I started shooting just as the car started to skid and continued shooting to get the whole sequence of the incident.

The most common DSLR technique for shooting action is to fill the frame with the main subject. However, you don't have to shoot all your action pictures like this. There are plenty of other composition styles that you can use to show the drama and excitement of sports and action events.

Shoot the wider scene
Don't always shoot the action in close-up; even if you are some distance from the subject you can still use wide lenses to show more of the event and surroundings. This usually works best when there are plenty of subjects in the frame, or when there is a lot of action going on. Try positioning the subject at the bottom of the frame and using grandstands, the sky, or crowds to fill the rest of the frame.

Include other competitors
In team sports look out for incidents or clashes between different competitors and frame your shot to include them. This not only adds to the story of the shot, but is also a good compositional tool. If the subject is positioned to one side of the frame, having another subject on the opposite side produces a more balanced image.

Photograph the crowd
It's not just on the track or field that the action takes place at sports events. The crowds themselves are full of emotion and energy, so look out for their reactions and expressions. Shooting with a DSLR means you are more likely to attract the attention of individuals, which should make it easier for you to establish eye-contact. If there is a large crowd, position your main subject at the bottom or to one side of the frame, and use the colors and shapes of the rest of the crowd to balance the composition. Using a wide aperture will throw the background out of focus to keep all the attention on the main person, but will still give a sense of the crowd behind them.

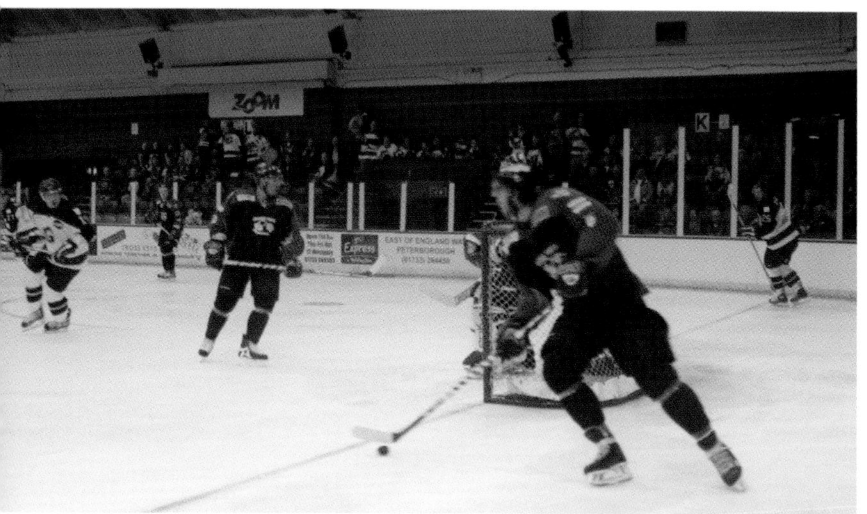

ABOVE
For sports where you can get closer to the competitors, use a wide-angle lens and shoot a wider view of the action, rather than the normal close-up composition.

RIGHT
The crowd at a sports event can give a flavor of the atmosphere. Try to frame individuals using the massed faces behind as a background.

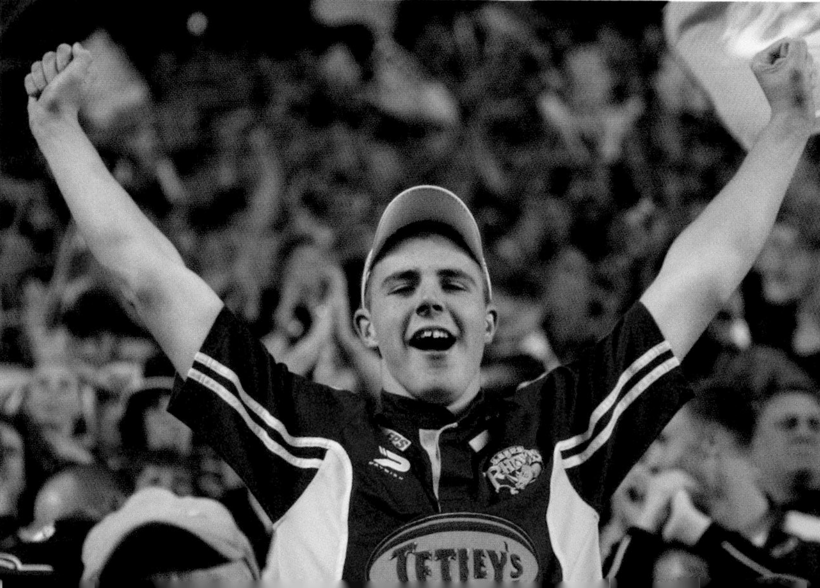

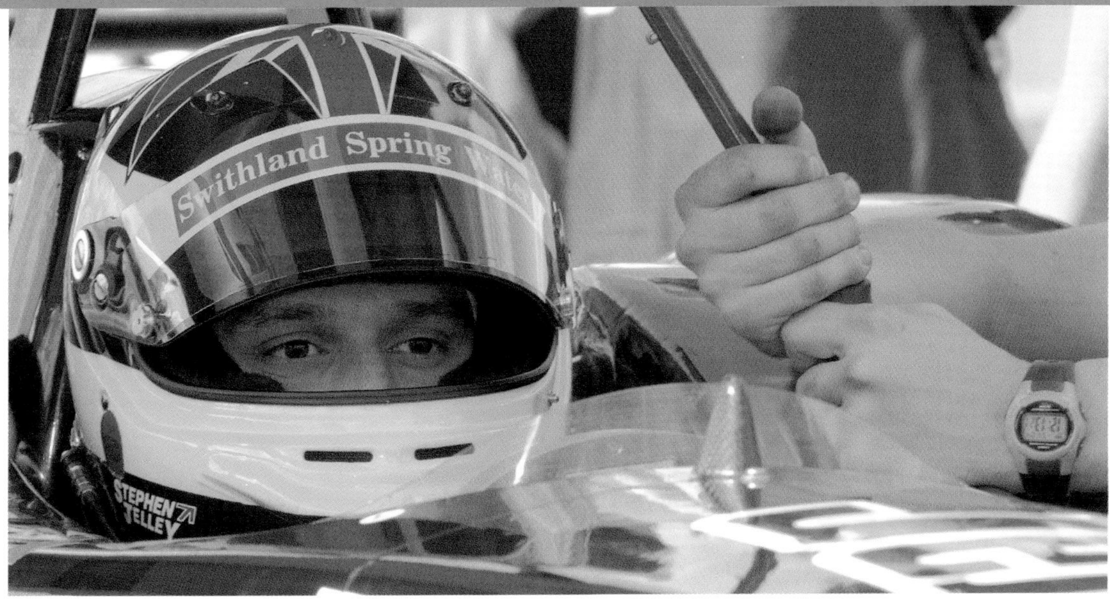

Before and after the action
The tension just before an event and the elation or despair after the finish can prove to be more eventful than the competition itself. You can often get closer to the competitors at these times, so try to capture their emotions by cropping in tight to emphasize their expression and actions.

Use unusual angles to add to the drama
While you would normally keep the horizon straight and level, action images can be enhanced by using unusual angles or viewpoints. Angle the camera when you shoot to create diagonal lines, which will add energy and drama to your images. When using this technique it's best to use large angles; if the horizon is only slightly off level, it can look like a mistake rather than an intentional framing.

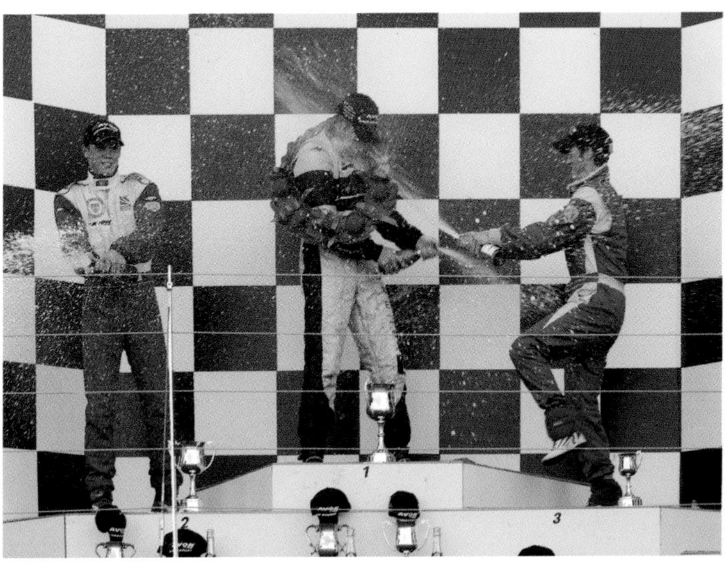

ABOVE AND RIGHT
For a different view of a sport, photograph the competitors before and after the main event. You can then concentrate on the emotion in their faces and gestures. For this shot of a driver before the race, I positioned his face on the left of the frame to allow plenty of space for him to look into. For the celebration photo, the position of the three figures creates a balanced image.

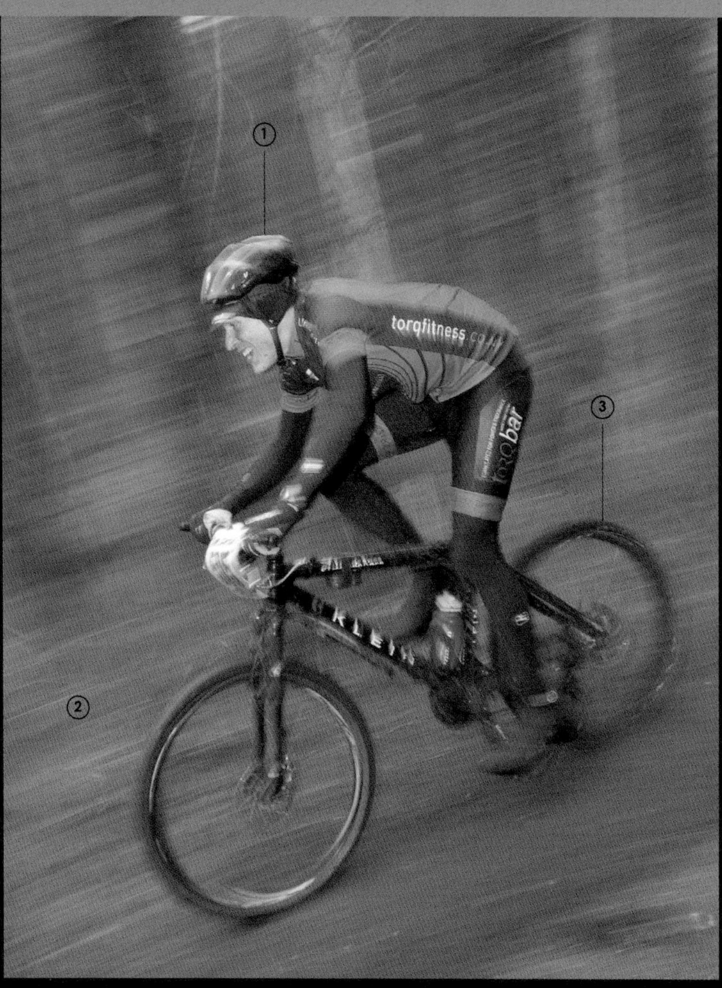

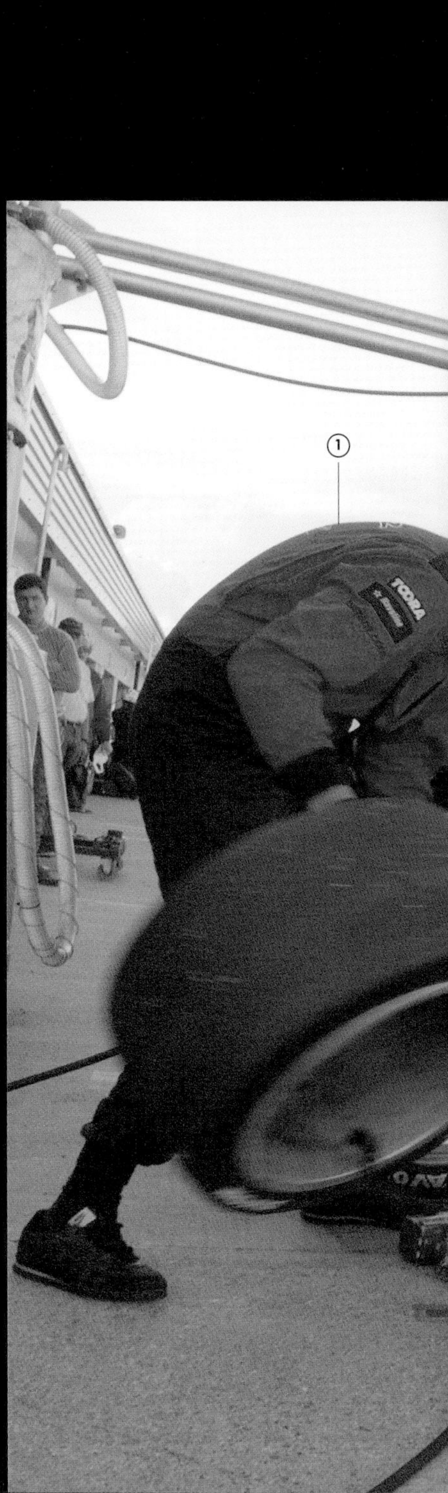

ABOVE

1. Positioning the main focal point—in this case the face—on the intersection of two third lines makes the most of the cyclist's expression.

2. Always leave space in front of moving subjects. This produces a more successful composition as it gives them a space to move into, rather than heading directly out of the frame.

3. Shooting at an angle makes this image more dynamic than a simple horizontal shot.

RIGHT

1. The timing of your action shots is crucial. Watch for moments when the subject is in the perfect position to give a balanced and interesting composition.

2. Using a wide-angle lens and getting in close gives a greater feeling of being part of the action.

3. Even a static subject can be made to look more dynamic by shooting at an angle.

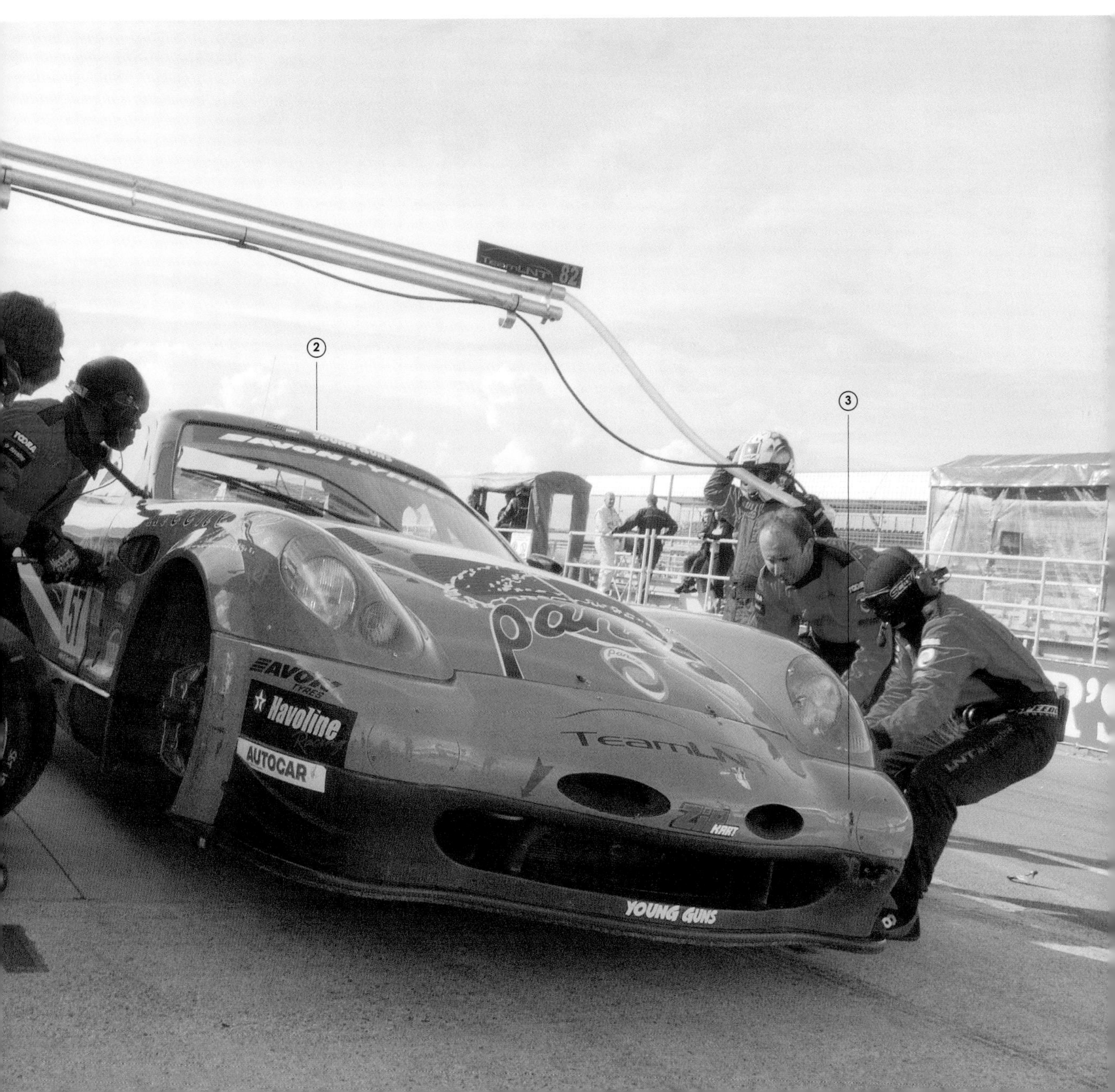

TeamLNT 82
AVON TYRES
Havoline
AUTOCAR
TeamLNT
YOUNG GUNS

Section 10

Specialist Techniques

From still life shots to portraits, studio photography gives you the ultimate control over the composition, framing, and lighting of your subject. In a studio you have the time and the opportunity to fine-tune every element of your shot, even down to being able to position each part of the image to achieve the best results.

The instant review facility on your DSLR makes it much easier for the newcomer to the studio to learn how to position the lighting. One of the major problems with using flash lighting is that you can't see the effect until you take the shot. Even though many studio flash units have continuous modeling lights to show where the light is falling, it can be difficult to visualize how the final image will look. Reviewing your shots on the DSLR helps you with the exposure and composition using studio flash.

Home studio considerations

Most photographers have to use a garage or spare room as a makeshift studio. You can still produce amazing results and tackle a wide range of subjects in even the most basic home studio, but space can be a problem. When you can't get far enough away from the subject to include it all with the lens you want to use, you can usually put on a wider lens to include more of the subject and carry on shooting, but in the home studio this can pose problems with both the composition and perspective.

Shooting at close distances with a wide lens causes distorted perspective, with the distance between the closer and more distant objects being apparently lengthened. While this can be a problem, it's an effect that you may want to use, particularly in product and still life photography. Where it does cause problems is with the background, because with a wide-angle lens, it's very likely that you'll be able to see the edges of whatever type of backdrop you are using.

ABOVE
Wide-angle lenses need to be used with care in the studio to avoid including equipment or the edge of the background in your shot. Here, shooting with a 17mm lens has meant that the legs of the lighting stand are visible on the left of the image.

BELOW
Using a short focal length macro lens, such as 50mm, can mean that you are too close to the subject, making it impossible to light the subject without the front of the lens creating shadows. A longer focal length, such as a 105mm lens will allow you to achieve the same magnification at a much more useable shooting distance.

Macro lenses in the studio

Shooting macro subjects in the studio gives you more control over the subject's position and lighting than out in the field. But because of the constraints of working distances and light positions, it's worth thinking about which focal length lens you should use. Shooting very small objects with a short focal length macro lens such as 50mm will mean that you are within a few inches of the subject, making it difficult to position the lights without the camera or lens causing shadows on the subject. At the other extreme, using a long focal length such as a 180 or 200mm macro lens can be difficult if your studio has limited space. For most users, a lens between 70 and 105mm is the best compromise. The shorter focal lengths are most suitable for DSLRs with the smaller sensor, and the longer ones are best for full-frame or 35mm cameras.

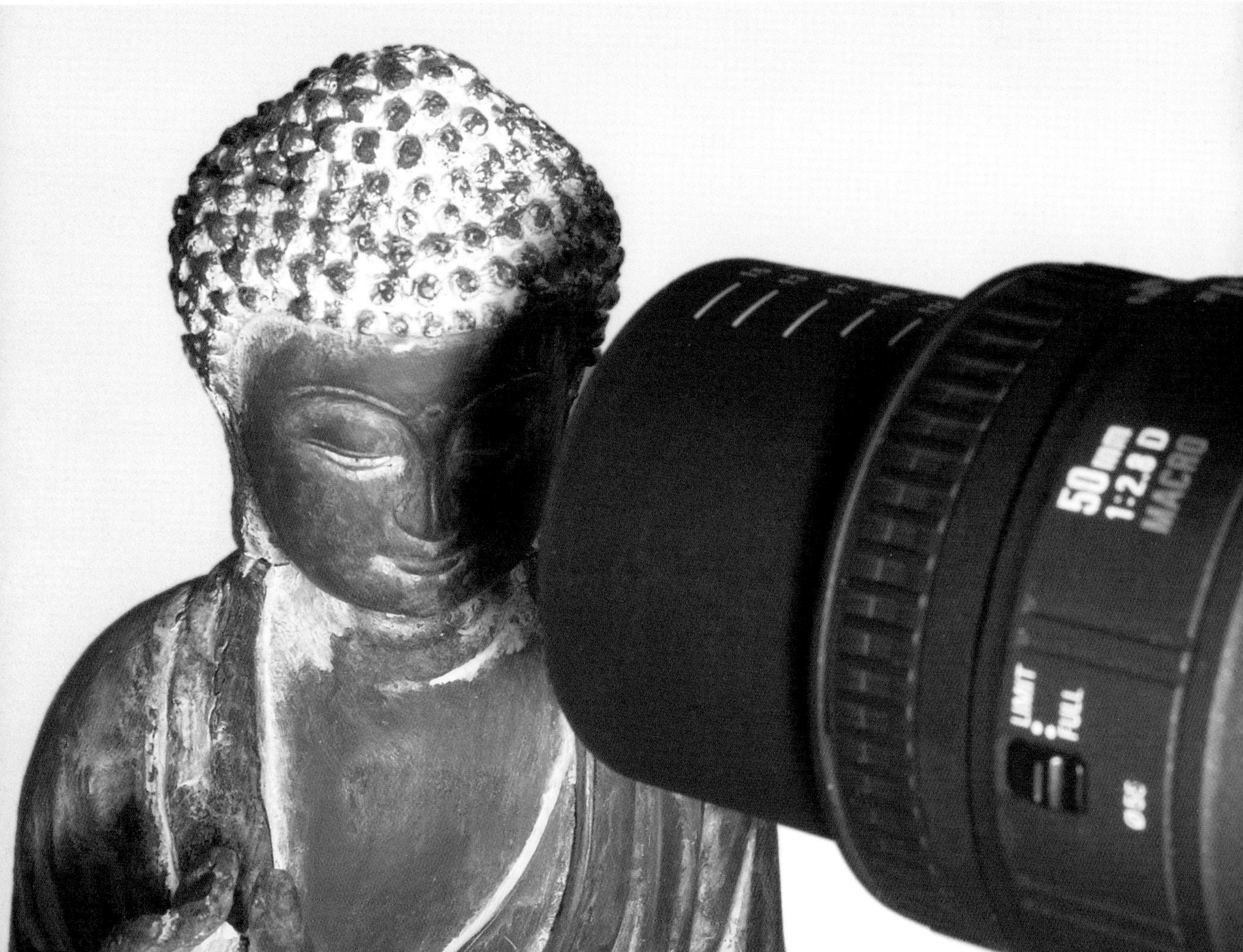

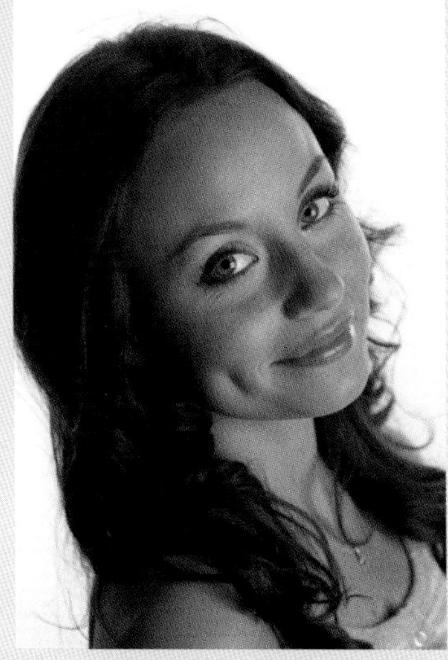

LEFT
A clean white background is perfect for portrait shots when you want your subject to really stand out in the frame.

BELOW
Simple white backgrounds are the most useful for many studio shots. They produce bright, fresh-looking images, without the background taking too much attention away from the main subject.

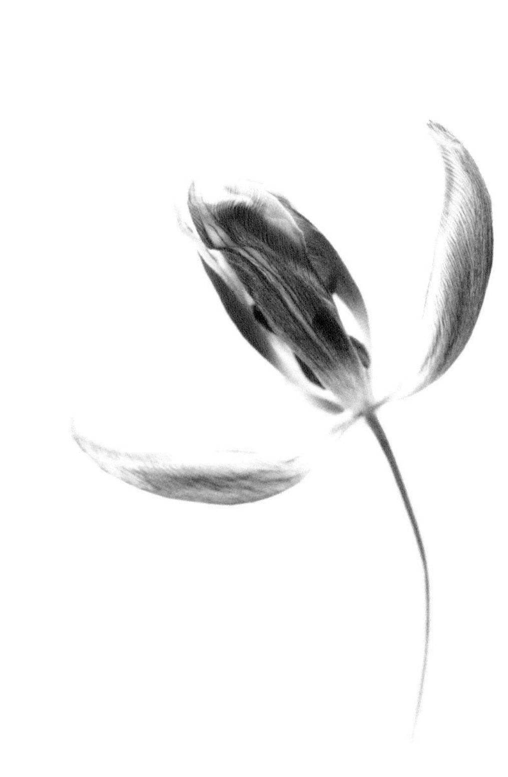

Unlike many other locations, you have complete control over the lighting and backgrounds in your studio shots. The background in particular plays a huge part in the overall look of your image and the type of composition you use.

When using studio flash, you need to set the white balance on your DSLR to the flash (or daylight) preset value. The automatic setting often doesn't work with the very short duration of the light from this type of lighting, so can give variable results. This is also true when using strong colored backgrounds under any type of light source. The white balance setting on your DSLR should be matched to the type of light that you are using to ensure the colors are correct.

When it comes to the exposure mode, the manual setting on your DSLR is perfect for most studio situations, as it's impossible to use automatic exposure with studio flash. Using white or black backgrounds can also affect the reading from automatic exposure systems. So for the best results set your DSLR to manual and use the image review facility to check your exposure.

White or black backgrounds
Neutral colors such as white and black give your shots a clean appearance, and tend to concentrate all the viewer's attention on the subject. These are perfect for many studio shots, where you don't want bright or saturated colors to influence the appearance of your images.

Blue or green
These colors are naturally recessive, so make excellent backgrounds for yellow or red subjects. They are also colors that we are used to finding in the natural world, such as blue skies or green foliage, so they create more believable images than stronger colors.

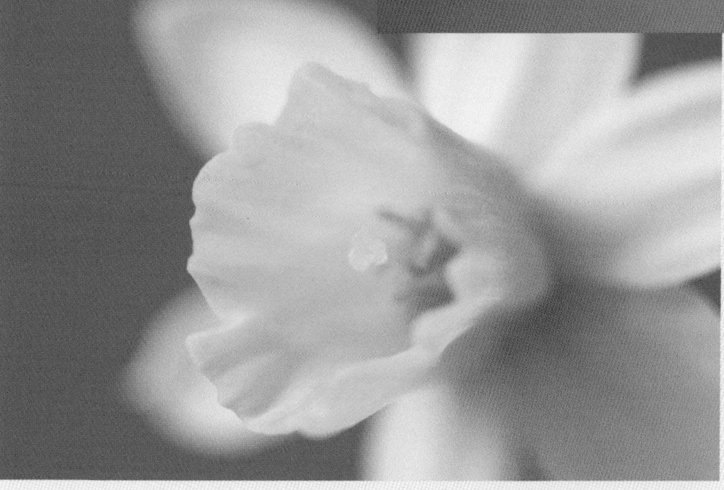

ABOVE
Recessive colors such as blue and green make excellent backgrounds for many natural subjects, especially brightly colored ones such as this yellow flower.

RIGHT
Strong background colors can be used to produce striking images. Because these colors tend to dominate you need to ensure that your main subject is strong in the frame to keep the viewer's attention.

Reds and yellows
Bright, vibrant colors tend to grab more of our attention than recessive ones, so they need to be used with care as background colors. For portraits in particular they can produce very energetic-feeling shots. Try to avoid other strong colors in the shot, or there will be too many elements vying for attention.

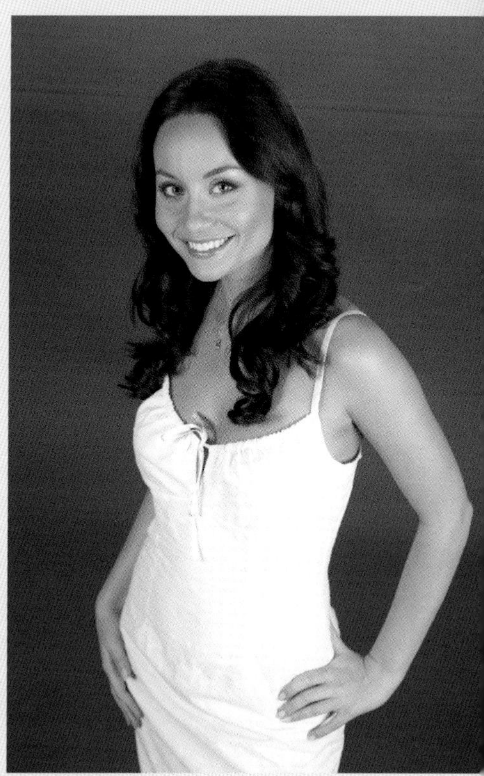

The popularity of internet sales sites such as eBay has meant that many people now need to produce basic product shots to illustrate their items online. Your DSLR is the ideal tool for producing these images, although you'll need to reduce the resolution of images before uploading them to the internet. Most DSLRs produce images that are perfect for high-quality prints, but you only need low-resolution images for the internet.

Main shot

You will need one main shot of your product, so try to make this as informative, interesting, and useful as possible. The best shot for most objects is a front three-quarter image. This means that you can see the front and one side of the object. This view will give the most information possible in a single shot, while also giving a sense of the height and depth. When it comes to lighting, it's best to steer clear of dramatic side-lighting. Although this will produce a more eye-catching image, it will create strong shadows that may make people think there is a flaw or problem that you are trying to hide. Instead, use a soft, even light on the subject.

A cluttered view will not enhance the aesthetic appeal of the object. Use a simple, solid background color. A white sheet or piece of card is ideal for most subjects to make sure that it gets all of the viewer's attention.

BELOW
For the main shot, choose an angle that shows off the majority of the subject and keep the background simple and uncluttered.

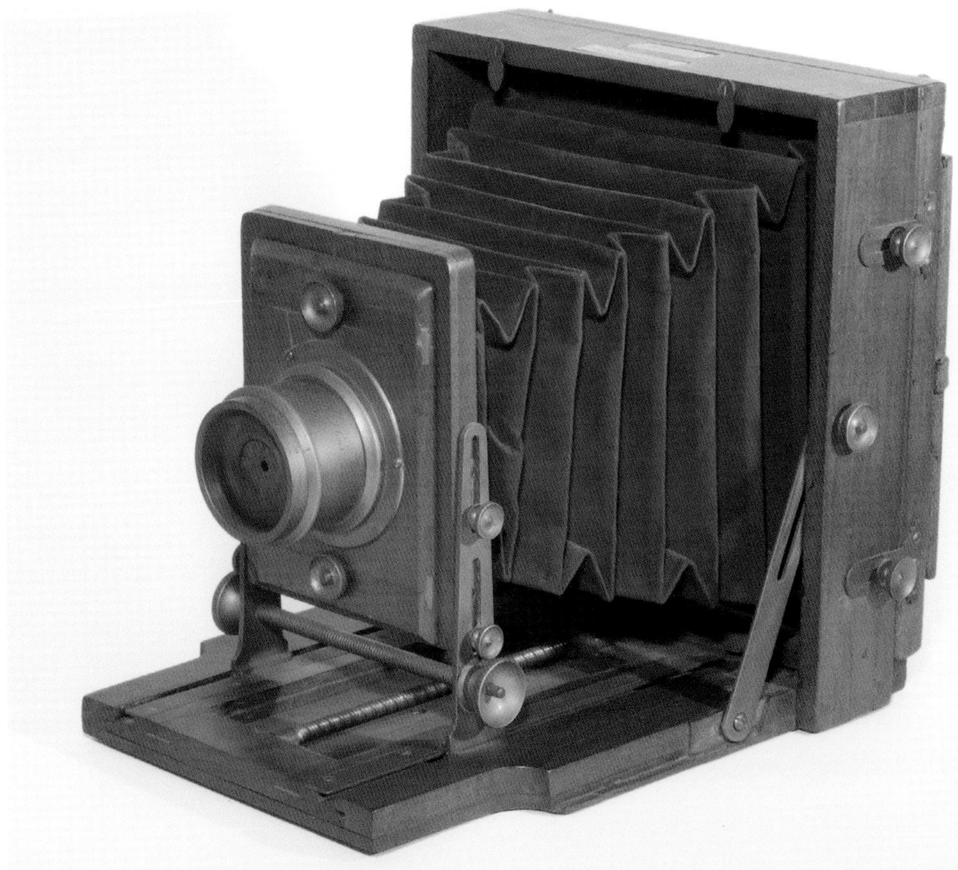

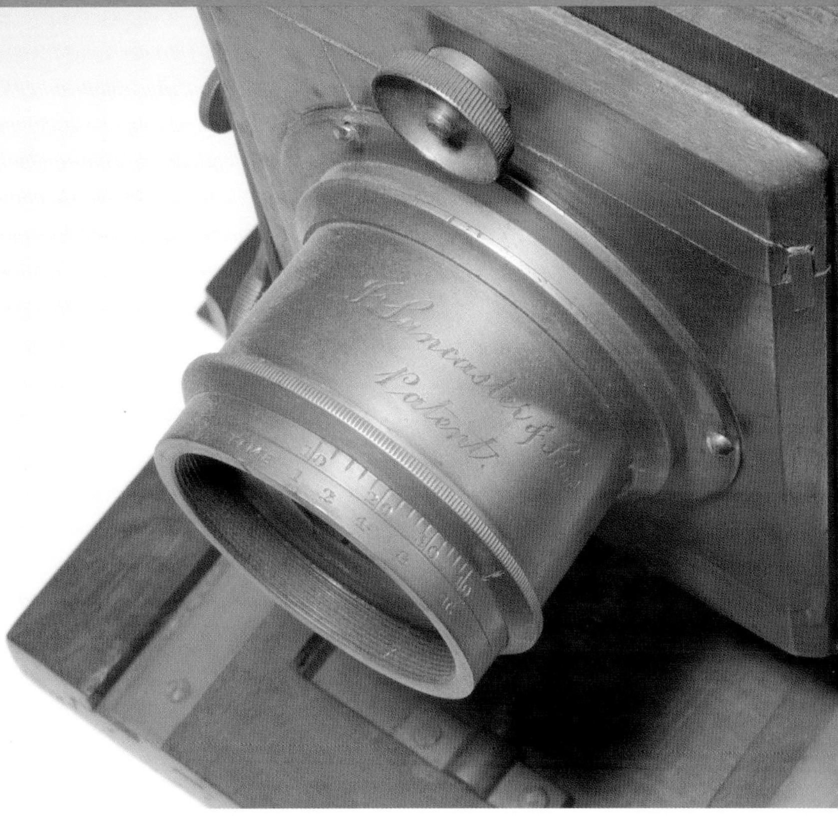

Other views
You can use straight-on views of the sides of the subject to show the condition and features. Again, keep the lighting soft and even to show the whole subject, and keep the background a simple white for clarity.

Detail shots
Here a macro lens can be ideal to get in close enough to show any important features or details of the object. However, because of the low-resolution needs of the internet, you can use the standard zoom on your DSLR and simply crop the image to achieve the close-ups you need.

Although it may be tempting to use jaunty angles and fancy lighting to liven up the images, simplicity and clarity are more important. Keep to straight, simple views and details to make sure that the buyer gets all the information that they need.

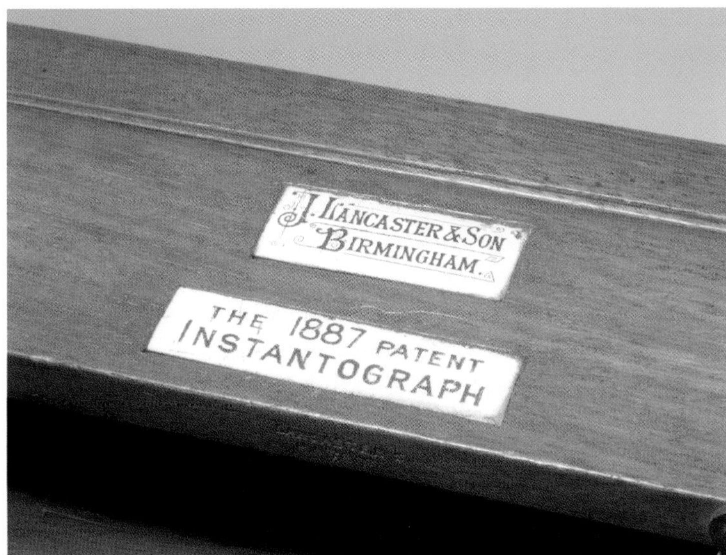

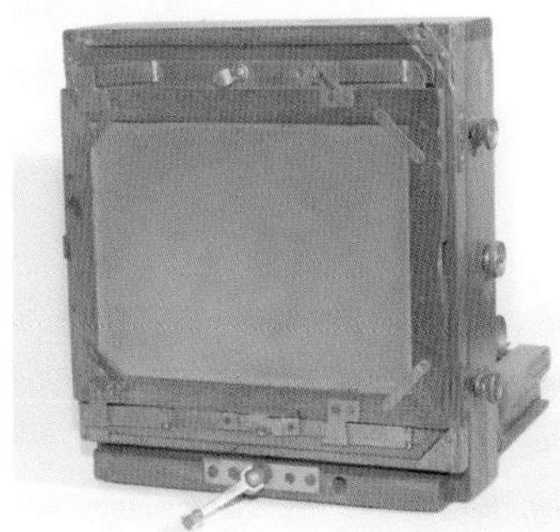

ABOVE AND LEFT
Don't shoot too many details, just show areas that are of particular interest, such as makers' marks or features.

Magazines, books, and brochures are great sources of freelance income for photographers. It is essential to research the potential markets, look at the sort of images that they are currently using, and ensure that your shots are technically first-rate. What your composition can do is ensure that your shots stand out from the crowd in this competitive market.

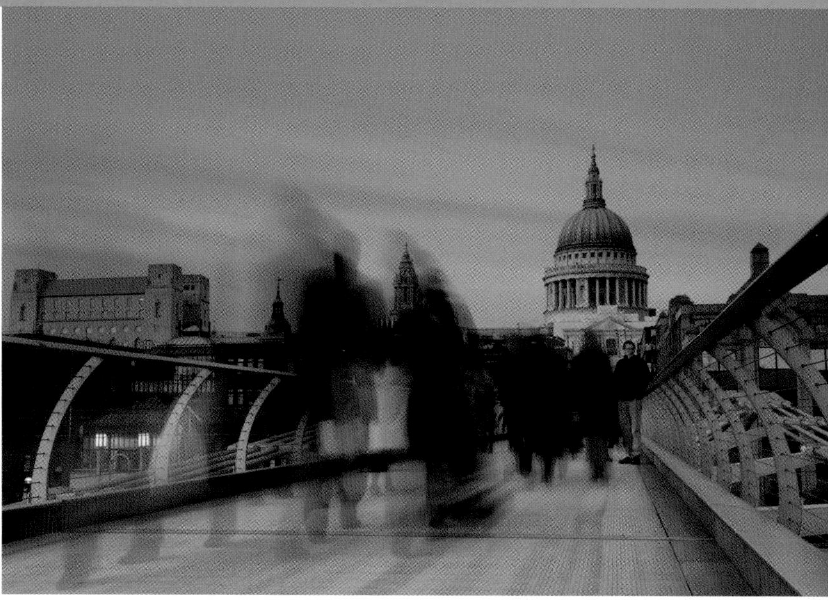

Go for impact
Picture editors and designers see thousands of images, so yours need to be memorable. Using the compositional tools that you've learned can give your images a head start. Simple techniques such as strong lead-in lines or adding foreground interest can help your images get noticed. For design or lifestyle-led publications, try breaking the rules to make an impact by using unusual angles or viewpoints.

Leave space for words
Because of limitations of space and layout, particularly in magazines, many images you see will have headlines, captions, or blocks of text on top of them. To many photographers this is almost akin to sacrilege, covering up beautiful images with words! But if you want to succeed in this market you need to be more realistic and start composing your images with this in mind. Leave clear spaces around the subject to allow the designers to fit the image to their layout. If they don't need the space, they can always crop into the image. This is especially important when it comes to covers. Take a look at most magazine covers and you'll find the picture is obscured by the logo of the magazine, text, and graphics. The choice of cover isn't always just down to the best image; often it's the one that works best with the words and graphics that need to be used.

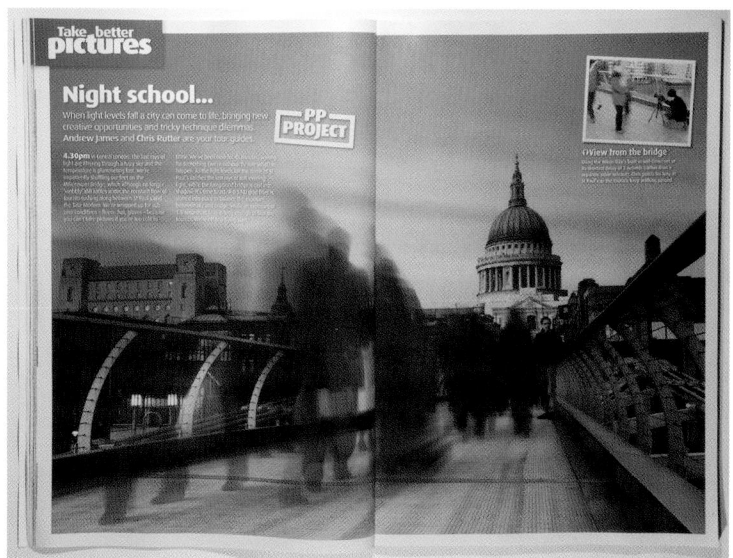
Take better pictures

Night school...

When light levels fall a city can come to life, bringing new creative opportunities and tricky technique dilemmas. Andrew James and Chris Rutter are your tour guides.

PP PROJECT

View from the bridge

ABOVE
This image, which I shot for *Practical Photography*, shows how essential it is to leave room for text on images used for magazines and books. If you are commissioned to shoot images, you should discuss specific requirements with the designer or art director.

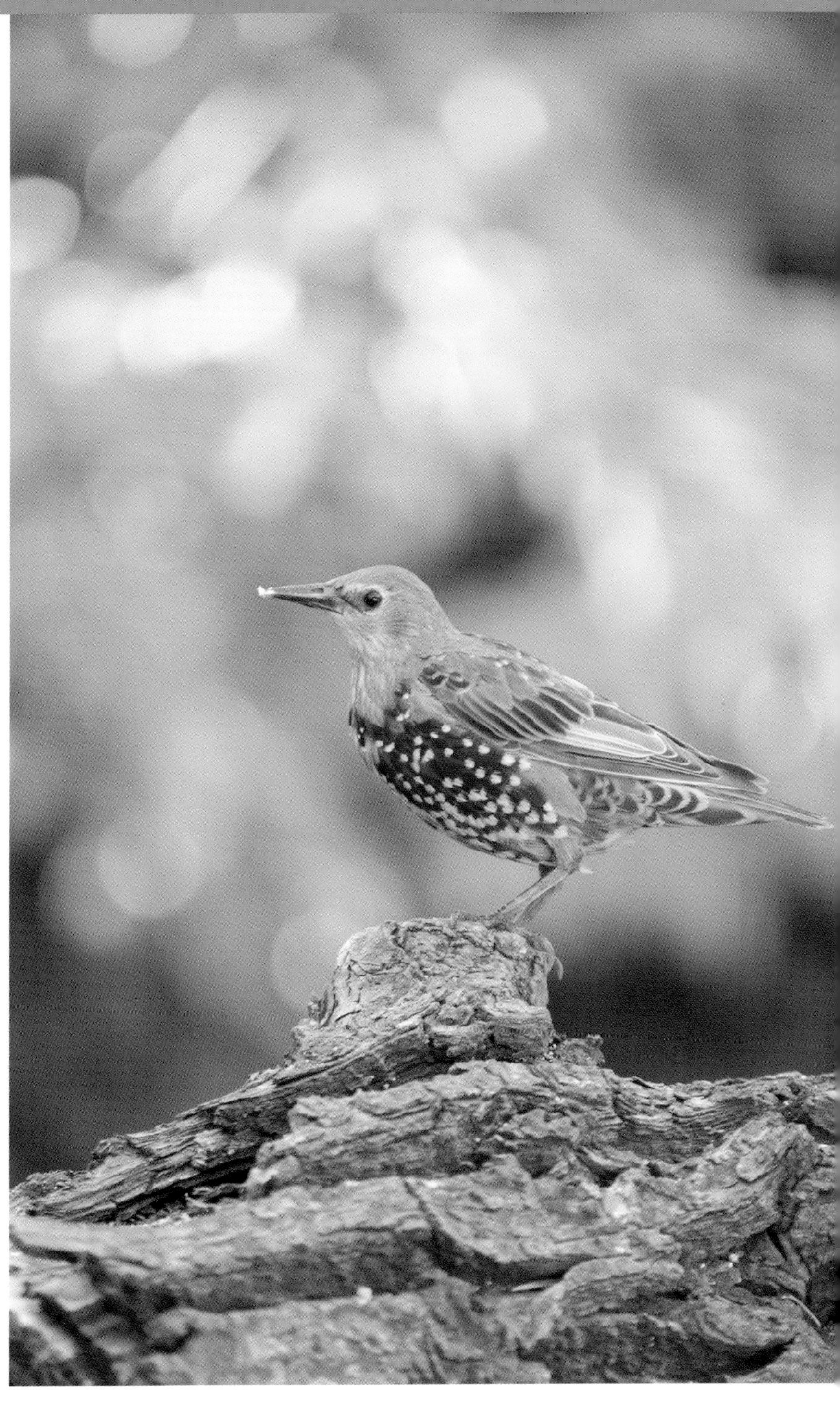

RIGHT
Even for images not specifically shot for editorial use, it's worth leaving space if you are submitting them to magazines.

Think about the page layout
Look at this book: if we were to put a picture across more than one page, part of the image disappears into the crease between the pages (known as the gutter). Good designers always try to ensure that the area of the picture that's going to be in the gutter is as plain as possible, with no objects that draw the eye. Try to keep this in mind when composing your shot, and keep a plain or clear area in the middle of the shot to allow it to go evenly across the two pages. Alternatively, leave a clearer area on one side of the image. This works especially well when you place an image on the left or right third of the frame, leaving the opposite third as clear as possible.

Don't submit any images that don't make the grade
Only send your very best images; most publishers would rather see 10 stunning images than 50 average ones. Also, check the publisher's resolution needs. Most use 300dpi as their standard, so the images from a six megapixel DSLR can be used at just under a full page of most magazines, while at least 12 megapixels are needed to cover a double-page spread.

Finally, don't be disheartened
It's common for pictures to be rejected for all manner of reasons, so don't be put off if your pictures are sent back. Take notice of any reasons that were given, and learn from them.

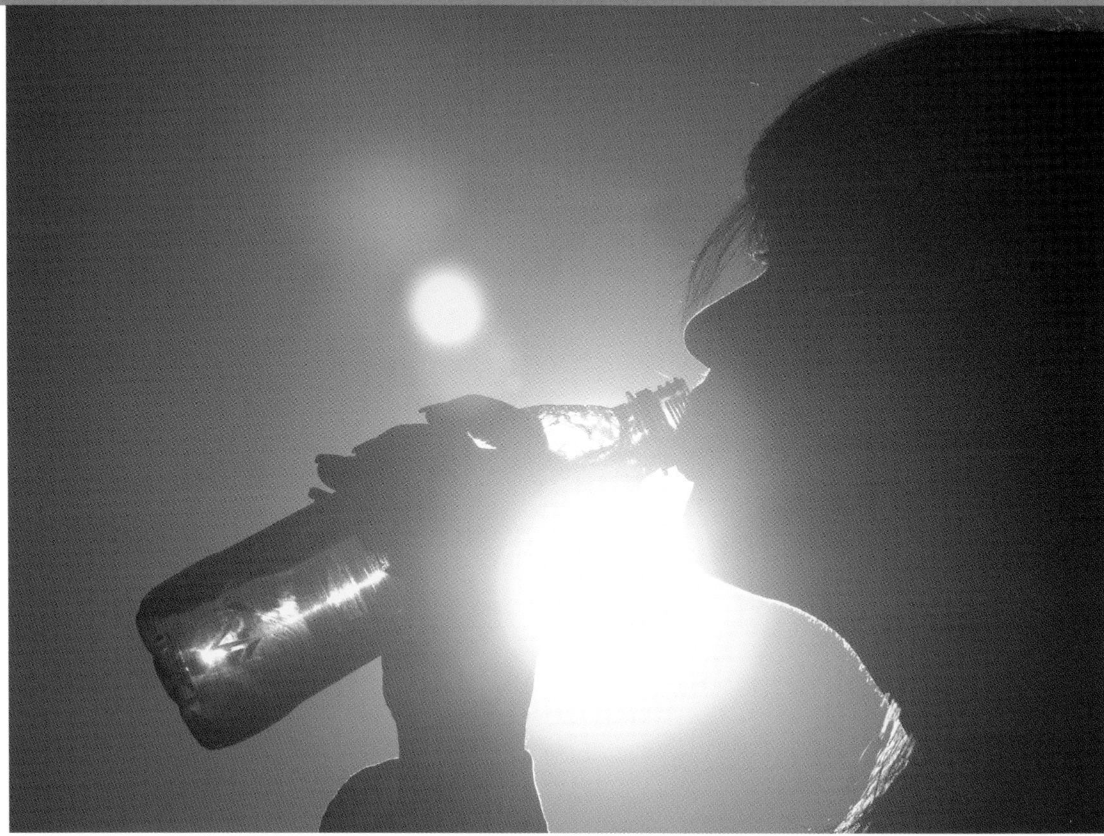

What is stock photography?
Stock photography is essentially any photography that is not shot for a specific market or client. These images are then sold either by the photographer or by a picture library. Picture libraries hold a supply of images from a number of photographers, which are then marketed and sold on their behalf. Obviously, the library will take a percentage of the proceeds from any sale, but the benefit for the photographer is gaining access to markets and resources that would be impossible to reach as an individual.

ABOVE
Simple, strong compositions will give your images a better chance of catching the eye of potential buyers.

DSLRs and the internet have revolutionized stock photography. The ability to store, view, and deliver images at relatively low cost and from anywhere in the world has opened up the market for photographers. But this has also increased the competition. As well as the traditional stock libraries, anyone can set up a website to showcase, publicize, and sell images. There are even several sources of free images to compete with, so you need to ensure that your shots stand out in this crowded market. The quality of your images is vital. While the six or eight megapixel resolutions of many DSLRs are perfect for your own requirements, many stock libraries demand that the shots should be taken on specific DSLR models. As long as your images make the grade, strong composition is one of the best ways you have of producing images that grab people's attention.

Keep the image simple
Simple, uncluttered compositions tend to have more impact and make the subject easier to see. Try to isolate your subject by using clear areas and narrow depth of field to make them stand out. Because of the high-resolution demands in this market, you need to get these compositions right in the viewfinder of your DSLR. Many libraries will not accept images that have been cropped, even if you use the highest-resolution DSLR.

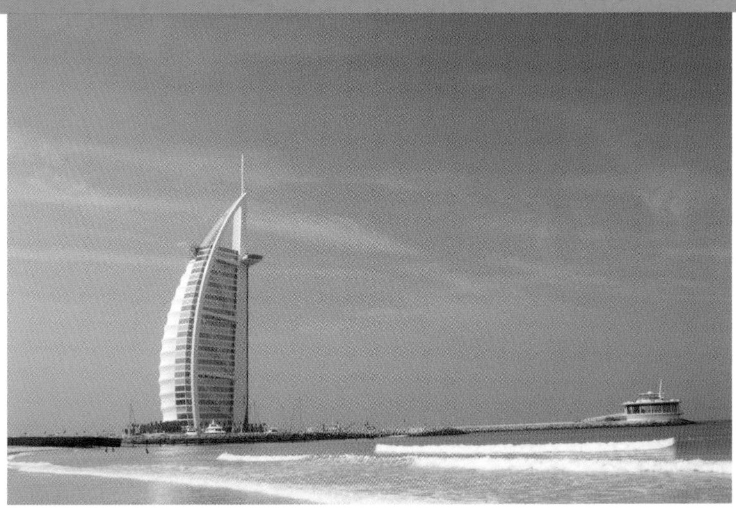

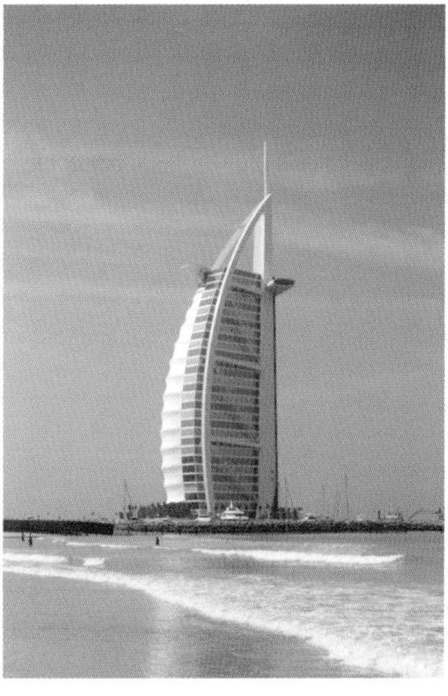

LEFT AND ABOVE
Whenever possible, shoot in both upright and horizontal formats. When shooting for stock you can never be sure in which shape the image will be used, so shooting both will double the chances of the image being used.

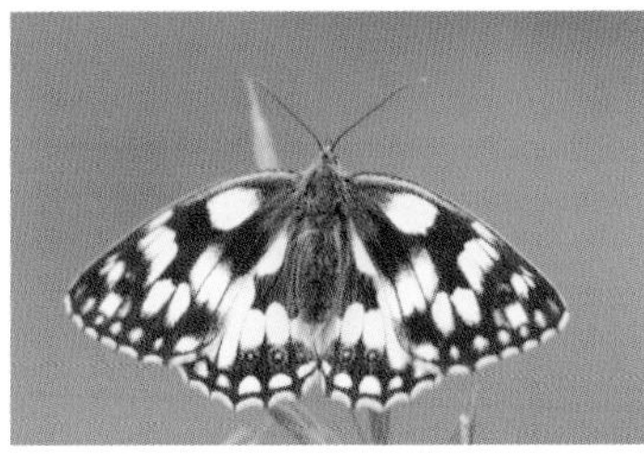

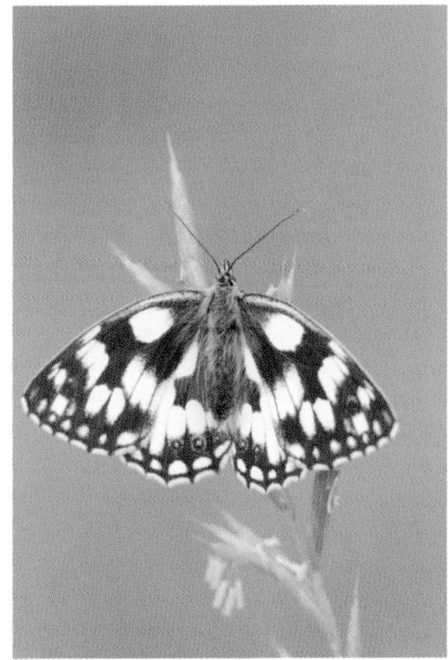

BELOW
Shooting from an unconventional angle can help your stock images to stand out.

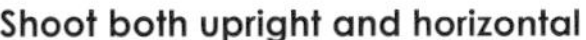

Shoot both upright and horizontal

Because you can't know how your images are going to be used, you should try to shoot the subject in both horizontal and vertical formats. This means that you will maximize the possible uses for your image in every market, as the buyer may want an image in a particular format to fit their design or layout. This can prove difficult as some subjects naturally tend to lend themselves to a particular format, such as a horizontal for landscapes. Try to use simple, clear areas such as a deep blue sky, or strong foreground interest to help balance the composition in a vertical format.

Try unusual angles

It's likely that there will be hundreds of similar images of many subjects available from various picture libraries and photographers. To make your shot stand out, look for unusual and dramatic angles to shoot from. For even more impact, use lenses that you wouldn't normally shoot a particular subject with to further differentiate your shots from others of similar subjects. These unusual viewpoints won't appeal to all buyers, so shoot them only in addition to the conventional views.

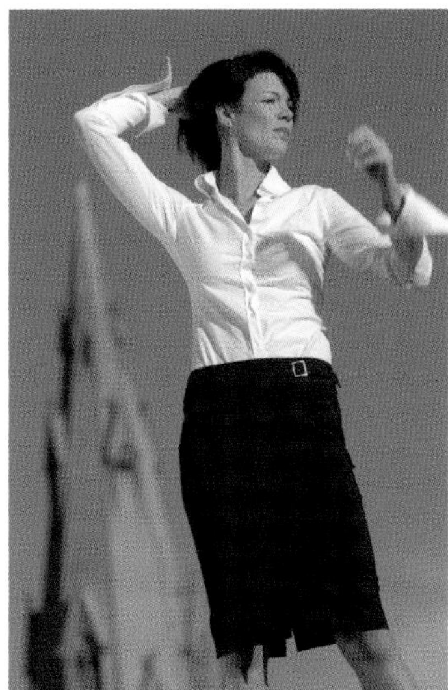

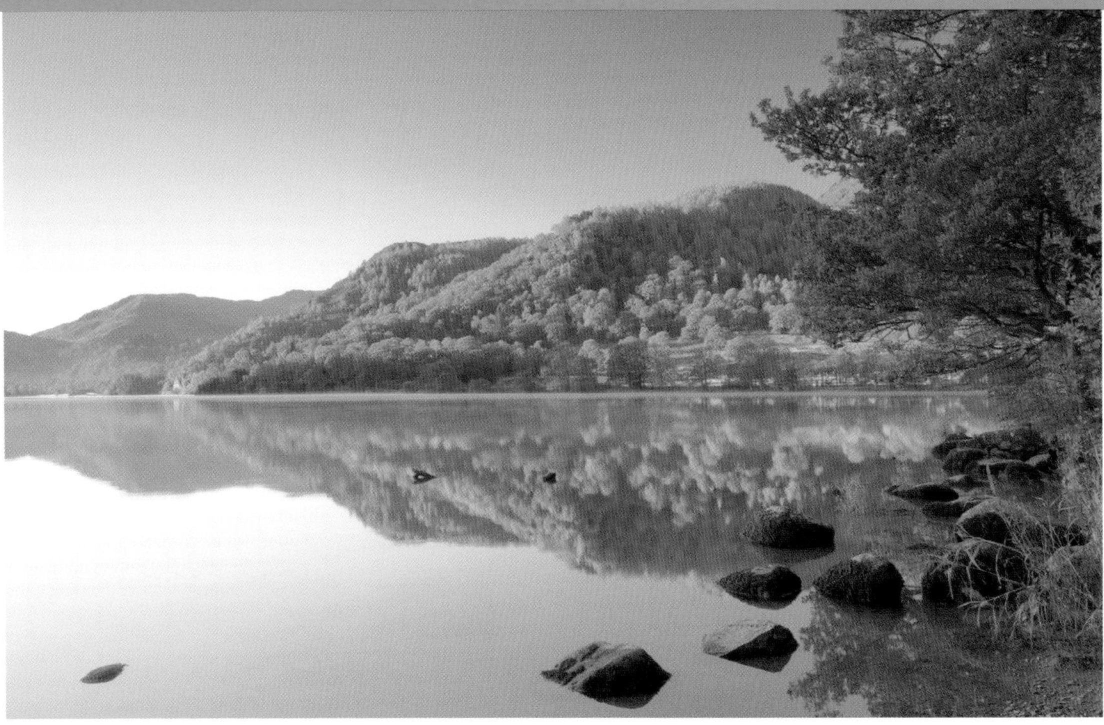

Use strong colors

Vivid and vibrant colors stand out more than subtle tones, so if you shoot a brightly colored subject make the most of it. The post-capture processing of your DSLR images makes it possible to add to this saturation, but use this facility with care as many libraries don't accept highly processed images.

Lead-in lines and foreground interest

Strong lead-in lines and foreground interest add a sense of depth to your shots. Objects in the foreground can also increase the potential uses of your shots. For example, if you shoot a picture of a harbor, try including boats or fishermen so that your shot can be used to illustrate other points.

ABOVE
Classic composition techniques, such as adding foreground interest, can help you to produce striking and saleable images.

BELOW
Shot at the same location as the main landscape, these images show how you can maximize the number of photos you get from a single location by looking for details that make strong subjects on their own.

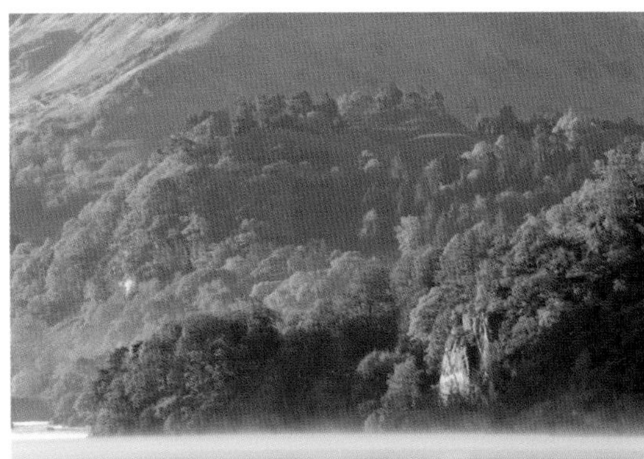

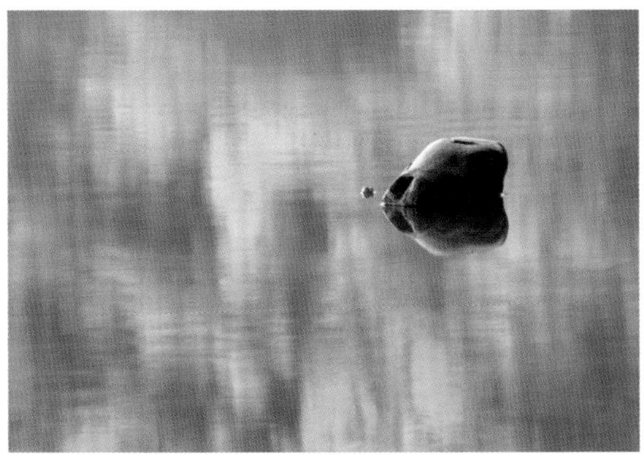

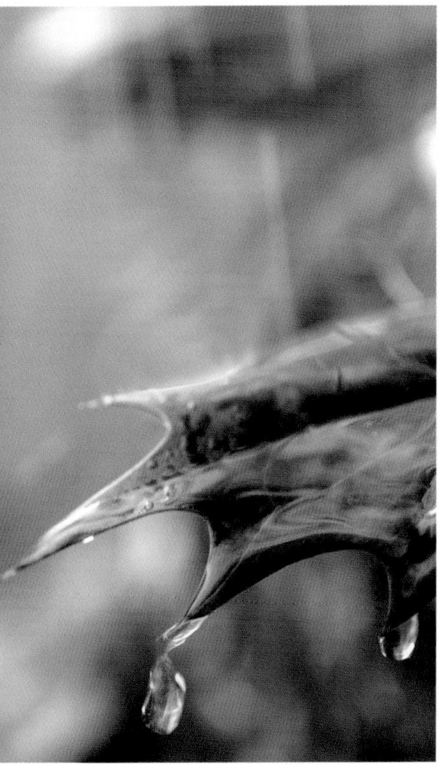

LEFT AND RIGHT
Using depth of field and shutter speeds creatively will make your shots stand out. For this shot on the left, I used a wide f/2.8 aperture to isolate the leaf from the background, and a shutter speed of 1/100th sec to freeze the movement of the water droplet while the rain behind was recorded as streaks of light. For the shot on the right, using a three second exposure highlights the swirls of the pool to add interest to the foreground.

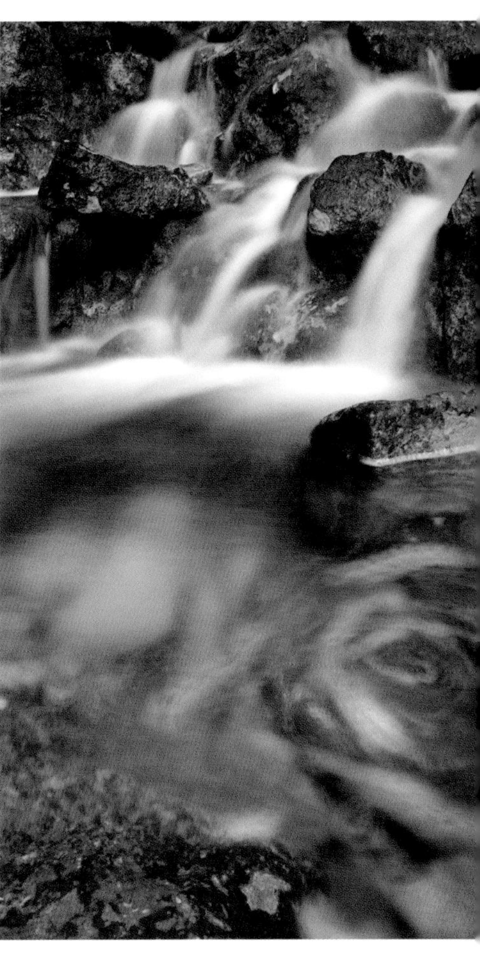

SUBMITTING YOUR IMAGES

Before you submit your images to stock libraries, you need to make sure that they are technically excellent, and that they conform to the requirements of the library. Check the submission guidelines for various libraries to see if your images are suitable. For example, Getty Images, one of the largest suppliers of stock images, requires uncompressed TIFFs at no less than 47.5 Mb.

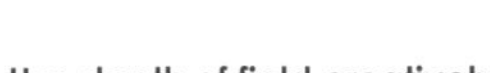

Use depth of field creatively
Both narrow and extensive depth of field can be used to ensure that all the important areas of your shot are sharp. If the background is as important as the main subject, use a small aperture and a wide-angle lens to keep the whole scene in focus. However, if you want all of the viewer's attention to be on a single point, blur the background by using a wide aperture and a longer focal length lens to minimize the depth of field.

Use shutter speeds creatively
The facilities available on your DSLR are ideal for adding a sense of movement to your subject. Using slow shutter speeds to blur parts of the image can be more dramatic than a sharp, clinical approach. Techniques such as panning and slow-sync flash keep the subject sharp and blur the background, and a strong, simple composition will give maximum impact. You can also use these blurred areas to ensure there is space for text to be added over the image.

Section 11

Software Techniques

SIMPLE CROPPING

While the ability to adjust, fine-tune, and manipulate your images using software should not be relied on as a substitute for getting your pictures right in-camera, it does offer the digital photographer an amazing level of control over their compositions. What software cannot do is make a great image out of a poor shot, so it doesn't take any of the skill away from the photographer. Rather, many of the tools available in image-editing software offer a simpler and more accessible way of getting your compositions just right.

In this section we'll look at how you can use these techniques to help you achieve compositions that are either impossible or extremely difficult to achieve in-camera.

Crop tool

The first—and most useful—technique for adjusting the composition of your images is using the Crop tool. This cannot rescue poorly composed images, but it can help you to make a good picture even better. It also gives you the opportunity to change the proportions of the picture, as not every image fits the 3:2 or 4:3 aspect ratio that your camera will produce.

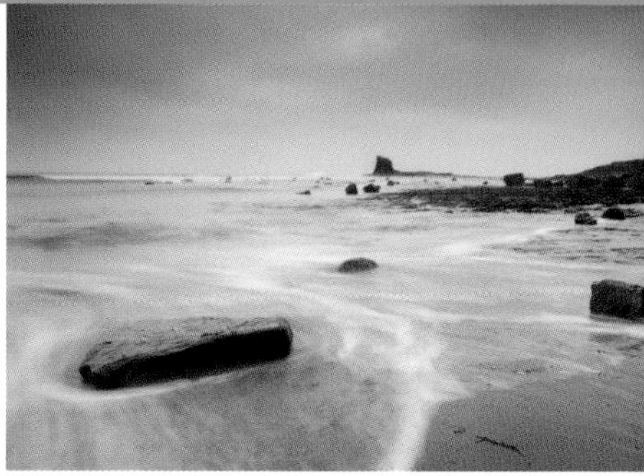

ABOVE
Although it's best to get your framing right in-camera, shooting digitally allows you to fine-tune your compositions very quickly and easily.

BELOW
Cropping this image has tightened up the composition for a much more effective result.

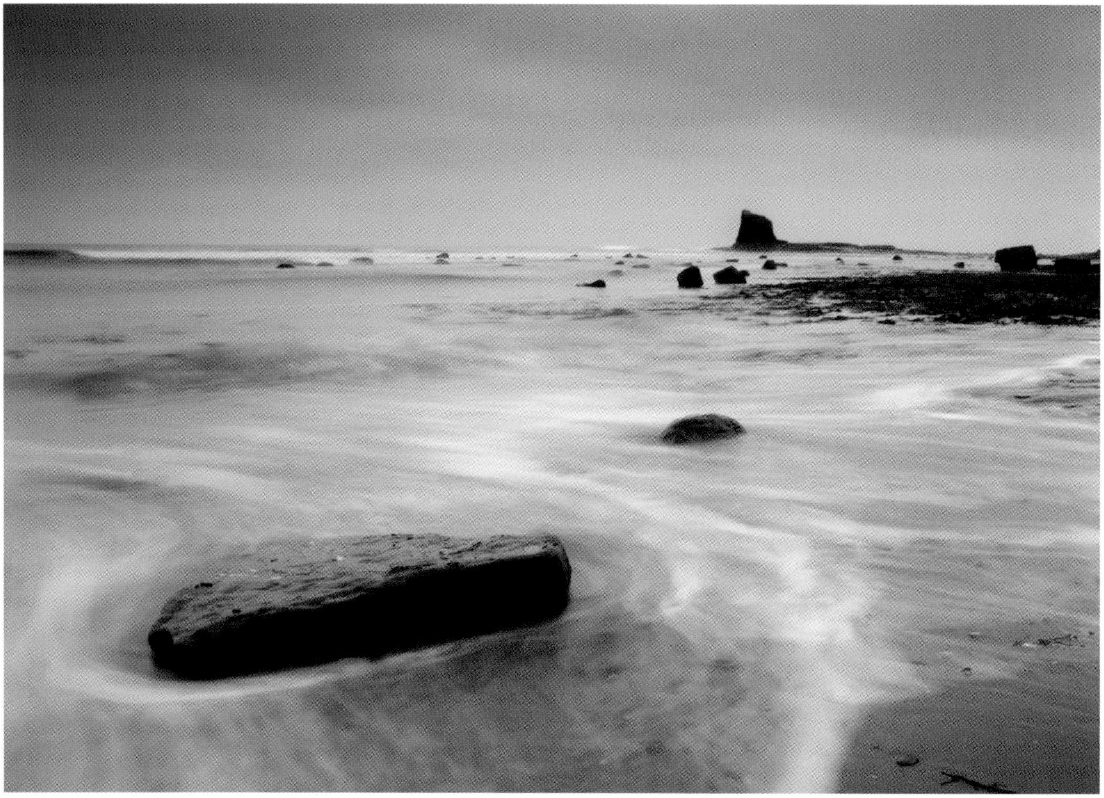

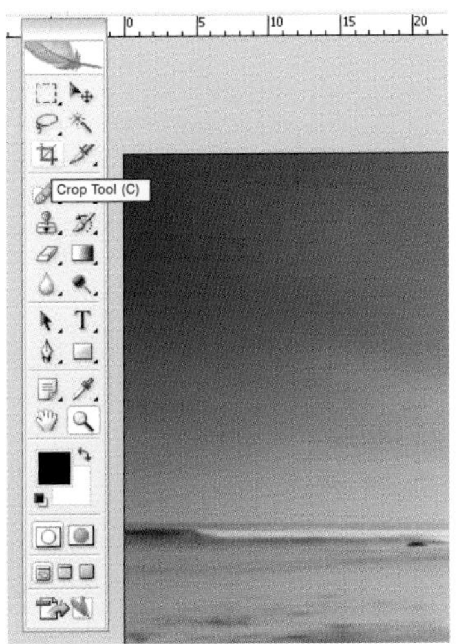

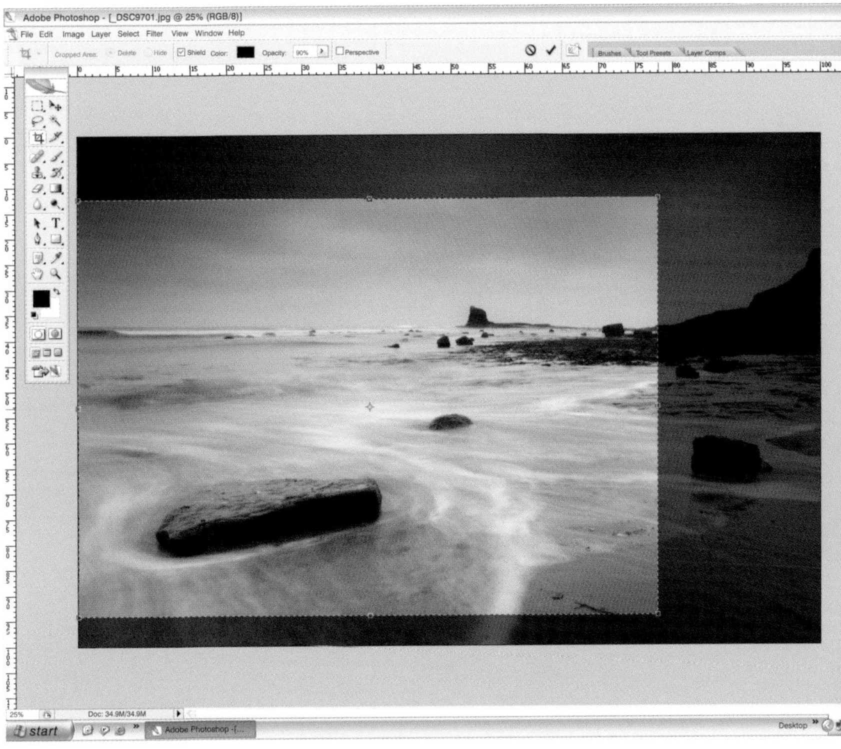

Simple cropping

Step 1
With your image open in Photoshop, select the Crop tool from the tool palette. Using this tool is simple: just place the cursor over the image and then left-click and drag the cursor across it to make the crop area appear on your image. Don't worry too much about the actual crop at this stage, as you can adjust this later.

Step 2
Once you have the crop area visible, you can fine-tune the actual area by dragging the middle tabs on each side of the crop markers until you achieve the composition that you want. Once you are happy with the framing, perform the crop by clicking on the tick button on the top tool bar, or by pressing return on the keyboard.

Crop tool settings
You'll notice that the area outside of the crop selection is darker than the rest of the image. This is known as the shield color and can be adjusted using the settings on the top tool bar once you have a crop area visible on your image.

This shield color can be set to anything from completely clear to pure black, but I use a setting of 95 percent gray. This allows you to just see the image behind the shield, but still makes the crop area obvious on-screen. Adjust the setting to find a color that you feel most comfortable with.

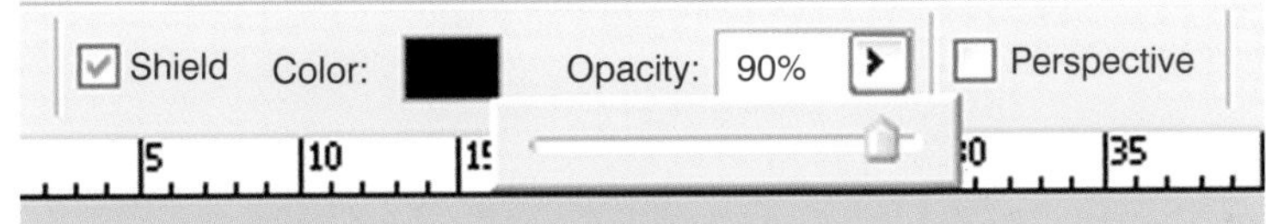

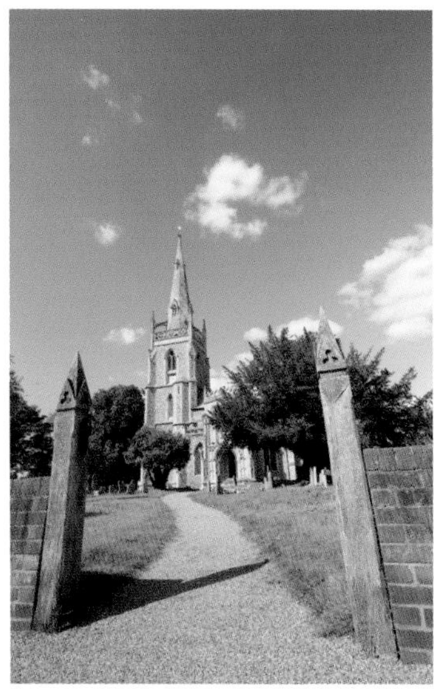

Photoshop CS2 allows you to make adjustments that would take hours in the traditional darkroom or would need specialized equipment to achieve in-camera. One of the most useful is the ability to correct the problem of converging vertical lines when the camera is angled up to include the whole of a tall building by using a combination of the perspective control and Crop tool. This correction can be achieved in-camera using a perspective control (or shift) lens, but these are too expensive for many photographers to consider.

ABOVE
Tilting the camera causes perspective distortion in images.

RIGHT
The perspective controls available with the Crop tool can correct these distortions on-screen.

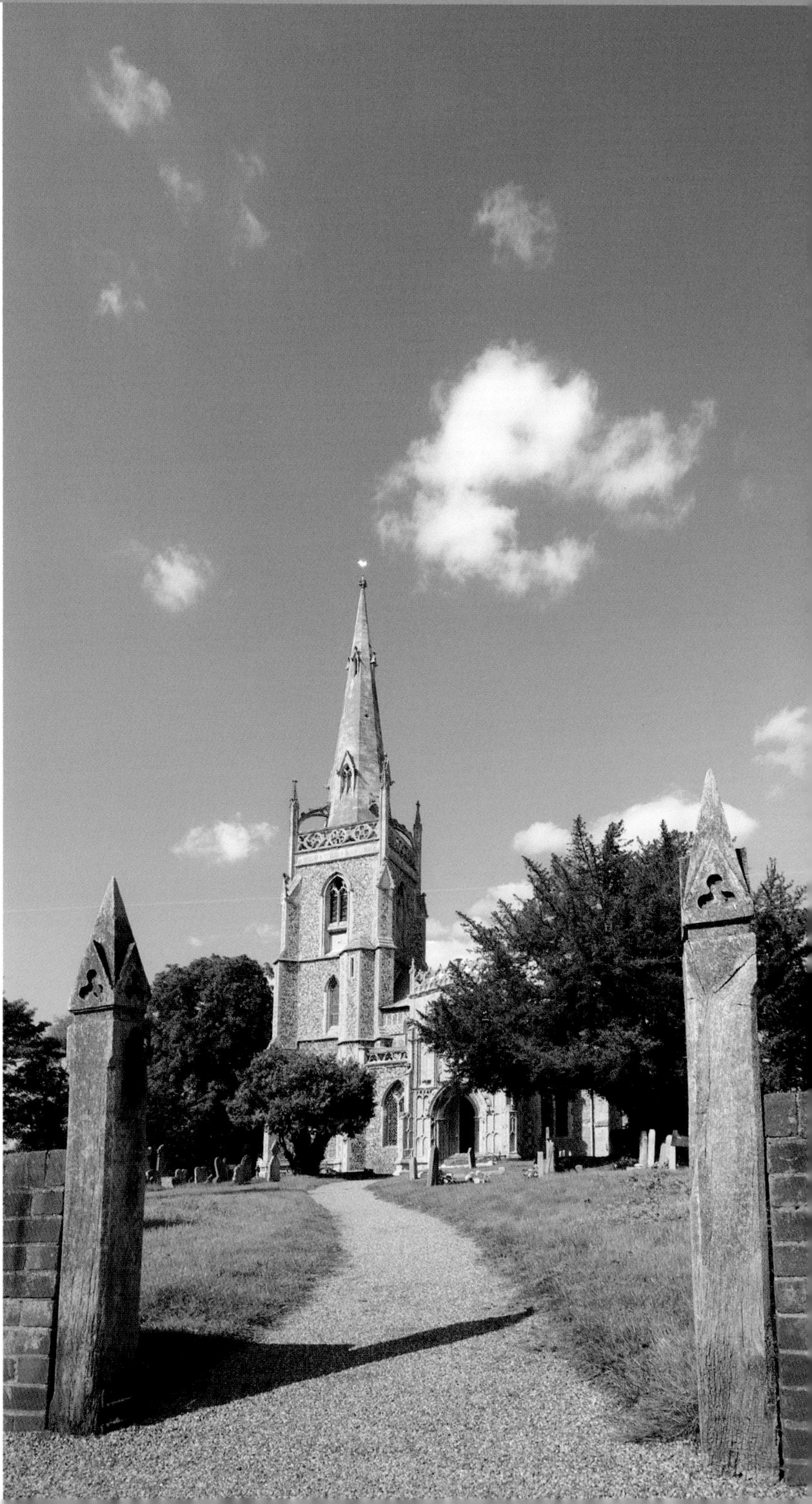

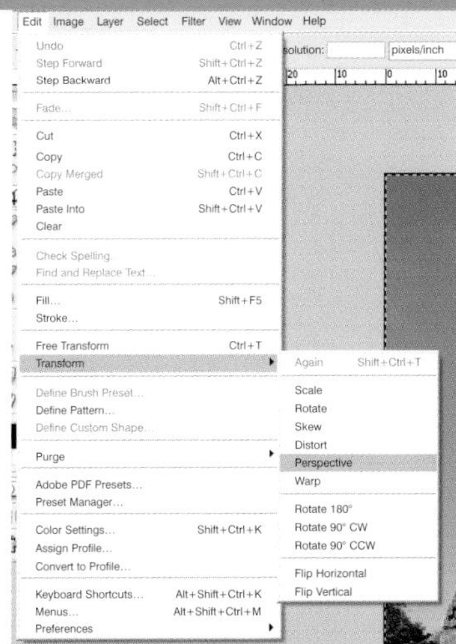

Correcting converging verticals

Step 1

Before you can start to make your corrections, select the whole image by going to Select>All (or pressing Ctrl+A). With the whole image selected you then go to Edit>Transform>Perspective, which will bring up a frame around the image with small tabs at each corner and in the middle of each side.

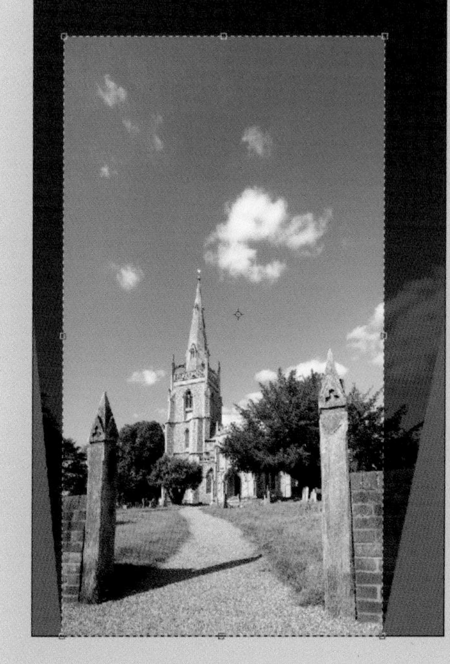

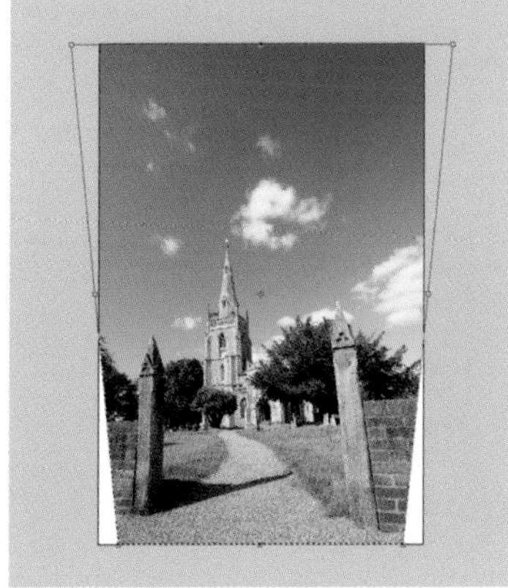

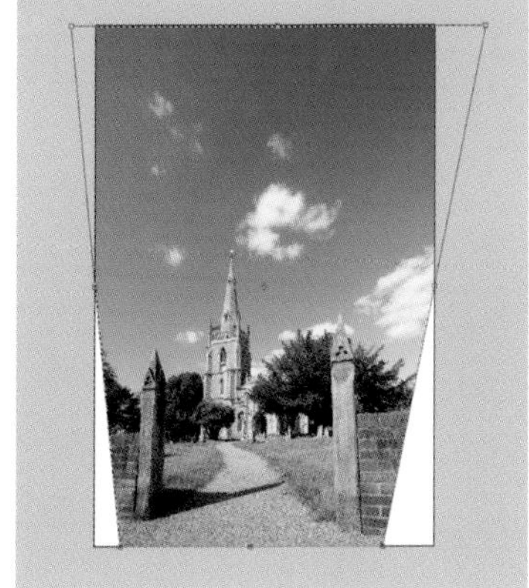

Step 2

To correct the converging vertical you need to use the tabs both at the bottom and the top of the image. Click and drag either of the top corner tabs until the distortion is around half corrected, then drag either of the bottom corner tabs until the vertical lines in the image are all perpendicular to each other. If you are lucky they will now be vertical, but as with this image, they may still be slanted to the left or right.

Step 3

To correct this slant, use the tabs at either the center of the top or bottom of the image. Drag one of these until the slanted lines become vertical. Before you confirm the transformation, check that the tabs on the center of the left and right sides of the image are positioned approximately on the edge of the original image. If not, repeat the previous steps until both the vertical lines are corrected and these tabs are aligned with the image, then press return to confirm the transformation.

Step 4

You'll notice that the image has some blank areas at the corners, so to finish the transformation, select the Crop tool. Then, using the technique described on the previous pages, simply crop out the unwanted blank areas. You may also want to use the Crop tool to restore the image to a more standard ratio as the proportions of the image can be distorted by the transformation.

As well as the more commonly used controls that adjust the overall saturation of colors, you can also target specific colors or areas of an image. This can help your composition because adjusting the color or tone of individual areas makes them appear more, or less, prominent in the frame. There are a number of ways to achieve this effect in your image-editing software, but this is the one that I've found to be the most useful and applicable to the majority of images. This allows you to increase the saturation and adjust the hue of your subject without affecting the rest of the image, but you could also use a similar technique to lower the saturation by using a negative value in the third step to make the subject less prominent in the image.

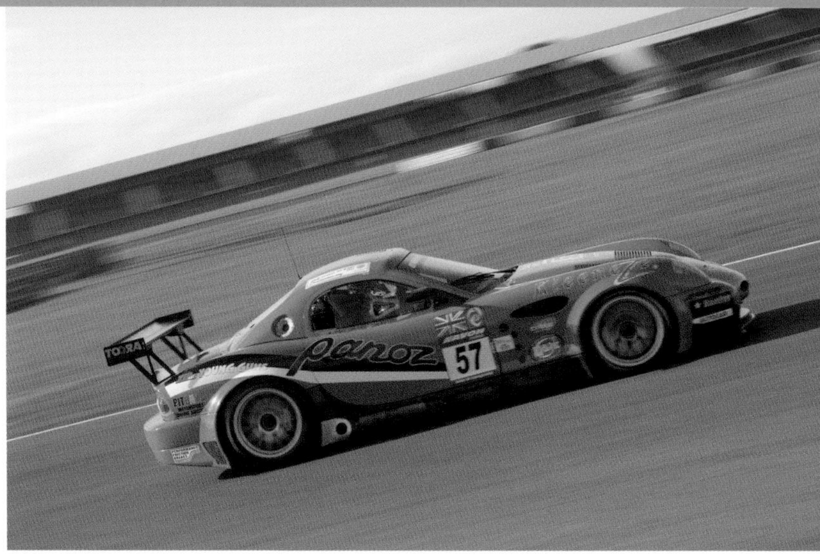

ABOVE
The saturation and hue of your subject affects how dominant it is in the frame.

You can adjust the individual colors to help to enhance the impact of your shots.

BELOW
Adjusting the color of the car makes it stand out more from the background.

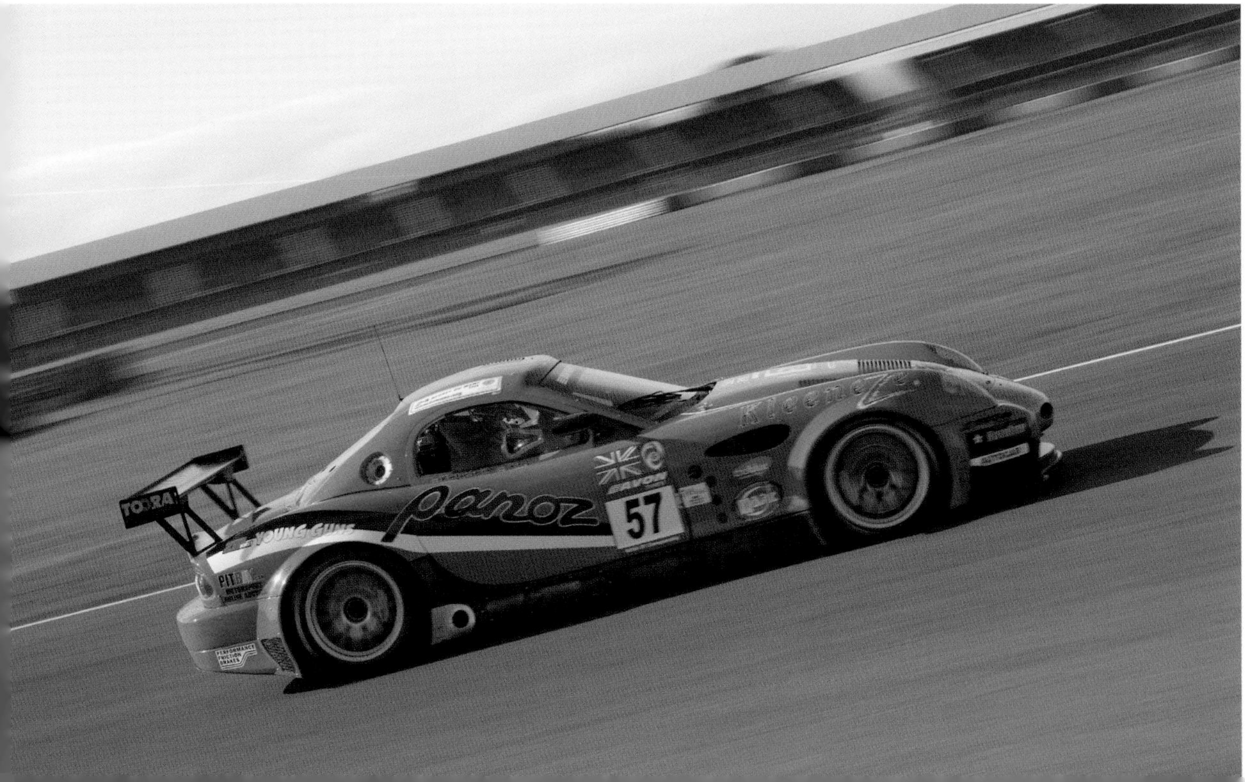

Correcting individual colors

Step 1

To ensure that you affect only the colors in the subject, you first need to select this area. The simplest way is to use the Lasso tool to loosely draw around the subject. You don't need to follow the outline precisely, but make sure that the selection doesn't include any areas of the color that you want to adjust. As long as there aren't any of these colors near the main subject, try to keep a gap between the selection and the outline of the subject so that the adjustments blend with the rest of the image.

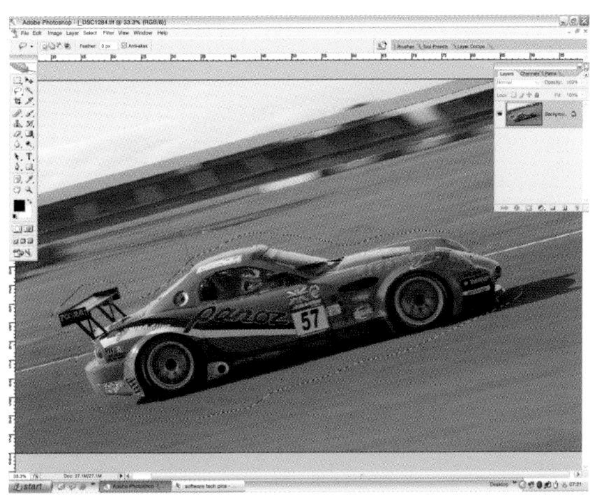

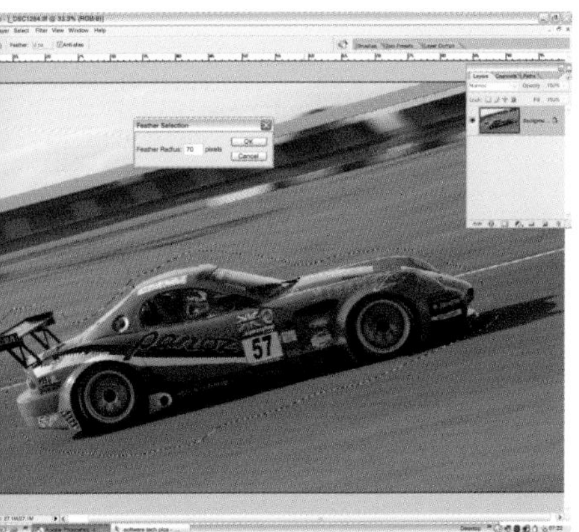

Step 2

To make sure that your adjustments blend smoothly with the rest of the image, use the Select>Feather Selection menu. In the dialog box, enter a value that is approximately the same as the distance between the outside of your selection and the object you want to adjust. In this case I used a value of 70 pixels to make the blending as smooth as possible. Once you've feathered the selection, it's safest to create a new layer from this selection by using Layer>New>Via Copy.

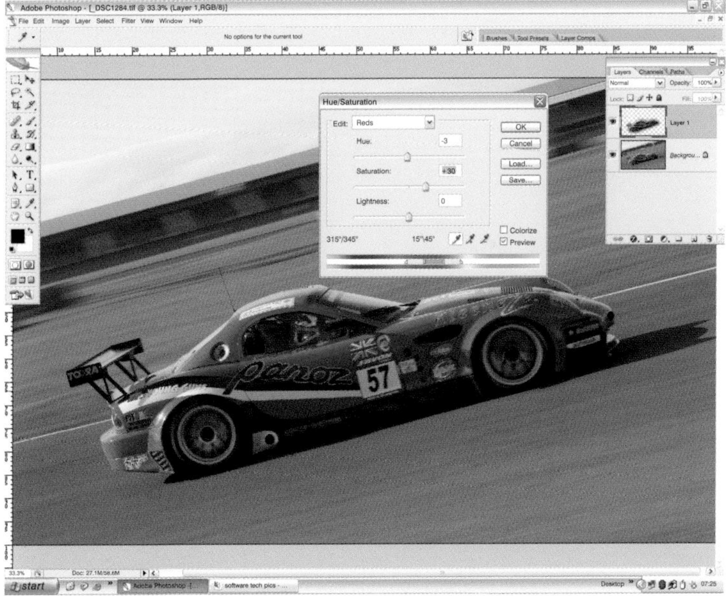

Step 3

To make your color adjustments, go to Image>Adjustments>Hue/Saturation. In the dialog box, use the drop-down menu to select the color that you want to adjust. In this case, I wanted to make the orange car stand out more against the background, so I selected red from the menu. With only this color selected, I entered values of -3 Hue and +30 Saturation. The Hue control allows you to change the color, and needs to be used carefully to avoid obvious color casts, so generally it's best to keep this between +/- 5.

Although many shots can be enhanced by adjusting the color and tone of the subject, this is not suitable for every image. As an alternative, you can achieve a similar effect by adjusting the tone or brightness of the background, rather than the main subject. By darkening the background, you immediately make the subject stand out more in the frame. This technique can also be used to minimize distracting elements in the background to make your composition simpler and more effective.

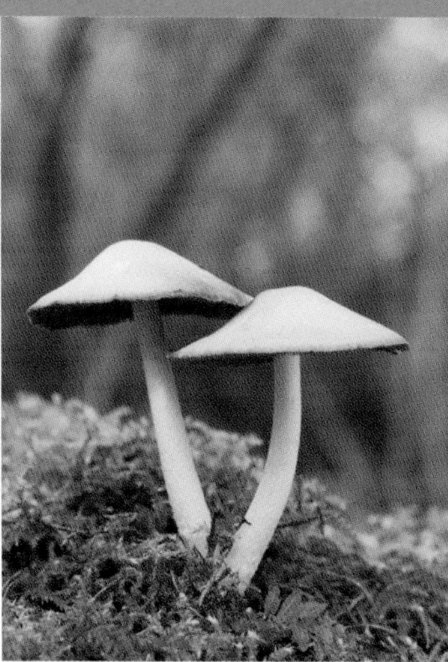

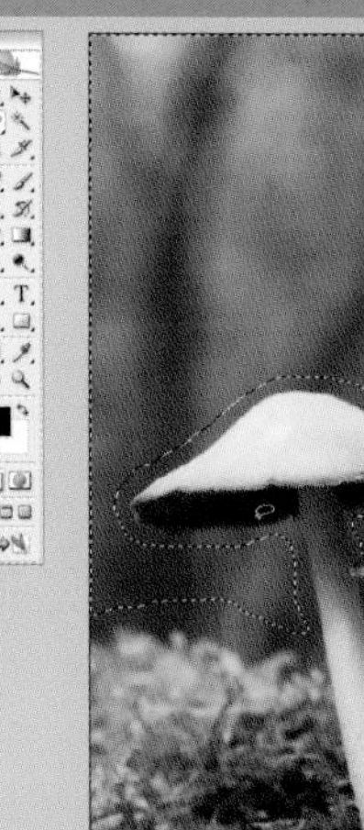

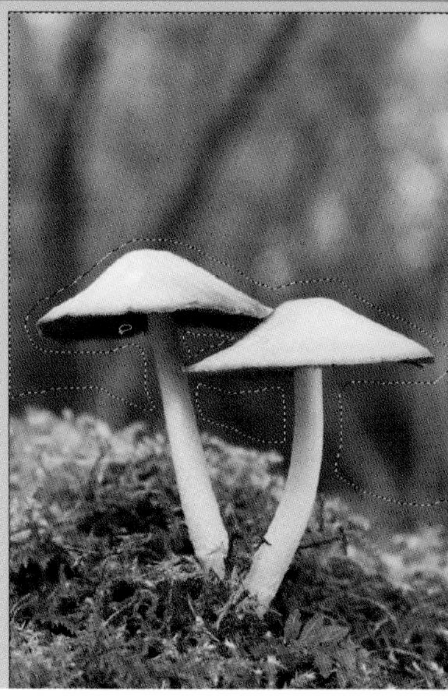

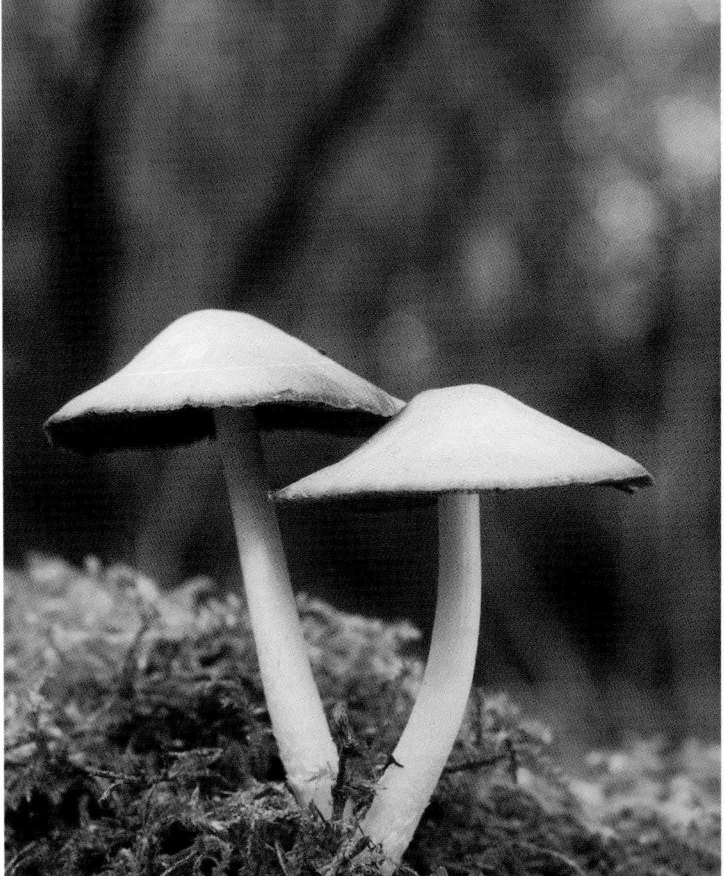

Darkening backgrounds

Step 1
To select the background of your image, you can use the rectangular Marquee tool for simple square or rectangular areas, but the most useful tool is the Lasso selection tool. This allows you to draw around quite complex shapes by simply clicking the mouse and dragging the cursor around the subject. You don't need to draw accurately, but try to keep a small distance between the edge of the subject and the selection, as above. You can also add to this by holding down the Ctrl key and drawing a new selection.

TOP LEFT
When you can't adjust the color of the subject to make it more prominent, darkening the background will give a similar result.

LEFT
This composition has been made stronger simply by reducing the brightness of the background to emphasize the main subject.

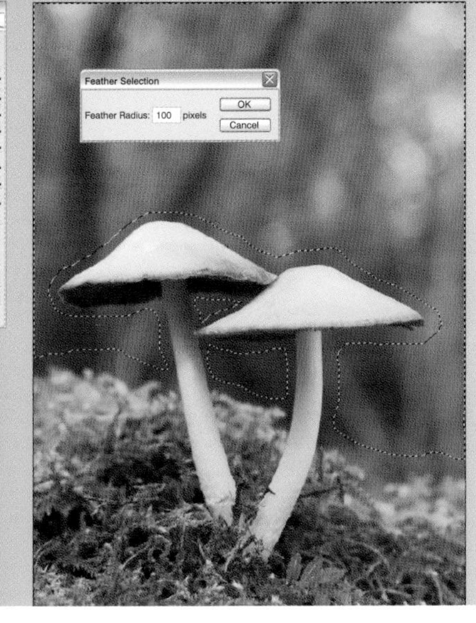

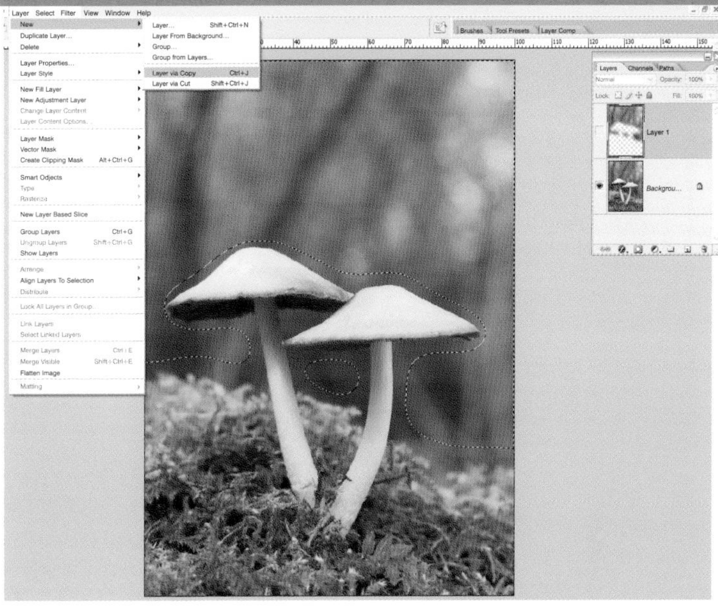

Step 2
Once you're happy with the selection, you need to "blur" the edges of the area to ensure that the changes that you make later blend smoothly with the other areas of the image. Go to the Select>Feather option and enter a Radius of around 100 pixels. This value depends on your image and selection: small selections need a smaller Radius and large selections can use a larger figure, but try to keep it between 70 and 150 pixels.

Step 3
To allow you to adjust the background but keep the original image intact so that you can fine-tune your adjustments, you need to create a new layer from this selection. Go to Layer>New>Layer via Copy, which will create a new layer containing only the areas of the image that you selected in the first two steps.

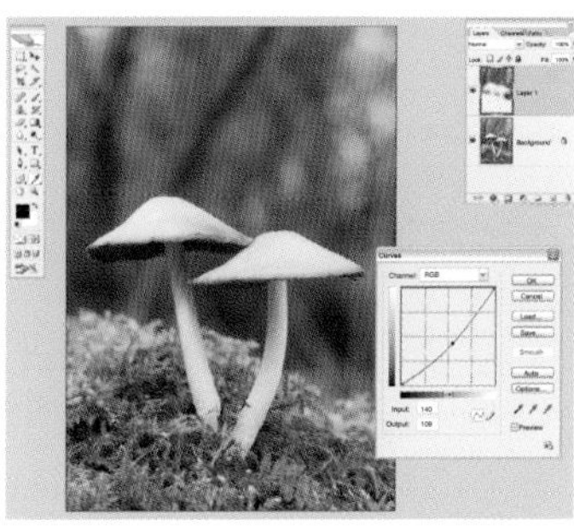

Step 4
To darken the background, ensure that you are working on the top layer containing only your selection by checking that it is highlighted in the Layers palette. Then go to Image> Adjustments>Curves, which will bring up the Curves dialog box. Click and drag the middle of the curve downward until you are happy with the result, although take care not to go too far. Then click OK to confirm the adjustment.

HALO EFFECTS

When you are using this technique, make sure that you don't try to darken the background too much. Otherwise, you'll get ugly and unnatural-looking "halo" effects around your subject, such as you can see in this image. As long as the image is still in separate layers, you can remedy this by reducing the layer opacity using the slider at the top of the Layers palette.

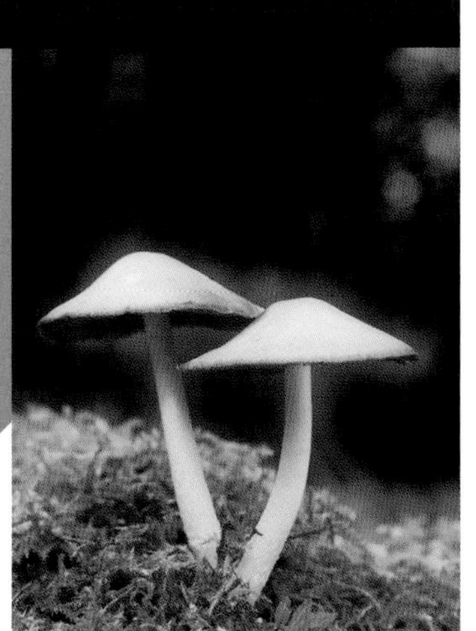

PANORAMIC STITCHER

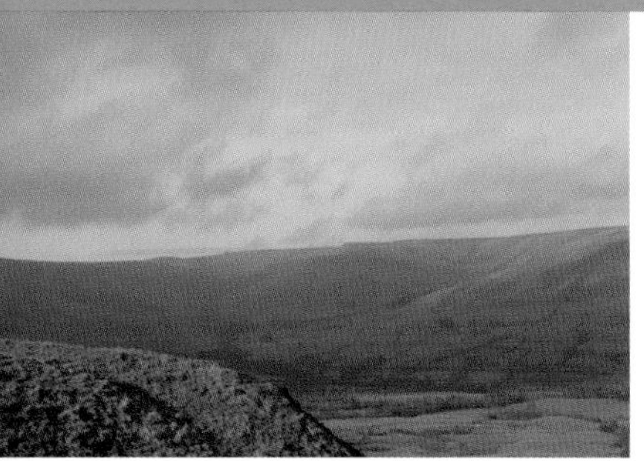

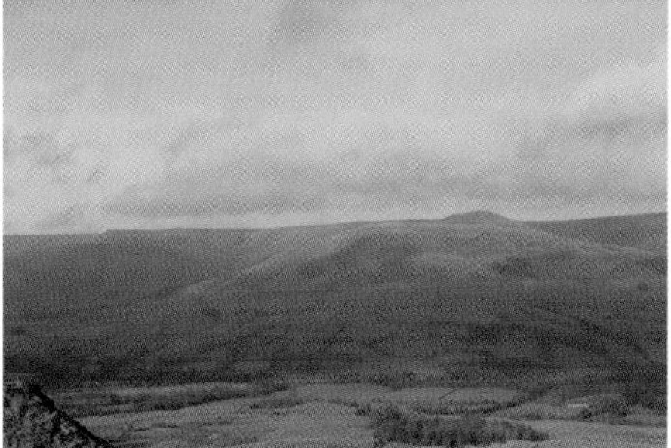

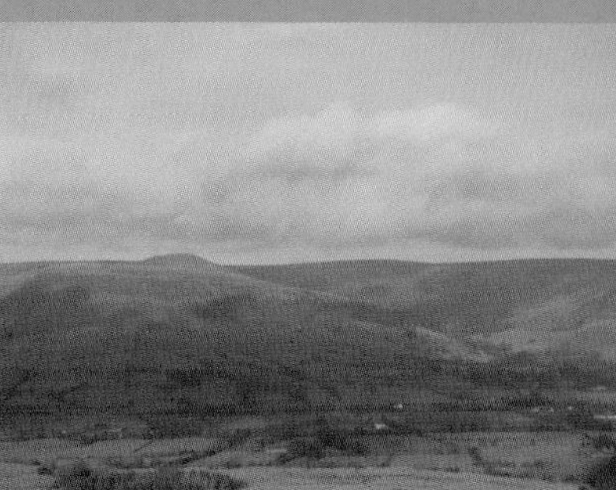

It is possible to simply crop your digital images to produce a panoramic format. However, every time you use the Crop tool you lose pixels, so you can end up with a low-resolution image that will only produce small-sized prints. By combining a series of images together (known as stitching) you can not only get much higher-resolution images, but you can also include more of the scene than you could using even the widest lenses available.

To make the most of this technique you need to think about how you shoot your images, rather than simply trying to stitch together any images that you have shot. We will first run through how to shoot the images that you are going to use, before moving on to the software techniques involved.

Shooting your panoramic stitcher image
The basic technique for shooting images to stitch together is simple; you shoot a series of pictures that overlap slightly. The main difficulty with shooting these images is matching the frames so that they go together easily and seamlessly. By planning your shots and following some simple techniques, you can make the job of stitching them together a much less difficult task for both the software and your image adjustment skills.

DSLRs are ideal for this technique as they offer a range of features that make the job much easier, such as manual exposure and focusing. Here are the top tips for shooting stitcher images with your DSLR.

Use a tripod
Fixing the camera to a tripod will help to ensure your movements are consistent and the camera moves only in a single plane.

Use a camera-mounted spirit level
Along with the tripod, a spirit level will help to keep the camera level for all your shots.

Avoid using wide-angle lenses
Even the highest-quality wide-angle lenses cause some distortion of the image that can make it impossible to match your shots together. Shoot at around 40mm to minimize this distortion in your images.

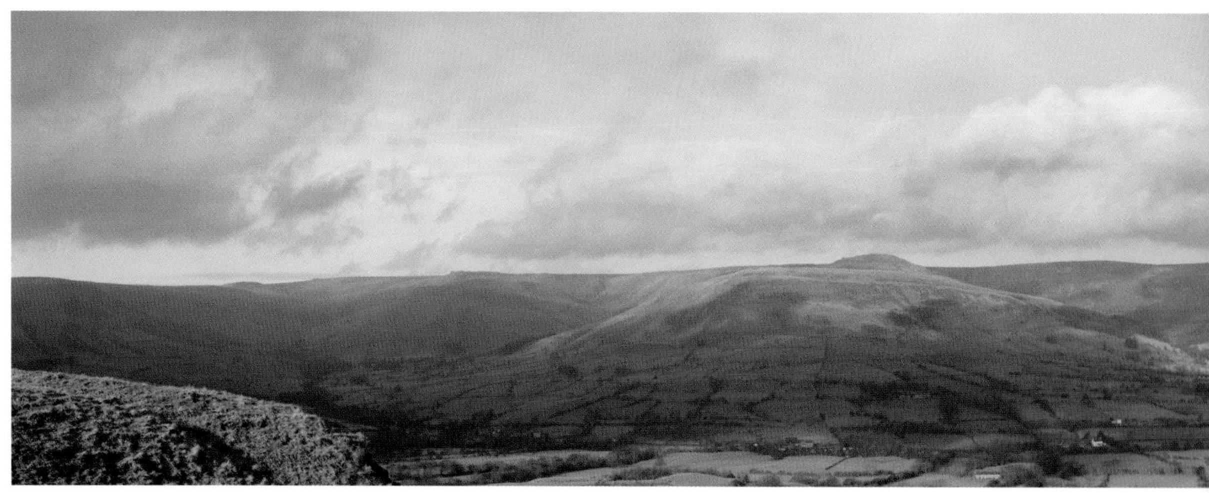

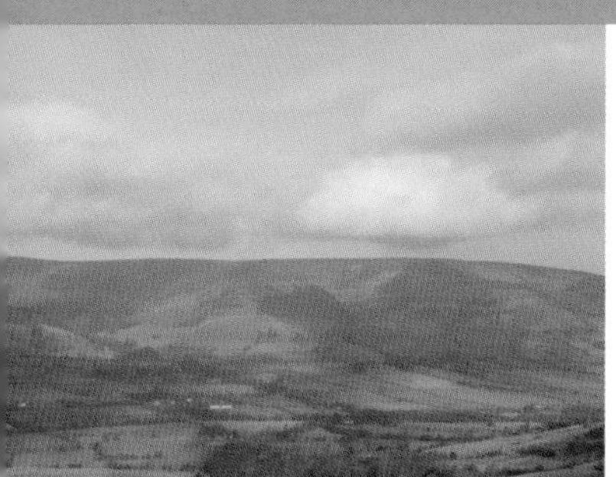

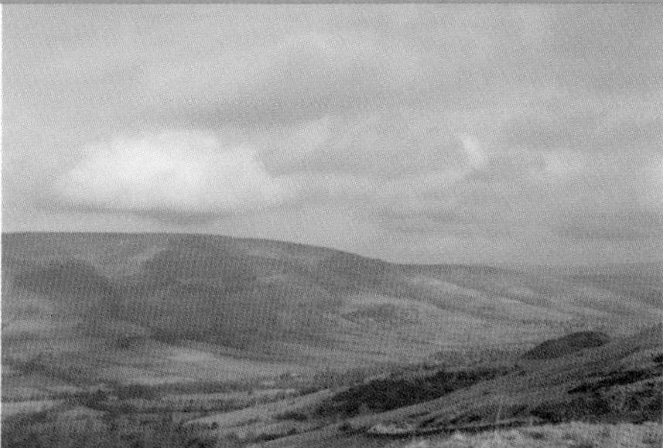

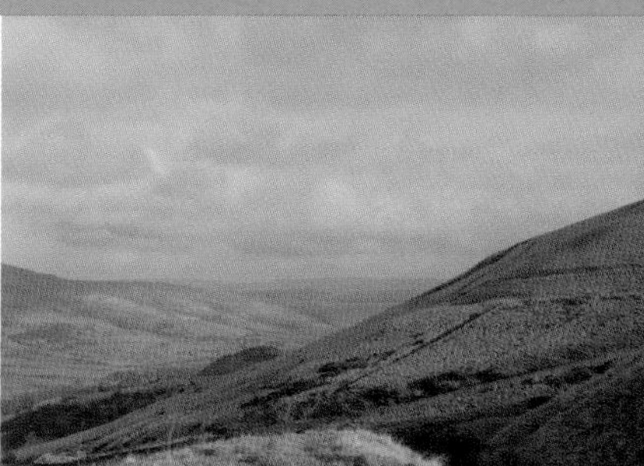

Make sure your images overlap by at least 30 percent
The more you overlap your images, the greater chance that they will stitch together successfully. Try to overlap your images by between 30 and 50 percent.

Use manual exposure
As you move the camera, the brightness of the scene will change. Using automatic exposure will mean that the exposure will vary between your shots, making them lighter or darker, so they will be difficult to stitch together. Use a manual exposure setting that will ensure that the brightest part of the whole scene will be recorded correctly to ensure that the exposure will cover all of your shots.

Don't use a polarizing filter
While it's tempting to use a polarizing filter, it can cause the tones and colors of the scene to be recorded differently between shots.

Use manual focus
For consistency, it will help if the focus of the lens remains the same through the whole series of images. Switch the camera to manual focus and choose an aperture such as f/16 or f/22 to give you a large depth of field.

Use manual white balance
Just like the exposure, using an automatic white balance setting could mean that the images in your sequence will be different. So use the appropriate manual white balance presets to ensure the results are a consistent color.

Plan your composition
As with any image, you need to think carefully about the composition of the shot. Because you can't see the whole image through the viewfinder, use a panoramic slot cut into card or paper to view the scene to show you how the final image will appear.

ABOVE
After shooting a sequence of images, you can combine them together to produce a high-resolution panoramic image, including much more of the scene than you can using most wide-angle lenses.

BELOW
With a few simple image adjustments, you can achieve stunning panoramas.

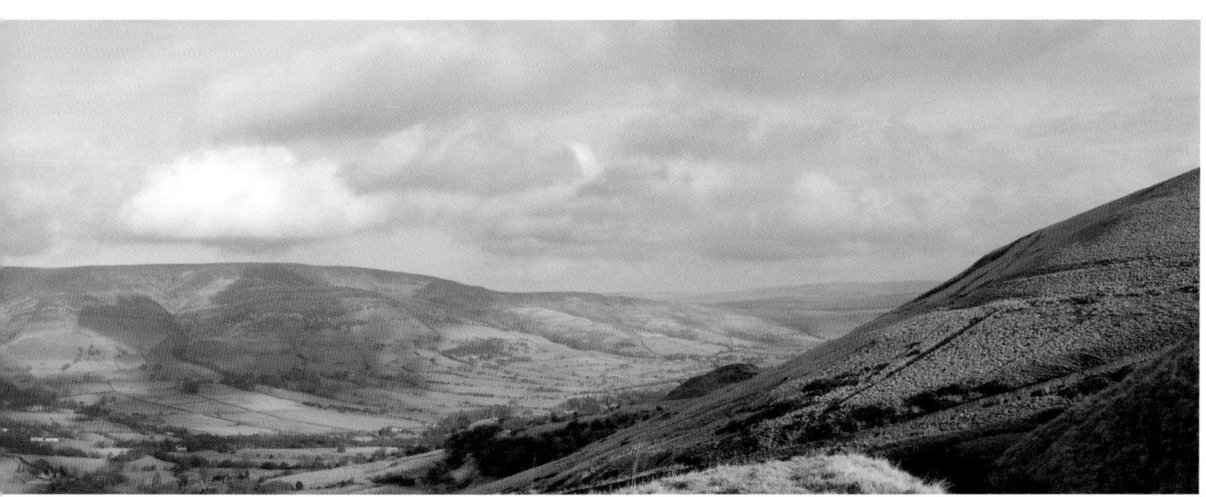

Software technique
There are many software packages available that can create panoramics. Here, I have used the Photomerge facility built into both Photoshop CS2 and Elements.

Step 1
In Photoshop CS2 you'll find the stitching option under File>Automate>Photomerge. This will open a dialog box allowing you to select the images to use for your panorama. You'll find this much easier if you've already moved the images together in their own folder and if they have sequential file names.

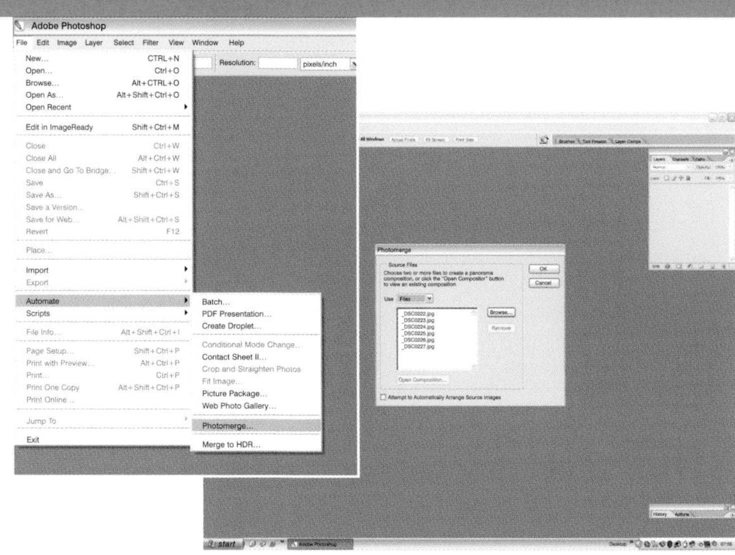

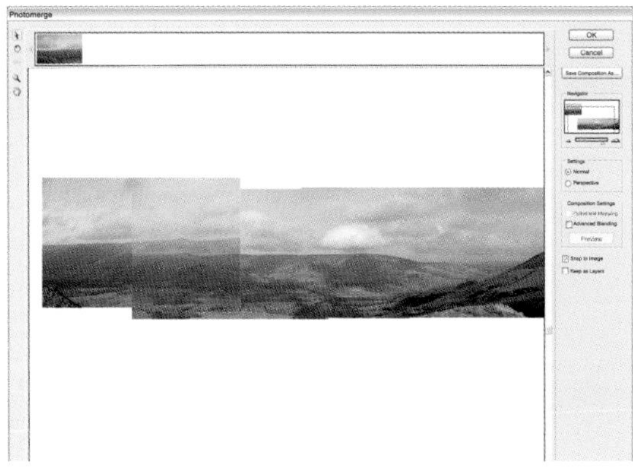

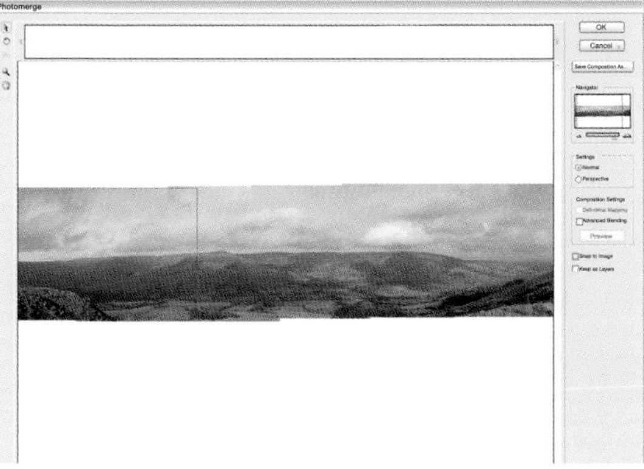

Step 2
Once you've selected the images and clicked OK, Photomerge will automatically try to combine the images to create the panorama. Even the most carefully shot sequence can run into problems though, and you'll usually find that either the merged image is incorrect or there are images left on the Lightbox area at the top of the screen.

Step 3
To manually arrange your images, you can drag them either onto the work area itself or from the Lightbox onto your image. The active image is indicated by a red outline, and you simply click on any individual image in the panorama to move it.

Step 4
When adding and moving images ensure that the Snap to Image option is ticked to allow the software to merge the images. You may find it easier to align them successfully if you use the Zoom tool to enlarge the area that you are working on.

Composition Settings
Cylindrical Mapping
Advanced Blending
Preview
Snap to Image
Keep as Layers

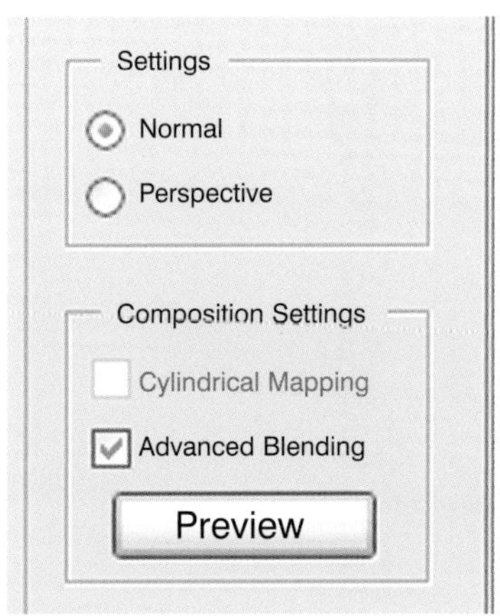

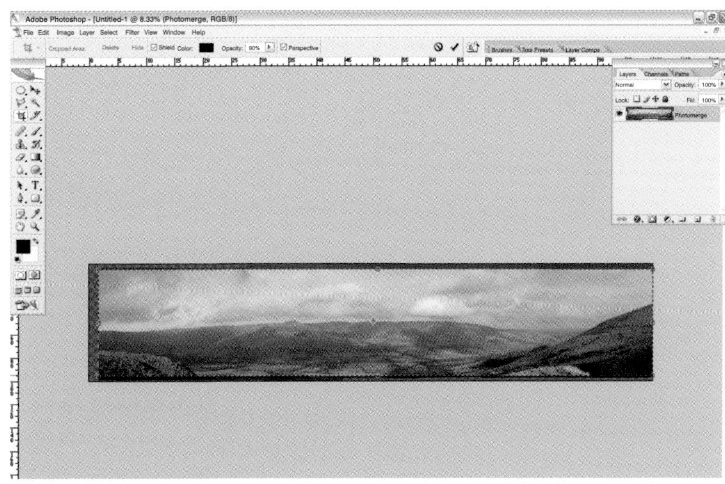

Step 5
Use the Advanced Blending option to even out any color and tone inconsistencies between individual images. Before you go on, click the Preview function to identify any problem areas.

Step 6
Once you are happy with the image, click OK, and after a while the whole panorama will appear in the main editing window. No matter how careful you have been both taking the shots and using the Photomerge controls, there are often areas of the image that need tidying up. The first thing to do is to use the Crop tool to remove any uneven areas around the edge of the frame.

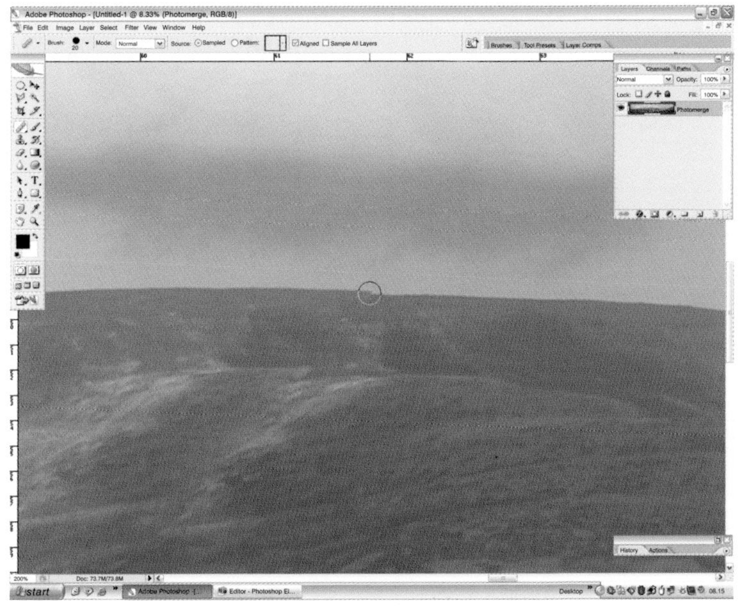

Step 7
The final steps are to use the Clone Stamp tool to clean up any areas that haven't merged correctly. If you've followed the shooting advice this shouldn't involve too much work; simply match areas and smooth out any inconsistencies in the image.

Final adjustments
Because the exposure settings you used to shoot the images were set for the lightest area of the scene, you will often find that you need to adjust the image more than normal. Use the Levels, Curves, and Hue/Saturation controls to fine-tune the exposure and color of your final image.

Section 12

Appendix

AERIAL PERSPECTIVE
The lightening of colors and tones due to their distance from the viewer. This is caused by particles in the atmosphere affecting the appearance of distant objects, so is more pronounced in misty and foggy conditions, and in heavily polluted areas. You can take advantage of aerial perspective to enhance the impression of distance in your images.

APERTURE
A variable opening inside a lens that governs how much light passes to the film or sensor. Numerically known as f-numbers, these are commonly arranged as f/2.8, f/4, f/5.6, f/8, f/11, f/16, and f/22, with f/2.8 letting in the most light and f/22 the least.

APERTURE PRIORITY
An automatic exposure mode where you choose the aperture setting and the camera sets the shutter speed needed according to the built-in light meter. Aperture priority is useful when you want to create a particular depth of field effect.

ARTIFACTS
Incorrectly valued pixels that are by-products of digital image-processing. Often visible as small marks or dots, similar to digital noise.

ASPECT RATIO
The ratio between the width and the height of an image. The sensors in most DSLRs have an aspect ratio of 3:2; the same as a 35mm frame. However, the sensors used in the Four Thirds system have an aspect ratio of 4:3.

AUTO EXPOSURE (AE)
An in-camera system for setting the shutter speed and aperture automatically. Selecting this option means that precise control over depth of field and movement cannot be guaranteed.

AUTOFOCUS (AF)
A system built into the camera that automatically focuses the lens by either measuring the distance to the object or analyzing the image. Most DSLRs offer a number of autofocus options including a choice of focusing from different areas of the image and either locking onto a single distance (single AF) or continually adjusting the focus to track moving objects (continuous or servo AF). Autofocus works best when locked onto an area with sufficient contrast.

BITMAP IMAGE (BMP)
A term used for any pixel-based image using a checkerboard-like arrangement. Also known as a raster image.

BRIGHTNESS
A measurable scale used in digital images with values from 0 (black) to 255 (white).

CALIBRATION
A technique that aims to match the characteristics of devices used in digital photography to ensure consistent colors and tones. It is most commonly used to match the image from the monitor to the printer in the digital darkroom.

CANDID
A picture taken when the subject is unaware that they are being photographed. The aim is to capture natural expressions and behavior. This technique must be used with care to avoid offending the subject, and to avoid possible ethical and legal issues in some countries.

CHANNELS
The individual color information used to form a digital image. In an RGB file, this consists of three separate grayscale images for the red, green, and blue components of the image.

CHANNEL MIXER
A tool in Photoshop that allows the color values for the channels to be altered. Especially useful for black and white conversions.

CHARGE-COUPLED DEVICE (CCD)
The most common type of light-sensitive sensor found in digital cameras and scanners.

CLIPPING
When tones in the image close to the highlight or shadow values are translated as pure white or black. The result is lost detail in the final image.

COMPLEMENTARY METAL OXIDE SEMICONDUCTOR (CMOS)
An alternative type of light-sensitive sensor to the CCD.

CMYK (CYAN, MAGENTA, YELLOW, AND BLACK)
An image mode used to prepare images for lithographic printing used in all magazines and books. CMYK has the smallest color space of the three color modes commonly used.

COLOR TEMPERATURE
A precise measurement of the color of a particular light source. This is commonly expressed in degrees Kelvin, with higher numbers indicating warmer light, and lower numbers denoting cooler colors.

COMPRESSION
A means of making digital files smaller by using a complex formula to group pixels together, rather than save every pixel. There are two types of compression: "lossy," where some information from the original file is lost during the process, and "lossless," where all the original data is retained.

CONVERGING VERTICALS
A perspective effect that is caused by tilting the camera upward to include more of the subject. It is especially noticeable in photographs of buildings. Because the sensor is no longer parallel with the subject, the building appears to fall over backward as the top appears much smaller than the base. This problem can be overcome by using a perspective control (or shift) lens, or by using the Crop tool in your image-editing software.

CROPPING
This usually refers to recomposing an image after capture by removing unwanted areas. This is achieved in digital images by using the Crop tool in image-editing software. In-camera, it can also refer either to getting closer to the subject or using a longer focal length lens to remove unwanted areas.

CURVES
A Photoshop tool that allows you to adjust the contrast, color, and brightness of images by setting points along a line representing the image.

CYAN
A blue-green color whose complementary color is red.

DEPTH OF FIELD
The area of sharp focus within an image. It is controlled by the focal length of the lens, the aperture, and the subject-to-camera distance. Short focal length lenses, small apertures (such as f/22), and greater distance between the camera and the subject produce the largest depth of field. Long focal lengths, wide apertures (such as f/2.8), and closer subjects produce shallower depth of field.

DIGITAL
The method used in computerized systems for storing and processing data. Information is converted into a binary code (a series of ones and zeroes) that can be interpreted by other devices using the same system. In photography, this involves the camera converting light into binary information that is stored on the memory card and then transferred to a computer or other device to produce an image.

DIGITAL DARKROOM
A generic term used to describe any computer and input or output devices used for digital imaging.

DYNAMIC RANGE
A measurement of the range of brightness in photographic materials or digital sensors. The higher the number, the greater the range of tones that can be recorded.

EXPOSURE
The amount of light that falls onto a digital sensor or light-sensitive material. In both photographic printing and shooting, exposure is controlled by a combination of time and aperture setting. The term is also commonly used to describe a single frame or shot taken.

F-STOP
Also known as f-numbers, this is an alternative expression for the aperture set on the lens.

FISHEYE
An extreme wide-angle lens that produces a circular or distorted image.

FOCAL LENGTH
An expression used to measure the distance between the optical center of a lens and the point where the image is focused. It can be used to indicate the angle of view of the lens, according to the size of the film or sensor. The shorter the focal length, the wider the view; the longer the focal length, the narrower the angle.

FOCAL POINT
The main subject or area of an image that draws the viewer's attention.

FOREGROUND
The area of the image closest to the camera. This is more prominent when using wide-angle lenses, as the greater angle of view makes more of the foreground visible than with longer focal length lenses.

GAMUT
An expression of the range of colors used to create, display, or output a digital image. Unexpected printouts often occur after CMYK mode images are prepared on RGB monitors and are said to be "out of gamut."

HARMONIOUS COLORS
Colors that are next to each other on the color wheel. Used together, these colors usually create gentle, harmonious images.

HIGHLIGHT
The brightest part of the image, represented by the value 255 on the 0–255 scale used in digital images.

HISTOGRAM
A graphic representation of a digital image showing the range of tones present as a series of vertical columns. Digital cameras can usually display the histogram of a shot to check the exposure recorded the correct level of tones.

HORIZON
The line between the sky and the land or sea in a landscape. Can also be used to express almost any intersection of two distinct areas.

HUE
An alternative expression for color that can be given a numerical value.

HYPERFOCAL DISTANCE
The shortest distance that a lens can be focused so that the depth of field extends to infinity. It is commonly used to give the maximum depth of field possible at any aperture on any lens.

INTERNATIONAL STANDARDS ORGANIZATION (ISO) SPEED
A rating used to determine the sensitivity of a film or sensor to light. A low number such as ISO 50 or 100 needs more light to form an image than a higher number such as ISO 400 or 800.

INTERPOLATION
The process of adding extra pixels to a digital image by assessing the existing information to create new data. This is usually used to increase the size of the image for printing. However, images that have gone through this process never have the same sharp qualities or color accuracy as original non-interpolated images.

JOINT PHOTOGRAPHIC EXPERTS GROUP (JPEG)
A universal image file type that uses compression to shrink the size of the file. Known as a "lossy" compression because some information is lost during the process.

LAYER
A means of stacking images on top of one another in Photoshop, used for creating composite images or creating copies of the original image to allow adjustments to be made without affecting the original.

LEAD-IN LINE
Diagonal lines that give an impression of depth to a two-dimensional image.

LEVELS
A tool in Photoshop allowing you to control the brightness of the image. Takes the form of a histogram with moveable points to allow adjustments.

MACRO
Generally used to describe any close-up photography, although strictly speaking it should refer only to photography where the image on the sensor or film is the same size or larger than the original subject. When the subject and image size are the same, this is known as life-size (or 1:1) reproduction. Many lenses offer a macro feature, but to get true macro images you need a dedicated macro lens or additional attachments to get life-size reproduction.

MAGENTA
A blue-red color whose complementary color is green.

MAXIMUM APERTURE
The widest aperture available with a particular lens. This lets in the greatest amount of light, allowing the fastest shutter speed to be used, and also gives the least depth of field.

MEGABYTE (MB)
The unit of measurement used to express the size of computer memory or hard disk space.

MEMORY CARD
A removable memory device used to store images on a DSLR. The most common types used are CompactFlash, SD, and xD cards.

MINIMUM APERTURE
The smallest aperture available with a particular lens. It lets in the least amount of light meaning that a longer shutter speed is required to achieve the correct exposure, and also gives the greatest depth of field possible.

NOISE
Unwanted, random pixels containing incorrect tone or color information that degrades the image quality. Most visible in shadow or even-toned areas of the image. Similar to grain in traditional film emulsions, this can be a consequence of shooting at high ISO settings. Can also be caused by using very long exposures.

OVEREXPOSURE
When too much light reaches the film or sensor due to incorrect exposure. Causes the image to look too light, with lost highlight detail.

PANNING
A technique used to capture moving subjects. It involves moving the camera to keep the subject in the same position in the viewfinder, then firing the shutter during this movement.

PANORAMIC
An image format where the dimension of one axis is at least twice that of the other. Can be created using the stitching technique in your image-editing software.

PERSPECTIVE
A composition technique for making a two-dimensional image appear to have depth. The term is also used to describe the view that you get from a particular viewpoint.

PHOTOSHOP
The industry-standard image-editing software produced by Adobe.

PIXEL
Short for "picture element," the pixel is the individual building block of a digital image. Arranged in a grid-like pattern called a bitmap to form the overall image, similar to the ink dots on a printed page that make up a photographic reproduction.

POLARIZING FILTER
A filter that only allows light through that is vibrating in a particular direction. Used to cut out reflections, increase color saturation, and darken blue skies.

PRIME LENS
A lens that only offers a single focal length. These lenses often offer wider maximum apertures and higher quality than many zoom lenses.

RAW
A file format that takes data directly from the image sensor and stores it in a format that needs to be decoded by dedicated software to form the image. Most camera manufacturers use their own proprietary RAW format.

RGB (RED, GREEN, AND BLUE)
The three primary colors used by most digital-imaging devices to form images.

RULE OF THIRDS
A composition technique that uses equally spaced imaginary lines to split the frame into thirds both horizontally and vertically. These lines can then be used to position objects in the frame to produce a balanced composition.

SATURATION
An expression for the purity of a color. The more white, gray, or black is present in a color, the lower the saturation.

SELECTIVE FOCUS
Using shallow depth of field and careful focusing to isolate the subject in the frame. This technique works best with longer focal length lenses and wide apertures.

SENSOR
The light-sensitive chip used inside a DSLR to convert light into a digital image. The most common types used are known as CCD or CMOS.

SHADOW
The darkest part of the image, in digital imaging it is represented by a 0 value on the 0–255 scale.

SHUTTER
The mechanism used to determine when the sensor or film is exposed to light. In an SLR camera it usually takes the form of a thin curtain in front of the sensor or film.

SHUTTER PRIORITY
An automatic exposure mode where the user selects the shutter speed, and the camera determines the exposure required according to the built-in exposure meter. Also known as shutter priority auto exposure.

SHUTTER SPEED
The length of time that the sensor or film is exposed to light. Short shutter speeds such as 1/1000 sec are used to freeze movement, while long shutter speeds such as 1/15 sec will produce some blur.

SINGLE-LENS REFLEX (SLR) CAMERA
A camera where the viewfinder image is seen through the same lens that is used to take the image. This is made possible by a series of mirrors called a pentaprism, which present a corrected scene to the viewfinder. The pentaprism is a more accurate tool for precise composing compared with rangefinder viewers.

STANDARD LENS
A lens of a certain focal length that gives a view that is most similar to human vision. The focal length varies according to the format of the sensor that is used, and is approximately equal to the diagonal measurement of the sensor. For most small-sensor DSLRs, this is around 30mm, while for full-frame or 35mm cameras it is 50mm.

STATIC
Used to describe a composition that makes the subject appear as if it is fixed in position. Placing the subject in the middle of the frame usually produces a static composition.

STITCHING
A technique used to combine a series of images taken of the same subject to give a wider view than would normally be possible. The most common use of stitching is to produce a panoramic image from a sequence of overlapping images taken from the same viewpoint.

TAGGED IMAGE FILE FORMAT (TIFF)
A high-quality file format used to store digital images, which is recognized by most imaging software. Can be uncompressed or compressed using a "lossless" system.

TELEPHOTO LENS
A lens with a focal length longer than 50mm. They are used to photograph small areas of a scene because it has the effect of magnifying the subject, making them ideal for wildlife and action photography.

UNDEREXPOSURE
When too little light passes to the film or sensor, giving very dark images with little or no shadow detail.

VANISHING POINT
An imaginary point where converging lines meet. It can be used to draw the viewer's attention to a particluar area of an image.

VIEWFINDER
The optical system on the camera used to compose your image.

VIEWPOINT
The point from which you take the photograph. Varying the viewpoint alters the perspective of the image.

WHITE BALANCE
A camera setting used to correct for changes in the color temperature of the lighting.

WIDE-ANGLE LENS
A lens with a focal length shorter than about 28mm giving a wide field of view. Used for capturing as much of a scene in one image as possible.

ZOOM LENS
A lens that offers variable focal lengths, allowing the photographer to alter the amount of the scene included in the final image.

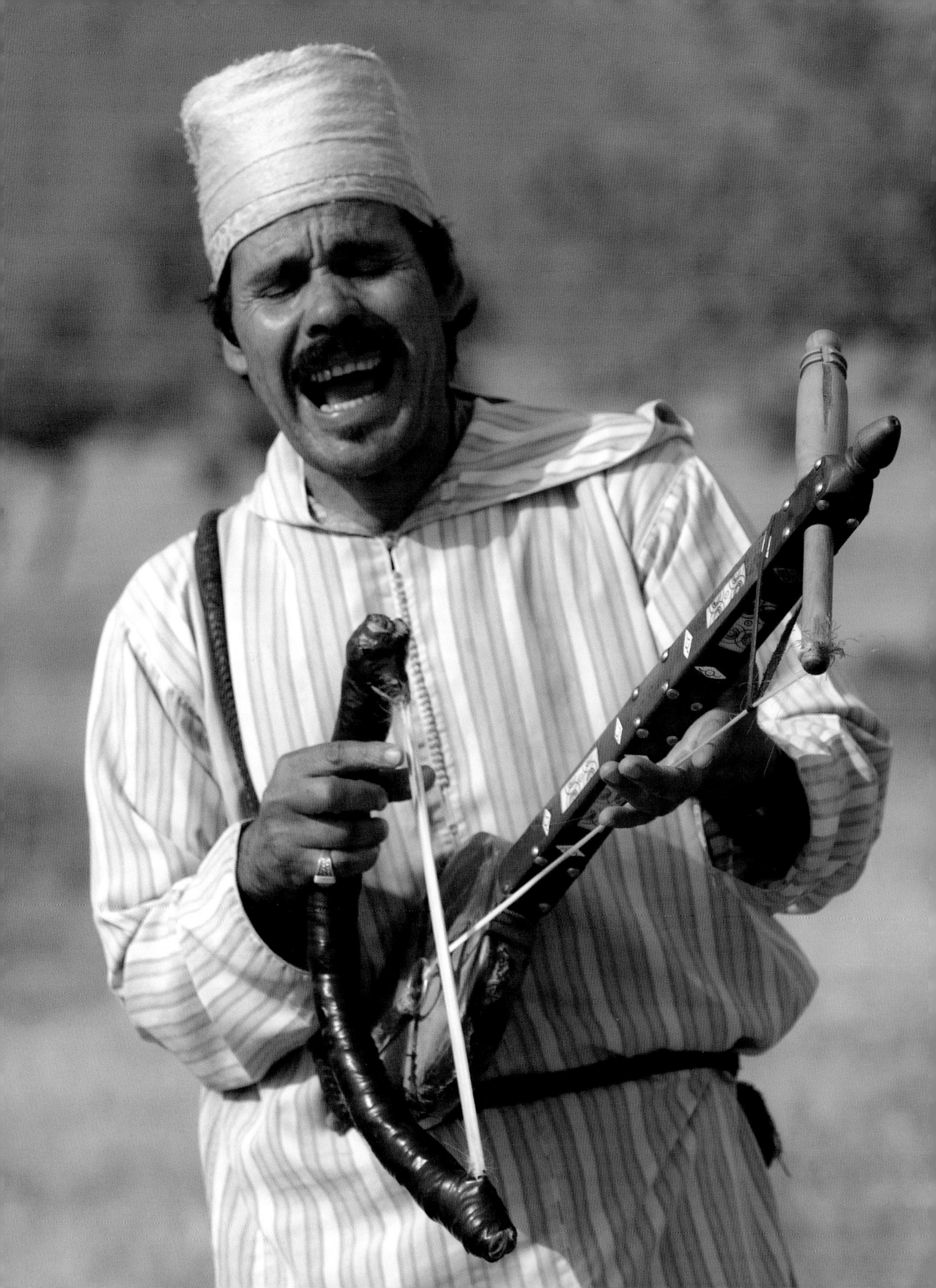

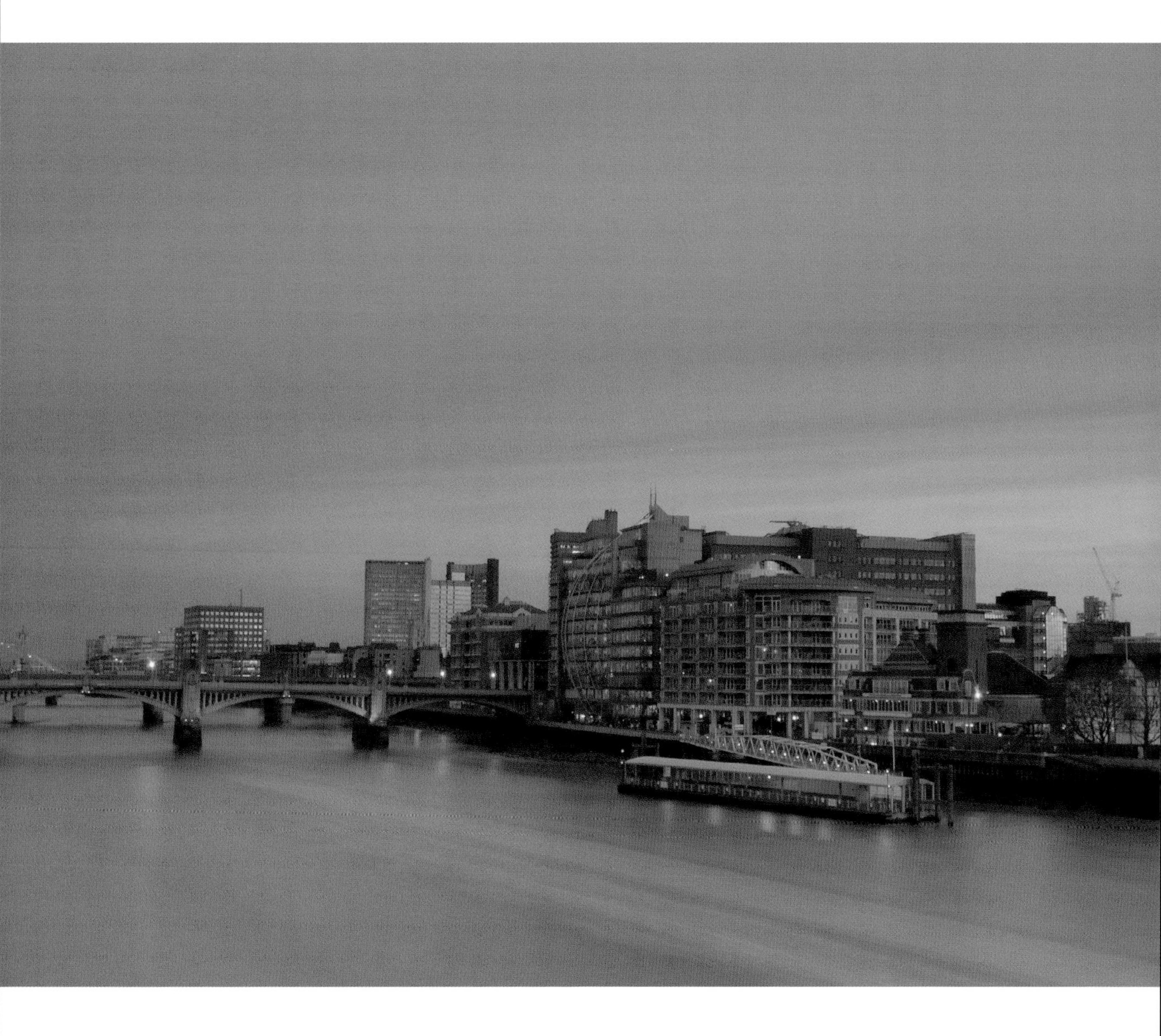

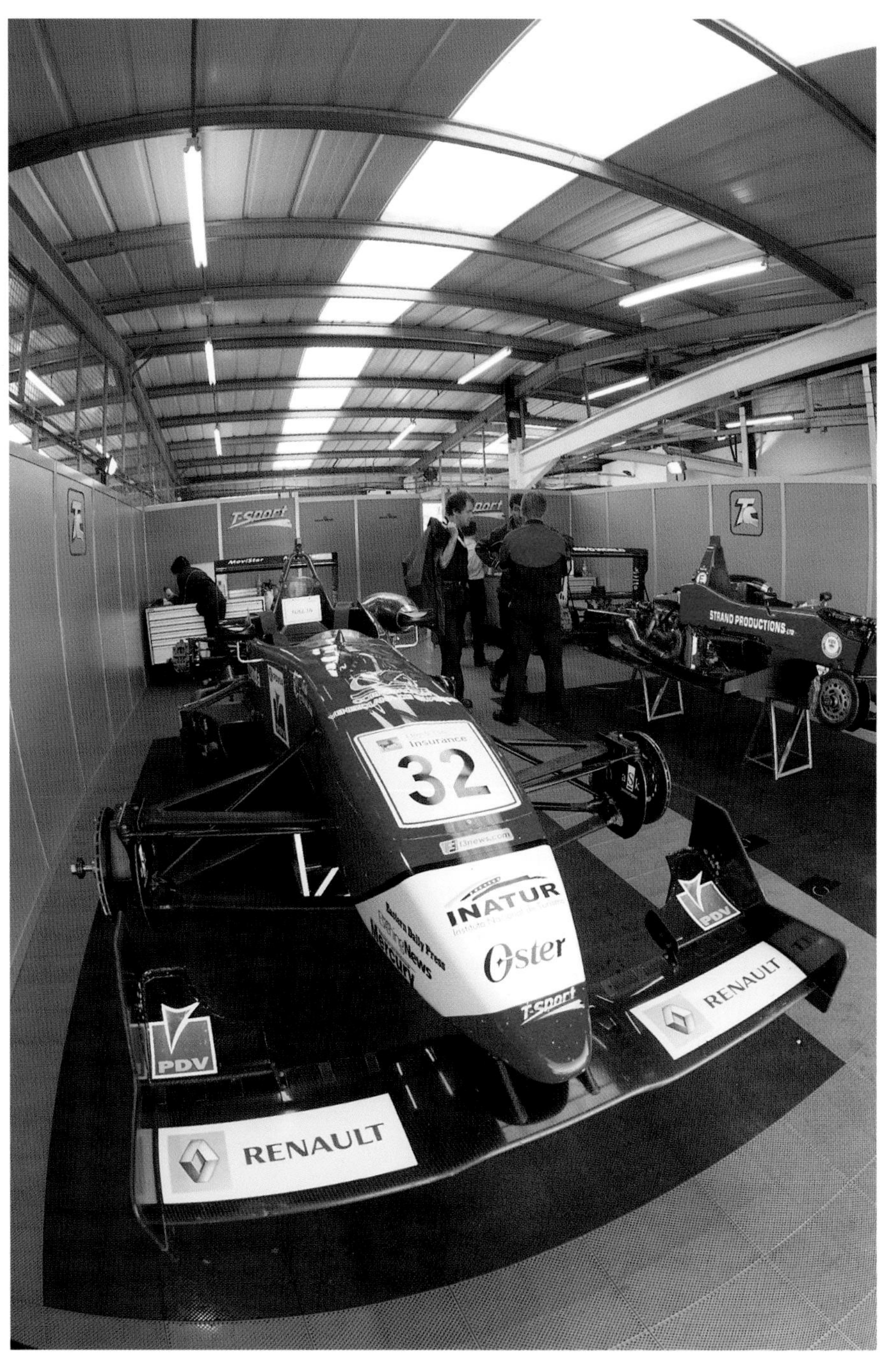
T-Sport
STRAND PRODUCTIONS LTD
Insurance
32
INATUR
Oster
Mercury
PDV
RENAULT
RENAULT
PDV

ACKNOWLEDGMENTS

There are countless people who have made this book possible, but particular thanks go to all at *Practical Photography* and EMAP for allowing me the time and opportunity to complete the project and use some images from the magazine. Thanks also to my commissioning editor Chris Middleton and Jane Roe at RotoVision, for getting the book underway in the first place, and continued help along the way.

Special thanks go to Paul Franks and Bob Martin for shooting a number of the portraits with little time to spare. Also to Len, Jo, Carrie, and all who allowed their portraits to be used in this book. Finally to all my friends and family for their continued support and help along the way, especially when I'm up against deadlines.